METAMORA
AND OTHER PLAYS

AMERICA'S LOST PLAYS

VOLUME XIV

A series in twenty volumes of hitherto unpublished plays collected with the aid of the Rockefeller Foundation, under the auspices of the Dramatists' Guild of the Authors' League of America, edited with historical and bibliographical notes.

BARRETT H. CLARK

GENERAL EDITOR

Advisory Board

ROBERT HAMILTON BALL, QUEENS COLLEGE
HOYT H. HUDSON, PRINCETON UNIVERSITY
GLENN HUGHES, UNIVERSITY OF WASHINGTON
GARRETT H. LEVERTON, FORMERLY OF NORTHWEST-
ERN UNIVERSITY
E. C. MABIE, UNIVERSITY OF IOWA
ALLARDYCE NICOLL, YALE UNIVERSITY
ARTHUR HOBSON QUINN, UNIVERSITY OF
PENNSYLVANIA
NAPIER WILT, UNIVERSITY OF CHICAGO

A complete list of volumes, with the names of plays contained in each, will be found at the end of this volume.

PUBLISHED AND DISTRIBUTED BY

PRINCETON UNIVERSITY PRESS
PRINCETON, N.J.

Metamora

& *Other Plays*

BY

JOHN AUGUSTUS STONE · SILAS S. STEELE
CHARLES POWELL CLINCH · JOSEPH M. FIELD
H. J. CONWAY (?) · JOHN H. WILKINS
JOSEPH STEVENS JONES · JOHN BROUGHAM

EDITED BY EUGENE R. PAGE

PRINCETON · NEW JERSEY
PRINCETON UNIVERSITY PRESS
· 1941 ·

19987

May - 1944

Requests for authorization of the use of any of the plays in this volume, on the stage, the screen, or for radio or television broadcasting, or for any purpose of reproduction, should be addressed as follows: for *Metamora,* to the University of Utah, Salt Lake City, Utah; for *The Spy,* and *The Usurper,* to the New York Public Library; for *Signor Marc, The Duke's Motto, Tancred, The Crock of Gold* and *The Battle of Stillwater,* to the Seymour Collection, Princeton University Library, Princeton, New Jersey; for *Job and His Children,* to Barrett H. Clark, in care of the Dramatists Play Service, Inc., 6 East 39th Street, New York City.

SET UP AND PRINTED
IN THE UNITED STATES OF AMERICA
BY PRINCETON UNIVERSITY PRESS
AT PRINCETON, NEW JERSEY

PREFATORY NOTE

THIS volume of *America's Lost Plays* includes eight dramas, and a fragment of a ninth, representing a forty-year period in the history of the American theatre. These plays were all written by men who made a considerable contribution to the drama of their time, and each play has a stage history. Beginning with the newly-discovered *Metamora* and a fragment of another play by Stone, the volume includes three patriotic melodramas, *The Spy, The Battle of Stillwater,* and *The Usurper,* followed by two "domestic" dramas, *The Crock of Gold* and *Job and His Children,* and concludes with two dramatizations of Continental plots, *Signor Marc* and *The Duke's Motto.*

The eight playwrights represented contributed some three hundred pieces to the stage. Yet two of them have never had a play printed, two more have had only one play printed, and the others have been almost as inadequately represented. These facts are especially remarkable in view of the long-continued popularity of some of the playwrights and their plays. Bringing these plays to print has been a cooperative venture in which many have assisted, and continuing the processes of discovery and identification will be a never-ending task in which many more persons can assist. It can only be hoped that additional plays and data will be brought to light and made available to all students of the drama, as a result of this tentative effort.

Of the plays included in this volume, *The Spy* and *The Usurper* are printed from manuscripts supplied by the New York Public Library; *Job and His Children* from a manuscript bought by the general editor of this series from a New Jersey dealer; *Metamora* from a manuscript owned by the University of Utah; and the others from manuscripts in the Seymour Collection at Princeton University. The introductions to each play provide complete information and acknowledgements of sources.

In general, the plays are printed as they have been found in the manuscripts. Obvious misspellings have been corrected, but the spelling has not been modernized. Illegible lines are marked by brackets, and occasional necessary explanations are made within parentheses. Stage directions have sometimes been simplified. Citations of such obvious sources as Quinn's *History of the American Drama* and Odell's *Annals of the New York Stage* are usually made merely by listing the author, and not including the full title of his work.

Concerning two of the plays, a word of explanation is needed. The assignment of the "anonymous" *Battle of Stillwater* to H. J. Conway, and the alteration of the title of the play formerly called "Saint Marc" to *Signor Marc* are discussed in the introductory notes on Conway and Wilkins.

Because no adequate lists of plays covering the playwrights represented in this volume have been made, the introductions to the plays include alphabetical or chronological lists for each author. These lists are not complete, for exact assignment is often impossible, but they provide by far the most extensive published record concerning some of the playwrights. For example, piecing together information from various sources brings the number of John Brougham titles to one hundred. Although Brougham has several times been mentioned as the author of at least a hundred pieces, no one list of more than sixty of his plays has previously been available. Wherever possible, dates of original production have been indicated for these plays, which run to a total of approximately two hundred and fifty for the eight authors.

Central College   EUGENE R. PAGE

CONTENTS

METAMORA;
Or, THE LAST OF THE WAMPANOAGS

An Indian Tragedy in Five Acts
as played by Edwin Forrest

By John Augustus Stone

METAMORA;

Or, THE LAST OF THE WAMPANOAGS

IT SEEMS especially appropriate that this volume of *America's Lost Plays* should open with the publication of nearly the whole of that long-lost classic of melodrama, *Metamora; or The Last of the Wampanoags*. One of the earliest, and certainly the most popular, of the dozens of "Indian" dramas of the last century, *Metamora* was also the favorite vehicle of America's greatest melodramatic actor, Edwin Forrest.

The discovery of this famous play is a romantic story in itself. Pursuing a vague reference in George D. Pyper's *The Romance of an Old Playhouse*, Mr. Barrett H. Clark wrote to Mr. Pyper, and also to Dr. Maud May Babcock in Salt Lake City, asking them to investigate the manuscripts mentioned in Pyper's book. The result was the discovery of four acts of the missing Stone play. Through the cooperative efforts of Professor Wallace A. Goates of the University of Utah, the manuscript was made available to the editors of this series. The original remains in the possession of the University of Utah, through whose courtesy this printing has been made possible. Thus, one of the most discussed and most valuable of "lost" plays is brought to light through the helpful cooperation of all concerned. The efforts of Professor Goates and of the Salt Lake City photographers, Hatch and Hatch, have made the University of Utah manuscript of *Metamora* an especially clean copy in microfilm.

Until the discovery of the University of Utah manuscript, *Metamora* was known only by the lines of the leading rôle, preserved in a manuscript in the Forrest Home, Holmesburg, Pennsylvania. This relatively inaccessible manuscript has never been printed. Through the courtesy of Mr. Frank H. Warner of Philadelphia, Secretary of the Board of Managers of the Forrest Home, the editor of this volume has been given permission to use this material. As a result, the University of Utah manuscript is supplemented in the following pages by a large part of the missing fourth act. In addition, one or two illegible speeches have been clarified from the Forrest Home manuscript.

Grateful acknowledgement is due to Mrs. Randolph S. (L. Ruth Murray) Klein, of Philadelphia, whose generous assistance in making for the editor a careful copy of the Forrest Home manuscript made use of this material possible.

Metamora was one of several plays written by actor-playwright John Augustus Stone. Born in Concord, Mass., on December 15, 1800, Stone made his début as Old Norval in *Douglas* on the stage of Boston's Washington Garden Theatre in 1820. From the beginning of his career, the youthful Stone specialized in the rôles of old men. His first New York appearance, at the City Theatre, on July 10, 1822, was in the part of Old Hardy (*The Belle's Stratagem*). For a decade, Stone was a popular though never a star performer at the City Theatre (1822-23), the Chatham Garden (1824 and 1827), the Bowery (1826 and 1831), and the Walnut Street and Chestnut Street Theatres of Philadelphia. His wife was the actress, Mrs. Legge, who later married N. H. Bannister.

Early in his career as actor-dramatist, Stone responded to Edwin Forrest's call for new native plays with his prize-winning tragedy, *Metamora*. In the *Critic,* for November 28, 1828, Forrest had advertised an offer of five hundred dollars and a half-benefit for "the best tragedy, in five acts, of which the hero, or principal character, shall be an aboriginal of this country." From fourteen plays submitted, the Committee of Award, headed by William Cullen Bryant, chose *Metamora*. Forrest's offer was one of the first attempts to encourage native dramatic talent with the promise of decent reward. In various prize competitions, Forrest received a total of two hundred plays, of which he used nine. Two of these nine, *Metamora* and *The Ancient Briton* (1833), were written by Stone.

The possibilities of the Indian theme had been faintly indicated by such plays as Custis's *The Indian Prophecy* and Bird's *Sagamore,* but it remained for *Metamora* to start a vogue which resulted in thirty-five such plays within twenty years. *Metamora* and its followers filled the stage with sentimentalized Indians of the Cooper pattern, "an extinct tribe which never existed." While Metamora declaimed through his tragic life in a stage wilderness, *Pocahontas, Oralloosa, Onylda, Osceola, Ontiata, Hiawatha, Oroonoka, Tuscalomba, Lamorah,* and many more romantic Indian plays followed in rapid succession. But none of them surpassed *Metamora*. If Forrest made it a success, it in turn provided Forrest with a sure-fire "vehicle." For nearly forty years, wherever he appeared, *Metamora* spelled popularity. In New York and Philadelphia, New Orleans and Saint Louis, the crowds came to see and be stirred. In twenty-five years Philadelphia had only two seasons without *Metamora*. In New York it was always in Forrest's repertoire. A twelve-day schedule in Saint Louis, featuring *Metamora,* brought a record profit of $2157. Even after Forrest's death, Metamora was played by Collier, and certain others, as late as 1887.

There were criticisms of the play, and Rees complained in 1845 that "Indian plays of late have become perfect nuisances," but not even Brougham's hilarious burlesque could stop *Metamora*. Its success was a remarkable impetus to American plays by American authors. The initial production, at the Park Theatre on December 15, 1829, was marked by a prologue and epilogue which begged the audience not to condemn the play merely because it was American. Groups of authentic Indians frequently attended productions of *Metamora,* and on one occasion, at the Tremont Theatre in Boston, such a group chanted a genuine Indian dirge! What a pity Stone could not have been present!

Stone had two lesser successes. His thorough revision of James Kirke Paulding's *The Lion of the West* kept that play on the boards, after its author had declined to make the revision himself. The play was rewritten except for the leading part, Colonel Nimrod Wildfire. In his *The Knight of the Golden Fleece,* Stone struck a popular note again. With George H. ("Yankee") Hill in one of his favorite rôles, Sy Saco, this play remained popular for fifteen years.

In contrast to these successes, Stone's life was tragic indeed. Despondency and ill health are the supposed causes of his suicide by drowning in the Schuylkill River, near Philadelphia, on May 29, 1834. His death was commemorated by Forrest, who erected a monument in Machpelah Cemetery, "To the Memory of John Augustus Stone, Author of Metamora, by His Friend Edwin Forrest."

Of Stone's plays only one, the unacted chronicle play, *Tancred; or, The Siege of Antioch,* has been published (1827). The scarcity of his writings has suggested the inclusion, following *Metamora,* of the only other material available, one act only of his *Tancred, King of Sicily* (a totally different play), first produced at the Park on March 16, 1831, with Stone in the cast.

Besides *Metamora* and the two *Tancred* plays, Stone wrote:

Restoration; or, The Diamond Cross.
                                    Chatham Garden (N. Y.), November 4, 1824.
The Demoniac; or, The Prophet's Bride.   Bowery (N. Y.), April 12, 1831.
The Lion of the West (revision).   Park (N. Y.), November 14, 1831.
The Ancient Briton.   Arch (Phila.), March 27, 1833.
The Knight of the Golden West; or, The Yankee in Spain.
                                    Park (N. Y.), September 10, 1834.
Fauntleroy; or, The Fatal Forgery.   Charleston.
La Roque, the Regicide.   Charleston.
Touretoun (?)

The University of Utah manuscript is the primary basis for the lines of *Metamora* as they appear here. In general, the differences between the Utah and the Forrest Home manuscripts are frequent but slight. There are many trivial variations, such as "white man" for "pale face," "were thirsty" for "thirsted," "tell you" for "say to you." The Forrest Home manuscript contains a total of ten lines not included in the Utah version.

The most conspicuous difference is in the names of the characters. The University of Utah manuscript cast, for a production at Salt Lake City on January 10, 1866, has several changes from the original names, as indicated by the play-bills of 1829 and by the Forrest Home manuscript. Guy of Godalmin has become Mordaunt, Horatio is changed to Walter, Holyoke to Goodenough, Kanshine to Kaneshine or Kaweshine, and Wisconeki to Annawandah. At least one of these changes must have been made prior to the production of Brougham's burlesque of *Metamora* in 1847. Brougham's burlesque character of Badenough obviously represents Goodenough and would be pointless as a reference to Holyoke.

Early reviews imply the discovery that Horatio (Walter) was actually the son of the villain, Fitzarnold, whereas this development does not occur in the copy here printed, and can neither be proved or disproved from the Forrest Home manuscript. In the fourth scene of the last act, the University of Utah manuscript refers to an action of Metamora's, which in the Forrest Home manuscript, is depicted in a brief appearance of the hero. These are the only important variations.

The original Park Theatre cast, December 15, 1829, had Forrest as Metamora, Richings as Lord Fitzarnold, Chapman as Sir Arthur Vaughan, Woodhull as Guy of Godalmin (Mordaunt), Barry as Horatio (Walter), Laughton as Errington, T. Placide as Church, Nexsen as Wolfe, Povey as Tramp, Wheatley as Holyoke (Goodenough), Blakely as Kanshine, Miss S. Parker as the child, Mrs. Hilson as Oceana, and Mrs. Sharpe as Nahmeokee.

CAST OF CHARACTERS

INDIANS

METAMORA, *chief of the Wampanoags*   G. B. WALDRON

KANESHINE, *an Indian prophet*   J. R. CLAWSON

ANNAWANDAH, *the traitor*   J. M. SMITH

OTAH, *an Indian boy*   H. MAIBEN

INDIAN BOY, *child of Metamora*   (MISS E. CLAWSON)

NAHMEOKEE, *wife of Metamora*   MISS ADAMS

INDIANS, WARRIORS, ETC.

ENGLISH

(Costumes)

LORD FITZARNOLD   *(rich shape, Charles II)*   N. S. LESLIE

SIR ARTHUR VAUGHAN   *(dark shape)*   E. G. WOOLEY

MORDAUNT   *(dark shape)*   J. S. LINDSAY

ERRINGTON, *chief of the council* *(Puritan shape)*   D. E. MCKENSIE

WALTER, *an orphan*   *(plain shape)*   J. S. SIMMONS

CAPTAIN CHURCH   *(breast plate, trunks)*   THOMPSON

WOLFE   *(plain)*   J. C. GRAHAM

GOODENOUGH   *(do)*   KELLY

TRAMP   *(do)*   MCINTOSH

OCEANA, *Mordaunt's daughter*   MRS. LESLIE

SOLDIERS, SAILORS, PEASANTS, ETC.

(The page above is, except for punctuation, a reproduction of the cast of characters, as they appeared in Salt Lake City, January 10, 1866, included in the manuscript itself, except for the name in parenthesis which has been copied from a playbill originally appearing in the *Deseret News Print*. The page from the original manuscript has been reproduced rather than the *Deseret News Print* playbill because of the descriptions of costumes contained in the former.)

ACT I.

Scene 1: *Sunset. A wild, picturesque scene; high, craggy rocks in distance; dark pine trees, etc. Rocks cross stage, with platform cross behind. Steps, etc., at back. A rude tomb, flowers growing around it. Half dark. Mordaunt discovered leaning on tomb. Slow music.*

Mor. The sun has sunk behind yon craggy rocks; and day's last beams are fading from the clouds that fleet in hurrying masses through the sky, like tattered banners of a flying host! England, my home! When will thy parent arms again enfold me? Oh! When for me will dawn a day of hope? Will not sincere repentance from my scathed brow efface the brand of regicide?

Tramp. [*Outside*] What ho! Good Master Mordaunt! [*Cannon*]

Mor. Ha! What mean those sounds? Now, your news? [*Enter Tramp*]

Tramp. A gallant bark, urged by the favoring breeze, makes for the crowded shore.

Mor. From England! Ha!

Tramp. St. George's banner floats from her high mast, and her long signal pennon gleams with green and gold.

Mor. 'Tis he—he comes and with him hope arrives. Go, hasten, fellow; seek my daughter; say the Lord Fitzarnold comes to greet her. [*Tramp crosses to R. behind*] Marshal my followers in their best array—away to the beach and let loud music welcome him ashore. [*Exit Tramp*] What mingled feelings crowd about my heart, blended so strange and wild? Sunned by his sovereign's smile, Fitzarnold comes to woo and wed my daughter. Born on the heaving deep, the child of storms, and reared in savage wilds, her worth and beauty well may grace the courtly halls of England. And yet, to force her gentle will, whose every thought has been to soothe my sorrows and relieve my cares! Yet must she wed Fitzarnold. His alliance can with oblivion shroud the past, clear from my scutcheon every rebel stain, and give my franchised spirit liberty. [*Exit. Slow music, four bars. Enter Oceana, looking around as if in search*]

Oceana. Sure, 'twas my father's voice, and loud in converse. Father! Dear father! Not here? And yet I thought—[*Flute heard, distant*] Ha! whence that strain? So soft yet strange. Methinks some pious minstrel seeks the moonlight hour to breathe devotion forth in melody. [*Music changes*] Hark! It changes place and measure, too. Now deeper in the woods it warbles, now it seems aloft floating in plaintive tones through the air. This place—the hour—the day—heavens! 'tis my mother's birthday, and her grave undecked with flowers! O my mother, my dear mother! Perhaps her angel spirit hovers here o'er her lone daughter's steps, a guardian still. [*Kneels to tomb*] Ah, what flower is this? "Forgetmenot!" [*Music ceases*] My mother, look from thy seraph home upon thy child, and when for those thou lovest on earth thou breathest a prayer, oh, then forget me not. [*Places flower in bosom. Enter Walter*]

WALT. Oceana!

OCEANA. Walter, was thine the strain but now I heard?

WALT. 'Twas but an humble tribute to thy beauty, but could not match the sweetness of thy voice, whose every tone, attuned to dulcet sounds, can melt the soul to nature's harmony.

OCEANA. Walter, this from thee.

WALT. Nay, blame me not; although dependent on Sir Arthur Vaughan, nameless and poor, yet do I not despair, for in my heart a sacred treasure lies I would not barter for my patron's gold.

OCEANA. What means't thou, Walter?

WALT. Thine own sweet image, which naught on earth can banish or efface—a whispered hope I dare not speak aloud—a light thine own bright eyes have kindled up.

OCEANA. Nay, Walter, you ask not of the danger I escaped!

WALT. Danger! What danger? When?

OCEANA. 'Twas yestere'en, when I was lingering on the eastern beach, all heedless of the coming night, a panther growling from the thicket rushed and marked me for his prey. Powerless I stood—my blood stood still—I shrieked as I strove to fly, when at the instant, from a ready hand, swift as the lightning's flash, an arrow came and felled the monster as he crouched to spring.

WALT. Didst mark who sent it?

OCEANA. Full well I did. High on a craggy rock an Indian stood, with sinewy arm and eye that pierced the glen. His bowstring drawn to wing a second death, a robe of fur was o'er his shoulder thrown, and o'er his long, dark hair an eagle's plume waved in the breeze, a feathery diadem. Firmly he stood upon the jutting height, as if a sculptor's hand had carved him there. With awe I gazed as on the cliff he turned—the grandest model of a mighty man.

WALT. 'Twas Haups great chieftain, Metamora called; our people love him not, nor is it strange; he stands between them and extended sway, ready alike with words of power to urge, or gleaming weapon force his princely dues.

META. [*Outside*]   Hah! Ha!

OCEANA. [*Going up*]   Behold his dread encounter with a wolf. His vanquished foe with mighty arm he hurls down the steep height where mortal never trod.

META.   Hah! Hah! [*Enters on rock, passes across and off*]

WALT. [*At Metamora's exit*]   'Tis Metamora, the noble sachem of a valiant race—the white man's dread, the Wampanoag's hope. [*Enter Metamora down R.*]

META.   Ha, ha, ha! Turned on me—brave beast; he died like a red man.

OCEANA.   Chief, you are hurt; this scarf will staunch the wound. [*Offers it*]

META.   No! [*Rejects it*]

WALT.   'Tis Oceana—she whose life you saved.

META.   Metamora will take the white maiden's gift. [*Oceana ties his arm with scarf*]

OCEANA.   But yestere'en thou savedst my life, great chief; how can I pay thee for the generous deed?

META.   Hearken, daughter of the pale face; Metamora forgives not a wrong and forgets not a kindness. In the days of his age, Massasoit, my father, was in the white man's dwelling; while there, the spirit of the grave touched him and he laid down to die. A soft hand was stretched out to save him; it was the hand of thy mother. She that healed him sleeps in yonder tomb; but why should Metamora let his arrows sleep in the quiver when her daughter's life was in danger and her limbs shook with fear? Metamora loves the mild-eyed and the kind, for such is Nahmeokee.

WALT.   Such words, and more than all, such deeds, should win you, chief, the love of all our people. Would you were more among us. Why never seek our homes? Sir Arthur Vaughan's doors will open to the Indian chief.

OCEANA.   My sire will thank thee for his daughter's life.

META.   The red man's heart is on the hills where his father's shafts have flown in the chase. Ha! I have been upon the high mountain top where the grey mists were beneath my feet, and the Great Spirit passed by me in his wrath. He spake in anger and the old rocks crumbled beneath the flash of his spear. Then I was proud and smiled, for I had slain the great bird whose wing never tires, and whose eye never shrinks; and his feathers would adorn the long black hair of Nahmeokee, daughter of Miantonemo, the great hunter. The war and the chase are the red man's brother and sister. The storm cloud in its fury frights him not. Wrapt in the spoils he has won, he lays him down and no one comes near to steal. The Great Spirit hears his evening prayer, and he sleeps amidst the roar of a mighty cataract.

WALT. Were all thy nation mild and good like thee, how soon the fire of discord might be quenched.

META. Metamora has been the friend of the white man; yet if the flint be smitten too hard it will show that in its heart is fire. The Wampanoag will not wrong his white brother who comes from the land that is first touched by the rising sun; but he owns no master, save that One who holds the sun in his right hand, who rides on a dark storm, and who cannot die. [*Crosses to L.*]

WALT. That lofty bearing—that majestic mien—the regal impress sits upon his brow, and earth seems conscious of her proudest son. [*Conch shell heard sounding, R.*]

META. Ha! My young men return from their evening toil, and their hands are filled with the sweet fish of the lake. Come to my wigwam; ye shall eat of fish that the Great Spirit of the waters sends, and your hearts shall be made glad. [*Going R. but returns and takes from his head an eagle plume*] Maiden, take this; it means speed and safety; when the startling whoop is heard and the war hatchet gleams in the red blaze, let it be found in thy braided hair. Despise not the red man's gift; it will bring more good to you than the yellow earth the white man worships as his god. Take it— no Wampanoag's hand will e'er be raised against the head or hand that bears the eagle plume. [*Crosses to Walter*] Young man, be thou like the oak in its spreading power and let thy tough branches shelter the tender flower that springs up under them. Look to the maiden of the eagle plume, and—come to my wigwam. [*Exit*]

OCEANA. Teach him, Walter; make him like to us.

WALT. 'Twould cost him half his native virtues. Is justice goodly? Metamora's just. Is bravery virtue? Metamora's brave. If love of country, child and wife and home, be to deserve them all—he merits them.

OCEANA. Yet he is a heathen.

WALT. True, Oceana, but his worship though untaught and rude flows from his heart, and Heaven alone must judge of it. [*Enter Tramp*]

TRAMP. Your father, lady, requires your presence.

OCEANA. Say I come. [*A distant drum*]

WALT. What is that?

TRAMP. The drum that summons Lord Fitzarnold's escort. He comes a suitor for my lady's hand. [*Exit Tramp*]

WALT. Deny it, Oceana—say 'tis false!

OCEANA. It is—

WALT. Untrue?

OCEANA. Oh, most unwelcome.

WALT. Heavens! You tremble—and your cheek is pale—my Lord Fitz-arnold, that most courtly gentleman, and must my hopes—

OCEANA. Walter, dost thou mean—

WALT. Obey thy sire. I cannot say farewell. But, oh, when highborn revelers carouse, and proud Fitzarnold lords it at the board, give one brief thought to me! That blessed thought shall soothe the fond complainings of my heart and hush them to repose. [*Exit Walter L. Oceana exit R.*]

SCENE 2: *Lights up. A room in Sir Arthur's house. Enter Sir Arthur and Walter.*

WALT. Yet hear me, sir.

SIR A. Forebear; thou art too hot.

WALT. 'Tis not the meanness of our state that galls us, but men's opinions. Poverty and toil and consciousness of lowly destiny sit lightly where no scorn is heaped upon them. But yesterday I was indeed content, for none despised, none had learned to scoff the son of charity, the wretched ship boy who could trace existence no further than the wreck from which you plucked him; but now 'tis changed, all suddenly begin to find me base.

SIR. A. Marry, go to! You wrong yourself and me. Have I not fostered you—like a father tutored you? In early life bereft of wife and child, wearied of discord and fierce civil strife, I left the haunts of wild and factious men, to woo contentment in this wilderness. My heart was vacant and received thee in. Do not by any rash, unworthy act forsake that heart. Who is it finds thee base?

WALT. All, since Fitzarnold is expected here.

SIR A. Fitzarnold! What a plague! There is naught talked of or thought of but Lord Fitzarnold! And yet this noble viscount, but for his coat and title were a man to look with scorn upon—a profligate and spendthrift as fame already has too truly shown him.

WALT. And 'tis for such a man that Master Mordaunt sets me aside—for such a man his daughter must cast me off.

SIR A. Tut! Master Mordaunt is too wise a man to give his daughter to this Lord Fitzarnold. Patience awhile, and watch the progress of this meteor. Patience, and trust to fortune. [*Exit*]

WALT. This lordly suitor comes to wake me from my cherished dreams, and crush the hopes which lately looked so fair. And shall I yield the glorious prize I deemed was wholly mine? Yield, and without a struggle? No, by heaven! Look to thyself, Fitzarnold. Let Oceana be but true, I heed not all thy power, thy wealth, thy titles, backed though they be by Mordaunt's selfish views. [*Exit*]

SCENE 3: *The harbor. Ships anchored in the distance. Military music. Mordaunt, Errington, Goodenough, Church, Soldiers, Citizens (male and female) discovered. A boat comes on from L., with Fitzarnold, Wolfe, and Sailors, who land. Shout.*

MOR. Long live the king! Welcome Fitzarnold! Rest to the sea-worn! Joy to each and all!

FITZ. I thank thee, Mordaunt! But I did not think to see such faces in the wilderness! Thy woody shores are bright with sparkling eyes, like Argonaut's adventurous sailors. But where's the golden boon we look for, sir? Fair Oceana—Mordaunt, where is she? [*Walter enters, L., and stands against wing*]

MOR. So please you, my lord, at home, eager to pay your lordship's kindness back, and prove she can discern thy courtesy.

WALT. [*Aside*] Indeed! Dost say so, worldling?

MOR. Pray thee, regard these gentlemen, my lord—our council's father, Errington—and this our army's leader; elders of the State. [*Introducing them severally; Fitzarnold salutes them, and at last approaching Walter, extends his hand; Walter bows coldly but does not take it. Music eight bars*]

FITZ. How now, young sir? Mordaunt, who is this?

MOR. My noble lord, I pray thee, heed him not! A wayward youth, somewhat o'er worn with study. [*Crosses to Walter*] Rash boy! Be wise and tempt me not; I can destroy—

WALT. Thy daughter's peace and wed her there. [*Mordaunt gives Walter a look of hate and turns from him*]

MOR. Forth to the hall—a strain of music there. [*Crosses to R.*]

FITZ. Young sir, I shall desire some further converse with you.

WALT. At injury's prompting, deeds, not words, were best. My lord, you shall find me. [*Touches his sword*]

FITZ. Now for thy fair daughter, Mordaunt, come. [*Music. Exeunt all but Walter and Wolfe. Peasants and Soldiers exeunt, R.*]

WOLFE. Thou goest not with them?

WALT. No, nor before, nor follow after. But why dost thou ask?

WOLFE. Because I know thee.

WALT. Then thou knowest one who will not take a lordling by the hand, because his fingers shine with hoops of gold—nor shun the beggar's grasp if it be honest. Thou knowest me?

WOLFE. Yes!

WALT. To know oneself was thought task enough in olden time. What dost thou know?

WOLFE. That thou wert wrecked and saved.

WALT. Aye, more's the pity! [*Aside*] Had I been drowned I had not lived to love and have no hope.

WOLFE. Thou art a good man's son.

WALT. A pity then, again. Were I a rascal's offspring, I might thrive. What more?

WOLFE. Thou shalt possess thy mistress.

WALT. Didst mark that lord?

WOLFE. He is my master.

WALT. Then I am dumb. Be faithful to him, and now farewell. [*Crosses to L.*]

WOLFE. Yet in good time I will say that you will bestow a blessing for.

WALT. Indeed! What mean you? [*Enter Tramp, L., with packet*]

TRAMP. News from the Indians. [*Shows packet*] 'Tis for the council by a horseman left, who bade me see it with all haste delivered. The Indian tribes conspire from east to west and faithful Sasamond has found his grave! This packet must be borne to Mordaunt.

WALT. Trust it with me.

TRAMP. That I will readily, so thou wilt bear it safely.

WALT. Aye, and quickly, too. [*Takes packet, crosses to R.*] Let me remember Metamora's words—"Look to the maiden of the eagle plume." [*Exit hastily, followed by Wolfe, and Tramp. Quick curtain*]

ACT II.

SCENE 1: *Music. Interior of a wigwam; a skin rolled. Stage covered with skins, etc. Child on skin near R. entrance. Nahmeokee near it. Metamora at L., preparing for the chase.*

NAH. Thou wilt soon be back from the chase.

META. Yes, before the otter has tasted his midday food on the bank of the stream, his skin shall make a garment for Nahmeokee when the snow whitens the hunting grounds and the cold wind whistles through the trees. Nahmeokee, take our little one from his rest; he sleeps too much.

Nah. Oh, no! But thou, Metamora, sleepst too little. In the still hour of midnight when Wekolis has sung his song, and the great light has gone down behind the hills, when Nahmeokee's arms like the growing vine were round thee—as if some danger lay waiting in the thick wood—thou didst bid me bring thy tomahawk and the spear that Massasoit had borne when the war cry of the Wampanoags was loudest in the place of blood! Why is thy rest like the green lake when the sudden blast passes across its bosom?

META. Nahmeokee, the power of dreams has been on me, and the shadows of things that are to be have passed before me. My heart is big with a great thought. When I sleep I think the knife is red in my hand, and the scalp of the white man is streaming.

Nah. Metamora, is not the white man our brother? And does not the Great Spirit look on him as he does on us? Do not go towards his home today because thy wrath is kindled and it spreads like the flames which the white man makes in the dark bosom of the forest. Let Nahmeokee clasp her arms around thee; rest thy head upon her bosom, for it is hot and thy eye is red with the thoughts that burn! Our old men counsel peace, and the aim of the white man will spare.

META. Yes, when our fires are no longer red, on the high places of our fathers; when the bones of our kindred make fruitful the fields of the stranger, which he has planted amidst the ashes of our wigwams; when we are hunted back like the wounded elk far toward the going down of the sun, our hatchets broken, our bows unstrung and war whoop hushed; then will the stranger spare, for we will be too small for his eye to see. [*Trumpet; enter Otah*]

OTAH. O son of Massasoit, the power of the white man approaches, and he looks not like one who seeks the Wampanoag's friendship! Look where the bright weapons flash through the clouds of his track.

META. Ha! Let the paleface come with the calumet or with the knife, Metamora does not fear their power. Where is Annawandah, skilled in talk? Let him approach me. [*Exit Otah*]

Nah. Our child would not rest in the mid-hour of night for the hidden snake had bitten him as he lay stretched in the rays of the sun. I rose from my seat to get the dried leaves the Good Spirit has filled with power to heal; the moon was bright and a shadow passed me. It was Annawandah passed our wigwam; his step was like the course of the serpent and he paused and listened. My eye followed him to the seaside, and his light canoe shot like an arrow across the slumbering waters.

META. Humph! Was he alone?

Nah. Alone.

META. And he went with fear?

NAH. Like one who goes to steal. [*Trumpet. Enter Otah*]

OTAH. Look! The white warrior comes. [*Enter Church, Sir Arthur Vaughan, and Goodenough, with musqueteers (sic)*]

CHURCH. Although we come unbidden, chieftain, yet is our purpose friendly.

META. Why do you bring your fire weapons if you come to hold a talk of peace?

CHURCH. It is our custom.

META. Well, speak; my ears are open to hear.

SIR A. Philip, our mission is—

META. Philip! I am the Wampanoag chief, Metamora.

SIR A. We are directed by our council's head, for the times are filled with doubt, and to make *sure* our bond of peace and love to urge your presence at the council.

NAH. [*Aside*] Do not go.

META. Daughter of Miantinemo, peace! [*To them*] I will go.

CHURCH. Our troops shall form thy escort there.

META. I know the path.

SIR A. We must not go without thee, chief.

META. I have breasted the cold winds of forty winters and to those that spoke kindly to me in the words of love I have been pliant—aye, very yielding like the willow that droops over the stream, but till with a single arm you can move the mighty rock that mocks the lightning and the storm seek not to stir Metamora when his heart says no. I will come! [*Crosses to R.*]

CHURCH. We shall expect thee, chief.

META. Metamora cannot lie.

CHURCH. Stand to your arms. [*Trumpet. Exit Church, Goodenough, Otah and Soldiers*]

SIR A. Be thou not rash, but with thy tongue of manly truth dispel all charge that wrongs thy noble nature. Throw not the brand that kindles bloody war lest thou thyself should be the victim. [*Sir Arthur going, L.*]

META. My father's deeds shall be my counsellors, and the Great Spirit will hear the words of my mouth. [*Exit Sir Arthur*] Now, Nahmeokee, I will talk to thee. Dost thou not love this little one, Nahmeokee?

NAH. Oh, yes!

META. When first his little eyes unclosed, thou saidst they were like mine; and my people rejoiced with a mighty joy, that the grandson of Massasoit, the white man's friend, should rule in the high places of his kindred; and hoped that his days would be long and full of glory. Nahmeokee, by the blood of his warlike race, he shall not be the white man's slave.

NAH. Thy talk is strange, and fear creeps over me. Thy heart is beating at thy side, as if thy bosom could not hold it.

META. Because 'tis full of thee—and thee, my little one. Humph! Bring me the knife thy brother wore in battle—my hatchet—the spear that was thy father's when Uncas slew him for the white man's favor. Humph! These things thou gavest me with thyself; thinkest thou this arm can wield them in the fight?

NAH. Ah! Thy bravery will lose thee to me.

META. Let not thy heart be troubled. If I require assistance from my people, I will lift up a flame on the lofty hill that shall gleam afar through the thick darkness.

NAH. I shall remember thy words.

META. Take in thy babe; I am going. [*Crosses to L.*]

NAH. Metamora, dost thou go alone?

META. No; Manito is with me. [*Exit. Nahmeokee exit*]

SCENE 2: *A room in the house of Mordaunt. Enter Oceana.*

OCEANA. Free from Fitzarnold's gaze, I feel myself again. Why came he here? His looks appalled [me] yet my father smiled—ah! he comes. [*Enter Mordaunt*]

MOR. How now, my daughter; how is this? Why have you left his lordship thus?

OCEANA. I thought 'twas time.

MOR. It is not time to play the prude, when noble men confess thy charms and come fair suitors to thee. Fitzarnold loves thee and his alliance is so dear to me, I'll have no scruples of a timid girl to weigh against it. For long years I've nursed this fondness and I now command obedience.

OCEANA. That union must remain unblessed wherein the helpless hand is giving no heart to bear it company. O my father, how at the altar can I take that vow my heart now whispers never can be kept.

MOR. Hear me, rash girl, now that none o'erhear our converse. Learn thy father's destiny—the name I bear is not my own!

OCEANA. My father!

MOR. Thou didst not know my former life and deeds. Hardy adventure and the shock of arms, civil contention and a monarch's death make up the past, and poison all who come! 'Tis thou alone can clothe my future days with peace and shed one cheering ray o'er a dark scene of terror.

OCEANA. Art thou distraught?

Mor. Do not deny me, girl, and make me so! I am an outcast and a man forbid. Fitzarnold knows me and he asks my child—has power, and gaining thee preserves thy sire. Speak, Oceana! Thy resolve: what is it?

Oceana. Thou canst not mean it, father! No, it cannot be!

Mor. Girl, it is as certain as our earthly doom. Decide, then, now between my honor and my instant death! For by thy mother's memory and by my soul, if my despair do find thee pitiless, my own right hand shall end a wretched life and leave thee nothing for a bridal dower but my curses and a blighted name. [Crosses to R.]

Oceana. My throat is parched! I pray a moment's peace, a moment's pause. [Business. Mordaunt paces the stage in great agitation, at last falls on his knee to Oceana. Walter enters, starts at seeing them and remains at back]

Mor. Look at thy father, lowly begging life of thee. I will not swear, I will not rave, my child, but I'll implore thee! If thou hast ever loved me and dost so still, show that affection now! Let not thy father's name forever stand a mark for men to heap their curses on—relent, my child.

Oceana. I can endure no more—rise, my father.

Mor. Dost thou promise?

Oceana. All, all!

Mor. Swear, by truth! by honor! By the dead—

Oceana. To wed Fitzarnold—

Walt. [Comes up] Hold! Hold, rash girl, forebear! Thou art ensnared and wouldst pronounce thy doom.

Mor. Lightning consume thee, meddling fool! What bringst thou here?

Walt. No pleasant duty, sir; a message which the council sends thee here. [Gives packet to Mordaunt] I am no spy, nor do I care to know secrets too dread for thine own heart to hold.

Mor. Beggar, begone! [Strikes him with packet and crosses to L. Walter draws swords. Oceana interposes]

Oceana. It is my father, Walter, mine.

Walt. A blow.

Oceana. Oh, thou wilt forgive him!

Walt. Never! I will forth, and ere he shall enforce thee where thou hast no joy, will rend the mask he cheats us with. [Crosses to L.]

Oceana. And if thou dost, by heaven I'll ne'er be thine.

Walt. [Sheathes sword] Old man, an angel's bosom shelters thine. Instruct Fitzarnold in our quarrel's cause. No daughter bars my way to him. [Exit. Enter Fitzarnold]

Fitz. How now, you tremble; what has chanced?

Mor. A moody beggar who abused my love and I chastised him for it—
that's all.

Oceana. My father—

Mor. Go to thy chamber.

Oceana. Would it were my grave. [*Exit*]

Mor. My noble lord, that moody stripling whom you saw last night—
whether set on by Vaughan, his patron, or by the vainness of his own con-
ceits, resolves to break my daughter's marriage.

Fitz. And wilt thou suffer this? What is the villain's state?

Mor. Dependence on Sir Arthur Vaughan; his wealth a goodly person
and the [law?] love of schools. [*sic*] [*Bell tolls*] Hark! I am summoned to
the council. Wilt thou along? [*Fitzarnold crosses to L.*]

Fitz. I trust he finds no favor with your daughter.

Mor. She shall be thine, my lord; thine with free will and full contentment. Now for the council. [*Exeunt*]

Scene 3: *Flourish. The council chamber. Errington, Sir Arthur and Church
on raised platform. Mordaunt and Fitzarnold seated at table, L. Elders, etc.
Goodenough and Soldiers, R. Villagers, etc. Walter and Tramp.*

Err. 'Tis news that asks from us most speedy action. Heaven has in sounds
most audible and strange, in sights, too, that amazed the lookers-on, fore-
warned our people of their peril. 'Tis time to lift the arm so long supine, and
with one blow cut off this heathen race, who spite of reason and the word
revealed, continue hardened in their devious ways, and make the chosen
tremble. Colleagues, your voices—speak—are you for peace or war?

Sir A. What is your proof your Indian neighbors mean not as fairly towards our settlements as did King Philip's father, Massasoit?

Err. Sir, we have full proof that Philip is our foe. Sasamond, the faithful
servant of our cause, has been dispatched by Philip's men, set on to murder
him. One of his tribe confessed the horrid truth—and will, when time shall
call, give horrid proof on't. I say this chieftain is a man of blood, and Heaven
will bless the valiant arm that slays him. [*Metamora enters suddenly and remains at C. When Metamora enters, all start and grasp their swords. The
soldiers prepare to fire. All are silent and confused*]

Meta. You sent for me and I am come. Humph! If you have nothing to
say I will go back—if you fear to question, Metamora does not fear to answer.

Err. Philip, 'tis thought you love us not, and all unmindful of our league
of peace, plot with the Narragansetts, and contrive fatal disorder to our colony.

META. Do your fears counsel you? What is it makes your old men grave? And your young men grasp their fire weapons as if they awaited the onset of the foe? Brothers, what has Metamora done that doubt is in all your faces and your spirits seem troubled? The good man's heart is a stranger to fear, and his tongue is ready to speak the words of truth.

ERR. We are informed that thou gavest shelter to a banished man, whose deeds unchristian met our just reproof—one by our holy synod doomed—whom it is said you housed, and thereby hast incurred our church's censure—and given just cause to doubt thy honesty.

META. Why was that man sent away from the home of his joy? Because the Great Spirit did not speak to him as he had spoken to you? Did you not come across the great waters and leave the smoke of your fathers' hearth because the iron hand was held out against you, and your hearts were sorrowful in the high places of prayer. Why do you that have just plucked the red knife from your own wounded sides, strive to stab your brother?

ERR. Indian, this is no reply for us. Didst thou not know the sentence of the court on him whom thou didst shelter?

META. If my rarest enemy had crept unarmed into my wigwam and his heart was sore, I would not have driven him from my fire nor forbidden him to lie down upon my mat. Why then should the Wampanoag shut out the man of peace when he came with tears in his eyes and his limbs torn by the sharp thorns of the thicket? Your great book, you say, tells you to give good gifts to the stranger and deal kindly with him whose heart is sad; the Wampanoag needs no such counselor, for the Great Spirit has with his own fingers written it upon his heart.

MOR. Why dost thou put arms into thy people's hands, thereby engendering mischief towards us?

META. If my people do wrong, I am quick to punish. Do you not set a snare for them that they may fall, and make them mad with the fire water the Great Spirit gave you in his wrath? The red man sickens in the house of the palefaces, and the leaping stream of the mountains is made impure by the foul brooks that mingle with it.

SIR A. Chieftain, since these things are so, sell us thy lands and seek another biding place.

META. And if I did, would you not stretch out your hand to seize that also? No! White man, no! Never will Metamora forsake the home of his fathers, and let the plough of the strangers disturb the bones of his kindred.

CHURCH. These are bold words, chief.

META. They are true ones.

Err.   They give no token of thy love of peace. We would deal fairly with thee—nay, be generous.

Meta.   Then would you pay back that which fifty snows ago you received from the hands of my father, Massasoit. Ye had been tossed about like small things upon the face of the great waters, and there was no earth for your feet to rest on; your backs were turned upon the land of your fathers. The red man took you as a little child* and opened the door of his wigwam. The keen blast of the north howled in the leafless wood, but the Indian covered you with his broad right hand and put it back. Your little ones smiled when they heard the loud voice of the storm, for our fires were warm and the Indian was the white man's friend.*

Err.   Such words are needless now.

Meta.   I will speak no more; I am going.

Mor.   Hold! A moment, Philip; we have yet to tell of the death of Sasamond, who fell in secret and by treachery.

Meta.   So should the treacherous man fall, by the keen knife in the darkness and not ascend from the strife of battle to the bright haven where the dead warrior dwells in glory.

Err.   Didst thou contrive his murder?

Meta.   I will not answer.

Err.   We have those can prove thou didst.

Meta.   I have spoken.

Err.   Bring in the witness. [*Exit Goodenough*] We, too, long have stayed the arm of power from execution. Come, we parley with a serpent and his wiles are deep.

Meta.   Injurious white man! Do not tread too hard upon the serpent's folds. His fangs are not taken out, nor has its venom lost the power to kill.

Err.   Approach! [*Goodenough returns with Annawandah*]

Meta.   Annawandah!

Err.   Behold, deceitful man, thy deeds are known.

Meta.   Let me see his eye. Art thou he whom I snatched from the war club of the Mohigan [*sic*], when thou hadst sung thy death song, and the lips of the foe were thirsty for thy blood? Has Metamora cherished thee in his wigwam and hast thou put a knife into the white man's hand to slay him! The foul spirit hath entered thee, and the pure blood of the Wampanoag has left thy veins. Thy heart is a lie, and thine eye cannot rest upon the face of truth, when like the great light it shines on thee in unclouded glory. Elders,

---

* Lines between asterisks are reprinted from the Forrest Home manuscript, because they are illegible in the University of Utah manuscript.

can he speak to you the words of truth, when he is false to his brother, his country and his god?

ERR. He was thy trusty agent, Philip, and conscience-smote revealed thy wickedness.

META. You believe his words?

ERR. We do, and will reward his honesty.

META. Wampanoag! No, I will not call thee so. Red man, say unto these people they have bought thy tongue, and thou hast uttered a lie!

ERR. He does not answer.

META. I am Metamora, thy father and thy king.

ERR. Philip o'erawes him—send the witness home.

META. I will do that! Slave of the white man, go follow Sasamond. [*Stabs Annawandah, who staggers off, R. All stand up, general movement*]

ERR. Seize and bind him. [*Soldiers make a forward movement*]

META. Come! My knife has drunk the blood of the false one, yet it is not satisfied! White man, beware! The mighty spirits of the Wampanoag race are hovering o'er your heads; they stretch out their shadowy arms to me and ask for vengeance; they shall have it. The wrath of the wronged Indian shall fall upon you like a cataract that dashes the uprooted oak down the mighty chasms. The war whoop shall start you from your dreams at night, and the red hatchet gleam in the blaze of your burning dwellings! From the east to the west, in the north and in the south shall cry of vengeance burst, till the lands you have stolen groan under your feet no more!

ERR. Secure him!

META. Thus do I smite your nation and defy your power.

ERR. Fire on him. [*Business. Metamora hurls hatchet into stage, and rushes out, C. Soldiers fire after him. Mordaunt, who has moved forward, receives a shot and falls in chair. Tableau. Drums, trumpets, and general confusion. Quick curtain*]

ACT III.

SCENE 1: *A chamber in Mordaunt's house. Enter Fitzarnold.*

FITZ. Mordaunt wounded, and perhaps to death, struck by a shot that was leveled at the chief; and the fierce storm of war at distance heard, which soon may burst tremendous o'er our heads! This is no place for me. She must be mine tonight! Aye, this night, for fear his death may snatch his gold and daughter from me. Within there, Wolfe! [*Enter Wolfe*] Go get a surgeon for this Mordaunt's wounds, a scribe and priest for me—wilt be silent?

WOLFE. I will observe! Does my lord wed tomorrow?

Fitz. No, this night; and with tomorrow's sun I spread my sail for England.

Wolfe. Ha!

Fitz. How now! What meanest thou? Wouldst thou to rival me?

Wolfe. My lord!

Fitz. Well, well; go see thy duty done. [*Exit*]

Wolfe. My lord, be sure on't. Now for young Walter. I will fulfill my duty but not to thee, my Lord Fitzarnold! Thou wilt not thank me for the priest I'll bring. [*Exit*]

Scene 2: *An Indian village, deep wood, set wigwam, R. Lights half down. Conch shell heard. Nahmeokee enters from wigwam.*

Nah. Sure 'twas the shell of Metamora, and spoke the strain it was wont when the old men were called to council, or when the scout returns from his long travel.

Meta. [*Outside*] Nahmeokee!

Nah. It is—it is Metamora. [*Enter Metamora*]

Meta. Is our little one well, Nahmeokee?

Nah. He is. How didst thou leave the white man with whom thou hast been to hold a talk?

Meta. Like the great stream of the mountain when the spirit of the storm passes furiously over its bosom. Where are my people?

Nah. Here in the deep woods where Kaweshine,* the aged priest, tells them the mighty deeds of their people, and interprets to them the will of the Great Spirit.

Meta. Otah! [*Otah enters*] Summon my warriors; bid them with speed to council. [*Exit Otah*] I have escaped the swift flight of the white man's bullets but like the bounding elk when the hunters who follow close upon his heels. [*Reenter Otah with Kaweshine and all the Indians. Indian march, eight bars. Indians form at L.*] Warriors, I took a prisoner from the uplifted weapon of the Mohigan, when the victor's limbs were bloody and the scalps at his belt had no number. He lived in my wigwam; I made him my brother. When the spirit of sleep was upon me, he crept like a guilty thing away, and put into the white man's hand a brand of fire to consume me, and drive my people far away where there are no hunting grounds and where the Wampanoag has no protecting Spirit.

Kawe. Annawandah?

Meta. Annawandah!

* From this point on, the manuscript reads *Kaweshine* instead of the original reading, *Kaneshine.*

KAWE. Where is he, chief of thy people, and where is the dog whose head the Great Spirit will smite with fire?

META. Where the ravenous bird of night may eat the flesh of his body. Here is the blood of the traitor's heart! [*Shows knife*] My people, shall I tell you the thoughts that fill me?

KAWE. Speak, Metamora, speak!

META. When the strangers came from afar off, they were like a little tree; but now they are grown up and their spreading branches threaten to keep the light from you. They ate of your corn and drank of your cup, and now they lift up their arms against you. O my people, the race of the red man has fallen away like the trees of the forest before the axes of the palefaces. The fair places of his father's triumphs hear no more the sound of his footsteps. He moves in the region his proud fathers bequeathed him, not like a lord of the soil, but like a wretch who comes for plunder and for prey. [*Distant thunder and lightning*]

KAWE. The chief has spoken truly and the stranger is worthy to die! But the fire of our warriors is burnt out and their hatchets have no edge. O son of Massasoit, thy words are to me like the warm blood of the foe, and I will drink till I am full! Speak again!

META. "Chief of the people," said a voice from the deep as I lay by the seaside in the eyes of the moon—"Chief of the people, wake from thy dream of peace, and make sharp the point of thy spear, for the destroyer's arm is made bare to smite. O son of my old age, arise like the tiger in great wrath and snatch thy people from the devourer's jaws!" My father spoke no more; a mist passed before me, and from the mist the Spirit bent his eyes imploringly on me. I started to my feet and shouted the shrill battle cry of the Wampanoags. The high hills sent back the echo, and rock, hill and ocean, earth and air opened their giant throats and cried with me, "Red man, arouse! Freedom! Revenge or death!" [*Thunder and lightning. All quail but Metamora*] Hark, warriors! The Great Spirit hears me and pours forth his mighty voice with mine. Let your voice in battle be like his, and the flash from your fire weapons as quick to kill. Nahmeokee, take this knife, carry it to the Narragansett, to thy brother; tell him the hatchet is dug from the grave where the grass is grown old above it; thy tongue will move him more than the voice of all our tribe in the loud talk of war.

NAH. Nahmeokee will not fail in her path; and her eyes will be quick to see where the stranger has set his snare.

META. Warriors! Your old and infirm must you send into the country of the Narragansett, that your hearts may not be made soft in the hour of battle.

NAH. Go you tonight, Metamora?

META. Tonight! I will not lay down in my wigwam till the foe has drawn himself together and comes in his height to destroy. Nahmeokee, I still will be the red man's father and his king, or the sacred rock whereon my father spoke so long the words of wisdom shall be made red with the blood of his race. [*Hurried music. Metamora and Indians exeunt. Nahmeokee goes in wigwam*]

SCENE 3: *A chamber in Mordaunt's house. Clock strikes twelve as scene opens. Thunder distant. Enter Oceana in plain attire.*

OCEANA. I know not how it is but every thunder peal seems to bear words portentous. The moaning blast has meaning in its sound and tells of distant horror—it is the hour when I bade Walter come! Can he have braved the tempest? Hark, I hear a step! [*Knock*] How my heart beats. [*Enter Fitzarnold*] It is—it is Fitzarnold!

FITZ. Fitzarnold, lady! Why this wonder? Is it fear? Can she whom thunder frights not shrink from me?

OCEANA. My lord, the hour is late; I feign would know who sent thee hither.

FITZ. Thy honored father.

OCEANA. Thy purpose?

FITZ. Read it there. [*Gives letter*]

OCEANA. Ha! Tonight! Be thine tonight?

FITZ. Aye, tonight. I have thy father's secret.

OCEANA. I know thou hast, and in that mean advantage wouldst mar his daughter's happiness forever—away! I blush that thus I parley words with thee—get thee gone. [*Crosses to L.*]

FITZ. Yes, when thou goest with me; not till then, lady. I will not waste the time that grows more precious every moment to me. [*Thunder*] What though the lightning flash and thunder roll—what though the tempest pours its fury down, Fitzarnold's soul does swell above the din! Nay more, dares brave the storm within thy breast, and shrinks not from the lightning of thine eye.

OCEANA. Would it could kill thee!

FITZ. It can do more—can conquer like the fiery serpent. It pierces, and as it pierces charms—Oceana!

OCEANA. Stand back! I will alarm my sire.

FITZ. And if thou dost, he will not aid thee. My treasures are embarked, aye, all but thee; thy father gives consent, the priest waits and ere morning, father, daughter, son, shall all be riding on the wave for England.

OCEANA. No, never!

FITZ. Convince thyself—[*Stamps his foot. Walter enters disguised as a priest*] Now, scornful lady, thy bridal hour has come; thy tauntings do but fan the flame that rages here.

OCEANA. Is there no refuge?

FITZ. None, but in these arms.

OCEANA. No hope—no rescue!

FITZ. None! None!

OCEANA. Walter, on thee I call—Walter, where art thou?

WALT. [*Throws off disguise*] Walter is here.

FITZ. Villain! Thy life or mine! [*Fitzarnold draws, Oceana throws herself between them*]

OCEANA. Forebear! No blood! [*To Walter*] Thou must come stainless to these arms.

WALT. Sayest thou? Wilt thou take me to them?

OCEANA. I will—I do. [*They embrace*]

FITZ. Thy father's blood be on thee; he is Fitzarnold's victim. [*Exit, R. Bell rings. Enter Tramp, L.*]

TRAMP. The savages approach! The Wampanoag chieftain and his crew, at distance, peal their startling yell of war! Haste, sir, to meet them.

WALT. Retire thee for a while, my Oceana—thou, sir, on the instant follow me—your sword! your sword! [*Exit, R. with Oceana, Tramp follows*]

SCENE 4: *A view of Mordaunt's house on the beach, R. Sea in distance, ship on fire. Garden and staircase leading down to the water. Lights down at opening of scene. Distant yells heard. Enter Fitzarnold hastily.*

FITZ. Almighty powers! Hemmed in on every side! No hope. [*War whoop*] Hark to their savage yells! No means are left for flight, for on the waves my precious vessel burns—by the fell savage mastered! No retreat! [*War whoops. Exit Fitzarnold hastily. Metamora and all the Indians enter up staircase entrances. Music hurried, forte till all are on.*]

META. [*Pointing to Fitzarnold*] Follow him! [*To others*] Go into the white man's dwelling and drag him to me that my eye can look upon his torture and his scalp may tell Metamora's triumph to his tribe—go. [*Otah and Kaweshine are about to enter the house when Oceana appears*]

OCEANA. Forebear, ye shall not enter.

META. Warriors, have I not spoken. [*Throws her around to L. Indians go in*]

OCEANA. Great chieftain! Dost thou not know me?

META. I am a Wampanoag in the home of mine enemy; I ride on my wrongs, and vengeance cries out for blood.

OCEANA. Wilt thou not hear me?

META. Talk to the rattling storm or melt the high rocks with tears; thou canst not move me. My foe! my foe! my foe!

OCEANA. Have mercy, Heaven! [*The Indians return dragging in Mordaunt and down R.*]

META. Hah!

MOR. Mercy! Mercy!

OCEANA. My father! Spare my father! [*Rushes to Mordaunt*]

META. He must die! Drag him away to the fire of the sacrifice that my ear may drink the music of his dying groans.

OCEANA. Fiends and murderers!

META. The white man has made us such. Prepare. [*Business*]

OCEANA. Then smite his heart through mine; our mangled breasts shall meet in death—one grave shall hold us. Metamora, dost thou remember this? [*Shows eagle plume*]

META. Yes.

OCEANA. It was thy father's. Chieftain, thou gavest it to me.

META. Say on.

OCEANA. Thou saidst it would prove a guardian to me when the conflict raged. Were thy words true when with thy father's tongue thou saidst, whatever being wore the gift, no Indian of thy tribe should do that being harm.

META. The Wampanoag cannot lie.

OCEANA. Then do I place it here. [*Places it on Mordaunt's bosom*]

META. Hah!

OCEANA. The Wampanoag cannot lie, and I can die for him who gave existence to me.

MOR. My child! My child! [*Red fire in house*]

META. Take them apart! [*Indians separate them*] Old man, I cannot let the tomahawk descend upon thy head, or bear thee to the place of sacrifice; but here is that shall appease the red man's wrath. [*Seizes Oceana; flames seen in house*] The fire is kindled in thy dwelling, and I will plunge her in the hot fury of the flames.

MOR. No, no, thou wilt not harm her.

OCEANA. Father, farewell! Thy nation, savage, will repent this act of thine.

META. If thou art just, it will not. Old man, take thy child. [*Throws her to him*] Metamora cannot forth with the maiden of the eagle plume; and he disdains a victim who has no color in his face nor fire in his eye. [*Bugle sounds*]

Mor. Gracious heavens!

Meta. Hark! The power of the white man comes! Launch your canoes! We have drunk blood enough. Spirit of my father, be at rest! Thou art obeyed, thy people are avenged. [*Exit hastily followed by the Indians. Drums and trumpet till curtain. Enter Walter, Goodenough, Church, Soldiers, Peasants, male and female, all from behind house. Soldiers are about to fire, when Walter throws himself before them and exclaims*]

Walt. Forebear! Forebear! [*Walter and Oceana embrace. Tableau. Curtain*]

ACT IV.

The fourth act of *Metamora* is missing from the University of Utah manuscript. Scene and property plots provided at the beginning of the manuscript, together with the Forrest Home manuscript, which includes Metamora's lines, cue lines, and a few stage directions, and clues from the rest of the play suggest the following summary:

The plot of Act IV is chiefly concerned with the capture of Nahmeokee by the white men, the capture of Walter (Horatio) by the Indians, and the demands and threats of the Indian chieftain, Metamora. There are three scenes: an oak chamber, a dark wood, and a landscape. The first scene, obviously located in one of the white men's houses—perhaps that of Errington, the head of the council—shows Nahmeokee a captive. Because Metamora does not appear in this scene, no part of it can be given here. Scene 2 introduces Walter (Horatio), captured by the Indians and about to be killed, until Metamora learns of the capture of Nahmeokee and decides to hold the youthful hero as a hostage. In the third scene Metamora, going to the rescue of his wife, meets the white men with Nahmeokee in the open country, and after several defiant speeches, accepts an offer of peace. Thereupon Nahmeokee is released and sent home to inform the Indians of the terms. (We later discover that Metamora keeps his agreement, but that an attempt to kill Nahmeokee is made by the white men.)

The following pages include the lines from the Forrest Home manuscript, together with a few parenthetical explanations and speculations. (See the introductory note to this play for acknowledgements and additional information concerning this manuscript.)

Scene 1: Missing from both the University of Utah manuscript and the Forrest Home manuscript.

Scene 2: Cue lines of other speakers than Metamora will be indicated by dashes. *Metamora disc^d., regarding the scene.*

————Captive's blood. [*The report of a pistol his [sic] heard. Horatio enters, the Indians raise their tomahawks to strike him*]

META. Forbear! Let the young man say why he has come into our country unbidden. Why does he tempt the ire of our warriors, when their weapons are red with the blood of the battle?

————white and red man, brothers. (Apparently this is Horatio's explanation of his hope to appease the opposing forces.)

META. No, young man, the blood my warriors have tasted, has made their hearts glad, and their hands are thrust out for more. Let the white man fear. The arrow he has shot into the mountain has turned back and pierced his own side. What are the elders' words?

————raised no more. (Perhaps the elders demur.)

META. Humph! And meanwhile he sharpens his bright weapons in secret and each day grows more numerous. When the mountain torrent first springs from the earth it is very weak, and I can stand up against its waters, but when the great rains descend it is swift and swollen, death dwells in its white bosom and it will not spare.

————avenge their countrymen. (The white men, it is feared, will come again in greater numbers.)

META. Well, let 'em come. Our arms are as strong as the white man's, and the use of the fire weapon he has taught us—my ears are shut against thee.

————[*Without*] Metamora!

META. Hah!

————Nahmeokee!

META. Dead?

————bore off the queen a captive.

META. Nahmeokee is the white man's prisoner. [*To Horatio*] Where is thy horse?

————near yonder tree. (Obviously Horatio's lying. Horatio, it should be remembered, is the Walter of the preceding acts.)

META. Unbind this captive. Young man, you must abide with the Wampanoag, until Nahmeokee return to her home. Woe come to you if the hard hand has been laid upon her. Bear these two to my wigwam.

————whose blood I bear. (Probably Horatio again.)

META. If one drop fall from Nahmeokee's eye, one hair from her head, the axe shall hew your quivering limbs asunder, and the ashes of your bones be carried away on the rushing wind.

SCENE 3:

————Take her child from her. (Spoken by one of the white men in charge of Nahmeokee and her child.) [*Enter Metamora*]

META. Stand back, or the swift death shall take wing. [*Pause*] Which of you has lived too long? Let him lift up his arm against her.

————What comest thou for? (The same speaker as at the beginning.)

META. Boy! Thou art a child, there is no mark of the war upon thy brows. Send me thy elder, or thy chief, I will make my talk to him. [*Bugle. Enter Errington and Soldiers*]

————Philip a prisoner! (Probably spoken by Errington.)

META. No. He has arms in his hand and courage in his heart. He comes near you of his own will and when he has done his work he will go back to his wigwam.

————you answer boldly. (Probably Errington again.)

META. What is there I should fear?

————man of blood. (Errington continues.)

META. Does he love mercy, and is he the white man's prince?

————Yes.

META. How did Nahmeokee and her infant wrong you, that you hunted her through the thorny pathway of the glen, and scented her blood, like the fierce red wolf in his hunger?

————sue for peace. (Probably Errington.)

META. Not till the blood of twenty English captives be poured out in sacrifice. Beware! the knife is sharpened, the stake is fixed and the captives' limbs tremble under the gaze of the prophet of wrath. Woe come to them! When my people shall hear their king has been murdered by the palefaces or is bound in the dark place of doom.

————standing in the midst. (Perhaps several speeches here omitted.)

META. Which can easier escape the hunter's spear, the tiger that turns upon it in its wrath or the lamb that sinks down and trembles? Thou hast seen me look unmoved towards a torturing death—shall mine eye be turned downward when the white man frowns?

————regard his words. (One of the councilors speaks.)

META. Yes.

————Wilt yield compliance. (A peace offering is made, whereby, among other things, Nahmeokee's release will be pledged.)

META. I will; Nahmeokee shall bear to my people the tidings that the prisoners shall return to their home, and the war whoop shall not go forth on the evening gale.

————remember thy words. (Errington.)

META. Grieve not that [I?] linger in the dark place of the condemned, for the eye of the Great Spirit will rest on me there.

————Nahmeokee shall return. (Probably Errington.)

META. 'Tis very good. The horse stand under the brow of the hill. Speak no more. I read thy thought in thine eye, but the white man must not know it. It will do. Go Nahmeokee. I am ready to follow you.

————forth to prison. (Apparently some business omitted here. Part of this speech seems addressed privately to Nahmeokee. The following stage direction supports the conclusion that at this point the white men attempt to seize the Indians, despite the previous agreement.) [*Soldier attempts to take his gun*]

META. No. This shall be to me as my child, and I will talk with it till I go back to my people.

————could it but talk.

META. It can! When the land of my great forefathers is trampled on by the foot of the foe, or treachery lurks round the Wampanoag when he bides in the white man's home, then—it *can talk*.

ACT V.

SCENE 1: *Same as Act I, Scene 1. Lights down. Oceana discovered leaning against tomb. Slow music, four bars.*

OCEANA. Tomb of the silent dead, thou seemest my only refuge! O Walter, where art thou? Alas! the kindly promptings of thy noble heart have led thee to captivity, perhaps to death! Welcome the hour when these dark portals shall unfold again, and reunite parent and child in the long sleep of death. [*Enter Fitzarnold*] Ah! Fitzarnold here!

FITZ. I come with words of comfort to thee and feign would soothe thy sorrow.

OCEANA. I do not ask your sympathy, my lord.

FITZ. A sea of danger is around thee, lady, and I would be the skillful pilot to guide thy struggling bark to safety.

OCEANA. Nay, but let me rather perish in the waves than reach a haven to be shared with thee.

FITZ. Thou hast no choice; thy father willed thee mine, and with his latest breath bequeathed thee to me. Walter, my stripling rival in thy love, has left thee here defenseless and alone. I deem as nothing thy unnatural hate, and only see thy fair and lovely form; and though thy flashing eyes were armed with lightning, thus would my arms enfold thee.

OCEANA. [*Clings to tomb*] Now, if thou darest, approach me—now whilst with my mother's spirit hovering o'er me—whilst thus with tearful eyes and breaking heart I call on Heaven to blast the bold audacious wretch, who seeks a daughter's ruin o'er her parents' grave.

FITZ. Aye, despite of all.

META. [*In tomb*] Hold! Touch her not!

OCEANA. Hark to that voice! Kind Heaven has heard my prayers. [*The door of the tomb opens, and Metamora appears. Oceana faints and falls*]

FITZ. Philip here!

META. He is the great spirit [who?] has sent me;* the ghosts are awaiting for thee in the dark place of doom! Now thou must go. Tremble, for the loud cry is terrible and the blaze of their eyes, like the red fire of war, gleams awfully in the night.

FITZ. I have not wronged thee.

META. Not? Didst thou not contrive the death of Nahmeokee, when the treacherous white man thirsted for her blood? Did she not with bended knees, her eyes streaming with woes of the heart, catch hold of thy shining broad garment thinking it covered man? Was not thy hand upraised against her, and thy heart, like thy hand, flint that wounds the weary one who rests upon it.

FITZ. No! no!

META. I saw thee when my quick step was on the hills, and the joy of Metamora's eyes felt thy blows. I feel them now! "Revenge!" cried the shadow of my father as he looked on with me. I, too, cried revenge and now I have it! The blood of my heart grows hotter as I look on him who smote the red cheek of Nahmeokee.

FITZ. As reparation I will give thee gold.

META. No! Give me back the happy days, the fair hunting ground, and the dominion my great forefathers bequeathed me.

FITZ. I have not robbed thee of them.

META. Thou art a white man, and thy veins hold the blood of a robber! Hark! The spirits of the air howl for thee! Prepare—[*Throws him around to R.*]

FITZ. Thou shalt not conquer ere thou killest me. This sword a royal hand bestowed! This arm can wield it still. [*Draws; Metamora disarms and kills him*]

---

* This is the actual reading of the manuscript. A more plausible reading would probably be: "He is. The Great Spirit has sent me."

META. Metamora's arm has saved thee from a common death; who dies by me dies nobly! [*Turns to Oceana*] For thee, Metamora's home shall screen thee from the spreading fury of his nation's wrath. [*Hurry till change. Exit bearing Oceana*]

SCENE 2: *A chamber. Enter Sir Arthur, meeting Errington and Church.*

SIR A. I have news will startle you.

ERR. Is't of the chief?

SIR A. It is; he has escaped our power!

ERR. Escaped! Confusion! How?

SIR A. But now we sought his prison and found it tenantless.

ERR. But how escaped he? There was no egress thence, unless some treacherous hand unlocked the door.

SIR A. And so we thought, at first; but on minute search we found some stones displaced, which showed a narrow opening into a subterranean passage, dark and deep, through which we crept until, to our surprise, we reached the tomb of Mordaunt.

ERR. The tomb of Mordaunt?

SIR A. The ruined pile which now serves as our prison was, years since, when first he sought these shores, the residence of Mordaunt, and this secret passage, doubtless, was formed by him for concealment or escape in time of danger.

ERR. Indeed!

SIR A. Yes, and he had cause to be so guarded, for once, unseen by him, I heard that wretched man commune with Heaven, and sue for pardon for the heinous sin of Hammond of Harrington!

ERR. Hammond! The outlawed regicide?

SIR A. Even so; it was himself he prayed for, the guilty man who gave to death the king, his lord, the royal martyr Charles. As Mordaunt, he here sought refuge from the wrath of the rightful heir now seated on the throne.

ERR. Think you the chieftain knew this secret way?

SIR A. 'Tis likely that he did, or else by chance discovered it and thus has won his freedom and his life.

CHURCH. We must summon our men. Double the guard and have their range extended. [*Exeunt Church and Errington*]

WOLFE. [*Without*] Where is Sir Arthur Vaughan?

SIR A. Who calls? [*Enter Wolfe*] Now, who art thou?

WOLFE. A suppliant for pardon.

SIR A. Pardon—for what?

WOLFE. A grievous sin, I now would feign confess.

SIR A. Indeed! Go on! Declare it then; I will forgive thee!

WOLFE. Long years have passed since then, but you must still remember when at Naples with your wife and child.

SIR A. Ha! Dost thou mean—

WOLFE. The flames consumed thy dwelling and thou together with thy wife and boy, escaped almost by miracle.

SIR A. Ha!

WOLFE. I there looked on midst the assembled throng, a stranger mariner. Urged by the fiend, and aided by the wild confusion of the scene, I snatched your boy and through the noisy throng I bore him to my anchored bark, thinking his waiting parents soon would claim with gold their darling. Next day came on a tempest and the furious winds far from the city drove us and thy child.

SIR A. Heavens! Can this be true?

WOLFE. He grew up the sharer of my sea-born perils. One awful night our vessel stuck upon the rocks near these shores and the greedy ocean swelled over her shattered frame—thy son—

SIR A. Go on—go on—

WOLFE. Was by mysterious power preserved and guided to his unconscious father. Walter is thy son.

SIR A. Man! Why didst thou not tell me?

WOLFE. I feared thy just anger and the force of law. I became Fitzarnold's follower but to this hour has memory tortured me.

SIR A. And Walter is a hostage to the savage foe; perchance they have murdered him!

WOLFE. No! Oceana's kindness to the Indian queen has purchased his freedom and my own.

SIR A. Where is he?

WOLFE. Looking for her he loves, fair Oceana! Whom, 'tis said, a party of the foe carried off.

SIR A. Quick, let us arm and follow him. For thee, this act of justice pardons thee. [*Exeunt*]

SCENE 3: *Indian village. Groups of Indians. Kaweshine and Otah discovered. Kaweshine has been addressing them. His looks are gloomy and bewildered.*

META. [*Outside, at change of scene*] Where are my people?

KAWE. Ha! 'Tis our chief—I know the sound of his voice, and some quick danger follows him. [*Metamora enters, bearing Oceana. Nahmeokee enters from wigwam*]

META. Nahmeokee, take the white maiden in; I would speak to my people; go in and follow not the track of the warrior's band.

NAH. Come in, my mat is soft, and the juice of the sweet berry shall give joy to thy lips. Come in, thou art pale and yielding, like the lily, when it is borne down by the running waters. [*She leads Oceana into wigwam*]

META. Warriors, I have escaped from the hands of the white man, when the fire was kindled to devour me. Prepare for the approaching hour if ye love the high places your fathers trod in majesty and strength. Snatch your keen weapons and follow me! If ye love the silent spots where the bones of your kindred repose, sing the dread song of war and follow me! If you love the bright lakes which the Great Spirit gave you when the sun first blazed with the fires of his touch, shout the war song of the Wampanoag race, and on to the battle follow me! Look at the bright glory that is wrapped like a mantle around the slain in battle! Call on the happy spirits of the warriors dead, and cry, "Our lands! Our nation's freedom! Or the grave!"

KAWE. O chieftain, take my counsel and hold out to the palefaces the pipe of peace. Ayantic and the great Mohican join with our foes against us, and the power of our brother, the Narragansett is no more! List, o chieftain, to the words that I tell of the time to come.

META. Ha! Dost thou prophesy?

KAWE. In the deep wood, when the moon shone bright, my spirit was sad and I sought the ear of Manito in the sacred places; I heard the sound as of one in pain, and I beheld gasping under a hemlock, the lightning had some-time torn, a panther wounded and dying in his thick red gore. I thought of the tales of our forefathers who told us that such was an omen of coming evil. I spoke loudly the name of Metamora, and the monster's eyes closed instantly and he writhed no more. I turned and mourned, for I said, Manito loves no. more the Wampanoag and our foes will prevail.

META. Didst thou tell my people this?

KAWE. Chieftain, yes; my spirit was troubled.

META. Shame of the tribe, thou art no Wampanoag, thy blood is tainted —thou art half Mohigan, thy breath has sapped the courage of my warriors' hearts. Begone, old man, thy life is in danger.

KAWE. I have spoken the words of truth, and the Great Manito has heard them.

META. Liar and coward! Let him preserve thee now! [*About to stab him when Nahmeokee enters from wigwam and interposes*]

NAH. He is a poor old man—he healed the deep wound of our little one. [*Gets to L. of Metamora*]

META. Any breast but Nahmeokee's had felt the keen edge of my knife! Go, corrupted one, thy presence makes the air unwholesome round hope's high places. Begone!

KAWE. Metamora drives me from the wigwam before the lightning descends to set it on fire. Chieftain, beware the omen. [*Exit*]

NAH. [*Aside*] Will he not become the white man's friend and show him the secret path of our warriors? Manito guard the Wampanoag!

META. Men of Po-hon-e-ket, the palefaces come towards your dwellings and no warrior's hatchet is raised for vengeance. The war whoop is hushed in the camp and we hear no more the triumph of battle. Manito hates you, for you have fallen from the high path of your fathers and Metamora must alone avenge the Wampanoag's wrongs.

OMNES. Battle! Battle!

META. Ha! The flame springs up afresh in your bosoms; a woman's breath has brought back the lost treasure of your souls. [*Distant march, drums and trumpet heard*] Ha! they come! Go, warriors, and meet them, and remember the eye of a thousand ages looks upon you. [*Warriors exeunt silently*] Nahmeokee, should the palefaces o'ercome our strength, go thou with our infant to the sacred place of safety. My followers slain, there will the last of the Wampanoags pour out his heart's blood on the giant rock, his father's throne.

NAH. O Metamora!

META. Come not near me or thou wilt make my heart soft, when I would have it hard like the iron and gifted with many lives. Go in, Nahmeokee. [*Distant trumpets. Nahmeokee goes in wigwam. Metamora kneels*] The knee that never bent to man I bend to thee, Manito. As the arm was broken that was put out against Nahmeokee, so break thou the strength of the oppressor's nation, and hurl them down from the high hill of their pride and power, with the loud thunder of thy voice. Confound them—smite them with the lightning of thine eye—while thus I bare my red war arm—while thus I wait the onset of the foe—[*Loud alarm*] They come! Death! Death, or my nation's freedom! [*Rushes off. Loud shouts. Drums and trumpets till change*]

SCENE 4: *Rocky pass. Trumpet sounds retreat. Enter Errington and Church.*

ERR. They fly! They fly—the field is ours! This blow destroys them. Victory cheaply bought at twice our loss; the red man's power is broken now forever. [*Enter Walter*] Is Oceana slain?

WALT. No; the chieftain Metamora rescued her from the base passions of the Lord Fitzarnold whom Metamora slew to avenge the wrongs he offered to his wife, and Oceana by the chief was borne in safety to his lodge.

ERR. In safety?

WALT. Yes; from the hands of Nahmeokee I received her, just as some Indians maddened by defeat, prepared to offer her a sacrifice.

ERR. Away then, Walter. [*Walter crosses to R.*] Sir Arthur now seeks thee out to claim thee as his own [son?]. (Parenthetical word *sic.*)

WALT. My father! I fly to seek him. [*Exit*]

ERR. The victory is ours; yet while Philip lives we are in peril! Come, let us find this Indian prophet whom Metamora banished from his tribe. He may be bribed to show us the chieftain's place of safety. [*Exeunt. Change*]

SCENE 5: *Metamora's stronghold. Rocks, bridge and waterfall. Nahmeokee discovered listening. The child lays under a tree, R., covered with furs. Slow music, four bars.*

NAH. He comes not, yet the sound of the battle has died away like the last breath of a storm! Can he be slain? O cruel white man, this day will stain your name forever. [*Slow music, sixteen bars. Metamora enters on bridge. Crosses and enters L.*]

META. Nahmeokee, I am weary of the strife of blood. Where is our little one? Let me take him to my burning heart and he may quell its mighty torrent.

NAH. [*With broken utterance*] He is here! [*Lifts the furs and shows the child dead*]

META. Ha! Dead! Dead! Cold!

NAH. Nahmeokee could not cover him with her body, for the white men were around her and over her. I plunged into the stream and the unseen shafts of the fire weapons flew with a great noise over my head. One smote my babe and he sunk into the deep water; the foe shouted with a mighty shout, for he thought Nahmeokee and her babe had sunk to rise no more.

META. His little arms will never clasp thee more; his little lips will never press the pure bosom which nourished him so long! Well, is he not happy? Better to die by the stranger's hand than live his slave.

NAH. O Metamora! [*Falls on his neck*]

META. Nay, do not bow down thy head; let me kiss off the hot drops that are running down thy red cheeks. Thou wilt see him again in the peaceful land of spirits, and he will look smilingly as—as—as I do now, Nahmeokee.

NAH. Metamora, is our nation dead? Are we alone in the land of our fathers?

META. The palefaces are all around us, and they tread in blood. The blaze of our burning wigwams flashes awfully in the darkness of their path. We are destroyed—not vanquished; we are no more, yet we are forever—Nahmeokee!

NAH. What wouldst thou?

META. Dost thou not fear the power of the white man?

NAH. No.

META. He may come hither in his might and slay thee.

NAH. Thou art with me.

META. He may seize thee, and bear thee off to the far country, bind these arms that have so often clasped me in the dear embrace of love, scourge thy soft flesh in the hour of his wrath, and force thee to carry burdens like the beasts of the fields.

NAH. Thou wilt not let them.

META. We cannot fly, for the foe is all about us; we cannot fight, for this is the only weapon I have saved from the strife of blood.

NAH. It was my brother's—Coanchett's.

META. It has tasted the white man's blood, and reached the cold heart of the traitor; it has been our truest friend; it is our only treasure.

NAH. Thine eye tells me the thought of thy heart, and I rejoice at it. [*Sinks on his bosom*]

META. Nahmeokee, I look up through the long path of thin air, and I think I see our infant borne onward to the land of the happy, where the fair hunting grounds know no storms or snows, and where the immortal brave feast in the eyes of the giver of good. Look upwards, Nahmeokee, the spirit of thy murdered father beckons thee.

NAH. I will go to him.

META. Embrace me, Nahmeokee—'twas like the first you gave me in the days of our strength and joy—they are gone. [*Places his ear to the ground*] Hark! In the distant wood I faintly hear the cautious tread of men! They are upon us, Nahmeokee—the home of the happy is made ready for thee. [*Stabs her, she dies*] She felt no white man's bondage—free as the air she lived— pure as the snow she died! In smiles she died! Let me taste it, ere her lips are cold as the ice. [*Loud shouts. Roll of drums. Kaweshine leads Church and Soldiers on bridge, R.*]

CHURCH. He is found! Philip is our prisoner.

META. No! He lives—last of his race—but still your enemy—lives to defy you still. Though numbers overpower me and treachery surround me, though friends desert me, I defy you still! Come to me—come singly to me! And this true knife that has tasted the foul blood of your nation and now is red with the purest of mine, will feel a grasp as strong as when it flashed in the blaze of your burning dwellings, or was lifted terribly over the fallen in battle.

CHURCH. Fire upon him!

META. Do so, I am weary of the world for ye are dwellers in it; I would not turn upon my heel to save my life.

CHURCH. Your duty, soldiers. [*They fire. Metamora falls. Enter Walter, Oceana, Wolfe, Sir Arthur, Errington, Goodenough, Tramp and Peasants. Roll of drums and trumpet till all on*]

META. My curses on you, white men! May the Great Spirit curse you when he speaks in his war voice from the clouds! Murderers! The last of the Wampanoags' curse be on you! May your graves and the graves of your children be in the path the red man shall trace! And may the wolf and panther howl o'er your fleshless bones, fit banquet for the destroyers! Spirits of the grave, I come! But the curse of Metamora stays with the white man! I die! My wife! My queen! My Nahmeokee! [*Falls and dies; a tableau is formed. Drums and trumpet sound a retreat till curtain. Slow curtain*]

END

TANCRED, KING OF SICILY;
Or, THE ARCHIVES OF PALERMO

By John Augustus Stone

ACT IV

TANCRED, KING OF SICILY;
Or, THE ARCHIVES OF PALERMO

O F John Augustus Stone's five-act tragedy, *Tancred, King of Sicily; or, The Archives of Palermo,* only a poor copy of the fourth act is extant. Publication of this fragment, however, adds to the hitherto meager evidence of Stone's work. With *Metamora* it brings into print the only known plays of Stone's except the chronicle play, *Tancred; or, The Siege of Antioch,* printed in 1827, but never acted.

Tancred, King of Sicily is completely different from Stone's other *Tancred* play. The present play was produced in New York at the Park Theatre on March 16, 1831, with Stone in the cast. It also had one performance in Philadelphia, on April 14, 1832. The fourth act, which is in blank verse, presents the climax of a melodramatic plot involving the enmity of brothers, a murder, and a dungeon scene. The manuscript copy, secured through the courtesy of Dr. Robert H. Ball, formerly of Princeton University, is confusing, with indications of many alterations and deletions. These will be marked and explained within parentheses. Odell's *Annals of the New York Stage* supplies the New York cast, reprinted here.

DRAMATIS PERSONAE

TANCRED	J. M. FIELD
EMANUEL (or IMMANUEL)	NEXSEN
ROMANO	RICHINGS
OFFICERS	HAYDEN, BISSETT
FRIAR	BANCKER
KAN WOGAN	SIMPSON
EL MORAD	POVEY
XENARCHUS	WOODHULL
ANGELO	BARRY
MALAZZO	T. PLACIDE
BISHOP	WHEATLEY
GIUSEPPE	BLAKELEY
AUGUSTA	MRS. WALLACK
CHILD	MISS TURNBULL
OLYMPIA	MRS. BARNES

(This cast, from Odell, is for the first performance, at the Park Theatre, March 16, 1831. At the third performance, a benefit for the author, Stone played Kan Wogan.)

ACT IV.

SCENE 1: *A private apartment. Angelo discovered pacing the floor.*

ANG. Why do such childish fears creep towards my heart,
  Like midnight stabbers round the brave they'd kill?
  I pant to know Malazzo's artifice—
  Perhaps ere this the mighty blow is struck
  Against the form the purple cannot shield,
  Kan Wogan's lips will utter threats no more—
  Olympia's fury has no terror in't—
  And soon I'll make disposal of the dame—
  The fair Augusta all my own—How now—
  [*Enter an Officer*]

OFF.   A lady muffled and with earnest speech
  Entreats a present interview.

ANG.   Who is't?

OFF. Lady Augusta, so she bade me say.

ANG. Is't possible? My love so near? 'Tis strange,
  Admit her straight—bid all retire—
  Let none break in upon our conference. [*Exit Officer*]
  Full of gratitude she comes to thank me,
  And for a life preserved devotes it all
  To Angelo. She comes—joy's bright herald
  At once divinity and sacrifice.
  [*Enter a Female, closely mantled*]
  Thy presence, fair Augusta, makes my hall
  A temple fit to kneel and worship in.
  Welcome as Iris in the hour of storm,
  Thou comest a rainbow spirit to me now,
  To say "Hope still be thine—" Joy of mine eyes,
  This mantle envies me.
  [*He gently removes the garment*]
  Olympia! [*Aside*] She goes not hence alone!
  [*Attempting to pass*]

OLYM. Stay, Lord Angelo! I command thee, stay!

ANG. Amazed I hear thou dost!

OLYM.   Look on me well—
Despair has made me daring and I'm armed.
[*Drawing a dagger*]
Behold a poisoned steel whose touch is death!

ANG.   Vain woman, should I call my guards—

OLYM.   Did'st thou
They could not hear thee, for thy own command
Confines them to the outer court—

ANG.   [*Coolly*] Indeed!
Then I'll wait their coming.

OLYM.   Thou'lt lack patience,
For I've barred the massive door and bear the key.
[*Showing it*]

ANG.   [*Furiously*]   I'll bid them beat it down.

OLYM.   And if they do,
Two bleeding corses shall affright them back.
I will not singly fall, nor unrevenged.

ANG.   [*Aside*]   First-born of Acheron! She withers me!
[*Gazes in wonder on her. Bell tolls*]

OLYM.   What sound is that?

ANG.   It is the knell of one
I would not live in fear of. Dread thine own!

OLYM.   Is it the Saracen's?

ANG.   Aye, his time is come.

OLYM.   Heavens! Rumour told truth, he goes to death!!
Another hour and succour came too late!

ANG.   His fate concerns not thee—or thine—Begone!

OLYM.   Never till my suit is granted.

ANG.   Suit—
What is thy suit?

OLYM.   Kan Wogan's liberty.
This instant let me bear thy sealed command
To snatch him from the flames enkindling. [*Pause*]
Resolve or else thy bond of blood I'll bear
Through street and palace, church and martial field.

ANG.   [*Aside*]   A *feigned* compliance now.
[*Bell tolls again*]

OLYM.   That peal again!
[*Pause; with sudden firmness*]

May mercy fly me, be despair my doom,
If to my purpose I remain not true.

ANG.   Then have thy wish—[*Aside*] but ere 'tis gained I'll make
Such use of time the boon is valueless.
[*Angelo goes up to the table and writes*]

OLYM.   The blight of age infect the villain's eyes
That he see not my treachery.
And tire of truth for suffering virtue's sake,
Make now my falsehood worthiness.
[*She exchanges the paper for one exactly resembling it*]

ANG.   [*Aside*] Ill fate that I should for a moment stoop
To parley with this outlaw's advocate.
[*He gives her the order. She glances at it and gives him the other*]

OLYM.   Thanks, thanks.

ANG.   Dumb witness of a deed
That sealed a proud oppressive brother's doom.
(Surcease. I rend thee part from part and give
Thy tiny members to the tongueless air!
Nor man nor devil now can conjure up
One black accusing line against me,
No, nor woman either, though of all things ill,
Most cunning, most accurs'd—ha, ha, ha!)*

OLYM.   [*Aside*] He rends a counterfeit. [*Aloud*]
Deceiver, thou art deceived—
Lord Angelo, fate smiles upon thee.
Olympia's ire will now as vainly fall.

ANG.   As hail on adamant.
[*Bell tolls. Olympia rushes out*]
Who's there? [*Enter Officer*]

OFF.   My lord.

ANG.   I've business for thee; mount thy steed,
Haste to the fields where execution waits
The Saracen—see him in death, dwell not
An instant—then by some devious path
Conduct the female who his pardon bears—
I do revoke the order—see it done—Away! [*Exit Officer*]
Her race is run, the grave her goal, or else—

* The last part of this speech has been pretty well crossed out in the manuscript.

One mortal form is *poison-proof*.
[*Enter Malazzo with other Officers in alarm*]
                                        My friends—

MAL.   O tale of horror. Hour that nature mourns!
I scarce dare trust my tongue to tell thee—

ANG.   What?

MAL.   Our royal master is no more!!

ANG.   Is't true?

MAL.   Alas! By ruffian steel he fell!

ANG.   [*Forgetting himself*] Then I'm king.
[*Aside*] What tho' the scepter beat some bloody stains,
'Tis mine—'tis mine!

MAL.   [*Checking him*] My lord, Lord Angelo!

ANG.   [*Aside*] I had forgot. [*Aloud*] No, I'll not believe thee.
Why forge a tale thou know'st will madden me?
Grief chokes thy utterance? Oh! 'Tis true—
And Sicily has lost a father!

MAL.   True!

ANG.   But she has sons will hunt the parricide
And terribly avenge a slaughtered king!
Where lies the body?

MAL.   I'll conduct thee to't.

ANG.   Oh, that my own heart's blood could fill its veins
And warm it into life again!
[*Exeunt Angelo, Officers and Malazzo*]

SCENE 2: *A palace. A dead body on couch. Nobles, Knights, Females and Monks crowd around it, mourning. Immanuel left. Enter Malazzo.*

IMM.   To mourn this deed enough, ye have not groans;
Where did'st thou find the body, officer?

MAL.   Headless as you see it, half immersed
In the green lake that turned to hue of blood
Seems blushing at this crime of monstrous man. [*Enter Angelo*]

ANG.   Where is it, where? [*Goes to body*]
                              Oh, deed to damn a world!
O royal leader—father—friend! [*Weeps and kneeling, kisses the feet of the body*]

MAL.   Alas! I fear so great his love and grief
That fatal blow stabbed mourner and the mourned.

ANG.   What fiend accursed has entered Paradise
And plunged mankind in woe and agony.

IMM.   This dagger buried in his breast we found—
Its fashion speaks its owner *Saracen*. [*Gives it to him*]

ANG.   O sons of blood! the serpent trampled on,
Expiring, darts a fatal sting and dies,
A conqueror—[*To the body*] We fall in thee!

MAL.   My lord,
Where shall we bear the body?

ANG.   My good friends—
'Neath my roof be its hallowed resting place.
With perfumes and libations fit it there
To meet the tearful gaze of multitudes.
Oh, if our tears could kill, cursed Africa
Should o'er slaughtered myriads of her sons
Bewail this deed with us. My friends—[*Bursting into tears*]
Go—go at once—Leave me to lamentations
And to prayer! [*Solemn music. The body is borne off*]
[*Solus*] Heaven-borne spirits, look in wonder on me.
Ambitious ones who in seraphic realms
The everlasting scepter warr'd to gain,
Look from your dwellings of eternal doom,
If such there are, look on and envy me,
As great my noble daring as your own.
The prize—wide earth can show no richer one—
I see it now aloft bedecked with gems
As bright and dazzling as the queen of stars.
I view thee, throne of royalty and power,
Mantled in glory, vacant, firm and *mine*,
My soul mounts upwards toward thee, seat of kings,
As if it winged its eager flight to Heaven
Like some bright goddess there you shine,
And ope your golden arms to welcome me.
Earth's grosser part begone—Oh, at one bound—
[*Darts forward but instantly recoils*]
Ha! What is this—
What wizard act is here?
A cloud comes o'er the glittering scene
And from its crimson bosom issues forth—

Of smoking blood—a deluge! Ha! Horror!
What ermin'd form lies prostrate there—
The King's!—another—his manly bosom
Scarred with wounds—his eye pours forth a flood
As it would beg mercy—Ha! *Romano,*
I cannot strike, I cannot pass him, no!
No! No! No! No! [*He stands shuddering at the scene his fancy
has raised. Enter Malazzo*]

MAL.   Lord Angelo.

ANG.   Who calls me—[*Starting*] Malazzo?

MAL.   What stirs thee? Good my lord?

ANG.   What stirs me?
Why that a child might look unmoved upon.
In the great fullness of my mighty joy
I rose on high to ecstasy. Some fiend
In envy plunged me thence to trembling.
For once, Malazzo, has this bosom quaked,
For once this cheek been blanched with fear.

MAL.   'Tis over now.

ANG.   It is—it is—it is.

MAL.   [*Aside*] Would it were so with me.

ANG.   My trusty friend,
Thou hast outdone my own imaginings—
That poniard used—Aye, 'twas a crafty deed,
Was't not? Suspicion cries "The Saracen,"
But why decapitate? Whose art was that?

MAL.   Ferrara's doubtless—to speak his work done
He'll show the head—it will not *lie,* my lord.
Tonight he meets me at St. Arno's cross.

ANG.   We'll speak anon of that. [*Aside*] That spot hath tombs.
[*Aloud*] Kind fate that threw Romano in my way.
He suspects me not?

MAL.   He thinks you friendly,
And straightway followed with a cheerful haste
As if I led him to his reverenced friend,
Guardenio—such was thy counterfeit
Of his ancient tutor's character.

ANG.   Well,
In what dungeon lies he?

MAL.   The Latomia,
  Which Dionysius in the olden time
  Made judgment seat and place of fearful doom.
ANG. I'll greet him there. Away, my friend, and know
  If wealth and honors can repay thy zeal,
  Sicilia's future *monarch* makes them thine.
MAL. At what a price I've bought them. [*Exit Malazzo*]
ANG.   He repents.
  Stops the great chieftain in his bold career
  To mourn the hapless fate of those who fall?
  No, not one that woman's part has played
  From Phrygia's victor down to Mecca's cheat.
  Glory be still my goal—my wrongs a spur;
  My earliest foe, I come. All furies now
  Fill me with ire. Oh, give me wrath as dread
  As that which drowned a new-born world in floods.
  Romano, tremble—fate's awful voice
  Shakes the dark caverns where revenge has slept,
  And bids the spirit, like a whirlwind, forth;
  It bursts—it swells—proud lord, it comes, it comes—
  Fate sends thee—*Angelo!* [*Rushes furiously out*]

SCENE 3: *A forest and byroad. Enter hastily Olympia conducting Kan Wogan.*

OLYM. Here thou art safe—they have not marked our course—
  Now let me rid thee of these manacles. [*She removes them*]
  Let thy betrayer wear them next, ha, ha!
KAN. How didst thou snatch me from the tyrant's grasp?
OLYM. Thou shalt know all anon. Treacherous knave!
  I wrung thy pardon from him—bore it forth,
  And as I rushed to snatch thee from the flames,
  Swift as the wind a horseman would have passed;
  I guessed his purpose. He bore thy death—thine.
  For Angelo revoked his kind decree.
  I barred the way. "On," cried the horseman, "on"—
  Oh! What was my horror then! I shrieked—
  Heaven heard and lent my woman's arm
  A champion's strength. I put it forth,
  And drove my poniard to the courser's heart!

His rider fell—thy guards released thee—thou—
Thou—art—free! [*She sinks on his shoulder*]

KAN.   O brave heroic woman! Dost thou faint?

OLYM.   I feel my weakness now—

KAN.   Then rest thee here.
            Through yonder trees I see a cottage roof.
            I'll seek its store and bring thee sustenance.

**   Come, lady, come. [*Exeunt*]

SCENE 4: *Dionysian Latomia. Wide excavations in the rock that have served for prisons. Romano discovered lying on the floor. One torch stuck in the back of the scene partially illumes the general gloom. Enter Angelo.*

ANG.   He sleeps, sounder than I do on my couch!
            He must not, shall not taste such luxury.
            Romano! Awake—arise, Romano!

ROM.   What voice—who calls? Guardenio, is it thou?

ANG.   It is not Guardenio.

ROM.   Comest thou from him?

ANG.   No.

ROM.   Will he not come?

ANG.   No!

ROM.   Then who art thou?

ANG.   Malfrondi!!

ROM.   My direst enemy!

ANG.   I am!
            Now, Lord Romano, has the moment come,
            Which through long years I've hourly prayed to know.

ROM.   Villain, begone—thy presence tortures me.

ANG.   I would have it so—nor would I hence,
            Though angels stayed to bear me up to Heaven,
            Till in thy wond'ring ear I rang a peal
            As terrible and true as the last trump,
            That bids the old and quaking earth dissolve.
            Oh, that thou hadst a hundred thousand ears,
            I'd rend them all with one dread word—*Revenge!*

ROM.   By heaven, I'll forth though fiends themselves oppos't—
            I will denounce thee, wretch.

** It is interesting to note that this entire scene was once crossed out, and then marked in the margin as follows: "All In—J. A. Stone."

ANG.   Thou darest not do 't.
For there is traitor written on thy brow.
Thou darest not for thy head's value cause
The fatal whisper, "Mark the banished one!"

ROM. Rail on—rail on—thou mayest in safety now.
Bore I the shadow of a weapon, slave,
Thy tongue had withered ere it dared revile.

ANG. Didst thou, boaster, wield a hundred blades,
Thou couldst not combat with my mighty hate.
Thou hadst a brother—

ROM.   Well—

ANG.   *That same am I!*

ROM. 'Tis false as perfidy—

ANG.   'Tis sure as fate.
Born to the same right noble sire, whose hand
Thrust me like an alien forth, for *thee*—
And for what reason? For thy *beauty's* sake!
Thy curled locks did charm the gossip tribe,
While my rude ringlets no adornment knew.
Thy comelier visage graced the gladdened hall,
While these ill-moulded features shrunk away
As noxious vapors from the glorious sun—
Like a nation's idol throned on all hearts wert thou,
While in despair I sought some dark retreat,
And filled it with my boyhood agonies!

ROM. And was this form's creation work of mine?
This heart did ever feel a brother's love,
Didst thou e'er cheer it with a brother's smile?

ANG. I could not to a Judas kiss conform the lip,
That I had taught to mutter *hatred* only.
I hated thee that nature loved thee so,
Laboring for thee in our mother's womb—
That gave thee to a joyful father's arms,
The earliest born and beauteous heir!
Closed were my father's gates and heart to me;
Until this tongue could humbly learn to say
"My best of brothers, I have done thee wrong,
Prostrate in the dust I ask forgiveness for't."

ROM. Our father did revoke his harsh decree,
And 'ere he died recalled thee.

ANG.   So he did.
When I had passed youth's ardent hour unknown,
Ploughing the distant ocean's foamy breast,
A wandering spirit courting enterprise!
Manhood at length I reached and then became,
Malfrondi.

ROM.   Aye, this scar upon my breast—

ANG.   'Tis true—was by my hand imprinted there,
When as thy humble vassal and unknown,
I followed my father's corse to burial—
Resolved to make his narrow mansion thine.
Curse on the hand that trembled when it smote,
Leaving to thee a dukedom, me the *rack!*

ROM.   And then, although I knew thee not I pitied,
I spared thy life.

ANG.   A precious gift indeed!
After thy slaves from torture's register
Had culled the keenest mortal agonies,
And heaped them all like burning coals upon me!
I feel them *now,* they rage in heart and limb,
On every sinew and in every vein!

ROM.   [*Aside*] By heaven, there is a raging fury in him,
No soothing tongue can qualify. [*Attempting to pass*]

ANG.   Ho, there! [*El Morad, and Saracens enter with arms and torches.
The scene lighted up instantly*] Let him not pass.

ROM.   Despair! Despair!

ANG.   I have rehearsed my sufferings only.
Now learn something of my victories.
Lightly will I touch on war's successes.
I will not count the steps by which I rose
To royal favor, honors, and command—
Nor say how cunningly I wrought thy doom.
Aye—'twas I! But tell at once my destiny.
The king is dead.

ROM.   The king!

ANG.   The king—the King of Sicily—
Last of the Norman line, no bold one comes,
To urge Constantia's doubtful claim, and I,
The army's idol, and a people's choice,
In triumph mount the throne of Sicily!

Rom.   Heavens!
Ang.   Here where the reckless dead repose
       Shall be henceforth thy gloomy dwelling place.
       Here mark the last sad end of nobleness,
       And shuddering think of thine!
Rom.   Thou canst not mean it—
Ang.   I have sworn it so.
Rom.   Thou wilt relent—
Ang.   These rocks as soon.
Rom.   Mercy!
Ang.   Found I any in your dungeon's gloom?
       Approach—[*Saracens advance*]
                    Ye live ye know but on my breath.
       Which of ye shows his head on upper earth,
       That moment loses it—so beware—
       Guard this prisoner—watch him night and day.
       Who shrinks rebellious from his duty dies!
       [*To Romano*] Adieu forever. The crown awaits me!
Rom.   I implore thee stay! [*Guards present their pikes*]
       O God of justice, succor, succor! [*Sinks down in agony. After Ro-
       mano falls, Angelo stands over him in triumph. Tableau*]
Ang.   Romano, I'm revenged!

END OF ACT IV

THE SPY

A TALE OF THE NEUTRAL GROUND
(FROM THE NOVEL OF THAT NAME)

A Dramatic Romance in Three Acts

By Charles Powell Clinch

THE SPY, A TALE OF THE NEUTRAL GROUND

CHARLES POWELL CLINCH was a New York business man who enjoyed a youthful career as dramatist and dramatic critic. During the early part of his life he was associated with the Knickerbocker writers, Bryant, Halleck, and others, and between the ages of twenty-four and thirty-two he contributed four plays to the New York theatre.

Clinch, the son of a wealthy ship chandler, was born in New York City on October 20, 1797. He entered business as private secretary to Henry Eckford, shipbuilder, made and lost a fortune in insurance stocks before he was thirty-eight, and served more than forty years as Deputy Collector and Assistant Collector of the Port of New York. He resigned this last position in 1876, and died in New York on December 16, 1880, at the age of eighty-three.

During his early years Clinch met the literary men of the day at the home of his first employer, Mr. Eckford. Their influence seems to have led the young man into the writing of plays as an avocation. Between 1822 and 1830 he wrote two melodramas, *The Spy* and *The Avenger's Vow,* and two farces, *The Expelled Collegian* and *The First of May in New York.* He also began to write essays and dramatic criticism, and gained great popularity as an orator. His most famous oration, *The Forty-Seventh Anniversary of American Independence,* was delivered at the New York Fire Department's Fourth of July celebration. Oratory apparently led to politics, for Clinch was later elected to the New York State Legislature.

Despite the fact that these activities were incidental to Clinch's major interests in business and finance, his plays were all successful, *The Spy* in particular holding the stage for thirty years. Less than ten weeks after the publication of James Fenimore Cooper's novel, *The Spy, A Tale of the Neutral Ground,* Clinch's dramatization was presented at the Park Theatre, on March 1, 1822. By that time the novel had reached a third edition, and novel and play proved equally popular. Audiences in New York, Philadelphia, Baltimore, and Washington enjoyed *The Spy.* As late as 1837 it was described as "a recent favorite," and in a shortened version it was a popular afterpiece until 1852.

Clinch followed up his first success with a two-act farce, *The Expelled Collegian,* also produced at the Park, on May 24, 1822. His next play was *The Avenger's Vow,* a melodrama of bandits, murder, and revenge, produced two years later at the Park, on March 25, 1824. For his last play Clinch returned to farce in *The First of May in New York,* which appeared at the Bowery Theatre on March 26, 1830.

The dramatization of Cooper's novel follows its source rather closely, except that Clinch concentrates the plot by having the death of Harvey Birch and the disclosure of his identity occur at the time of the main action, instead of many years later. Nearly all of the characters of the novel are retained, and some of their dialogue is reproduced almost identically. The songs in the play are taken directly from Cooper.

The Spy is printed in this volume from a manuscript in the New York Public Library, through the courtesy of Mr. George Freedley of the Theatre Collection. It is the only Clinch play known to be in existence, and it has never before been printed. The copy is good, except for a few lines, which are indicated in the following pages by bracketed spaces or explanations. The title-page and *dramatis personae* are from the manuscript, the cast from Odell.

DRAMATIS PERSONAE*

Caesar	BANCKER
Colonel Singleton	REED
Mr. Wharton	WHEATLEY
Henry Wharton	WOODHULL
Major Dunwoodie	SIMPSON
Captain Lawton	KENT
Lieutenant Mason	RICHINGS
Dr. Sitgreaves	COWELL
Sergeant Hollister	WENT
First Sentinel	
Second Sentinel	
Harvey Birch	MAYWOOD
Rawson	PHILLIPS
Smith	ANDERSON
Sanders	NEXSEN
First Cowboy	
Second Cowboy	
Judges	
Soldier	
Sarah	MISS JOHNSON
Frances	MISS JONES
Betty Flanagan	MRS. BATTERSBY
Katy Haynes	MRS. WHEATLEY

* The parts in the play are listed in the order given in the manuscript; the cast is from Odell's *Annals of the New York Stage*, for the first production at the Park Theatre, New York, on March 1, 1822.

ACT I.

SCENE 1: *Storm. The open country in the distance. A post-rail fence crosses the back of the stage. On one side, the dwelling of the pedlar. Enter Harvey Birch from behind with his pack, etc., crosses the stage and knocks at the door of the hut.*

BIRCH. Holla! within there! Holla, I say! Open the door. [*Comes forward*] Home! Yes, there was a time when even to me, the thought of returning to my *home* brought the fullness of expected happiness! When *its* attendant comforts answered my every wish, and hope looked not beyond its circle for enjoyment! There is a wide and woeful difference now! I have no home— and for my former hopes—but wherefore call these up? My mind is wearied —I am not myself tonight. It is these broodings that destroy me. Would I could cease to dwell upon the past or guess the future! But wherefore would I read it? I have chosen this life of peril—then be it perilous as fate can make it! And be my ending what it may! Let those that ought to bless me, curse me! *He, he* will know and honour me, and if not to the world, at least to Heaven, will witness for me! [*Stands a moment lost in thought, then renews his application to the door*] Holla! within there! 'Tis I, Harvey—open the door, I say. [*Enter Katy Haynes above at the window*]

KATY. What is wanting this time o' night? It's quite unbearable to be banged out of one's sleep when there's no good to come of it to nobody. It would be improper for a forlorn lone woman to let lodgings, and there is nobody in the house but the old gentleman, and so—

BIRCH. Peace, you babbling fool! Come down and open the door. Will you keep me standing here till morning?

KATY. Bless me! Harvey Birch, is it you? Why didn't you tell me before? Bless me, what a rainy night—I'm sure—

BIRCH. Open the door instantly. [*She descends and opens the door*]

KATY. Certainly, Harvey Birch, it is very right and proper—

BIRCH. Peace, I say. How is my father? [*Exit into the cottage*]

SCENE 2: *The interior of Birch's dwelling, a large fireplace in the center, a door on either side. Enter Birch and Katy Haynes.*

BIRCH. How is my father? I hope he has not been disturbed by your want of attention to the door.

KATY. As I was saying, Mr. Birch, it is certainly very right and proper for a man to be admitted into his own house when he desires it, especially when he is in it so seldom as you are, Mr. Birch. But still, I will say it is quite dispisable [*sic*] conduct in a man to get in a passion with a woman, Mr. Birch. But this comes of your wandering, vagabonding, vagranting life—never letting daylight find you within your own doors. What good is to come of it? I'm sure, Harvey Birch, if you would but take advice and leave off your unsteady courses and settle in life, it would be much more convenienter to yourself and the old gentleman; and I am free to confess, Harvey, more agreeable to me.

BIRCH. It would be much more agreeable to me, Katy, if you would leave off talking and get me some refreshment. I must away by daylight.

KATY. 'Mercy on us! Harvey Birch, you will be more dispisable than the wandering Jew if you think of leaving the house and your father on his dying bed!

BIRCH. What do you say? Is my father ill?

KATY. Indeed is he, Harvey Birch, and been so this three weeks; and you wandering about for no good to yourself nor him, as I'm bold to say my mind misgives, Harvey Birch.

BIRCH. [*Aside*] My father! Must you, too, leave me—must I alone bear up against the wrath that's fallen on you and yours. Well—be it so. I should not murmur at your escape from sorrow—but to be left alone—

KATY. [*Who has busied herself in preparing supper during this dialogue*] Nay, Harvey, don't stand sulkying [*sic*] there, but come to your supper. Tho' I did say your father was on his dying bed, I can't say I do positively think he is dying on it, for he's better today than he was a fortnight ago.

BIRCH. Fool! Have you seen anybody going toward the Locusts today?

KATY. Yes, I sent a traveler there this evening, who wanted lodgings here.

BIRCH. Lodging here? What kind of man? How dressed?

KATY. A very strange man, Harvey.

BIRCH. With a red wig, black patch, and an old, brown greatcoat?

KATY. I can't say I know what's become of your seven senses, Harvey Birch, to think I'd be sending that kind of a man to the Locusts. No, indeed! A very differenter sort of body from such, I guess.

BIRCH. What kind of a man?

KATY. Such a man as I never see before, nor look to see again, Harvey, till I see a king, which I don't think is over likely now, since—

BIRCH. Was he within doors?

KATY. No, never got off his horse. But tho' I told him I did not like to give lodgings to a stranger, there's few I would wish to accommodate sooner.

I have ever since been in a wonderment about him. There was something in his ways that made me wish to do him a service. And when I mention'd your not being home, he asked me suddenly if this was the dwelling of Harvey Birch.

BIRCH. Aye? Indeed? [*Aside*] Could it have been *he*? [*Aloud*] When was this? This evening? Did he go to the Locusts? Give me my supper. I must away in the morning. [*He sits at the table, leaning his head upon his hands in a thoughtful mood*]

KATY. I charge you, Harvey Birch, as you value honest advice, not to go abroad again till you have seen your father, nor not till he has made his last will in the testament. You would be the most unregardful, undutiful—

BIRCH. Peace! Peace, I say.

SCENE 3: *A wood. Enter Rawson, as leader of the Skinners. He whistles, then enter Sanders, Smith and other Skinners from different parts of the wood.*

SMITH. Well, captain, what's the news?

RAW. Are we all here?

SMITH. Some few stragglers not come in yet. Any luck tonight?

RAW. Yes, plenty of it! Only not of the right sort.

SAND. Devilish bad luck, I suppose.

RAW. Aye, our scheme of plundering old Wharton's house is blown to the devil!

SMITH. How so?

RAW. The Virginian Horse move up tomorrow. I overheard a dragoon below say that they had received orders to keep the dwelling of Harvey Birch constantly watched and so—

SMITH. What, the pedlar spy?

RAW. Aye, and that mad Virginian Lawton will come on the business, and quarter himself at Whartons, for he's damned fond of looking out for No. *one* when good cheer is in the way.

SAND. Yes, and I suspect would be apt to look out for No. *one* if our band came in his way. So do you look out for yourself, captain.

SMITH. But what the devil! Are you afraid of one man? The detachment will not be at Wharton's. The pedlar's hut is half a mile distant. We shall have time enough before they can be upon us.

SAND. To be sure we shall, and as for Captain Lawton, a bullet won't be over and above particular about turning to the right as the law directs to avoid making a hole thro' him, provided your nerves don't give it St. Vitus' dance before it sets out.

Raw. You're about as wise as usual, both of you! And your famous foresight can't see the reason why I won't quarrel with the Virginian or his troop?

Sand. Say it's fear and you'll not go to hell for lying about it.

Raw. Fear! You cowardly fool—raise but the skin of one of that corps, and you'll never see another peaceable night's foraging again. And as to that mad Virginian, Captain Lawton, I know there is not one of you that would not sooner oppose a score of cowboys than stand up before that single man! So let's have no more jabbering. If you've got any wits, use them in finding out some employment that may be profitable to us.

Smith. Why, I don't know about my wits, captain, but I think I employed my eyes today to a better purpose than you did your ears.

Raw. What do you mean?

Smith. What do I mean? Why, I mean that in the dusk of the evening as I was skulking along to our rendezvous, I saw the pedlar bending under a well-filled pack, tho' with a devilish quick step, moving across the country with his nose pointed homeward.

Raw. Aha! then, by heavens, we'll have him!

Sand. The devil you will!

Raw. Aye, will we, Sanders! And have the reward of fifty guineas offered for his capture, too! But the best of the whole will be that we'll get on friendly terms with Lawton and the Virginians, and, damn-me, lads, in that case, our future is made! That's what I've been wishing for and driving at this long time. If we can only be covered with a troop now and then, we'll do a glorious business this fall!

Sand. Covered with Lawton's troop! They'd sooner a devilish deal put us in a state to be covered with a few shovels full of dirt.

Raw. Pshaw! Never fear, my lads. Such an opportunity of filling our purses should not be lost for want of courage and industry!

Sand. Didn't your grandmother use to count her chickens before they were hatched, captain?

Raw. I don't know what kind of a chick your grandmother counted on before *you* were hatched but if she didn't look for a goslin [*sic*], she was disappointed a few, I take it.

Smith. Well, but captain, if you think it an easy matter to take the pedlar and keep him long enough to get the reward, let us go about it without flinching. But I think it will be labour lost. Harvey Birch is not to be taken by us when he has slipped thro' the fingers of Captain Lawton.

Raw. Didn't you say you saw him on his way home?

Smith. I did, but if *you* heard that his dwelling was to be constantly watched, the devil a doubt but that he has heard it, too, and we'll be apt to find Harvey Birch at home when we meet with a snowstorm in July. However, I'm for visiting his house. We may pick up something at any rate.

Sand. And I'm for keeping out of sight of it. I've no doubt we'll make more money by keeping "hands off" than by laying them on him.

Raw. How the devil will you make that out?

Sand. By making out that a live man is better than a dead one. That the pedlar spy is worth more alive to Sir Henry Clinton than he will be worth to Washington when he's dead. We'll get a much better *reward* by aiding him to escape.

Raw. To say nothing of the chance of slipping our necks into a noose by going to fetch it! No, no, I'm for making hay while the sun shines. We are certain of the fifty guineas if we take him, beside the plunder of his pack and his hoard; for Sir Harry's a liberal fellow, they say, and Birch is as closefisted a pedlar as ever gripped a yard stick. So let's be off and keep an eye upon his house before the dragoons come up. If he's abroad now, let him wander to his heart's content; but if we take him, his movements will be contracted to the swing of a four-foot rope. Come, lads—march!

Sand. Well, for my part, captain, I never could bring myself to talk so familiarly of swinging, and ropes, and nooses.

Smith. Ha, ha! You seem to have a great antipathy to a rope, Sanders!

Sand. Oh! to be sure I have. I never hear of one but I immediately think my neckcloth is too tight, and instantly clap my hand up to feel if the knot hasn't slipped around under my ear!

Scene 4: *The parlour at the Locusts. Mr. Wharton, Henry, Harvey Birch, Frances and Sarah discovered, the purchases of the ladies visible.*

Birch. [*Adjusting his pack*] And now, Captain Wharton, may I ask you, do you go in tonight?

Henry. Tonight! not I, faith!

Birch. Excuse me, Captain Wharton, I think you had better.

Henry. What, Mr. Birch, would you have me leave such company so soon? And that, too, when I never may enjoy it again.

Whar. Henry, my dear boy—

Fran. My dear brother! Jesting on such a subject is cruel.

Henry. There, Mr. Birch, you see the effect of that grave face of yours. Dismount it, will you?

BIRCH. I rather think, now the storm is over, the Skinners may be moving. You had better shorten your visit, Captain Wharton.

HENRY. Oh! a few guineas will buy off those rascals at any time, should I fall in with them. No, no, Mr. Birch, I'll run the risk of being "taken as a spy, tried as a spy, and hanged as a spy" as old Putnam says, rather than leave this dear society so soon after so long an absence and the risks I have encountered to enjoy it. No, sir, here I stay, today, tonight, and perhaps tomorrow morning.

BIRCH. Money could not purchase the liberty of Major André.

FRAN. But my dear brother, hear me.

SARAH. Brother, you had better take the advice of Harvey. Rest assured, his opinion in such matters ought not to be disregarded.

FRAN. Yes, if as I suspect, Mr. Birch assisted you to come here, your safety, our happiness, dear Henry, require you to listen to him now.

HENRY. Now, don't frighten yourself, my dear sis. I brought myself out and can take myself in. Our bargain went no further than to procure my disguise and let me know when the coast was clear, and in the latter particular, you were mistaken, Mr. Birch.

BIRCH. I was! Captain Wharton, and the greater is the reason why you should go back tonight! The pass I gave you will serve you but once.

HENRY. Well, cannot you forge another?

BIRCH. [*Aside*] Forge! Well, what matters it!

HENRY. Here I stay till this time tomorrow morning, come what will.

BIRCH. And here I do not hold it safe for me to stay another hour. Tho' it *may be* safe for you, Captain Wharton, beware a tall Virginian with huge whiskers. He is below you to my knowledge, perhaps much nearer than I am aware of. Take care of him. The devil can't deceive him. I never did but once myself.

HENRY. Let him beware of me! But, Mr. Birch, I exonerate you from further responsibility.

BIRCH. Ah, will you give me that in writing?

HENRY. Oh! cheerfully. Caesar! Bring pen, ink, and paper. [*They are brought*] While I write a discharge for my trusty attendant. [*Exit Caesar*] Harvey Birch, pedlar, etc., etc.,—How many et ceteras are there, Mr. Birch?

BIRCH. [*With meaning*] Possibly two or three that will one day astonish you, Captain Wharton.

HENRY. Hum! [*Delivers Birch the writing, who makes a silent bow and exit. Aside*] There's something damned mysterious about that fellow after all! This Harvey Birch with his knowing looks gives me more uneasiness than I am willing to allow.

Whar. How is it that he is able to travel to and fro in these difficult times without molestation?

Henry. Why, I don't know, father. I have often wondered why the rebels suffer him to escape so easily. But Sir Henry would not permit a hair of his head to be injured.

Fran. Indeed, is he then known to Sir Henry Clinton?

Henry. I have heard people say so, my dear.

Fran. Ah!

Whar. Do you think there is no danger of his betraying you?

Henry. Why, no. I reflected upon that before I trusted myself in his power. He seems to be faithful in matters of business. The danger to him should he return to the city will of itself prevent such an act of villainy.

Fran. Why, yes, my dear brother, I hope you are sure of him. For my part, I think Harvey Birch is not without good feelings.

Sarah. Oh! Harvey has loyalty and that's a cardinal virtue with me. [Here occur several lines crossed out in manuscript.]

Fran. I think that Harvey Birch—

Henry. Has more love for his money than for his king. I think so, too, Fan.

Whar. Then, my dear boy, you cannot be safe while in his power, for no love can withstand the temptation of money, when offered to avarice.

Henry. Surely, my dear sir, there must be one love that can resist anything—is there not, Fan? [*She turns away, humming an air: "Though that same love is not so omnipotent when glory is arrayed against it." Enter Caesar in haste*]

Caes. Run! massa Harry—run! run—

Whar. What's the matter, Caesar? What's the matter?

Caes. Oh! run, massa Harry—if love old Caesar, run—here come the rebel horse!

Henry. Run! No, Mr. Caesar, running is not my trade.

Fran. Oh! Heaven! what's to be done!

Henry. Where are they, Caesar? How near?

Caes. Oh! massa Harry, see 'um from piazza. Golly! How 'um do gallop! [*Exit Henry*]

Whar. Fly, Henry! fly to the wood!

Caes. 'E' too late, Massa. See 'em go dare.

Sarah. What! Are they so near?

Whar. Run, girls. Run. Fanny, my dear. Persuade your brother to hide himself.

Fran. No, father—the disguise. [*Exeunt Frances and Sarah*]

WHAR. Oh! Heaven—that he should be taken here before my eyes. How many of them, Caesar? Are they coming to the house? [*Enter Henry, disguised, Sarah and Frances*] Well, my dear boy, is it so? Are they the rebel horse?

HENRY. Even so, sir. But be under no apprehensions for me—there! Caesar, go to the door. [*Knock is heard. Caesar exit*] Now, my dear father, don't be alarm'd. Cheer up, girls. My dear Fan, don't tremble so. Dear Sarah, don't look at me. Appear as indifferent as you can. Holla! Here they are! Hem! [*Enter Caesar, followed by Captain Lawton, Mason and Hollister*]

LAW. Good morning, ladies. Good morning, gentlemen.

WHAR. Good morning to you, gentlemen. [*Henry and the ladies bow*]

FRAN. [*To her sister*] Oh! Heaven support me! The very man that Harvey mentioned.

LAW. You have no cause for alarm, ladies—none whatever. My business will be confined to a few questions which, if freely answered, will remove us from your dwelling.

WHAR. And what may they be, sir? [*In great agitation*]

LAW. Has there been a strange gentleman staying with you during the storm?

WHAR. This gentleman here favour'd us with his company during the rain and has not yet departed.

LAW. This gentleman! [*Looks scrutinizingly at Henry, then turns to Mason with a smile of meaning. Then returns*] Have you been long afflicted with it, sir?

HENRY. Sir!

LAW. I am very sorry for it. The late bad weather, I presume.

HENRY. Sorry for what, sir?

LAW. For the severe cold you have in your head, sir.

HENRY. I—I have no cold in my head, sir.

LAW. Oh! I beg your pardon, sir. I must have fancied it then, from seeing you had covered such handsome auburn locks with that ugly old wig. [*Turns to Mason*]

WHAR. [*Aside*] He is lost! [*Sinks into chair*]

SARAH. My father!

HENRY. [*Putting his hand to his head, where his own hair is visible. Aside*] Provoking! Was ever anyone so foolishly caught!

LAW. [*To old Wharton*] Then, sir, I am to understand there has not been a Mr. Harper here within the week?

FRAN. Mr. Harper!

WHAR. [*Rising suddenly*] Harper! Oh, yes, sir, yes! I had forgotten. But he is gone and if there be anything wrong in his character, we are in entire ignorance of it. To me, he was a total stranger.

LAW. You have little to apprehend from his character, sir. But he is gone —how—when—whither?

WHAR. He went as he came, on horseback, last evening and he took the northern road.

LAW. Ah! Then all is well! [*To Mason*] Tom, draw off your division and pursue our route. You see, I've something in the shape of business here— farewell. Now, sir, my principal affair settled, may I beg leave to examine the quality of that wig? [*Exeunt Mason and Hollister*]

HENRY. [*Handing him the wig*] I hope, sir, it is to your liking.

LAW. I cannot, without violating the truth, say it is. I prefer your brown hair, from which you seem to have combed the powder with great industry. But that must be a sad hurt you have received under that enormous black patch.

HENRY. You appear so close an observer of things, I should like to be favoured with your opinion of it, sir. [*Removes the patch*]

FRAN. O my brother!

LAW. Upon my word, sir, you improve most rapidly in externals! Shall I trouble you to exchange this old surtout for that handsome blue coat by your side? [*Henry makes the exchange*] Thank you, sir! I think I never witnessed a more agreeable metamorphosis since I myself was changed from a lieutenant to a captain. You're a newcomer on the scene. It is usual you know, for strangers to be introduced. I am Captain Lawton, sir, of the Virginian Horse.

HENRY. And I, sir, am Captain Wharton of His Majesty's 60th regiment of foot!

LAW. Is it possible! Captain Wharton, from my soul I pity you!

HENRY. [*Haughtily*] Indeed! Sir, I am not conscious of having any particular claim upon your sympathy, but perhaps you can inform me better.

WHAR. Oh! Then if you pity him, dear sir, why molest him? He is not a spy. Nothing but a desire to see his friends prompted him to stray so far from the protection of the regular army. Leave him with us. There is no reward, no sum which I will not cheerfully pay.

LAW. Sir, your anxiety for your friend excuses your language, but you forget I am a Virginian and a gentleman. Were you ignorant, Captain Wharton, that our picquets have been below you for several days?

HENRY. I did not know it until it was too late to retreat. I came out, as my father has mentioned, to see my friends, supposing your parties to be at Peeks-kill, or surely I would not have ventured.

LAW. All this may be very true, but the affair of André has made us on the alert. When treason reaches to the grade of general officers, Captain Wharton, it behooves the friends of liberty to be vigilant.

HENRY. Well, sir, you must do what you imagine to be your duty. I have nothing more to say.

SARAH. Let me observe, Captain Lawton, that you have found my brother in the bosom of his own family—in a situation where, whatever might have been his intention, he had not the power to—

LAW. Pardon me for the interruption, madam, and allow me to observe that I am not the commander of the party. Major Dunwoodie will decide what must be done with your brother.

FRAN. Dunwoodie! Thank heaven! Then Henry is safe.

LAW. Upon my soul, I hope so, madam! And, with your permission, we will leave the matter for his decision.

SARAH. May we expect the pleasure of Major Dunwoodie's company shortly, sir?

LAW. Immediately, madam. I was detached in advance for the purpose of apprehending a neighbour of yours, the pedlar, Harvey Birch. But I believe he seldom visits the valley.

WHAR. At times only, I believe, sir. I may say he is seldom here. In fact, we scarcely ever see him.

LAW. That is strange, too! Considering he is your next neighbour. It must be somewhat inconvenient to the ladies. I dare say that muslin on the table cost twice as much as he would have ask'd for it.

WHAR. [Aside] 'Tis impossible to deceive him! [Trumpet]

LAW. Ha! 'Tis the major. [Exit Frances, Sarah following. Enter Mason]

MASON. Major Dunwoodie has arrived and brings intelligence that the enemy are upon us, horse and foot.

LAW. Aha! How near, Tom?

MASON. Why, the major says we'll be upon them in half an hour.

LAW. Bravo!

HENRY. Be not alarmed, father! This may benefit us, but cannot make our situation worse. [Lawton gives hasty direction to Mason, referring to Henry and exit. They retire to the windows]

SCENE 5: *A room at the Locusts. Dunwoodie and Frances meeting.*

DUN. Frances!

FRAN. Ah! Dunwoodie! How happy I am on many accounts to see you! I have met you here to prepare you to meet an unexpected friend in the next room.

DUN. To what ever cause it may be owing, dear, dear, Frances, I am happy, too, in being able to see you alone.

FRAN. Hear me, Peyton!

DUN. Frances! The probation you have decreed to my love is cruel. War and distance may shortly separate us forever.

FRAN. We must submit to necessity, Peyton. But it is not love speeches which I would hear now. I have more important matter for your attention.

DUN. What can be of more importance than to make you mine by an indissoluble tie? Frances, you are cold to me! Me! from whose mind all my days of battle and my nights of alarm have never banished your image!

FRAN. Dear Dunwoodie! You know my sentiments. This war once ended, and this hand is yours forever! But I never can consent to be yours while my brother and yourself are arrayed in arms against each other. Even now that brother is waiting your decision to restore him to liberty or conduct him to a probable death!

DUN. Your brother! Speak, dear Frances—your brother! What dreadful meaning is concealed in your words!

FRAN. Have you not learn'd that my brother was arrested this very morning as a spy by Captain Lawton?

DUN. I heard of his arresting a captain of the 60th in disguise, but not where—or whom—[*In great agitation*]

FRAN. Dunwoodie! Dunwoodie! What means this agitation! Surely you will not betray your friend—my brother—your brother—to an ignominious death!

DUN. Frances! Ah, Heaven! What can I do! What can I do!

FRAN. Do! Would Major Dunwoodie yield his friend to his enemies—the brother of his betrothed wife?

DUN. Ah, speak not so unkindly to me, dearest Miss Wharton, my own Frances! Heaven knows I would this moment die for you—for Henry—but I cannot forget my duty, cannot forfeit my honour. You, yourself, would be the first to dispise me if I did!

FRAN. Peyton Dunwoodie! You have told me—you have sworn that you love me—

DUN. I do! I do!

Fran. Do you think I can throw myself into the arms of a man, whose hands are stain'd with the blood of my brother?

Dun. Frances! You wring my heart! [*Trumpet*] Ha! Even now I must leave you! Instantly! [*Going, returning*] After all, dearest Frances, we may be torturing ourselves with groundless fears. Henry, when I hear all, may be only a prisoner of war and I can liberate him on parole! [*Trumpet. Enter Soldier*]

Sol. Captain Lawton—

Dun. I come! I come! [*Exit Soldier*]

Fran. Oh! There can be no just grounds to doubt that he is innocent! I knew—I knew, Dunwoodie, that you would never desert us in our greatest need.

Dun. Hope everything, my dear Frances. Farewell!

Fran. Ah, Dunwoodie, you are about to risk your life in battle. Remember there is one heart whose happiness depends upon your safety.

Dun. Dearest love!

Fran. Brave I know you are—be prudent.

Dun. For your sake?

Fran. For my sake! [*Sinks in his arms*]

Dun. Heaven forever bless and comfort you, my love! Farewell! [*Rushes out. Exit Frances*]

Scene 6: *The lawn before the Locusts. On one side, the house of Wharton, with piazza in front and Sentinel pacing to and fro on piazza. On the other, Dr. Sitgreaves, with preparations, bodies, etc., about him. Open country in distance. Alarums and firing without. Caesar appears at the door.*

Sent. Go within, blacky, or I'll shave off one of your ebony ears with this razor.

Caes. There, Mister Light-horseman, why you rebels don't fight. See—see how King George's men make Major Dunwoodie run. Good gentlemen, too, but don't like fight reg'lars.

Sent. Damn your regulars! Wait a minute, blacky, and you will see Captain Lawton come out from behind that hill and scatter them cowboys like geese!

Caes. Oh, golly! Dere he come, too. He ride like de devil. Old Nick no stand afore him. [*Retires into house. Dr. Sitgreaves comes forward, smoking a cigar*]

Sit. Now I know that man to have been kill'd by Captain Lawton just as well as if I had seen him strike the blow. How often have I strove to teach him the manner in which he can disable his adversary without destroying him. It is cruel thus unnecessarily to cut off the human race. And further- more, such blows as these render professional assistance unnecessary. It is, in a measure, treating the lights of science with disrespect. My art is of no avail with the wounded Captain Lawton sends me. I did put in the brains of one patient today, but I rather think the man was dead before I saw him. Such blows as Lawton's men give, alighting on the human frame, are fatal and set at naught all the lights of science. [*Wounded brought in at a distance*] Ah! That looks like a good subject! [*Rolls up his sleeves. Enter two Cowboys*]

FIRST Cow. Ha! Sinister! I told you luck was in the way! Here are two damned fine horses.

SECOND Cow. They're ours, by heavens!

SENT. Here's a receipt for the pay, you rascals! [*Fires his pistols, but misses. Rushes upon them with his sword. They fight*]

SOL. [*At the window*] Hollo! Ned! [*Henry seizes him from behind. Throws him out of the window*]

HENRY. Attempt to enter here and you die!

SENT. There, Tom, never mind *him!* Save the horses! [*Tom runs to his comrade's assistance. Enter from the house, Caesar and Henry*]

CAES. Run! Now—run! Massa Harry, run!

HENRY. Yes, my honest fellow, now indeed is the time to run. [*Enter Birch, disguised*]

BIRCH. Bravely done, Captain Wharton—mount that horse there! Don't spare the whip and turn to your left before you cross the brook!

HENRY. Bless you, Birch! Good-by, Caesar. Salute the girls. [*Exeunt Birch and Henry*]

CAES. Hey, golly! How well he ride. Hurrah! Hurrah! Hurrah! ["*Yankee Doodle." Curtain falls*]

ACT II.

SCENE I: *Same as the last. Sitgreaves discovered at the back of the stage, exam- ining a body; comes forward.*

SIT. No hope—life's extinct. More of Lawton's work—severed the jugular. Generally does that or lets out the brains—both so difficult to remedy. Gen- erally die before I can get to them or they to me. Never had success but once in replacing a man's brains, tho' I tried three this very day—ah! It's easy to tell where Lawton's troop charge in a battle, they cut so at random—[*Henry, who has entered in charge of two Soldiers during the soliloquy, now speaks*]

HENRY. If, sir, your leisure will admit, I must beg your attention to this slight hurt of mine.

SIT. Ah! [*Starting*] You are from the field below. Is there much business there, sir? [*Assisting Henry to take off his coat*]

HENRY. Why, it has been a very stirring time, I assure you, sir. But now—

SIT. Stirring! I like that! You give me great pleasure, sir. For so long as they can stir there must be life and while there is life, there must be hope. Stirring—good! Take a cigar, sir? [*Offering his box*]

HENRY. I thank you, sir. I never—

SIT. No? It is a very good habit, sir—that is to say, sir, it depends upon your habit of body. It's a sort of burning of the exhalations of the stomach, sir —same effect, sir, as burning bogs and marshes. Distroys [*sic*] the obnoxious vapours of mind and body both, sir. Ah, the ball has glanced round the bone without shattering it—a circumbendibus, as Captain Lawton would say—a route never taken by the swords of his men. You are fortunate in falling into the hands of an experienced surgeon or you might have lost this limb. [*Busied with dressing*]

HENRY. Indeed! I did not apprehend the injury to be so serious.

SIT. Oh, the hurt is not bad, but you have such a pretty arm for an operation, the pleasure of the thing might easily tempt a novice! [*Binds up the arm*]

HENRY. The devil! Can there be any pleasure in mutilating a fellow creature?

SIT. Sir, let me inform you, a scientific amputation is a very pretty operation, and doubtless might tempt a younger man in the hurry of business to overlook all the particulars of the case.

HENRY. Ah! Here comes my father. [*The Doctor retires. Enter Wharton, Sarah, Frances and Caesar from house*]

WHAR. Henry, my son, what is it I see? Are you again a captive and in danger of your life?

FRAN. O my brother—

SARAH. We were so happy in the thoughts of your escape.

HENRY. The better fortune of these rebels has prevailed. I strove nobly for my liberty, but the spirit of rebellion has even lighted on their horses and I was carried by the steed I mounted, sorely against my will, I acknowledge, into the very center of Dunwoodie's men.

CAES. Why you didn't hold 'em in, Massa Henry?

HENRY. That was a thing easier said than done, Mr. Caesar—especially as I had been deprived of the use of my better arm.

SARAH and FRAN. Wounded!

HENRY. Oh, a mere scratch, but it disabled me at a most critical moment. [*Enter Dunwoodie hastily*]

DUN. Mr. Wharton, in times like these it is useless to stand on idle ceremony. One of my officers, Captain Singleton, is hurt mortally and, presuming on your hospitality, I have ordered him to be brought to your door.

WHAR. I am happy, sir, that you have done so. The necessitous are always welcome, and doubly so in being the friend of Major Dunwoodie.

DUN. Sir, I thank you for myself and in behalf of him who is unable to render you his thanks. But Frances—Miss Wharton [*Takes a hand of both the ladies*] what say you—will you not bid my friend an equal welcome; it is at moments like these—in sufferings like his, that the soldier most finds the want of female tenderness.

SARAH. All the attention that can with propriety be given to a stranger, your friend shall receive.

DUN. Ah! That cold word, propriety, would kill him. He must be fostered, cherished, soothed.

FRAN. These are offices for a wife or sister.

DUN. Ha! He has a sister and she might be here with tomorrow's sun.

FRAN. She will be welcome to us.

SARAH. We will prepare for your friend's comfort. [*Exeunt Ladies*]

DUN. Eternal thanks for your kindness, Sitgreaves! What can delay the litter? Sitgreaves! Hasten this way or George Singleton will bleed to death! [*Exit. Henry and his father retire into the house. Guard follows*]

SIT. What! Singleton! Heaven forbid! Bless me, is it George, poor little George? [*Looking out*] He is alive, tho', by the care they take in moving him and while there is life, there is hope! This is the first serious case I've had today where the patient was not already dead. Captain Lawton teaches his men to strike with so little discretion! Poor George. [*Exit, followed by Dunwoodie*]

SCENE 2: *A wood; twilight. Enter Harvey Birch with his pack.*

BIRCH. There is still too much light to venture. Lawton has been dispatched to watch the enemy to their boats. He will be returning. He will never give me *time* to escape again from him, if taken. I think I can elude any vigilance but his, but never again his, I fear. And shall I continue to risk an ignominious death—a death sudden and unvouched for by even the mockery of a trial? Will any after benefit to me or mine reward me for it? No! I am alone—deprived of kindred by the hand of Heaven. And shall I labour to restore my hold on life? I have no thoughts that whisper me I can be happy here. But then, my country—ah! she receives the benefit. And *he—he* knows the heart of him that's call'd a traitor, and one day yet, when the grave's silence sleeps around me, he will tell the world my truth. But come! An hour's delay may deprive me of my father's blessing! The shades of evening gather slowly. I will venture. [*Exit*]

SCENE 3: *The open country.*

MASON. [*Without*] Halt!

LAW. [*Without*] Dismount Tom! We'll wait here 'til Hollister comes up with his guard. [*Enter Captain Lawton and Mason*] Then it struck you, too, eh? By my faith, Tom, the girl does no discredit to the major's taste.

MASON. She would do honour to the corps. And the other, captain, I think she is well worthy to be called the sister of the major's wife.

LAW. Don't trouble yourself to cast a thought that way, Tom! She's mine, if she's anybody's. There's a sort of high-toned, dignified remnant of royalty about her disposition that I should glory in conquering. No! There is no chance for you! I'm as tough as a peperage [*sic*] log and have as many lives as a cat!

MASON. Faith! the log may yet split and Grimalkin lose his lives if you often charge as madly as you did this morning. What think you of many raps from such a beetle as laid you on your back today?

LAW. Ah, don't mention it, Tom! It is what I call forestalling night.

MASON. The night of death.

LAW. No, the night that follows day. I saw myriads of stars—things which generally hide their faces, you know, when the sun shines. I do think nothing but this thick cap saved me.

MASON. That, or the skull must have had a comfortable portion of thickness, I admit.

LAW. Ah, you're a licensed joker, Tom! It surprises me, however, that as Singleton and I both fell at the same time, the men behaved so well.

MASON. Oh! I thank you for the compliment, but my modesty forbids. I did my best to stop them, but without success.

LAW. Stop them! Would you stop men in the middle of a charge?

MASON. I thought they were going the wrong way.

LAW. Aha! Our fall drove them to the right about, eh?

MASON. It was either your fall or apprehensions of their own. Until the major rallied us, we were in admirable disorder!

LAW. Dunwoodie! Why the major was on the crupper of the Dutchman!

MASON. Aye, but he managed to get off the crupper of the Dutchman. He came in at half speed with the other two troops and, riding between us and the enemy, with that imperative way he has when roused, brought us into line in a twinkling! Oh, it was a sweet charge, heads and tails, until we were upon them.

Law. The devil! What a sight I miss'd! [*Harvey Birch is seen crossing the stage in the distance, among the rocks*]

Mason. Yes, that spent bullet was as good a soporifick [*sic*] as you could have wished for. You slept thro' it all most famously!

Law. Well, Tom, there is no curing your license of speech—but what animal is that moving among the rocks there?

Mason. 'Tis a man.

Law. By his hump, 'tis a dromedary—Harvey Birch! Take him, dead or alive! [*Draws his sword and dashes off in pursuit*]

Mason. [*To the Soldiers without*] Holla! There! Join the pursuit among the rocks! [*Exit*]

Scene 4: *A more rocky part of the country. Dragoons searching among the rocks. Birch rushes down the stage from the rocks. Dragoons perceive him. A sudden discharge of their pistols lights the scene, then all is darkness. Lawton, without:* "*Harvey Birch, take him, dead or alive!*"

Birch. Hunted like a beast of the forest! Life, thou art a burden to me. I resign myself to my fate. But no! I have promised *him* never to dispair [*sic*] while life—ha! [*Enter Lawton, furiously*]

Law. Stop or die! [*About to strike. Birch sinks at his feet. The blow in descending is intercepted by the limb of a tree directly over Lawton's head and the sword flies from his grasp. Birch, as quick as lightning, springs up, overthrowing Lawton, claps his foot upon his breast, seizes his sword and raises it to strike*]

Birch. Now then, my wrongs—but—no! no! no! Heaven, I thank thee. [*Throws down the sword and rushes out. Lawton on his knee*]

Law. Eternal providence! What does this mean? [*Enter Mason, Hollister and other dragoons*]

Mason. Help Captain Lawton there. And some of you follow me and search these rocks. The villain lies here conceal'd.

Law. Hold! If one of you stir, he dies! Tom, my good fellow, you will help me to straddle Roanoke.

Mason. I dread your impetuosity among these rocks. You are much hurt, I fear.

Law. Something so, I believe; I wish our bonesetter was at hand to examine into the state of my ribs.

HOLL. Captain Lawton, we will pass the house of the pedlar on our way. Is it your pleasure that we burn it?

LAW. No! Are you an incendiary? Would you burn the house in cold blood—Hollister are you mad? Let but a spark approach it and the hand that carries it will never light another!

HOLL. Zounds! There's life in the captain, notwithstanding his tumble. [*Exeunt*]

MASON. [*Without*] Prepare to mount. Mount—forward!

SCENE 5: *Parlour at the Locusts. Enter Dunwoodie, Henry and Frances.*

DUN. Henry Wharton, to me, honour is dearer than life, but in your hands I know it can safely be confided. Remain here, unwatch'd, until we leave the country.

HENRY. Your generous confidence, Peyton, will not be abused, even tho' the gibbet on which your Washington hung André be ready for my own execution.

DUN. Henry! Captain Wharton, you little know the man who leads our armies or you would have spared him that reproach. And now, Henry, tell me the circumstances of this disguise in which Captain Lawton reports you to have been found. And remember, Captain Wharton, your answers are entirely voluntary.

HENRY. The disguise was used by me, Major Dunwoodie, to enable me to visit my friends without incurring the danger of becoming a prisoner of war.

DUN. But you did not wear it until you saw the troops of Lawton approaching?

FRAN. Oh, no! Sarah and myself placed them on him when the dragoons appeared. It was our awkwardness that led to his discovery.

DUN. Ah! [*Takes her hand*] Probably some articles of your own which were at hand and were used on the spur of the occasion.

HENRY. No, the clothes were worn by me from the city. They were procured for the purpose of disguise and I intended to wear them on my return.

FRAN. Oh, heaven! I had forgotten—

DUN. But the picquets—the party at the plains—

HENRY. I passed them, too, in disguise. I made use of this pass. It bears the name of Washington; I presume it is forged.

DUN. [*Seizing the paper eagerly and perusing it*] Captain Wharton, whence did you procure this paper?

HENRY. That is a question, I presume, Major Dunwoodie will concede he has no right to ask.

DUN. Your pardon, sir. My feelings have led me into an impropriety.

FRAN. Surely, Dunwoodie, the paper cannot be material. Are not such artifices daily used in war?

DUN. This name is no counterfeit. Is treason still among us?

HENRY. [*Aside*] No counterfeit! New mysteries envelope [*sic*] that man!

DUN. The confidence of Washington has been abused, for the fictitious name is in a different handwriting from the pass. Captain Wharton, my duty will not suffer me to grant a parole. You must accompany me to the highlands.

HENRY. I did not expect otherwise. I will seek my father. [*Exit*]

FRAN. Major Dunwoodie, I have already acknowledged to you my esteem. Even now, when you most painfully afflict me, I wish not to conceal it. Believe me, Henry is innocent of everything but imprudence. Our country can sustain no wrong. I have promised, Dunwoodie, when peace is restored to our country, to become your wife. Give to my brother his liberty on parole, and I will this day go with you to the altar, follow you to the camp, and in becoming a soldier's bride, learn to endure a soldier's privations.

DUN. Frances, say no more, I conjure you, unless you wish to break my heart!

FRAN. You then reject my offered hand?

DUN. Reject it! Oh, heaven, have I not sought it with entreaties, with tears—has it not been the goal of all my earthly wishes! But to receive it under such conditions would dishonour us both. Yet hope for better things. Henry must be acquitted—perhaps not even tried. Believe me, Frances, I am not without favour with *Washington* and my intercession—

FRAN. That very paper—that abuse of his confidence—will steel him to my brother's sufferings. If threats or entreaties could move him, would André have suffered? Oh, heaven! There is no hope? [*Rushes out*]

DUN. Frances! my beloved Frances! Hear me! Merciful Heaven! This is a trial almost beyond my strength! [*Exit opposite side*]

SCENE 6: *A room in the pedlar's hut. Caesar and Katy Haynes discovered.*

CAES. Berry true, but I wish Harvey get back.

KATY. It is very disregardful in him to be away at this time. Suppose now his father wanted to make his last will in the testament—there's nobody to do it for him. Harvey is a very wasteful and a very disregardful man.

CAES. Maybe he make him afore?

KATY. It would not be a wonderment if he had. He is whole days looking in the Bible.

CAES. Den he read good book. Miss Fanny read him to Dinah berry often.

KATY. Yes, but he wouldn't be forever studying it if it didn't contain something more as common. [*She fetches Bible*] Where abouts is Matthew? [*Turning the leaves*]

CAES. Never see him. [*Holding a candle*]

KATY. Ah, here it is, and here is the very words themselves. Now I would give the world to know who he has left them there big silver shoe buckles to.

CAES. Read him—why 'e don't read him?

KATY. And the black walnut drawers, for Harvey could never want them.

CAES. Why he no want him, as well as he fader?

KATY. And the six silver tablespoons, for Harvey always uses iron.

CAES. I guess he say dere—read him! [*Pointing to the writing*]

KATY. [*Reading*] "Chester Birch, born July 12th, 1757."

CAES. Well, what he give him?

KATY. [*Reads*] "Abigail Birch, born Sept. 1st, 1759."

CAES. I guess he give her de spoons.

KATY. [*Reads*] "June 1st, 1760—on this day the awful judgement of offended Heavens lighted upon my house. By a dreadful conflagration, in one hour, competence and kindred were swept from before me and but one child —[*A groan behind. She shuts the book suddenly*]

CAES. He 'bout to go—[*The Pedlar appears at the door. Caesar perceives him and exhibits signs of affright*]

BIRCH. Is he alive?

KATY. Surely, he will live till the tide is out or the first cock crows in the morning! [*Birch deposits his pack and exit into the inner room*]

CAES. I tink he 'bout to go. [*Enter Rawson, Smith and Sanders, with the gang. They seize upon the pack. Katy screams. Reenter Birch*]

BIRCH. What is the matter? Ha! Villains! [*They cut off his retreat*]

RAW. What the devil has become of the contents of your pack, Mr. Birch? It's as light as a feather!

SAND. You didn't look as often behind you as usual, Mr. Birch, on your march home this time.

SMITH. I think we've housed you neatly, my worthy pedlar.

BIRCH. Hear me. In the next room is my father, now in the agonies of death. Let me go to him, receive his blessing and close his eyes, and you shall have all—aye, all!

RAW. Answer me as I put the questions or this musket shall send you to keep the old driveller company. Where are your goods?

BIRCH. I will tell you nothing unless you let me go to my father.

RAW. You won't? Then, by jingo, you shall never answer another question! [*Takes aim at him*]

SMITH. Hold! Captain, what would you do? You surely forget the reward! Tell us where are your goods and you shall go to your father.

BIRCH. I have disposed of them.

RAW. Aye! but there's gold somewhere for what the pack contained. Give us your gold, Mr. Birch.

BIRCH. You break your faith—

RAW. Give us your gold or—[*Pricking him with bayonet. Voice within—"Harvey"*]

BIRCH. Oh, for heaven's sake! Let me go to my father and you shall have all!

RAW. I swear you shall go then!

BIRCH. Here, take the trash. [*Throws down his purse. Sanders seizes it*]

RAW. Ha, ha, ha! but it shall be to your father in Heaven!

BIRCH. Oh! Villain—diabolical villain! Have you no faith—no honesty?

SAND. Why, to hear him now, one would think there was not a rope round his neck already. No necessity for your being uneasy, Mr. Birch. If the old man gets a few hours the start of you, you'll be sure to follow him before noon tomorrow. [*Voice within—"Harvey! Harvey!"*]

BIRCH. Hush! father—hush! I come—I come! [*Attempts to run past Smith, who makes a plunge at him with his bayonet and pins him to the wall by his clothes*]

SMITH. No—no, Mr. Birch, we know you too well for a slippery rascal to trust you out of our sight. Your gold—your gold!

BIRCH. You have it.

SAND. Don't struggle so, Mr. Birch, you'll tear your clothes and I want that coat myself.

RAW. Aye, we have the purse, but you have more purses. King George is a prompt paymaster and you've done him many a piece of good service. Where is your hoard? Without it, you'll never see your father.

BIRCH. Remove the stone underneath the woman. Remove the stone.

KATY. He raves! He raves! [*Changing her place. They tear up the stone, but find nothing*] He raves! You have driven him from his right mind. Would any man in his senses think of keeping gold under a hearth stone?

BIRCH. Peace, babbling fool. Lift the corner stone and you will find what will make you rich and me a beggar! [*They lift it*]

KATY. And then you will be dispisable—a pedlar without goods and without money is sure to be dispisable. [*They produce the gold*]

SAND.   There will be enough left to pay for his halter!

RAW.   And now, Mr. Birch, march—forward! [*Presenting his bayonet*]

BIRCH.   What would you more—is it not enough to harass the last moments of a dying man—to impoverish me—what more would you have?

RAW.   Your blood!

BIRCH.   And for money, like Judas, you would grow rich with the price of blood!

RAW.   Aye! and a fair price it is, my worthy pedlar. Fifty guineas—nearly the weight of that scarecrow carcase of yours in gold.

KATY.   Here—here are fifteen guineas and them drawers and that bed in the other room are all mine. If you will give Harvey one hour's start from the door, they shall be yours.

RAW.   One hour! [*Sanders snatches the purse*]

BIRCH.   Hold! Put no faith in the miscreants.

RAW.   Damn her faith and yours, too! We have the money in safe keeping. As for you, Mr. Birch, we will bear your insolence for the sake of the fifty guineas that are to pay for your gallows.

BIRCH.   Lead on! Take me to Major Dunwoodie. He, at least, may be kind, altho'—

RAW.   Not so fast, if you please, my worthy pedlar. I'll not go so far in such bad company. Captain Lawton's troop is quartered nearer. How would you like to sup with the captain this evening, Mr. Birch?

KATY.   Give me my money! Or set Harvey free!

SAND.   Your bribe was not enough, good woman.

KATY.   If there's law in the land, I'll be righted!

RAW.   The law of the neutral ground is the law of the strongest. Here Sulky, take this candle and set fire to that straw bed in the next room. Let us have a bonfire in honour of ourselves! Having succeeded in capturing the renown'd pedlar spy, Harvey Birch!

BIRCH.   Oh, for mercy—hold, hold!

RAW.   Away and do it! [*Exit Sulky*]

BIRCH.   Mercy! Mercy! [*Sinking at Rawson's feet*] You forget—my father —my old father—is bedridden there. He will perish in the flames! Oh, for heaven's sake, hold!!

RAW.   Blaze away, Sulky! [*Birch rushes towards his father's room. They intercept. He throws himself on the ground. They drag him roughly up and force him away, he struggling*]

SMITH.   Don't be in such a devil of a passion about it, Mr. Birch. You say the old gentleman is going—the fire will keep him warm.

RAW. Away with him!

SAND. Yes, and as the old gentleman is bound on a dark voyage, this will light him on his way.

BIRCH. Curses! Overwhelming and everlasting light on you and yours till—

RAW. Whew! Away with him!

BIRCH. Help! Mercy! O Heaven—my father—my father! [*Bursts into convulsive laughter*]

RAW. Away with him, I say. [*They drag him out. Katy and Caesar exeunt hastily into inner room*]

SCENE 7: *The exterior of Mrs. Flanagan's hotel, an old country building which extends entirely across the stage. Outbuildings supposed to be continued on the left. Sign, "Elizabeth Flanagan, her hotel." Sentinel parading before the door. Enter from the house, Betty, from the left, Lawton and Sitgreaves.*

SIT. Slight, but muscular—good subject, that pedlar spy. Damn him, Jack, I should like to dissect him. I wish you'd catch and hang him.

LAW. I have *caught* him, you know, Sitgreaves, once or twice, but the difficulty seems to be to keep him long enough to hang. Mysterious man! [*Aside*] I wash my hands of all future attempts to bring you to justice. Ah! By my hopes of promotion, my fair Elizabeth! How are you this evening?

BETTY. Sure, Captain Jack, why didn't you ride up to the door? An't it myself that's always here to tend upon you?

LAW. Yes, but the doctor would not think of allowing a lady to attend upon his horse, so we rode to the stable.

BETTY. Is it you, doctor—joy?

LAW. Oh, the doctor is petrified with the cold, but he'll soon be thaw'd. The sight of your fiery countenance, Elizabeth, is as cheering as a Christmas fire.

BETTY. Now sure, Captain Jack, you are always coming over one with your complimentaries. But hurry in for the life of you, darling. The fences here are not so strong as in the highlands and there's that within will warm both soul and body.

LAW. So you've been laying the rails under contribution, have you. Well, that will do for the body, but I shall not relish your whiskey for a month. I've been drinking from a cut-glass bottle with a silver stand, my charming widow.

BETTY. Och! If it's silver or goold that you're thinking of, it's but little I have, tho' I've a trifling bit of the Continental, Captain Jack. But in, darling, there's that there that's fit to be put in vessels of di'monds.

LAW. What can she mean, Sitgreaves? The animal looks as if she meant more than she says.

SIT. 'Tis probably a wandering of the reasoning powers, created by the frequency of intoxicating draughts.

BETTY. Faith, my dear jewel of a doctor, but that's well said of you. [*Aside to Lawton*] I'll bother him now. I've been stirring about like a lark for ye, doctor, and fadeing the wounded in your absence with the fat of the land.

SIT. Barbarous stupidity! To feed men labouring under the excitement of a fever with powerful nutriment! Woman! Woman! You are enough to defeat the skill of Hippocrates himself.

BETTY. [*To Lawton*] Didn't I tell ye? Pooh—pooh! Doctor, dear, what a botheration you make about a little whiskey. There was but a gallon betwixt a good half-dozen on them and I gave it to the boys to make them sleep asy —sure, jist as slumbering drops. But come in, I tell you. Ye'll be all in a botherment to hear about what's there. [*Exit in the hotel*]

SCENE 8: *Interior of the hotel; a long table at which some are drinking; some laying on benches round the fire. Dunwoodie seated at the fire. Mason at table. Enter Lawton, Sitgreaves and Betty.*

BETTY. Belave your own eyes now, Captain Jack.

LAW. Ha! Tom—why, what have you got in that demijohn that keeps you so long at the table?

MASON. [*Coming forward*] Oh, a royal gift, captain—some of the real amber-coloured juice of the grape—sent as an offering to Major Dunwoodie from his friend, Captain Wharton, of the royal army. The major gives us an entertainment in honour of our victory and the expense, you see, as it should be, is borne by the enemy.

LAW. Well, bravo! I've already had a sip of the same cup and have no objections to continue the draught!

MASON. That's right—let us keep it up. The major bade us be merry, altho' I never saw a man farther from it than he is himself.

LAW. What is the matter?

MASON. His friend, young Wharton, is to be tried tomorrow. Colonel Singleton has just arrived as president of the court-martial.

LAW. Indeed! Tomorrow?

MASON. Tomorrow morning—here—and I'm afraid it will go hard with the young captain. But come—let us have a song and endeavour to drive away the gloomy anticipations of the major. Room, gentlemen, for Captain Lawton. Silence for Captain Lawton's song.

Sit. [*Who has been drinking at the table*] Now, Jack, remember the air I taught you, and—stop, I've a copy of the words in my pocket.

Law. Oh, no! Never mind, doctor. I never could wheel round those hard names. Gentlemen, I'll give you an humble attempt of my own.

Mason. Silence for Captain Lawton's song! [*Lawton sings*]

> Now push the mug, my jolly boys,
>   And live while live we can.
> Tomorrow's sun may end our joys,
>   For brief's the hour of man
> And he who bravely meets the foe,
>   His lease of life can never know.
>
>   Old mother Flanagan,
>   Come and fill the can again,
>   For you can fill and drain at will.
>   Good Betty Flanagan.
>
> If love of life pervades your breast,
>   Or love of ease your frame,
> Quit honour's path for peaceful rest,
>   And bear a coward's name;
> For soon and late we danger know
>   And fearless on the saddle go.
>
>   Old Mother, etc.
>
> When foreign foes invade the land
>   And wives and sweethearts call,
> In freedom's cause we'll bravely stand
>   Or will as bravely fall.
> Of this fair home the fates have given,
>   We'll live the lords or live in Heaven.
>
>   Old Mother, etc.

[*Loud applause by knocking on table, etc.*]

Betty. [*Who has been much delighted*] Here's to you Captain Jack, in a drop of the gift myself. [*Drinks*] Faith, 'tis but a wishy-washy stuff, after all.

Sit. [*Who has been very uneasy during song*] Captain Lawton, I marvel that a gentleman and a gallant officer can find no other subject for his muse in these times of trial than such beastly invocations to that notorious follower of the camp, the filthy Elizabeth Flanagan.

BETTY. Heyday! And is it one of your dirty trade, doctor, that calls me filthy? I'll make ye ate your words, mister.

DUN. Peace! Woman, leave the room. He who criticizes, doctor, ought to be able to perform. I call upon Doctor Sitgreaves for a song. [*Exit Betty*]

MASON. Doctor Sitgreaves, sing! Doctor Sitgreaves, sing!

LAW. A classical ode from Doctor Sitgreaves.

SIT. [*Sings without voice or tune*]

> Hast thou e'er felt love's dart, dearest,
>   Or breath'd his trembling sigh—
> Thought him afar, was ever nearest
>   Before that sparkling eye.
> Then hast thou known what 'tis to feel
> The pain that Galen could not heal.

LAW. Hurrah! The doctor eclipses the muses themselves. His melody is a crossbreed of the nightingale and the owl. Holla! What's coming? [*Noise without. Enter the Skinners, dragging in Birch, preceded by the Sentinel. The company rise*]

RAW. Which is Captain Lawton?

LAW. He waits your pleasure, sir.

RAW. Then here I deliver into your hands a condemned traitor. This is Harvey Birch, the pedlar spy.

LAW. [*Aside*] Ha! By heaven, he is lost. [*Aloud*] And who are you, sir, that speak so freely of your neighbours? But your pardon, sir. [*Bowing to Dunwoodie, who advances*] Here is the commanding officer. To him you will please address yourself. How is this—arms in our quarters? Stack them instantly.

RAW. No, it is to you I deliver the pedlar and from you I claim my reward. This is Harvey Birch and—

DUN. Are you Harvey Birch?

BIRCH. I am. [*With pride*]

DUN. And a traitor to your country! Do you know that I should be justified in ordering your execution tonight?

BIRCH. 'Tis not the will of Heaven to send a soul so hastily to His presence.

DUN. You speak truth, and a few brief hours shall be added to your life. But, as your offense is most odious to a soldier, so it will be sure to meet the soldier's vengeance. You die tomorrow.

BIRCH. 'Tis as Heaven wills.

DUN. You have already been tried, Harvey Birch and the *truth* has proved you too dangerous an enemy to the liberties of our country to be suffered to live.

BIRCH. The truth!

DUN. Aye, the truth—you were charged with communicating intelligence to the enemy, which frustrated the intentions of Washington.

BIRCH. Will Washington say so, think you?

DUN. Doubtless he would. Even the justice of Washington condemns you.

BIRCH. No—no—no—Washington can see beyond the hollow views of pretended patriots. Has he not risk'd his all on the cast of the die? Is a gallows ready for *me?* There was once one ready for *him* also! No, no, no! Washington would never say "lead him to the gallows."

DUN. Have you anything, wretched man, to urge to the commander-in-chief why you should not die?

BIRCH. [*Slowly draws from his bosom a tin box, opens it and takes out a paper which he holds toward Dunwoodie. Suddenly recollects himself and exclaims*] No! It dies with me! I knew the conditions of my service and will not purchase life with their forfeiture! It dies with me.

DUN. Deliver that paper and you possibly yet may find favour.

BIRCH. It dies with me.

DUN. Seize the traitor and wrest the secret from his hands! [*They seize him. Birch, quick as lightning, swallows the paper*]

LAW. Astonishing, mysterious being!

[SIT. Hold him while I administer an emetic.]

DUN. Forbear! If his crime is great, so will also be his punishment.

RAW. I have spent many a good hour to entrap the villain and I hope you will give me a certificate that will entitle us to the reward. It was promised to be paid in gold. [*During this speech Lawton gives directions to Hollister to take the flint muskets of the Skinners. He accordingly does this in view of the audience*]

LAW. Major Dunwoodie, I second the request of this worthy gentleman and crave the office of bestowing the reward on him and his followers.

DUN. Take it; and you, miserable man, prepare for the fate which will surely await you before tomorrow's sun goes down.

BIRCH. Lead on!

DUN. Whither?

BIRCH. To the gallows.

DUN. No! My duty requires that I order you to be executed, but surely not so hastily. Take till nine tomorrow morning to prepare for the awful change you are to undergo. [*Exit Dunwoodie*]

Law. Come, my worthy patriots. Follow and receive your reward.

Raw. Farewell, Mr. Birch, I hope you—

Law. [*Furiously*] Silence! Listen now, my band of worthies.

*[Raw. Will you not pay us now, Captain Lawton?

Law. Oh! Pay you. Yes you shall have [   ] measure of your reward. There is the money that Washington sent down for the captors of the spy. [*Dashing the bag on the floor*]

Sand. Don't let us stay to count it, captain; I don't like his [   ].

Raw. Thank you, sir. I don't doubt it is all right. Let us go to our homes.

Law. Hold! So much to redeem our promise. Now [   ] we pay you for taking the spy, but we punish you for [   ], robbing and murdering. Seize them, my lads!

Raw. How! Are we betrayed? Are you then our enemy? Look to yourselves, men. Our arms will save us—fire!] [*Exeunt Birch and Officers on one side, Lawton and Skinners on the other*]

ACT III.

Scene 1: *The outside of Birch's prison, apparently a shed at one end of the Hotel Flanagan. No opening but a small door in C. First Sentry on duty. Enter Hollister from shed with lantern.*

Holl. [*Speaking as he enters*] Well, good night! I have left you my Bible. You had better read it, for 'tis that only can be of service to you now. What noise was that a while ago?

Sent. The lamentations of the Skinners. Captain Lawton ordered each a flogging on their bare backs in addition to the reward of fifty guineas.

Holl. Ah, the rascals! If they had their deserts, they'd hang on the same gallows with the pedlar spy tomorrow. Well, my lad, look well to your prisoner. Suffer no one to speak to him. And remember, your life depends upon his not escaping.

Sent. But Lieutenant Mason ordered me to let Betty Flanagan pass in and out when she pleases.

Holl. Well, let her then, but be careful this wily pedlar don't pass out in the folds of her petticoats. Give the same instructions to your relief, and tell him to do the same to his. I'll give similar orders to the whole guard and if Harvey Birch escapes this time, we are either worse than fools, or Sir Henry

---

* Bracketed lines indicate an inserted addition in the manuscript, some lines of which are incomplete.

Clinton has made a league with the devil and sent him here in the shape of a pedlar. [*Exit*]

SENT. [*Listening*] Why, damn the fellow. A halter already about his neck and he sleeps as comfortable as a Hessian sentinel on his post. [*Enter Betty, drunk*]

BETTY. The divil burn the rascals—the rapscallions—the villains.

SENT. What's the matter, Betty? What's the matter?

BETTY. Ye divil, ye—don't ye be after axing what's none of your business to know. Be asy, won't ye? Is it that way ye kape still upon yeer post—whisking about like a jacky-lantern? Be asy, can't ye till I spake to you—ye won't? Faith, then, and ye may dance. I'll be no looker-on. [*Goes into the shed. Enter Corporal* with relief guard. The sentry is changed in silence*]

FIRST SENT. You may keep yourself warm by dancing, John. The pedlar spy has tuned his fiddle, you hear, and it will not be long before Betty will strike up in her turn. [*Guard laugh*]

CORP. Forward. [*Exit guard. Enter from the shed Birch in the dress of Betty Flanagan, as drunk. Birch drinks from bottle*]

SECOND SENT. Stop! Are you sure the spy is not in your pocket?

BIRCH. Can't ye hare the rascal snoring in my room, ye dirty blackguard? And is it so you would sarve a dacent female that a man must be put to sleep in the room with her, you rapscallion.

SECOND SENT. Pooh! What do you mind a man that's to be hung in the morning for? You see he sleeps already. Tomorrow he'll take a longer nap. [*Seizing the bottle*]

BIRCH. Hands off! ye villain. [*Relinquishing the bottle*] But I'll go to Captain Jack and know if it's his orders to put a hang-gallows spy in my room, aye, even in my widow'd bed, you thief.

SECOND SENT. Silence! you old Jezebel, or you'll wake the gentleman. Would you disturb a man in his last sleep.

BIRCH. I'll wake Captain Jack, you riprobate villain and bring him here to see me righted. He will punish ye all for imposing on a dacent widow'd body, you marauder. [*Exit staggering*]

SECOND SENT. Away with you, you old devil!

SCENE 2: *A wood. Enter Skinners in disorder.*

SMITH. Well, this is an end of our business in West Chester. The Virginian Horse will soon make the county too hot to hold us.

RAW. I'll have his blood if I am tormented by furies the next instant!

* Not listed in cast of characters.

SMITH.   Oh, you are very valiant here in the wood! Why did you who boast so much of your aim, miss your man tonight at thirty yards?

RAW.   A devilish good shot it was by starlight—to shoot a horseman on a brisk gallop. 'Twas the person next him I hit, tho!

SAND.   A woman, you say.

RAW.   So it seem'd by the shrieking. Some of the Whartons, I suppose, that he was attending home. The cold had set me a shivering or I'd have made worm's meat of *him!*

SAND.   The cold! Damn me if I think I shall ever be cold again! My back burns as if a thousand red-hot gridirons were laid on it about as softly as a flail shakes hands with buckwheat.

RAW.   And you would tamely submit to such usage, and kiss the rod that beat you?

SAND.   Why, as for kissing the rod—it wouldn't be an easy matter, I'm thinking, the one that paid its compliments to me was broke into such small pieces on my own shoulders that it would be difficult to find a part big enough to kiss. But captain, you'll excuse it—it's a way I've got. I'd rather lose half my skin than the whole of it with my ears into the bargain. By the Lord, I'd at any time give Captain Lawton enough of my hide to make a pair of jack boots to get out of his hands with the remainder! If you had known when you were well off, you would have stuck to Major Dunwoodie, who don't know half so much of our evil doings.

RAW.   Silence! You talking fool! Your jabbering is sufficient to drive a man mad. Isn't it enough to be rail'd at and beaten, but we must be tormented by your folly. Help to get out the provisions if any are left in the wallet and try to stop your mouth with food. [*Birch, as Betty, behind the scenes exclaims*]

BIRCH.   This way, Captain Jack. Here are the rascals. This way and murder the thieves. Quick—leave your horses and shoot your pistols.

SAND.   Ha! The mad Virginian!

SMITH.   Holla! Away! [*Noise without*]

RAW.   Off! Off! Save himself who can! Meet at the rendezvous! [*They fly. Enter Birch carrying the dress of Betty which he hides*]

BIRCH.   Oh, miscreants! May Heaven's hoarded wrath fall quickly on you! But let me not think of them. Heaven be praised. He has again enabled me to escape a horrid death. [*Clasps his hands in energetic devotion and looks silently up to Heaven for a moment*] Now my desolation is complete! And what is left me but to die! But no! I'll never leave the service *He* has honour'd me with, and the last words of my poor murdered father were, go on and serve the cause of your country. I will live to obey thy injunction, my father! and be content to be known only by *him*. But then, to endure the contempt, the detestation, of those gallant men by whom I was surrounded last night, and of all who, like them, fight for their country's liberty! I had overrated my strength when I thought I could endure the obloquy which my service heaps upon me without repining. Ha! It's daylight. I must retire further. Those miscreants are conceal'd among the rocks and hatching mischief, I doubt not. Every principle bids me to thwart their designs, if possible, and vengeance may grow out of it. But hold! I have destroyed my only safeguard, should I again be captured. Ha! The mountain hut! I'll meet *him* there to-night. [*Exit*]

SCENE 3: *A more open part of the wood. Rocks, etc., in the back part of the stage; morning twilight. Enter Dunwoodie and Lawton, meeting.*

LAW. Good morning, sir.

DUN. Captain Lawton! You are an early riser, sir.

LAW. Not more so than Major Dunwoodie.

DUN. I have not been in bed. The fate of Henry Wharton—

LAW. True! He is to be tried today. I had thought that the murder of his daughter would have prevented Colonel Singleton from being able to preside at the court today, but he has sent me hither to prepare.

DUN. How does he bear the fatal tragedy?

LAW. I have not seen him since he arrived at Wharton's. His servant brought his message to me.

DUN. Are you clear, Captain Lawton, as respects the person who committed this atrocious deed?

LAW. I have not the shadow of a doubt, Major Dunwoodie, that it was the leader of the Skinners.

DUN. And the ball was aim'd at you?

LAW. At me, undoubtedly.

DUN. We must take immediate measures to bring the villain to justice. But let us away. The spy is to be executed at nine—and—[*Birch appears above on the rocks with a musket*]

BIRCH. Stand or die!

LAW. By heaven! It is the spy, himself—and free!

DUN. Escaped? Impossible!

LAW. 'Tis he.

DUN. If we are to be murder'd, fire.

LAW. We will never become your prisoners.

BIRCH. No, it is not my intention to capture or to slay.

DUN. What then would you have, mysterious being?

BIRCH. Your good opinion!

DUN. To you, it must be indifferent what men may think of your actions; for you seem to be above the reach of their sentence.

BIRCH. Heaven spares the lives of its servants to its own time. 'Tis but a few hours and I was your prisoner, threatened with the gallows. Now you are mine, but you are free. There are those abroad who would treat you less kindly. Of what service will that sword be to you against my weapon and a steady hand? Take the advice of one who never injured you, and who never will—do not trust yourselves in the skirts of any wood, unless in company and mounted.

LAW. Have you comrades who have assisted you to escape and who are less generous than yourself?

BIRCH. No—no—I am alone truly. None know me but Heaven and *Him!*

DUN. And who?

BIRCH. None! But such is not your case, Major Dunwoodie. There are those that are dear to you. Danger is near them. Double your watchfulness. With your opinion of me, should I tell you more, you would suspect an ambush. Remember and guard those you love best. Farewell.

LAW. Hold! But a word—are you what you seem—can you—are you—

BIRCH. A spy! a royal spy!

LAW. Then go, miserable wretch! Either avarice or delusion has led a noble heart astray. [*Birch fires his musket in the air, throws it at their feet. When the smoke clears away, he has disappeared*]

DUN. Unaccountable being! How can he have escaped!

LAW. How has he escaped so often before? There is an unfathomable mystery that surrounds him.

DUN. Away then. We can at least develop it in this instance. He cannot have escaped without treachery. [*Exeunt hastily*]

SCENE 4: *The outside of Birch's late prison. Second Sentry, etc. Enter Dunwoodie, Lawton, Mason, Hollister, and the whole troop of Dragoons, marching.*

DUN. Well, sir, I suppose your prisoner is safe.

SECOND SENT. He is yet asleep, and makes such a noise that I could hardly hear the bugles sound the alarm.

DUN. [*To Hollister*] Open the door and bring him forth. [*Exit Hollister into the shed*]

HOLL. [*Within*] Gone! Hell and the devil! Wake up, here! [*Enter Hollister*] The pedlar has fled!

MASON. Impossible.

DUN. Someone's life must answer for him!

MASON. Muster all the guard without. [*Enter Betty from hut*]

BETTY. Is it breakfast that's wanting? Well faith, ye look as if you would ate myself. But patience a little, darlings, and ye'll see sich a fry as never was.

HOLL. Fry! We'll have you roasted, you jade! You've help'd that damned pedlar to escape!

BETTY. Jade back again in your taath! And damned pedlar, too, Mister Sargeant, what have I to do with pedlars and escapes? I might have been a pedlar's lady and worn my silks, if I'd a had Sawny McTwill, instead of tagging at the haals of a parcel of dragooning rapscallions, who don't know how to trate a lone body with dacency.

HOLL. The fellow has left my Bible. In place of reading it, he has been busy in labouring to escape.

BETTY. And who would stay and be hung like a dog? It is not everyone that's born to meet with such an ind like yourself, Mister Hollister.

DUN. Silence! This business must be enquired into closely, gentlemen. There is no outlet but the door and there he could not pass unless the sentinel connived at his escape, or was asleep on his post. Examine all the guard. [*Enter First Sentry*]

FIRST SENT. Major Dunwoodie, Mr. Wharton and his family have arrived to attend the young captain's trial and have asked for you.

DUN. Ah! 'tis well. Captain Lawton, will you attend me? Lieut. Mason, you will examine strictly into this business and make report to me this afternoon. [*Exit Dunwoodie and Lawton*]

HOLL. Here is Hinder, sir, confesses that the washerwoman there, passed out about twelve o'clock last night. But he says he had orders to let her pass out and in.

BETTY. It's false, you thief, it's false! Would you slanderize a lone woman by saying she walks a camp at midnight? Here have I been sleeping the long night as swately as a sucking babe.

HOLL. Here, sir, is something written in my Bible that was not in it before.

MASON. [*Reads*] "These certify that, if suffered to get free, it is by Heaven's help alone, to whose divine aid I humbly recommend myself. I am forced to take the woman's clothes, but in her pocket is a recompense. Witness my hand. Harvey Birch." Can this be possible?

BETTY. What! has the thief robbed a lone woman of her all. Hang him! Catch him and hang him if there's law in the land.

HOLL. Examine your pocket, Betty.

BETTY. [*Pulling out a guinea*] Ah! Faith, but he's a jewel of a pedlar! Long life and brisk trade to him, anyway, say I—he is welcome to the duds—and if he is ever hung, many a bigger rogue will go free. [*Exit*]

MASON. Were this certificate from anybody else but so notorious a villain as the pedlar spy, it might benefit you something, Hinder—but as it is, it is hardly to be believed that you could have been thus deceived, with your eyes open and sober. Bring him away, and secure him till I bring you orders from the major. [*Exeunt*]

SCENE 5: *The interior of the Hotel Flanagan, fitted up for the sitting of the court-martial. Colonel Singleton as president and two Judges at table on one side, the Wharton family on the other. Dunwoodie, Lawton, Mason, with other Dragoons fill up the back of the stage.*

SING. Now, sir, proceed. You are at liberty to explain what your motives were, in entering the ground held by our army, in disguise.

HENRY. I am the son of this aged man; it was to visit him that I encounter'd the danger, and I feel that my father is entitled to my affection, and I would run much greater hazard to prove it to him in his old age.

SING. A very commendable spirit! Come, gentlemen, this business brightens. I confess at first it was very bad. Have you proof that to see your parent was your only intention?

HENRY. Yes, here—here is proof—my father, my sister—Major Dunwoodie, all know it—

SING. Then indeed we may be able to save you. You are the father of the prisoner?

WHAR. He is my only son.

SING. And what, sir, do you know of the visit he made to your house on the 29th day of October last?

WHAR. He came as he told you, sir, to see me and his sisters.

SING. To see his sisters, too! Have you daughters, sir?

WHAR. I have two—both are with me.

SING. How long had you been separated?

WHAR. One year and two months.

SING. And you think it was to see you, only, that he came out?

WHAR. And my daughters.

SING. [*To Judge*] A boy of spirit. [*To Wharton*] Do you know that your son was entrusted with no commission from Sir Henry Clinton, and that the visit to you was not merely a cloak to other designs?

WHAR. How can I know it—would Sir Henry entrust me with such business?

SING. 'Tis well. Major Dunwoodie, you gave it as your opinion, on your examination, that the prisoner had no other object than what he has avow'd.

DUN. None other, I will pledge my life! I have known this gentleman from a boy—he is above deceit!

SING. You say that he escaped and was retaken in open arms?

DUN. He was. Would he, think you, sir, have trusted himself where he could fall again into our hands, had he been guilty?

SING. Would André have deserted a field of battle, had he encounter'd such an event near Tarry-town? Is it not natural to youth to seek glory?

DUN. Do you call this glory—an ignominious death and a tarnished name?

SING. Major Dunwoodie, you have acted nobly; your duty has been arduous and severe, but it has been faithfully and honourably discharged—ours must be no less so.

JUDGE. Let that black come forward. [*Caesar advances*] You know the prisoner?

CAES. I think I ought.

JUDGE. Did he give you the wig, when he threw it aside?

CAES. I don't want 'em—got a berry good hair he'self.

JUDGE. Were you employ'd in carrying any letters or messages while Captain Wharton was in your master's house?

CAES. I do what a tell me.

JUDGE. But what did they tell you?

CAES. Sometime a one ting—sometime anoder.

SING. Enough! [*To Judges*] We have the noble acknowledgement of a gentleman—What more can we get from this fellow? Captain Wharton, you perceive the unfortunate impression against you—have you other testimony to adduce? [*Frances comes forward*] Ha! Your sister? To you then, your brother communicated his intention of paying your family a secret visit?

FRAN. No! No! we knew not of the visit until he arrived—but can it be necessary to explain to gallant men, that a child would incur hazard to meet his only parent?

SING. But was this the first time? Did he never even talk of doing so before?

FRAN. Certainly, certainly! This is but the fourth of his visits.

SING. I knew it! an adventurous warm-hearted son—I warrant me, gentlemen, a fiery soldier in the field; in what disguises did he come?

FRAN. None—for none were then necessary; the royal troops covered the country and gave him safe passage.

SING. And was this his first visit out of the uniform of his regiment?

FRAN. Oh! the very first! His first offense I do assure you, if offense it be.

SING. But you wrote him—you urged the visit—surely young lady, you wish'd to see your brother?

FRAN. That we wish'd for it, and prayed for it—oh! how fervently we prayed for it—is true, but to have held communion with the royal army, would have endangered our father, and we dare not.

SING. Did he leave the house until taken, or had he intercourse with any out of your own dwelling?

FRAN. With none—not one, excepting our neighbour, the pedlar Birch.

SING. [*Rising from his seat*] With whom!

DUN. He is lost! [*Rushes out*]

FRAN. But Harvey Birch—

SING. Harvey Birch! [*The Judges repeat, "Harvey Birch!"*]

HENRY. To you gentlemen it can be no new intelligence to hear that Harvey Birch is suspected of favouring the royal cause, for he has already been condemned by your tribunals to the fate which I now see awaits myself. I will therefore explain that it was by his assistance that I procured the disguise and passed your picquets—but to my dying moment and with my dying breath, I will avow that my intentions were as pure as the innocent being before you!

SING. Captain Wharton, the enemies of American liberty have made mighty and subtle efforts to overthrow our power. A more dangerous man for his means is not ranked among our foes than this pedlar of West Chester. He is a spy—artful—delusive and penetrating, beyond the abilities of any of his class. Sir Henry could not do better than associate him with the officers in his next attempt. He would have saved him André—indeed, young man, this is a connexion that may prove fatal to you.

FRAN. O heaven! I have ruined him! Do you desert us? Then he is lost indeed!

SING. Forbear, lovely innocent, forbear! You injure none, but distress us all.

FRAN. Is it then such a crime to possess natural affection? Would Washington—the noble, upright, impartial Washington, judge so harshly? Delay but till Washington can hear his tale.

SING. It is impossible.

FRAN. Impossible! Oh! But for a week suspend your judgment—on my knees I entreat you! As you will expect mercy yourself, where no human power can avail you, give him but a day!

SING. It is impossible—our orders are peremptory, and too long delay has been given already. [*He comes forward*]

JUDGE. Remand your prisoner. Colonel Singleton, shall we withdraw?

FRAN. Singleton! Singleton! Then you are a father and know how to pity a father's woes—you cannot, will not wound a heart that is now nearly crush'd! Hear me, Colonel Singleton—as God will listen to your dying prayers—hear me and spare my brother. [*Still kneeling and holding his hand*]

SING. Remove her.

FRAN. Colonel Singleton how lately was your own son in suffering and danger; under the roof of my father he was cherish'd, under my father's roof he found shelter and protection. Oh! suppose that son the pride of your age, the solace and protection of your orphan children, and then pronounce my brother guilty if you dare!

SING. What right has Heath to make an executioner of me! But I forget myself. Come, gentlemen, let us mount—our painful duty must be done.

FRAN. Mount not! Go not! Can you tear a son from his parent—a brother from his sister, so coldly? Is this the cause I have so ardently loved! Are these the men that I have been taught to reverence! But you relent, you do hear me—you will pity and forgive!

SING. Lead on! Gentlemen.

FRAN. Lead not on but hear me! Colonel Singleton you are a father! Pity! mercy! mercy for the son! mercy for the daughter! Yes, you had a daughter—on this bosom she pour'd out her last breath—these hands closed her eyes—these hands that are now clasp'd in prayer—did those offices for her that you now condemn my poor brother to require!

SING. [*Overcome by his feelings*] May Heaven bless you for the deed! [*She faints in his arms, her father and sister receive her from him*] Come, gentlemen, we have still our duty to perform as officers; our feelings as men may be indulged hereafter. What is your pleasure with the prisoner? [*They hand him a paper*] Ha! is it even so? But this is a short notice—not a day to fit one so young for Heaven.

JUDGE. The royal officers gave Hale but an hour. We have extended the usual time, but Washington has power to extend it, or to pardon.

SING. Then to Washington will I go! and if the services of an old man like me, or that brave boy of mine entitle me to his ear, I will yet save the youth! and cheer the heart of Heaven's own innocence! [*Exeunt*]

SCENE 6: *The rendezvous of the Skinners among the rocks; fire burning in a cleft, they seated round it.* *[*Sanders sings; as the scene draws, the chorus is heard, all join in.*

Chorus

Drink, comrades, drink! let mirth endure,
    Nor e'er your joys delay;
We're of the present only sure,
    Be jovial while you may!

Ours is the life to pleasure known,
    Our thoughts are in confine,
Tomorrow's cares ne'er bid us moan,
    Nor present joys decline.
For distant cares we distant know,
    And dont their coming fear!
For while for us our goblets glow
    We'll drown them when they're here!

Drink, etc.

Jade conscience in her woman-freaks
    The gibbet doth display.
Pshaw! of tomorrow 'tis she speaks,
    We only know today!
Send round the wine—give life fair play,
    Let mirth with time still flow—
If we but keep thought far away
    We ne'er shall sorrow know!

Drink, etc.

SAND.   Drink away, lads! here's wine sufficient to perform an operation on the phizzes of a whole legion of monks! Down with it!]

RAW.   'Twill be a glorious night for our business! As dark as hell; the house will blaze like a furnace, ha, ha! We'll fire it in the chambers, and while we're at work, there will be light enough to see if the coast is clear for half a mile round. There is plate and money enough to make you all gentlemen—aye! and revenge, too!! You all know your posts—

SAND.   Aye, aye, captain, we've had noise enough made about that—let's say no more till the time comes. [*Whistle without*] Ha! who is that?

* The bracketed lines, including the song, were apparently omitted from the stage production, which begins the scene with Rawson's speech.

Raw. [*Whistles*] 'Tis Smith—he has been on the lookout at Wharton's. [*Enter Smith*]

Sand. Well, comrade, what's the news?

Raw. Have you learn'd anything of consequence to us?

Smith. Aye, have I, captain—and better luck than we ever deserved at fortune's hands I'll swear. Major Dunwoodie and Captain Lawton are off to the highlands in search of Washington, to entreat a pardon for the royal captain.

Raw. Then the coast is clear! By Heaven! the rich plunder of Old Wharton's house is ours! Come lads, away! It's already dark enough for us to move in safety—now for fortune and revenge! [*Exeunt Skinners*]

Scene 7: *The room at the hotel. Night. On one side enter Sitgreaves, Katy Haynes, Betty; Mason, Hollister and Dragoons on the other.*

Mason. How is your prisoner?

Holl. He is very quiet—tho' a little anxious I presume for the return of the major and Captain Lawton.

Mason. He may expect them every minute—they cannot be detain'd much longer.

Katy. As I was saying doctor, Captain Lawton told me you could tell me all about the matter, being learned in these things betterer than nobody else.

Sit. Hem! He said so, did he?

Katy. Yes, sir—and what I want to know is if a woman a'nt got no dower in her husband's property unless they be actually married?

Sit. I judge not, madam—if death has anticipated your nuptials I am fearful you have no remedy against his stern decrees.

Katy. I did think he only waited the death of the old gentleman before he married—but now he is nothing more than dispiseable [*sic*]—or what's the same thing: a pedlar without house, pack, or money.

Betty. What? and is it the pedlar that ye're making all this bother about? —Belike then, good woman, ye're knowing whether or no he's a kin to Beelzeboob—it's Sargeant Hollister there who's saying there's a relationship atwixt him and the ould one, and it's no fool the sargeant is neither.

Katy. It's a scandalous disparagement! There's no kinder soul nor Harvey that ever carried a pack. Beelzebub indeed! What for would he read the Bible if he had dealings with the evil spirit?

Betty. He's an honest divil ony way, as I was saying before—the guinea was pure—but then the sargeant thinks him amiss, and it's no want of larning that Mister Hollister has.

KATY. He's a fool. Sargeant Hollister would be glad to hold a candle to Harvey in the way of learning I guess.

BETTY. Pooh!—do you hear that, sargeant dear? Pooh! pooh! ye're no thinking that Mister Hollister is an officer and stands next the cornet in the troop—ye're no thinking of that, Mrs. Beelzeboob.

KATY. I'm a single woman and my name is Haynes, and I'd thank you to use no disparaging terms when speaking to me—it's what I isn't used to—and Harvey is no more of Beelzebub nor yourself.

SIT. It is compulsatory upon us all, madam, to tolerate a degree of license in the speech of Mrs. Flanagan—but go on with your business, madam.

BETTY. Och! Doctor, if its bis'ness ye have with the divil or his consort, I'll not interript ye.

KATY. As I was saying, sir, it might be hard for a man to get a wife at all in such a predicary as Harvey is—but before the old gentleman's death—

SIT. Pray, ma'am, who administered to the case?

KATY. No one yet; I expect he made his last will in the Testament.

SIT. Um! You don't comprehend me, madam. Under whose care was the sick man during his indisposition?

KATY. Under mine, and care thrown away it was.

SIT. How did you treat him?

KATY. Why kindly, you may be sartain.

MASON. The doctor means medically, madam.

KATY. Oh! I doctor'd him mostly with yarbs.

SIT. With simples—ah!—safer than more powerful remedies in the hands of the unlettered, but why had he no regular attendant?

KATY. I'm sure Harvey has suffered enough from having consarns with Rig'lars, without having one to tend upon his father.

MASON. The doctor does not mean a rig'lar soldier, madam, but a regular physician.

KATY. Oh! For the best of all reasons—there was none to be had, so I took care of him myself. Oh! I'm clear for doctoring, tho' Harvey says I am killing myself with medicines.

SIT. [*Talking* at *Mason*] Therein you shew your sense, madam—you appear to be a sensible, discreet woman—and some who have had opportunities of acquiring more correct views, might envy you your respect for knowledge and the lights of science!

KATY. Pray, sir, may I ask if them lights that you speak of are what we call northern lights in these parts? [*Mason roars*]

BETTY. Och! to be sure they are—the rory-bory-ails-us as I've heard the doctor call 'em for himself. [*Exit Sitgreaves. Birch appears at the door*]

BIRCH. Why stand you idle here, when the cry of murder breaks on the silence of the night!

KATY. [*Shrieking*] Harvey!

BETTY. Faith, but ye're welcome, Mister Pedlar or Mister Birch, or Mister Beelzeboob, or what's yeer name—ye're an honest divil anyway!

MASON. The pedlar spy! Seize him! Cut him down!

BIRCH. Who lays a hand upon me dies! [*Draws pistol, and shows himself fully arm'd*] Mount! mount! and fly to the Locusts! All that your commander holds dear is in danger—arm, and mount, and that instantly or you will be too late!

MASON. What! villain—you would have us leave the royal captain unguarded, that you may contrive his escape? Miscreant! your artifice is too shallow! Advance and seize him! or—

BIRCH. Fool! think you I would have trusted myself here if—

MASON. You are my prisoner! Fire and you die! [*Rushing toward him. Birch fires the pistol, and exit*] Pursue him! By heaven! that was either a blank charge, or a miracle has saved me! [*Katy, Hollister, and Dragoons rush out*]

BETTY. Faith! and ye're wrong ony way, Lieutenant Mason, not to do as ye're bid. Ye had better be off with the troop or the major will never forgive ye the longest day ye're alive!

MASON. Silence! I shall not stir till the major and Lawton arrive, though all—[*Reenter Hollister and Dragoons*]

HOLL. He has escaped—'tis useless to pursue him—the night is so dark you can't see an inch before you.

MASON. Very well, mount the guard and surround Captain Wharton's prison; we may calculate upon some stratagem to scotch him—away! [*Exit*]

BETTY. Faith, then, it's a big fool or a big coward ye are, Mister Mason. By the powers I'll just hitch the mare to the tills and ride down to the Wharton's myself. No, I won't aither—I'll foot it—it's no rasonable for the baste to be hurted. [*Exeunt Dragoons one way, and Betty the other*]

SCENE 8: *The lawn before the Locusts; the roof, etc., of the building, and plunder lying in front. Skinners bringing it out. Enter Rawson and Smith with bundles which they throw down with the rest.*

RAW. Aye! aye! my lads—smoking ruins tell no tales—bring the women in—let us have no news abroad—the coast is clear—time enough, lads—we'll all get sufficient to make us comfortable in this world—and more.

SMITH. Aye, that we will, captain—long life*——lived like a prince and its only fair that a little*——[*Enter Harvey Birch*]

BIRCH. Accursed villain—you at least shall not escape!

RAW. Ha! Mister Birch! You here! By heaven, we have had trouble enough at your hands—you die! [*Rawson snaps a pistol at Birch, it misses fire, Smith rushes upon him with his sword, they fight, off*] What the devil brought *him* here? But never mind, the rascal Smith will give a good account of him. Muster up now men, muster the plunder and let us be off—the light will bring the troop down upon us. [*At this moment the flames burst thro' the windows of the second story*]

LAW. [*Without*] Onward! onward! give quarter when you have done justice!

RAW. By hell! 'Tis the Virginian and his troop—off—off—leave all and fly! [*They rush out tumultuously, L.*]

LAW. Holla, forward!

DUN. [*Without*] Die! Miscreant, die! [*Enter Skinners driven before Dunwoodie's party; Rawson and Dunwoodie, fighting; Lawton and his men enter from R., some firing. Some of the Skinners are killed, others made prisoners*]

LAW. Major Dunwoodie! Fly to the cottage, the females are within; leave these hellhounds to me. [*Exit Henry and Dunwoodie into the house*]

RAW. Must I be murdered—then away all thoughts but vengeance. [*He and Lawton fight; after an obstinate resistance, Rawson is killed. Enter Dunwoodie, bringing Frances*]

FRAN. Fly! fly—my sister—Oh! save her—save her. [*Lawton rushes into the building. Enter Henry, Old Wharton, and Caesar, from the house*] Henry! my brother!

HENRY. Aye, Frances! and safe from the fear of death. The exertions of Dunwoodie have procured me a pardon.

DUN. Say rather the wisdom of the "father of his country" has condemned not where there was no cause for condemnation.

HENRY. But my sister Sarah, is she not here?

CAES. She come dere, Massa Harry [*Enter Lawton bringing Sarah*]

SARAH. My preserver! Ah! my father—my sister—and my dear brother.

FRAN. Pardoned! Sarah, pardoned! Oh! join us in blessing the benign being who leads the armies on to victory! and ennobles our nature by acts of wisdom. Would that we might see him.

DUN. You have seen him, dearest Frances, and received his blessing—for Harper and he are one.

* Manuscript imperfect at this point.

FRAN. Ah! merciful Heaven! is it so indeed! [*The Whartons express astonishment. Enter Doctor Sitgreaves*]

SIT. [*Running to the dead body of a Skinner*] Ah! it's all over—had I been in time to have stopped the effusion from the jugular he might have been saved; yes, life is extinct, indeed. Well, are there any more wounded? [*A shot is fired without*]

MASON. The spy!—the spy!—the pedlar spy! [*Birch rushes in, wounded; he tears open his clothes, exposes the wound in his breast; the action forces the tin box from its concealment, it falls on the floor. He sinks down, points with eagerness to the box*]

LAW. By heaven! 'tis Harvey Birch!

DUN. Murdered!

LAW. Mysterious man! What didst thou here?

A SKINNER. [*Who is brought in by Dragoons, a prisoner, immediately after the entrance of Birch*] He was killed by me—I claim my life as the reward.

MASON. I fear I wronged him greatly. May Heaven repay him if his intentions were good in giving us the information. [*Birch in the agonies of death exhibits impatient signs to have the box examined*]

LAW. Ha! what is here? [*He takes up the box, looks at a paper, and gives it to Dunwoodie with a wild air of astonishment*] Read! read!

DUN. [*Reads*]

"Circumstances of political importance have kept secret what this paper reveals. Harvey Birch has been for many years a faithful and unrequited servant of his country. Though man does not, may God reward him for his conduct.

GEORGE WASHINGTON."

BIRCH. [*Collecting himself for a last exertion, his countenance one of gratitude and exultation, exclaims*] Eternal providence! [*Dies*]

DUN. Rest in peace, injured patriot. Thy country and the world shall know that hearts like thine beat and break to serve it! Comrades! friends! let it be our most cherished pride throughout this struggle, and our proudest boast to Heaven—our consolation whenever death may overtake us—that the approbation of the "Father of his Country" is ours, ours the confidence of WASHINGTON!

ALL. Huzza! Huzza! Huzza! [*Flourish. The Dragoons fill up the back of the stage. In front, old Wharton in C., Dunwoodie and Frances on one side, Lawton and Sarah on the other, etc.*]

THE END

THE BATTLE OF STILLWATER;
Or, THE MANIAC

In three acts, founded on national events, by the author of Pirate of the East, Black Douglass, Ida Stephanoff, The Fatal Prophecies, etc.

By H. J. Conway (?)

THE BATTLE OF STILLWATER;
Or, THE MANIAC

THE *Battle of Stillwater; or, The Maniac* was first produced at the National Theatre in Boston on March 16, 1840. No satisfactory assignment of authorship has hitherto been made, the only reference being Quinn's remark (*History of the American Drama,* Vol. I, p. 282) that "it has been attributed to Rufus Dawes but shows no trace of his style." The evidence for ascribing its authorship to H. J. Conway, though not conclusive, appears valid. The title-page of the Seymour Collection manuscript of the play reads as follows: "*The Battle of Stillwater or The Maniac,* In Three Acts, founded on National events, by the Author of *Pirate of the East, Black Douglass, Ida Stephanoff, The Fatal Prophecies, Nix's Mate,* &c. &c. &c." Of these last plays, three are assigned to Conway by Wilson in his *History of the Philadelphia Theatre 1835-1855.* These three are *Ida Stephanoff, The Fatal Prophecies,* and *The Arab Chief; or, Pirate of the East,* all produced in Philadelphia, the last one also having a New York production recorded by Odell. Further, Conway's career, as evidenced by many plays, includes plays written for various theatres in Philadelphia, Boston, and New York, at such periods as would fit in with the time of the Boston and New York productions of *Stillwater.* Many plays already ascribed to Conway are of the same pattern and style as *Stillwater.* Odell lists a number of Conway's "moralized melodramas." His *New York Patriots; or, The Battle of Saratoga* even uses the same theme, for Stillwater is but a fictitious name for Saratoga.

Conway had a long career in the theatre, as playwright, prompter, and business-office man. He was for several years, beginning in 1835, prompter at the Walnut Street Theatre in Philadelphia. After a brief period in the 1840's apparently spent in Boston, he became active in New York, writing plays for Barnum's, The Old Bowery, and occasionally other theatres until 1862 or later. In the year 1852 he held the position of treasurer at the Castle Garden Theatre, New York. His wife was the popular British actress, Miss Courtney, who made her American début in 1832.

Conway's early Philadelphia plays were not very successful, but *The Battle of Stillwater* won ready acclaim. Its New York production on May 3, 1841 was followed by a very successful adaptation, *Charles O'Malley; or, The Irish Dragoon,* and in later years by such popular pieces as *Uncle Tom's*

Cabin, The Old Brewery, Anna; or, The Child of the Wreck, and *The Orphan's Dream.* The *New York Patriots,* mentioned above, won Conway a five-hundred dollar prize.

The Battle of Stillwater is a turgid melodramatic mixture of patriotism, rustic humor, and a sensational love plot, climaxed by the surrender of Burgoyne, and a pageant of the "Genius of Liberty." The author's primary interest seems to be in the rustic humor of his "character" part of Uzzial, although the New York production of the play featured the parts of the heroine's parents, played by Mrs. Thorne and the Bowery idol, J. H. Kirby. *The Battle of Stillwater* is printed in this volume from the National Theatre (Boston) copy in the possession of Princeton University, and supplied through the courtesy of Dr. Robert H. Ball. The manuscript copy, which is very clean, was obviously that used by the prompter, J. B. Wright, for whose benefit the production was given.

With some definite evidence in favor, and none to the contrary, the assignment of this play to H. J. Conway has been made. Accordingly, a chronological list of Conway's plays is included, with dates of first productions.

The Arab Chief; (and the) *or, Pirate of the East.* Bowery (N.Y.), July 5, 1834.

A Miser's Miseries. Walnut (Phila.), November 9, 1835.

The Spanish Pirates; or, A Union of the Flags. Walnut (Phila.), November 14, 1835.

Fatal Prophecies; or, The Smuggler's Daughter. Walnut (Phila.), December 5, 1835.

Ida Stephanoff. Walnut (Phila.), January 1, 1836.

The Battle of Stillwater; or, The Maniac. National (Boston), March 16, 1840.

Charles O'Malley; or, The Irish Dragoon. National (Boston), January 20, 1842.

The Mysterious Chief; or, The Heroes of 1812. National (N.Y.), July 21, 1851.

Hiram Hireout; or, Followed by Fortune. Chicago Theatre, 1851.

The Orphan's Dream. Barnum's (N.Y.), August 30, 1852.

Charlotte Corday. Chestnut (Phila.), October 14, 1852.

The Last Nail. Barnum's (N.Y.), November 1, 1852.

Our Jemimy; or, Connecticut Courtship. Chestnut (Phila.), May 9, 1853.

Uncle Pat's Cabin. Burton's (N.Y.), May 23, 1853.

Uncle Tom's Cabin. Barnum's (N.Y.), November 7, 1853. (Advertised as "written eighteen months previously," and as having been in rehearsal for twenty weeks, probably by way of proving originality in comparison with several other contemporary versions of this plot.)

The Black Douglass. (burletta) (N.Y.), 1853. (Obviously, if this is the play mentioned in the *Stillwater* manuscript, the date of first production cannot have been 1853.)

The Old Brewery. Barnum's American Museum (N.Y.), February 27, 1854.

Anna; or, The Child of the Wreck. Barnum's (N.Y.), May 8, 1854.

New York Patriots; or, The Battle of Saratoga. Barnum's (N.Y.), June 2, 1856.

Dred. Barnum's (N.Y.), October 16, 1856. (One of several versions of this popular plot.)

Like and Unlike. Laura Keene's (N.Y.), May 4, 1857. (Authorship doubtful.)

Nature and Art. Laura Keene's (N.Y.), May 11, 1857. (The same play as that produced at the Olympic Theatre (N.Y.), September 25, 1848?)

Our Irish Cousin. Barnum's (N.Y.), March 1, 1859.

Pike's Peak; or, The Search for Riches. Old Bowery (N.Y.), August 12, 1859.

Out of the Depths. Barnum's (N.Y.), October 3, 1859.

Wills and Ways to Make and Break. Barnum's (N.Y.), October 24, 1859.

Dick, the Newsboy. New Bowery (N.Y.), January 4, 1860.

Wicomiket; or, The Indian's Curse. New Bowery (N.Y.), February 27, 1860.

Half a Dollar. Laura Keene's (N.Y.), May 26, 1862.

DRAMATIS PERSONAE

British

GENERAL BURGOYNE	MR. HAYNES
MAJOR ACKLAND	MR. BROWN
CAPTAIN VALCOUR, *alias Singleton*	MR. HAMILTON
SERJEANT BOMB	MR. SAUNDERS
CORPORAL PRIMINGWIRE	MR. G. H. (?)
SIDEARMS	MR. YOUNG (?)
BRITISH OFFICERS, SOLDIERS	
SOLDIERS' WIVES	
MRS. SERJEANT BOMB, *alias Moll Flaggon*	MRS. NAPP (?)

Americans

ADAM COTTON	MR. MARSHALL
HARRY COTTON	MR. LEMAN
UZZIAL PUTNAM	
MYNHEER SNIGGLEFRITZ	MR. SPEAR
AZARIAH LAMBSON	MR. SAMUELS
SILENCE SAMSON	I. GEORGE (?)
GENERAL GATES (don't speak)	
AMERICAN OFFICERS, SOLDIERS, ETC.	
ROSE COTTON	MRS. CRUMER
JULIA VALCOUR, *The Maniac*	MRS. PELBZ
LUCE LAMBSON	MRS. MEER
GENIUS OF LIBERTY (don't speak)	

First produced March 16, 1840 for the benefit of J. B. Wright, prompter, at the National Theatre.

(This page and the title-page are reproduced from the manuscript. Some names in the original cast cannot be fully identified.)

ACT I.

SCENE I: *Moonlight view of the American camp previous to the Battle of Still-water, October 1777. In the distance, fires lighted, etc. On the right, the farmhouse of Adam Cotton. A light is seen burning through the casement. Enter from the house Captain Singleton (Captain Valcour in cloak, disguised) and Rose. Musick.*

CAPT. S. But Rose—only listen to me, my dear Rose!

ROSE. No more, Edward, no more. Leave me—it is already midnight.

CAPT. S. Cruel, cruel girl, is the sight of me already grown so hateful to you that you drive me hence with indifference? Can you, you whom I so devotedly love, shorten the hours I have stolen to pass with you? Ah, you know not what joy your dear presence gives me. If you did, you would not, could not, be so cruel. You do not love as I do.

ROSE. Edward, you wrong me, indeed you wrong me. But you must leave me; my father will return ere long and should he find you here, he will force an explanation from you, and I tremble for the consequence.

CAPT. S. Would that moments could be lengthened into years. 'Tis death for me to go. Tomorrow the clang of arms will thrill upon my startled ear, drowning all dreams of love. Rose, I go to battle, perhaps to death! [*A child's voice from house calls, "Rose." Starts*] Ha!

ROSE. Edward, leave me. 'Tis Henry's voice. His mother perhaps has awoke—my poor sister, who but yesterday returned from England a maniac from grief. At an early age she married, unknown to her family. Her husband proved a villain, deserting her and her infant boy, leaving them to the charity of the world. Heavens, are you ill? Edward, you are trembling. What agitates you so fearfully?

CAPT. S. Nothing—nothing—a—a—pain from—from military fatigue. I am subject to it at times. [*With effort*] 'Tis over now; do not alarm yourself. I am better—well, quite well. [*Child's voice again, "Rose"*]

ROSE. Hush. I am called again. I *must* go. [*Going*]

CAPT. S. Stay—stay—let me first kiss this dear hand and swear once more how true I love you, be you but true to me. I ask of Heaven no higher joy. Let stern war press me in its iron grasp, my heart is still for thee. My mistress is more fair than glory and should it be my fate to fall, my last sigh shall breathe for thee, dear Rose, for thee! [*Kissing her hand*]

JULIA. [*Sings within house*]

> Yes, he was false—yes, false to me,
> Though he looked so true and bold,
> Yes, he was false—yes, false to me,
> And his heart, untrue and cold.

CAPT. S. [*Starts, then listens with intense feeling*] Ha! What voice was that?

ROSE. Alas, my poor mad sister's.

CAPT. S. [*Aside*] It cannot be, sure I am deceived. *She*, she here, impossible!

ROSE. Edward, what disturbs you?

CAPT. S. [*Agitated*] I must away—the—the morning is near breaking. I have scarce time to reach my quarters and—and [*Aside*] I'll know the worst. [*Aloud with effort*] Thy sister's name?

ROSE. Julia, and her husband's, Valcour!

CAPT. S. Eternal Heaven!

ROSE. [*Placing her hand on his arm*] Edward—Edward, for mercy's sake! Why are you thus agitated?

CAPT. S. [*Breaking from her*] Girl, girl, let go thy hold; thou dost cling unto a serpent! Villain! Villain! Would'st thou destroy another? Is not one victim enough?

ROSE. Art mad? Edward, Edward, why dost thou rack me thus?

CAPT. S. Thou know'st me not—thou—! [*Recovering himself*] Rose, I know not what I utter; weep not—I am distracted. I—I knew the villain Valcour—I was once in England. 'Twas him I meant, he, that villain! He was too vile to tread the earth. He is dead.

ROSE. May Heaven forgive him!

CAPT. S. [*Suddenly*] Infernal villain! May all—[*Checks himself*]

ROSE. You are not angry with me for that wish?

CAPT. S. Angry with thee? No, no, devil that I am. No—no, the memory of bygone times discomposed, tortured me.

JULIA. [*Sings*]

> His hair was of the raven dye,
> His lips like roses cleft apart,
> Bright as the eagles was his eye
> But false and icy was his heart.

CAPT. S. Death and hell! Where shall I hide? Cover me, night! Open earth and swallow me! [*Rushes out*]

Rose. Is this reality? Do I dream? Can this be caused by the memory of Valcour's villainy? What am I to think? Ah, he returns. [*Enter Adam*] Father—I thought that—

Cotton. Well, what did you think?

Rose. You did not intend returning so soon.

Cotton. Hark ye, girl! What do you up here? Why are you out at this time of night? Was it to meet your father, child? Did you sit up to welcome the old man? Rose, Rose, if *you* desert me, you, the last prop of my age, my heart will break. I cannot choose but die.

Rose. Oh, I know not what you mean, but do not speak of death; no, no, you cannot think so hardly of me! Desert you, shall your poor Rose desert her dear father? How have I deserved this? By these tears, you do not mean it, you cannot be so cruel! [*Takes his hand*]

Cotton. Let go my hand; it is rough and scarred by honest labour and weather beaten; 'tis not fit for your dainty lips to kiss.

Rose. Dear, dear father! Your unkindness cuts me to the heart, have I not ever been dutiful? Have I not laboured to gain your smiles? Toiled for no greater reward than your lips could bestow? Have I, by word, thought, or action, offended you? If I have indeed lost a father's affection, here let me atone, here at your feet [*Kneels*] nor will I rise without your pardon!

Cotton. Rise. Remember, my child, virtue can hold no intercourse with vice!

Rose. What mean you, father?

Cotton. Have I not doated on thee, girl? But now—now—I cannot say more. Ought there to be mystery between father and child, and that child the only one now left to him?

Rose. Indeed, dear father—

Cotton. Have I not seen—have I not heard—why art thou here? O Rose, Rose, better be a maniac like thy sister, better braid straws and sing the songs of madness than be that—that which I dare not think of. Rose, that man is one of our oppressors. I have double wrong to avenge! What, are they not satisfied by heaping insult, scorn and oppression on us; but must they drive daggers into our very hearts, creep to our firesides, and lay desolate our hearths! My hand and eye have somewhat failed me, but not my heart. Let the destroyer dare cross my threshold, and, by heaven, his blood be upon his own head!

Rose. Father, do you wish to drive me frantic, thou dost suspect me most unjustly. Have you not always known my most secret thoughts—save this alone—at his most earnest solicitation. I concealed his visits, but only for a time. Father, I am innocent; I swear, by all the bright saints above, I am innocent!

Cotton. Concealment, yes, serpent-like he wished concealment that he might seize his prey defenseless. But I will not judge too harshly. Rose, my child, deceive not thyself. Where there is secrecy and deception, honour cannot dwell. Now, my child, to rest, to rest.

Rose. Bless me, father?

Cotton. I do, my child, I do. [*Musick. She kneels*] Good night. [*She goes into the house*] And has the spoiler come a second time—must I lose—both —all—no, never! This arm can still protect my honour. [*Exit into house. Stage has gradually become light*]

Scene 2: *A front wood, outposts of the British camp. Flourish. Enter General Burgoyne, Major Ackland, and British Officers. Uzzial speaks outside.*

Uzz. What in all creation is the use o' dragging on me. You'll smash my seed pumpkin all to squash! [*Enter Uzzial, dragged in by two Soldiers. He has a very large pumpkin and squash slung by a straw band over his shoulders. Sidearms precedes them*]

Side. [*Saluting*]   General, a prisoner! [*Officers laugh*]

Gen. B.   Why, major, this is our old ostler of Boston memory. What old acquaintance, Uzzial. How came you to let my men catch you, eh?

Uzz.   Why, damn it, I don't know. They came along when I didn't think of it and tuk my cart and horse, pumpkins, squash and all, as quick as you could say Jack Robinson, and not particler perlite neither. I only saved two for seed, 'cause they are all killin' good uns for pies.

Gen. B.   Well, Uzzial, since you are taken, you must make the best of it. What are they doing in your camp?

Uzz. [*Scratching his head*]   Why, I don't know—I don't exactly know. They're eating taters, whittling, making pandowdy, and telling stories; and some on 'em talking like fools about what they shall do with all the fine things they s'pose they shall get hold on when they take all you officers prisoners.

Gen. B. [*Laughs*]   Major, what do you think of this, eh?

Major.   His last observations are rather personal, general. And perhaps too amusing to any ears but our own. [*Looking at Sidearms*]

Gen. B.   Sidearms, wait without. [*Sidearms salutes and exit with the two Soldiers*] So they talk in this way, do they? We shall see. Come here—take this spy glass and tell who some of your officers are I see in your lines. [*Uzzial puts down pumpkin and squash and takes the glass, looking thro' the wrong end*]

Uzz. Why damn it—it looks all swush—like under water. [*They laugh. He finds he has the wrong end*] Du tell, why it's got two ends to it.

Gen. B. Who is that heavy man on horseback, riding as slow as a snail? [*Uzzial looks thro' the right end and staggers back, falling over the pumpkin*]

Uzz. All pisen! If the likeness an't so strong it knocked me down.

Major. Whose likeness?

Uzz. Why major, Ben Lincoln's. You know Ben Lincoln that used to come to the "Bunch of Grapes" with Warren and them good patriots, as they were called in Boston. He sleeps half the time, but, by gosh, he knows a thing or two about fighting they tell me.

Gen. B. Who is that short stout man who seems to be rather careless of his dress, talking very vehemently with General Gates? I know Gates.

Uzz. [*Aside*] Guess you'll know suthin more on him, too. [*Aloud*] That old cock of the walk is General Stark that walked into Count Baum's men and mauled 'em till they all peeled like a log [*sic*] of basket stuff. Look at his men—some of them chaps as live up among the rocks of New Hampshire. Them's the chaps. When they want fresh meat they go out and kill a bear. Look at their mouths. They can eat granite and drink a mill stream. They're real snowgers [*sic*]! They can live on the feed of a mule and carry more than a horse when their dander's up.

Gen. B. Excellent qualities for a soldier. I wish ours could subsist for a time on the same food. Who is that stout tall man with a light-coloured frock on, and stands without a hat?

Uzz. That's Virginia Morgan. He's got the true mountain stuff about him. He can hit a squirrel on the full gallop with his rifle ball. You can hear him farther off than you can the roar of a wild bull. He's a real roarer. And if you have a tough fight, he'll be up knee-high in business. I had rather fight a catamount than that 'ere Morgan.

Gen. B. Well, Uzzial [*Taking glass*], you rascal, I suppose you are a spy and I ought to have you hanged in ten minutes. By the bye, major, it is reported to me that daring young rebel, Harry Cotton, as he is called, has escaped to the American lines. Our outposts must be on the alert. Now Uzzial, are you sure you're not a spy, you rascal?

Uzz. No, I ain't a spy, general, but I believe a *little* bit of a traitor. Guess I could have got out of the way, but I had always a sneaking liking for you, general—whatever the Boston folks said about you—and I ain't afeared but I shall get my horse and cart again, whoever eats up the notions I had in it.

Gen. B. [*Smiling*] Uzzial, how came you to know all these Yankee officers so well?

Uzz. Why, I have heard father, and Uncle Jo and the town clerk, and Deacon Doughnut talk a heap about 'em. Then, I have tended horses ever since I was ten year old, and I shall be twenty-six year old next grass, and you know there's nothing in creation like a stable to get introduced to gentlemen. You know, general, that's w'ere you fust saw me.

Gen. B. [*Laughs*] Uzzial, you shan't be hanged this time. I will see that your horse and cart are returned to you for old acquaintance sake. [*Takes out tablets and pencil*] That will pass you thro' our lines. Now, gentlemen, to the business of the day, our fates will soon be decided. [*Flourish. Exeunt all the Officers*]

Uzz. Well, I calculate you ain't too cute anyhow. I never was in a stable long. Guess about long enough to shed my colt's teeth. Perhaps I've come the gum game over you, general, straight up and down like a sheep's foreleg in a mud puddle or a pole in the centre of a haystack. I reckon I'll know suthin about all on you and what you're agoing to do afore long. [*Serjeant Bomb and Corporal Primingwire speak outside. He conceals himself behind wing*]

Bomb. But Gay, you know nothing. [*They enter*]

Corp. Zounds, serjeant, you make as much noise as an eighteen-pounder. Why, you'll rouse the enemy—they'll all be on the march.

Bomb. By the right hand of Mars, do you parley with me, sir? Am I not a non-commissioned officer in his most gracious majesty's Grenadiers and therefore entitled to respect? Corporal Primingwire, I want none of your advice. I have read Turenne, sir—I can command an army, sir, if Frederick of Prussia had me in his service.

Uzz. [*Aside*] He'd have one more to flog.

Bomb. What do you say, sir? Only let General Burgoyne ask my advice. I say, only let him ask my advice.

Uzz. [*Aside*] What about—feedin' hogs?

Bomb. Corporal, do you mean any disrespect to me. Answer—do you mean it?

Corp. I didn't say anything. Of course, I didn't mean anything.

Bomb. Spoken like a soldier. Well, Gay, discretion is the better part of valour. Above all, let no man boast of what he can do. Only let my advice be followed, and General Burgoyne wins the field.

Corp. It's surprising how you gained so much knowledge.

Bomb. By Mars, Gay, it is *not* surprising. I wonder who first invented gunpowder? Why one of my ancestors. And who, sir, was it first invented cannon? Why another of my ancestors, sir. And who do you suppose was my mother, sir?

Uzz. [*Aside*] Another of your ancestors!

Bomb. My mother, sir, was the seventh living wife of a third serjeant of the Horse Guards. And where, sir, did I lose my right eye? Why, in a duel with a fifth fifer in the Sepoys. And above all—who is now my tenth wife? Why, Moll Flaggon that was, widow of cut-and-thrust Jack. By Mars and Moloch, I am a very extraordinary man, sir—[*Looking off*] Speak—who goes there? [*Enter Captain Singleton*]

Capt. S. Ha, Serjeant Bomb! I am fortunate in falling in with you, serjeant.

Bomb. [*Salutes, winking at Primingwire*] Captain, if the general will only—

Capt. S. No doubt, no doubt. But, at present, I have a little business for you. Mars must excuse you. I wish you to serve under the banner of Cupid.

Bomb. [*Nudging and winking to Corporal*] Ahem! Captain, if to make love, you could not have pitched on—

Capt. S. Very probably. Listen, the daughter of a farmer near here, a wild bud of the forest, has for some time past engaged my attention. I will point out the house to you and will at the same time have a small party of men dispatched to an outpost of the enemy's near it. And a feigned attack will give you an opportunity to carry off the girl to my quarters. You must bring her *at all hazards*. And here's the king's head as part of your reward. [*Gives piece of money*]

Bomb. I'll see it done, captain.

Capt. S. I rely on you. Follow me. [*Exit*]

Corp. I say, serjeant, think we had better divide the king's head at once?

Bomb. What, divide the head of his most sacred majesty? I am his majesty's officer and will take care of his head. Would you be a rebel—would you destroy the crown? No, no. [*Pockets it*] Attention! Forward, march. [*Exeunt. Uzzial comes forward*]

Uzz. Make tooth powder of my toenails if you ain't nice officers and no soldiers. Only a farmer's daughter. Well, guess it don't want no more to make my dander upriz. I feel as if I could stand afore six common chaps. Oh, I'll be there and if I'm ketched in the rear ranks when there's any fightin' to do, why call me skunk. Only a farmer's daughter to be carried off. Guess I'm a farmer's son of this 'ere soil, and darn my kidneys, if you take the daughters, you shall take some of the sons, too. [*Pauses*] Swaggers, I never thought on it afore, but now it strikes me right on the noggin, hard enough to floor a New Hampshire bull, that it's the pretty Rose, Farmer Cotton's daughter, they're arter. Well, guess I shall be there. [*Exit*]

SCENE 3: *Another view of Adam Cotton's house, his barn and haystack conspicuous, to burn. Wagon under shed, etc. A tree near C., with an overhanging branch that has had a swing attached to it with parts of the ropes hanging down. A party of American soldiers discovered, some under the shed cooking, others burnishing their arms, etc. Silence Sampson walking up and down. Azariah Lambson, a stiff puritanical serjeant, comes forward. Azariah is at a grindstone. A man is turning it while he grinds a very long sword. Musick.*

AZAR. Dost thou behold aught, Silence? [*Feeling edge of his sword*]

SILENCE. Nay.

AZAR. Feelest thou of strong heart?

SILENCE. Yea!

AZAR. Peradventure, if the enemy come suddenly, wilt thou not flee?

SILENCE. Nay.

AZAR. Verily, thou art as a lion. Thou refreshed thy body with the spirit.

SILENCE. Yea.

AZAR. Verily, the hosts of the enemy will not find us sleeping, when their captains of thousands and captains of hundreds approach us! Verily, we will smite them hip and thigh with the edge of the sword. [*Comes to guard with his sword*]

SILENCE. Stand. Who cometh?

UZZ. [*Sings outside*]

> Cape Cod is all afloat,
> Marblehead is sandy,
> Charlestown is a spunky place,
> And Boston is the dandy.
>
> Corncobs twist your hair,
> Cart wheel surround you,
> Fiery dragons carry you off
> And mortar pestle pound you!

[*Enters singing and carrying a very long rifle*]

AZAR. Verily, 'tis Uzzial.

UZZ. Well, shouldn't wonder if it warnt me, myself. Well, Serjeant Azariah, you had better put some lead atop of your powder right off.

AZAR. Our weapons are keen-edged—'tis already so ordered.

UZZ. There's some confloberated varmints a coming here to do a little outrageousness. So just make your men get behind the barn. Keep quiet and wide awake as weasles.

AZAR. Silence, betake thee with the men of war, to thy weapons.

SILENCE. Yea. Fall in! [*The men take their guns, fall into rank. Azariah goes to the head. Silence to flank*]

AZAR. March.

SILENCE. Yea! [*They march off behind the barn. Uzzial marches in time till they are off*]

UZZ. There. I'll be antidolrollified into a crab apple jam, if this sort of business don't agree with my constitution. I vow, we've got serjeants that don't talk but do. If that chap that has sich wonderful ancestors comes here, I'll fix the skunk. [*Takes a rope from the shed, makes a noose on one end and throws it over the branch of the tree, placing a block of wood under it to stand on*] There. That's what I call a mantrap. Shouldn't stifle with wonder if somebody's ancestor should get ketched. [*Takes his rifle from the tree and examines the priming*] Make alligator-skin boots of my hide if I don't make the fire fly out of some o' their eyes worse than it does out of the stone of a razor grinder! [*Places it against the tree again*] Holloa—here comes ancestors, and if I don't larn him something besides carrying off farmers' daughters afore I get through, and get him twice the length of a ten-foot pole into suthin' that he won't relish quite so slick as a good clam chowder, why tread on my sorest corn. [*Whistles. Takes out knife and whittles. Enter Serjeant Bomb*]

BOMB. What are you doing here, you stupid Yankee?

UZZ. What'll you give to know, you damned skunk, you?

BOMB. I'll give you six inches of cold steel or a bullet thro' you.

UZZ. Hold on—don't be so pesky spunky. My business here is to lick you and I only wish there was a half dozen more sich, as I always like to do a full job, whilst my hand's in.

BOMB. Mars, Vulcan and Beelzebub, must I, Serjeant Bomb, whose ancestors invented gunpowder, submit to this from a raw Yankee. Never, by the blood of Moloch. [*Clubs his gun and is about striking Uzzial*]

UZZ. [*Springing on one side as gun descends, seizes it*] I cal'clate I can do this job. [*Twists gun out of his hand, throws it down, seizes him by the collar*] You see, you can't do it. If you want to see me licked, you must get some full-blooded chaps to do it, by gravy. Come here, foot to foot. Toe the mark. [*Trips him up under the tree, gets the noose over his arms and around his body. Hoists him up to the block of wood*] I have often heard of horses having the flounders [*sic*], but I never know'd jackasses ketched 'em afore.

BOMB. Quarter—quarter!

UZZ. Quarter—no, it an't only the beginning, and you shall have the hull on it. I say your ancestors invented gunpowder and cannon—mine planted hemp and invented spinning. Cal'clate what my ancestors made—that rope— will hold you till some of your ancestors come and cut you down. Damn your karkiss, you'll find us raw Yankees just as quiet as kittens, only let us alone; but just git their ebenezers a little riz—and then, Jehu! They'll have satisfaction if they cross the Atlantic on a raft of grindstones! [*Takes rifle and retires behind barn*]

BOMB. By Mars, this comes of my departing from my general rule: Discretion is the better part of valour. Holloa! Corporal Primingwire! [*Enter Corporal Primingwire*]

CORP. Why, serjeant, what are you doing up there? [*Assists him to get down*]

BOMB. Cannons! Thunder! Fire! Must I, Serjeant Bomb, suffer this. No. Corporal, bring up the men. I'll have revenge, I'll fire the barn, and carry off the girl in spite of the devil. [*Corporal brings on four Men, one with lighted torch*] Fire that hayrick. [*Corporal takes the torch and is going towards it when Adam Cotton, with a gun, rushes out*]

COTTON. And if he does, I'll lay him dead at my feet.

BOMB. How dare you oppose us, rebel?

COTTON. Rebel! I stand here as a man! To protect our wives, our children, and our homes. In this house, my father's father lived and died, and defending it—here will I die, too! Stand back, I say!

BOMB. Take away his gun—fire the barn. [*Corporal fires the barn. Two Soldiers rush on Cotton, he fires. They seize him. Serjeant levels his piece at him. Rose rushes from house between them*]

ROSE. Spare him—spare him! Take my life—not his!

BOMB. That's the girl. Lay hands on her. [*Drum beats without. The house, barn and rick are in flames. Red fire. Cotton struggles with the Soldiers. Corporal and one Man seize Rose. British Soldiers enter, are met by Azariah's men and Uzzial, fight in background. Serjeant Bomb fires his piece, Cotton falls wounded. Rose shrieks, breaks from the Men and falls over him. Serjeant is going to seize her when Julia, dressed wildly with flowers, etc., rushes from the house between him and Rose*]

JULIA. Hold, I command you—her false husband doth not call her to the grave! [*Spreads her white veil before Rose. Picture and flames and red fire till quick drop*]

ACT II.

SCENE 1: *A rustic chamber in Azariah Lambson's house. Enter Lucy, knitting.*

LUCY. Patience sake—I want to know, what has come of father—nobody to fodder down the cows, nor do nothing. Go for a soldier—I always told him to let soldiering alone and mind his family. If he don't I shall sartinly get somebody to mind me. [*Enter Uzzial, takes off his hat and flings it down. Has rifle*]

Uzz. By Satan, if it warn't for two or three things, I'd be off like a streak of lightning acrost a New Hampshire logging chain. One thing is sartin, I mustn't sneak off and leave Miss Rose and that poor critter, her sister, chin deep in a quagmire without a soul to help 'em out. No, I swough, it ain't Uzzial Putnam that lets such nasty notions get the upper hand of him. By Judas, Luce Lambson wouldn't like that and she is one of the loveinest and slickest critters I've seen since Ben Hannaford's darter, Jerushy, died eatin' artichokes when she had the hifenudins. [*Lucy comes down*]

Lucy. Well—and do you think so still, Uzzial?

Uzz. You there—do I—don't I—Wal, guess I do.

Lucy. And what in the name of patience have you been doing with such a long gun?

Uzz. I an't been doing nothin' in the name of patience with it, but I cal'-clate suthin' in the name of knock down and drag out! I made two chaps streak it so, there warn't nothin' to be seen but now and then the ends of their red coat tails through the dust and gravel stones that flew like chaff out of a winnerin' mill, and if neither on 'em warn't ketched, it was narrow dodging, as the chap said when the cannon ball took his wig off. But I shouldn't have cared the heft of a corncob about what they could have done to me. If they hedn't burnt up the house and come so rotten nigh killin' of old Adam Cotton. I never felt so bad in my life. Why the time I was shipwrecked warn't a circumstance to it.

Lucy. And where is Miss Rose and her poor sister?

Uzz. Why prisoners—but they ain't agoing to stay so long. It won't be long afore it's night. Where's Azariah—an't he come home?

Lucy. Why, no. I wish he was. But you spoke of the time you were shipwrecked. Do tell me all about it.

Uzz. Well, I'll tell it to you if you'll—[*Looks sideways at her*]

Lucy. If I'll what?

Uzz. Why—a—I—I suppose you know bread don't go real slick without butter?

Lucy. What do you mean?

Uzz. Seems to me you're darned clumsy at taking a hint, so I guess I'll have to speak it right out. I wants a smack to ile my lips afore I start, so't not git stuck in my story.

Lucy. Oh, Uzzial, don't be aplaguing me with your nonsense, don't.

Uzz. [*Picking up hat, going*] Wal—conclude I shan't—

Lucy. Here, you needn't be so huffish. I'll give you a kiss.

Uzz. [*Turns around*] Will ye?

Lucy. Why, ain't I said so?

Uzz. [*Opening his arms*] Meet me halfway then. [*Embrace and kiss*] O Jerusalem! Fill my eyes with splinters if that warn't as refreshin' to my feelings as a cord of gingerbread and a swig of sweet cider arter a skirmish.

Lucy. Now Uzzial, tell me about your shipwreck and all that. [*They sit*]

Uzz. Well, here goes like a hand sled downhill on a good crust, or a weazel arter a barn rat. Hem! You see I was born in the upper part of New Hampshire about twice the length of grandsire Emerton's fishpole from Bakers River. I guess you didn't know grandsire Emerton, did ye?

Lucy. Why, how should I?

Uzz. Wal, wish you had, for he was an old soldier in the French War— killed more Injuns than any other chap of his size and there warn't no end to his ketchin' pickerel in Loveyer's Cove, just back of Fearly's house on the Alexander road. Wal, as I was saying before, I was born jist by the river, but I didn't stay ther long. I was an orfin afore I was six and got put out to bring up at Rufus Pikes, and a tarnations good place it was, too—dreadful pretty location just at the head of Newfound Pond and about fifteen miles below Uncle Bill Willoughby's, and suthin' like a quarter of a mile from grandsire Jim George's and Elijah Blood's mills. Make souse of my ears if I didn't pass ten happy years there. Well, at sixteen I started off for Boston to seek my fortin'. I didn't find it—plenty of misfortin' tho'. Well, when I got to Boston, the fust thing I did was to hire out in a genteel family, Britishers, I guess, and not long from the old country. I went to work like a streak—did everything they told me till dinner was ready.

Lucy. And then you was ready, too.

Uzz. Get out. Maybe I warn't! So when the rest begun to set down, I squat right down alongside the lady. Says I, "Mister, shan't I karve that 'ere turkey? I'm afraid you'll spatter Missus's yaller gownd." But before I had time to speak, Miss What's-her-name rared right up on end like a two-year-old colt, and busted out in a bilin' passion, and calls me a sarsy greenhorn.

Lucy. Goodness—why, she warn't a lady.

Uzz. Says I, "Look here [*Puts finger to nose*], guess I an't quite so green as you've an idee; and as for sarse, I guess you've got your share on it." So, at that, the old chap himself got me by the collar and begun to kick like a cow that warn't used to being milked.

Lucy. Yes, just like our Brindle.

Uzz. Well, hug me to death in a pretty gal's arms, if he didn't find he'd ketched the wrong animal that pull anyhow. By gol! I wonder if his legs and the legs of the table didn't get into a snarl. Down went the table—chaw-wallop; and spilt the gravy all over the best carpet; and then down came the old chap, all over the floor like a barrel of soft soap. And, to wind up the con-sarn, just by way of bringing the old woman out of her fainting fit, I doused a pitcher of water in her face, and then backed out a leetle too abrupt for manners.

Lucy. Do tell.

Uzz. Well, then I hired out in a stable at the "Bunch of Grapes" and stuck to the horses like a gob of maple sugar afore it's cool, for six years—put a leetle suthin' in a puss, and then concluded I'd see suthin' of foreign parts, and tuk a shine to be a sailor. But I was took in the wust kind. There warn't no shine about it. Well, I went down to the wharf and struck a bargain with a chap to go to the West Indies and was off to sea next day like a frog into a moat. Well, in about two hours I begun to feel dreadful alloverish at my stommick, so I got up off a pile of rope I'd been a squatting on to go and tell the captain I was used up and wanted to bunk in. But the tarnal savage critter bust out aswearin' enough to take the tail off a Newfoundland dog; said he didn't hire me to idle away my time by two chalks and if I warn't up to the mast-head in two minutes, he'd ropesend me.

Lucy. What, hang you?

Uzz. No, worse—wallup me. Says I, "Captain, reason is reason, and there an't a stick of reason in my going up them ropes feelin' so all-killin' bad as I do now! And I'm a chap what always adheres to its dictates, so ropesend or no ropesend, I shan't do it!" Well, at that, he gin me a cut. I didn't want an-other, I tell ye, for I was abilin' over like a kittle o' syrup the day Zeek Pyke sugared off. Gosh almighty, you'd ought to have seen me tuk him up and give him the all-firedest kick, clean across the deck, just like a football.

Lucy. Served him right.

Uzz. Well, at that, the hull crew run foul on me, yelling like screech owls, "Mutiny, mutiny." Well, I warn't going to be pounded into jelly for nothin', so I went into 'em like a chirping squirrel into a stone fence; floored six on 'em in jest about two winks of a toad under a harrow, and then I got a claw acrost the skillet with a handspike, what made me think the heavens and airth were acoming together, and that was the last I knew about the mutiny for three weeks.

Lucy. My, Uzzial, you warn't senseless all that time.

Uzz. Clean out o' my head. Well, when I come to, wonder if I didn't feel nasty suthin' like an old wooden clock run down but the doctor wound me up agin in a few weeks. But I warn't allow'd to do any work; nor stir a peg with-out two or three to guard me. Cause they said I was under an arrest. And they calculated I should get run up for attempting to kill the captain when we got back to Boston, but all their calculations kicked the bucket. You see, just as we got near the coast here, there cum a gale what peeled the bark off anything I ever see afore. Down come masts, spars, rigging and all, like lightning; and before I had time to collect my scatterin' idees, the vessel went right over— slap-dab carouse! And I found myself holding onto a hencoop out in the open water.

Lucy. Goodness, a hencoop?

Uzz. Guess you'd have thought I had a dreadful liking for poultry, if you'd seen me hug the old hencoop. But it warn't no joke, for I kept myself atop of water all night with it.

Lucy. Do tell—where did you sleep?

Uzz. Guess I didn't sleep much, had rocking enough, too. Well, next mornin' there was a small schooner—a pilot boat, coming right down like a streak of lightning, and a chap standing in the fore end of her alooking at me. When I was tuk aboard, don't suppose I was as stiff as an oak rail. But when they got me ashore to the "Bunch of Grapes," warn't I tuk the best care on. Harry Cotton was all-killin' kind to me and had me rubbed and basted and soaked in Jamaica spirits till I felt just like a new critter.

Lucy. Uzzial, didn't a small grain of the Jamaica run down your throat?

Uzz. Why, you—shouldn't wonder if a small trifle did leak in. Well, Mr. Harry made me tell him all about the wreck. He tuk a kind o' likin' to me and I tuk a dreadful likin' to him. And the war bruck out in a fresh place, I jined the army with him. That is, I kind o' hang on to it. I swough, I feel striped when I hear folks say Harry Cotton has jined the Britishers. I say, "No, by gosh!" I have been in their camp disguised more than once to hear suthin' on him, and I have heard he was a prisoner and has escaped, and he'll come right side up. I do love him, by Judas—only wish *somebody* loved me as well. [*Looks at Lucy*]

Lucy. Now, Uzzial, how do you know *somebody* don't love you?

Uzz. Well, guess 'tain't the *somebody* I want to.

Lucy. How do you know?

Uzz. I should like some proof on it.

Lucy. Guess you want too many proofs. Ain't you had one already?

Uzz. I'll put the question to her right off. Luce, do you love me?

Lucy. Why, Uzzial, I don't know what to say, you are so blunt-like.

Uzz. Well, I'll put it to you in another shape if that don't suit you; will you be my wife—Mrs. Uzzial Putnam.

Lucy. Why, you never asked me before.

Uzz. Well, that was cause I was afraid to.

LUCY. What was you afraid of?

UZZ. Afraid you wouldn't have me if I did, but now see'n the ice is broke, I want you to tell me in one word—yes or no. Out with it or it'll be too late. [*Going*]

LUCY. Well then, yes.

UZZ. Enough said! But we mustn't get married till these Britishers are banged off our ground here, and Rose Cotton is placed in her father's arms. I expect old Adam will be down here and when he hears Mister Harry's coming, it'll cheer him up apiece. I'm agoing to do the thing up nice. Luce, just fill my hunting bag with suthin' to eat. [*Takes gun*]

LUCY. And drink, Uzzial?

UZZ. A taste, I reckon, like this. [*Kisses her*] Bumble bee's honey, by Jerusalem! [*Exeunt*]

SCENE 2: *Front wood. Enter Adam Cotton. Musick.*

COTTON. The pain of the wound that scars my flesh I feel not. No, no, 'tis here, here inflicted on my heart. Where is my son, whose arm I fondly hoped should avenge his father's and his country's wrongs? Has he deserted me, has he leagued with the spoilers, is he so doubly base? My children, all, all torn from me and I am left to go down to the grave childless and broken-hearted. What, tears? Shame, Adam Cotton, shame. Let thy wrongs arouse thee. Why, let all perish—every spark of flame that flashes from our burning dwellings shall light a fire against these tyrants that will never be quenched till they are driven from our soil. [*Enter Serjeant Bomb and Corporal Primingwire*]

BOMB. By Mars, here is the old rebel. Seize him, corporal.

COTTON. Oh, had I but a weapon. Cowards, slaves, where are my children?

BOMB. Our captain's fond of children and he'll take care of *one*. As for the mad girl, she's loose in the woods somewhere.

COTTON. Are there such monsters? Alas, alas, my poor Julia! And Rose, blooming in health and beauty, my pride, my darling is in the hands of such a monster. Oh, the thought raises a hell within my brain and mads me. By heavens, I'll be revenged upon ye yet! [*Musick. Suddenly rushes on Serjeant and seizes his gun. Struggle. Corporal gets L., Adam's back is toward him*]

BOMB. Shoot the old rebel—fire, I say! [*Harry Cotton rushes on suddenly in a British captain's uniform. Strikes up the Corporal's gun as it goes off. At the same moment seizes him and flings him off stage. Cotton has struggled round to R., leaving Serjeant still holding him in C. next Harry, who seizes him*]

HARRY. Scoundrel! Villain, let go your hold or I'll pass my sword thro' your body. [*Serjeant lets go the gun which Adam retains. Harry flings him round to L.*] Away, thou disgrace to the name of man!

BOMB. By Mars! [*Harry makes toward him. He runs off. Harry looks at his father earnestly*]

HARRY. Adam Cotton, do you not know me?

COTTON. [*Gazing on him*] Do my eyes deceive me? Can it be my boy—my son—

HARRY. [*Going toward him*] Father! Dear father!

COTTON. Hold off! Touch me not, pollute me not! Why that dress? Why have you come to save my life, if only to witness thy disgrace. Better that ball had penetrated my heart! Begone traitor! Leave me.

HARRY. Traitor! Father, father, you know not the heart that beats in this bosom. Would that I could lay it bare before thee. No, traitor I am not; but true, heart and soul, to my country! This dress is but assumed; in this disguise, I effected my escape from the British camp, where since our last action, I have been a close prisoner. Father, do you not believe your son?

COTTON. [*Drops the gun. Embrace*] I do, my boy, I do!

HARRY. I dare not ask why you are here—some new outrage—

COTTON. My son, my heart is full. I cannot tell the tale—nature bursts her trammels and grief will have way, my boy. My boy—[*Falls on his shoulder*] Our home is burned—your sister, my darling Rose, a prey to the ravisher!

HARRY. Great heavens, grant me patience. Who has done this? Where is she convey'd?

COTTON. I know not. A party of British soldiers, like bloodhounds in a body, come upon us, fired our dwelling and tore her from my arms.

HARRY. No more—no more! A thousand thoughts rush quick upon me. Oh! had I a thousand hands, I could employ them all—all! Our home destroyed! A father houseless! A sister dragged to disgrace and infamy! Action—action, if I have not quick revenge, I shall go mad! Father, I will bring her back to your arms or die! [*Going. Enter Uzzial with his rifle and a canvas bag slung over his shoulder; followed by Azariah*]

UZZ. [*Leveling rifle*] Hold on, or I'll drill a hole right into you with Uncle Zeek's drilling iron. Oh, I'll be through you like pison!

HARRY. What, Uzzial! Don't you know me? [*Azariah picks up the gun dropt by Adam Cotton*]

Uzz. [*Recovering gun*] Eh? I have heard that voice. [*Stares*] Why no—why yes—why do tell—why Master Harry. I am all-killin' glad to see you. [*Shakes hands*] I heerd you had escaped.

HARRY. Escaped, yes, to witness greater misery.

Uzz. Just hold on a spell. I'll make all come out as fair and as white as the wool on Hitty Coburn's Cosset lamb, the day Uncle Zeek washed sheep. [*To Adam*] Adam Cotton, give us your hand. [*Grasps it*] You believe me to be an honest man and a true Yankee?

COTTON. I do. None dare dispute it.

Uzz. Well, I don't know about that. But I do know you shall have Miss Rose safe back again. But Mr. Harry and myself must fix up the job. I guess I'm provided here with the tools. [*Points to bag*] I know where she is.

COTTON. Heaven be praised!

Uzz. And we must have her down to Azariah's tonight. Tomorrow I reckon there'll be fightin' on a large scale, and then I guess you can have your hands full, but tonight you can stop at Azariah's and wait till we come.

COTTON. But why cannot I share the danger—who so great a right as a father?

Uzz. Nobody as I knows on, but we don't go by right these times. If we did, none of these Britishers would be here. But I can pass the lines—I have the general's pass, and Master Harry—

HARRY. Will be, with a little circumspection, free from suspicion. Father, be persuaded. The time is precious. Even now, perhaps—

COTTON. Heaven be with you. I will await your return. [*Aside*] I dare not tell him of poor Julia. [*Aloud*] Farewell, my son, and if our tyrants triumph it shall be over our prostrate bodies. Farewell. [*Exit with Azariah who has shouldered his gun*]

AZAR. Yea, verily. [*Exit*]

Uzz. True grit, by gosh! Only let Yankees know they're afightin' in a good cause and then, by Jerusalem, they won't flinch while there's an eye in their heads to take aim or a finger left to pull the trigger with. [*Exeunt*]

SCENE 3: *English camp by sunset. Tents painted on the wings. Set tents partially on stage; set cannons, a tumbril or covered wagon. On the canvas, painted, "Moll Flaggon, Spirituous liquors, Flour, Charcoal, etc." A part of a fort projecting onto stage, with a practicable iron-bound door. The flats representing a continuation of the tents, and a part of the Hudson River seen. English colours flying on tents. Small steps up to the back of the wagon. A table and two stools; drinking cups and flask on table. A Sentry pacing up and down near the fort. Serjeant Bomb, Corporal Primingwire, Sidearms and*

Soldiers with their Wives grouped, drinking. Moll Flaggon serving out liquor. Some playing cards. They come forward.

> *Chorus* (air, "With Helmet on His Brow")
> Fill soldiers, fill the can!
> And let the toast then be,
> . . . Dear woman! Bless them all,
> And that with three times three!
>
> Full cans make merry lives,
> In camp, from care we're free!
> Here's to our smiling wives,
> And that with three times three.
> Hurrah, hurrah, hurrah.
> Hurrah, hurrah, hurrah.
> Hurrah, hurrah, hurrah.
> Hurrah, hurrah, hurrah!

[*At the conclusion of chorus, drum beats "Go to Bed Tom"*]

BOMB.   There's "Go to Bed Tom." Now Moll, my darling, lock up for the night. You may leave that. [*Takes a flask, leaves it on table. Moll removes everything into wagon*] I'm on guard tonight. Corporal, relieve guard. [*The men take their arms which were stacked. The Women go off with Moll who locks up the wagon doors. Corporal counter-marches his men and relieves the Sentry at the fort in military style. He falls into ranks, they all march off, when Captain Singleton enters from the tent*]

CAPT. S.   Serjeant, my honour is in your keeping. Let it not be known *who* I have there. [*Pointing to door*] Give me the key. On some pretense dismiss the sentry for a few moments. [*Serjeant salutes, goes up to Sentry. They both retire*] What fiend is it prompts me to urge this girl's ruin? No matter what, I have gone too far to retract. [*Musick. Unlocks door. Rose enters*] Can all my protestations not convince you, have I not rescued you from the rude grasp of a common soldier? I love you most ardently—what sacrifices will I not make—at your feet, I lay riches, rank—

ROSE.   Hold, sir, nor dare insult me further with shame, with deep humiliation. I confess I thought I loved you, but you have basely deceived me. I have been reared in obscurity but I have been taught to respect honour, to love virtue. I am but a poor farmer's daughter, a farmer of that soil that is debased by bearing such as you, with all your rank, upon its surface.

CAPT. S.   But listen only—

Rose. I will not listen. You would ruin their daughters. But a day of retribution is at hand, and even now their sons are in arms to drive you hence, and withered be that arm that wields a sword in such a cause as thine.

Capt. S. Girl, remember, you are in my power. Force may—

Rose. You dare not use it. You know you dare not. Although you have debased yourself, libertine as you are, and forfeited the character of man, there are those, even in this camp, who will not be deaf to the cries of injured woman!

Capt. S. Beware—taunt me not beyond endurance. None are within hearing of thy cries. And by heaven—[*Approaching her. She suddenly draws a dagger from his [sic] bosom*]

Rose. [*Resolutely*] Stand back! Advance one step, one inch, and this steel is in my heart! [*Pause*] What, so you pause? Are you aw'd—you the polished British officer—by a wild American girl? Remember, their virtue is as sacred to them as their liberty, and an attempt to violate the one or the other will meet with that vengeance it deserves! You may deprive me of my liberty, you dare not injure my honour! I am resolute, beware how you drive me to despair. [*Exit into fort*]

Capt. S. By heavens, I am paralyzed. Is this the gentle being formed for love alone? Beware! Do you beware of me; I am not used to be defied, and tonight, if all the fiends of disappointment league not against me, beware of me! [*Goes up R. Calls. Stage has gotten darker*] Serjeant. [*Serjeant Bomb enters*] Lock that door. [*Serjeant does it*] Let none have access there. You have the guard tonight. I shall be back at twelve. [*Exit. Distant drum beats. Serjeant places the Sentry, goes to table and sits as scene closes*]

Scene 4: *Dark, rocky pass. Musick. Julia rushes on as if pursued, speaking as she enters.*

Julia. Whither would you drag me? Not unto the grave! He is there, the false one! Off! Off! [*Enters*] Come not to me with those eyes of fire, those hands of death. Away—away—you shall not have my babe! [*Presses her veil or drapery to her bosom. Enter Singleton. She turns and gazes on him*]

Capt. S. Horror! Horror—what do I behold? Is it a spectre come to blast me from the grave? I dare not look on her! [*Hides face in his hands*]

Julia. [*Approaches him*] No, thou wilt not harm me. Thou art gentle—weep not for me. Keep your tears to shed them o'er the grave of her you love. Beware mankind! They're devils in the form of angels. Mark me! One false one made me what I am!

CAPT. S. Hell—Hell, where is thy torment! Gaze not on me thus. Those eyes penetrate my very soul.

JULIA. The moon is up—see there she is—her beams will dance merrily on the green sward over me, and I shall smile—may not the dead smile? Come, come, thou too shalt go with me; we will wander among the tombs.

CAPT. S. Wretch, wretch, that I am, she does not know me. Thank Heaven, she is spared the agony of recognizing her destroyer.

JULIA. Thank Heaven! Can *he* thank Heaven? *You* can look to Heaven, but *he* cannot. [*Suddenly seizing him*] Where is my child, my boy! False one, thou hast borne him from me. [*Falls on her knees*] Give me my boy! Can you look upon a poor distracted mother pleading for her boy unmoved? Canst thou look upon a sight so pitiful, does thy heart not bleed like mine? Give me my boy, and I will die even here!

CAPT. S. Were racks to tear my quivering flesh, 'twere naught to this. Nature cannot bear it. Oh, hide me, Heaven, from this sight!

JULIA. [*Rises gradually*] See, see, where my sister beckons me. Look, look at her hair all wild upon her bosom. Oh, she too has a tale of woe to tell. But not like mine—no, not like mine; and see her eyes are full of tears—mine are dry, quite dry. I cannot weep, I cannot weep! [*Suddenly*] Hark! that scream. See the flames rage. Now, now they reach him, my boy, my child! [*Screams*] Oh, save him, save him! [*Rushes out*]

CAPT. S. Stay, Julia, my wife—stay! [*Follows her*]

SCENE 5: *Same as Scene 3, the British camp, but dark. Transparent fire lighted a little up the stage and others seen on the flats in perspective. Serjeant Bomb discovered seated at a table. Pen and ink, paper, drinking cup, and flask. Sidearms on guard as before.*

BOMB. By the great toe of Mars! I can't see what the captain wants with so much useless baggage. Women are well enough in their way. Now, my wife, that is, Moll Flaggon that was, is useful. She finds me in bed, board, and liquor and money besides. She's always making money. [*Noise outside*]

CORP. [*Outside*] I don't care. The serjeant must read it, so come along.

UZZ. [*In an assumed voice*] Mein Gott—what for a usages is dis? Dere ish mein passport! [*Enters disguised as Mynheer Snigglefritz, a Dutch pedlar with a pack on his shoulders, in charge of two soldiers, with Corporal Priming-wire. A short blue Dutch frock, a hanging cap, Dutch pipe slung around his neck, trunks and large high boots. The same canvas wallet he had in last scene hung under his arm*]

BOMB. Who are you, sirrah? Stand before me, Serjeant Bomb, and answer without equivocation, or by the thunder of Mars—

Uzz. Mein Heimmel, what for a usages is dish. I have not so moshe Englishe. I am no thunder of Mars, I am one poor German pedlar, Hans von Snigglefritz. Mein Gott, what for a country is dish!

BOMB. Poor pedlar, if you deceive me, tremble! Let me see your passport. [*Takes it*] What cursed cramped hands all great folks write. Our general's, here, looks like an enemy's line just broke in by cavalry. The letters are nowhere in particular. [*Reads with difficulty*] "The bearer has permission to pass thro the camp and outposts." Burgoyne. [*During the reading and while the Sentry's back is turned, Harry appears for a moment and exchanges signals with Uzzial*] Poor pedlar, you have not deceived me. Therefore, tremble not. [*Returns the passport*]

Uzz. [*Taking it*] No, I never dosh.

BOMB. Dismiss the men, corporal. [*Corporal and the two Soldiers exeunt*] Now what have you worth looking at, poor pedlar?

Uzz. I have everytings what is goot, and plenty more beshides. But I am tired very mosh. I have dravel on mine foots more as dirty mile today and dro' so mosh woods. Mein Gott, what for a country ish dish?

BOMB. I have another stool here under my tent, so we can look at your wares and be comfortable till the guard's relieved.

Uzz. [*In his natural tone while the Serjeant is upstage*] Comfortable— guess you shall, and have headache enough to carry a double-breasted grist- mill or a rifle ball a hundred and eighty yards. I'll sew up the darned critter as tight as a sack of sawdust. [*Takes off his pack*]

BOMB. Come sit down. You may sit. When nobody is here I condescend to be d—d familiar.

Uzz. [*Sitting R. of table*] Ha, ha! Dot ish goot. Dot damn your family ish goot. [*Drinks deeply of the Serjeant's flask*] Und dat ish more petter ash goot.

BOMB. By the thunder of Mars! What do you mean by drinking out of the bottle. Can't you drink like a gentleman. [*Pours out liquor into cup and finds it nearly all gone. Shakes bottle*] What in the devil's name has got into your Dutch throat? Why, you've swallowed all my best cognac at one drink.

Uzz. Yesh, 'tish the swallow what makes me drink. I have dust in mine throat, but tish gone. I feelsh petter now! I have some liqueur here what ish distilled for de Emperor of Germany more ash two hunder yearsh ago. [*Takes out flask from canvas wallet*] I shells it very dear! And here I have von leetle roast fowl!

BOMB. I hope that wasn't hatched for the Emperor of Germany two hun- dred years ago.

Uzz. [*Laughs*] Ah, dat ish goot—dat ish damn goot.

CORP. [*Outside*]   Good night, Moll, good night. [*Enter Moll Flaggon. She has two empty sacks and a lighted stable lantern. Goes to the wagon, puts sacks under it, then gets up the steps, opens the door and goes into wagon. Serjeant turns around to her and nods. Uzzial pours some of his mixture into the Serjeant's cup*]

BOMB. [*Drinks*]   Did you see that woman, sir? That woman, sir, is my wife—always making money. Now those sacks are to be filled with something I know. She is the greatest woman, sir.

UZZ.   Yesh, I see she is a very great 'omans. Very pig 'omans as I never see. If your wife shall lend us some blates we shall eat supper. I am hungry as one wolf. [*Serjeant gets up and goes to wagon. Uzzial writes on a piece of paper*] Guess Rufus Pike did suthin' for me when he made me larn writin'. And the old German Corporal Donderdonk give me some idee of the Dutch. [*Conceals paper. Serjeant, who is a little unsteady from drink, brings down two plates, knives and forks, and bread. They sit and eat*] Dat ish goot, Serjeant Bumbs. I drink your goot helt. [*Drinks*] And Mishtresh Bumbs, [*Pretends to drink*] And all the little Bumbs. [*Again. Serjeant drinks*] What is dat poor fellows dere walking up and down so mosh?

BOMB.   Oh, that's the sentry. [*Drinks*] You're a pretty pedlar—not know a sentry. He's got something to look after—a woman, but mum.

UZZ.   Mein Gott, what dosh he look after, Mishtresh Bombs?

BOMB. [*Starting up*]   Death and the devil! Ha, ha, ha! don't be frightened —look after my wife! No—no—after the captain's mistress. [*Drinking*] Here's the key. [*Touches it in his waist belt*]

UZZ.   Oh, ho! Yesh, yesh. In dere, hey? [*Points to door. Serjeant nods*] Dem soldier fellows is der deyvill for dem women fellars. I shall make dat sentinel drink his serjeant's goot helt. [*Musick. Takes his flask and a cup, goes up to the Sentinel. Serjeant attempts to rise and turn around but can't. Sits again and yawns. Sentry places his musket near the door, drinks twice, saluting military style behind Serjeant upstage. Uzzial contrives to slip the paper into Harry's hand up behind. Harry thrusts it through the door crack and immediately retires. Uzzial lights his pipe at the fire upstage. Sentry yawns several times. Uzzial comes down. Aside*] If you an't both on you got a dose now that'll glue your eyes up so close it'll take a yoke of oxen to pull 'em apart. Serjeant, what for you don't eat, eh?

BOMB. [*Sleepy drunk*]   Sir, I'll see you d—d be—be—before I'll eat on my post. I won't eat, sir, by the great toe of Mars. No, nor slee—slee—sleep, sir. [*Gradually leans on table. Asleep, repeating*] Nor sleep, sir. [*The Sentry has yawned several times and at last sits down near the door. Sleeps. Uzzial knocks ashes out of his pipe, gets up, looks around. Silently takes key of wagon from*

Serjeant's belt. Locks door. Beckons on Harry. Takes the other key from the Serjeant's belt, gives it to Harry who unlocks door and goes in. Uzzial takes Sentry's gun, points it at Serjeant who is uneasy in his sleep]

Uzz. [*In undertone*] Hold on, or I'll send a dose into you shall operate quicker than tother one. [*Harry enters with Rose*]

Rose. My dear, dear brother, liberty is doubly dear when given by you.

Harry. [*In undertone*] We are still in danger here, dear Rose. We must pass the outposts. He must fight well that takes you from me. Uzzial, follow me as soon as you can. We owe you eternal gratitude. Now, my dear sister, we have not a moment to lose. [*Exeunt*]

Uzz. I hain't felt so slick since I was soaked in Jamaica spirits. Darn me, if I had a horse, if I wouldn't put these two critters into that 'ere waggin along with old Mother Bomb! And take 'em all prisoners. I must do suthin'. Calculate I'll *sack* the camp. [*Musick. Takes the two sacks from under the wagon, puts one over the Sentry's head, covering him, and the other over the Serjeant, who has turned and got his back to the table, sleeping nearly upright*] Now when you wake up, guess you'll find yourselves dry goods. [*Gun fires*] By Jerusalem, they're arter Mister Harry. [*Rushes out with gun. Drum beats, voices. "Fire upon 'em." Corporal Primingwire and Sidearms, with Soldiers and their Wives rush on, Women in night caps, etc. Moll Flaggon cries "Murder," tumbles out of the wagon in nightgown and cap. Corporal Primingwire, R., pulls sack off the Serjeant, who is covered with flour, and Sidearms pulls sack off the Sentry, who is covered with charcoal. Drum continues, another gun is fired. Soldiers and Wives laugh and shout at Serjeant. Quick drop on picture*]

ACT III.

Scene 1: *Interior of Azariah's house. Front scene. Enter Adam Cotton.*

Cotton. This suspense is beyond endurance. I have passed a dreadful night. Visions of blood and horror have visited me with fearful distinctness. My poor Julia, with her hair all wild and streaming in the wind and her white garments dabbled with blood, shrieking in mine ears, "Save me! Save me!" Her infant in the flames appeared as on that dreadful day. I felt my arms again pinioned by the monsters that held me then. With fearful struggles I tore myself away, and rushing to my burning dwelling, I awoke! awoke to find the misery real. Where is my daughter, Rose—where my son? I cannot bear it longer. [*Going. Enter Uzzial*] Where is my daughter—my son? Speak, tell me.

Uzz. Well, 'tain't no use akeeping on it from you. They've ketched Mr. Harry, and—and—I can't speak. My heart's as big as a meetin' house and fills my throat so full the valve won't work.

Cotton. [*Stand quiet*] You see I am calm. Affliction's heavy hand is on me. I can bear it. Tell me the worst. You say my boy is taken. Well, what more?

Uzz. And they'll execute him as a spy.

Cotton. Execute him! What, in cold blood! They cannot, dare not do it. Follow me. I will save my son or perish with him. [*Rushes out*]

Uzz. You shan't perish alone, by gosh! [*Calls*] Luce, Luce Lambson. [*Enter Lucy*] Luce, my heart is sunk down as low as a bullet in a bag of feathers.

Lucy. Why, Uzzial?

Uzz. Guess my eyes look like two red onions in a fish chowder, but I ain't got time to tell you. Just fill that chuck full of the strongest brandy, right off, and tell Azariah to meet me down at the old tree where Zeb Ferrin's ducklegged cow died with the horn ail. Be spry. [*Lucy takes flask. Exit*] When I heard Mister Harry was taken as a spy, I swan every hair on my head got so stiff you might use it for a hatchel to comb flax on. [*Reenter Lucy with flask. Tastes*] Melt the buttons off my Sunday coat if that ain't better than pandowdy. Now, Luce, good-bye, and if you don't hear by night, I've done suthin' you can be proud on. Never look at me agin. Shall I have one more kiss afore I go? Come say the word and the wool flies.

Lucy. Yes.

Uzz. [*Kisses her, shakes his rifle, knocks his hat on his head, looks fierce*] I feel as if I could wallow knee-deep thro' fire and brimstone without boots or buskins. Now look out, for I'm acoming, by Jerusalem! [*Strides off in long strides*]

Lucy. Patience—gracious! If anything should happen to Uzzial, I shall cry a churn full. [*Exit*]

Scene 2: *Interior of General Burgoyne's tent. Table, chairs, pen and ink, paper, etc. General Burgoyne, Major Ackland and four other British Officers discovered seated. Harry on R. in American uniform (captain's) guarded by Sidearms and four Soldiers with fix'd bayonets. Musick.*

Gen. B. Prisoner, you have been taken in arms a second time, a rebel against your king and country, crimes alone enough to condemn you to death. It is moreover proved you have acted as a spy, an office a soldier should despise, and has a right to refuse. Plans of our forces have been found on your person. It remains now with me to pass on you the sentence of death, which—

HARRY. Hold one instant. Be it remembered I do not fear death, I do not supplicate for life. I have already explained that those papers came into my possession in the uniform I wore as a disguise to effect my escape. You brand me with the name of rebel, I fling back the charge with honest indignation. Have we not declared our independence? We have, and we will maintain it spite of British tyranny. Have we not cause to be in arms? Look abroad; behold our country, once so smiling, now lies desolate, trampled on by the foot of tyranny. Look at our dwellings, once our contented homes, now lying crumbled into ashes—our fathers houseless, butchered, dead! What—

GEN. B. We cannot listen—

HARRY. You must, or drag me hence by force, for, by all the powers above I will speak! What blood can wash away our wrongs? And you would have us submit, and tamely stifle the remembrance of our injuries! Never, never, we are now a free nation, our country is our mother. Can we see her sufferings and listen to her groans calmly? Show me the man—the American that can, and I, too, will brand him villain, rebel, traitor! No, rebel I am none! I fight for my country and if we are but true to her, the whole world will soon behold Liberty shake off her galling chains! Our country will be free! I have done—lead me to death! [*Folds his arms*]

GEN. B. Prisoner! To ameliorate the sentence as much as in our power lies, you will be allowed to die a soldier's death. You will be shot. [*Musick. Harry bows, Sidearms and Soldiers conduct him off. Muffled drum with musick very piano. General Burgoyne comes down C., Officers, R. Rose speaks outside*]

ROSE. Let me pass, I say. No power on earth shall stay me. [*She rushes in, looks about wildly*] Where is he, where is my brother? You have not murdered him. [*Falls on her knees to General Burgoyne*] Give him to me, I implore you! Oh, sacrifice him not, let him not die for me! What prayer can I use to soften thee? Are there none here will plead for me, have ye no sons, no brothers, daughters, are nature's ties all dead within you? Cast your eyes abroad, behold the glorious sun, see all nature nourished by his beams, is smiling, all is life! Let it soften thy stern hearts—take not that life ye cannot give. Oh, let me not plead in vain—only for one, one life—ye are stern men, men of war and bloodshed, but ye are human. He is not guilty, he came to save me—me, his sister, from dishonour. Which of you would not have done the same? Spare him, spare him!

GEN. B. It cannot be. He is guilty.

Rose. "Cannot! He is guilty." [*Starts up*] He is *not* guilty! Guilty of what? Rescuing his sister from the grasp of the ravisher! What code of honour, of arms, of manhood can condemn a brother for protecting a sister's honour, yet allows the miscreant life that attempted it—oh, shame! shame!

Gen. B. Girl, you are mad to—

Rose. I am not *mad!* Would that I were. Where is the villain that hath done this, where is he that "pulled this ruin on our heads?" Our home destroy'd, a brother slain. Show him to me, let me look upon him. Woman as I am, I would strike him dead. [*Distant drum. Shrieks*] Ha! That signal —my brother, my brother. I am mad! [*Rushes out. Distant trumpet*]

Gen. B. [*Addressing one of the Officers*] Captain Lowden, be it your care to see that young girl safely returned to her home. Major Ackland, Captain Valcour of your regiment will attend to the execution of this court's sentence. [*Trumpet*] Now gentlemen, for the attack. We must expect determined opposition. All must be convinced, from the specimen of character we have just been compelled to witness, we have to contend with noble spirits. Come, gentlemen, to arms. [*Flourish. Exeunt*]

Scene 3: *A rocky pass or wood. Enter Julia.*

Julia. Oh, if I could but weep. What is it dries my tears? The flames, yes, the flames—they rage here—here. [*Placing her hand on her forehead*] Hark! Hark! that voice, that little voice, calls "Mother, mother, save me! Save me!" [*Bursts into tears, sobs*] Oh, where was that mother? [*Hides her face. Rose enters hurriedly. Musick. Julia starts, runs to her, lays hold of her arm and gazes steadfastly upon her*]

Rose. What a sight is here. Oh, heart, heart, hold firm. Sister, sister, stay me not. I fly to save a brother's life. Alas, alas, I know not what to do.

Julia. Look, here are tears. Oh, *let* me weep, *let* me weep! Dost think I *cannot weep,* does think my heart is broke, my brain dry? 'Tis *not dry*—I *can weep,* I *can weep.* [*Sobs on her sister's shoulder*] I know you—you are young and beautiful—do they not tell you so? Heed them not—they will betray you. Fly with me to the grave. There is rest, yes, there is rest.

Rose. Even now the fatal word is spoken and my brother is no more, and here—

Julia. You shall not leave me. I will go with you. Hist, I will tell you all. Ah, me! mine is a sad and sorrowful tale. It will make you weep. *I* have learned to weep of the *Heavens,* for they send forth plenteous tears for the *evil doings* they look down upon. [*Captain Singleton speaks outside*]

Capt. S. Serjeant, bring up the men quick.

JULIA. [*Crouches close to Rose*] Hush! [*Pause*] 'Tis my husband, hide me, hide me, let him not see me, he will kill me. [*Rises gradually, looking but retreating, followed by Rose*] Nay, gaze not so upon me; 'tis thy wife, thy Julia. His eyes are upon me. They penetrate my brain—it burns, it burns! Now—now—softly—softly—steal away—his eyes are closed—now—now—softly—softly—[*Exit, looking L., as if on some object. Rose a little above her follows her off, expressing her affliction by action*]

SCENE 4: *A rocky pass in second grooves. A projecting rock on stage. Muffled drum, piano and a dead march behind scenes. Enter Corporal Primingwire and Soldiers, reverse arms, conducting Harry to execution. Harry is in a white dress. They form on L. with Captain Valcour (alias Singleton).*

CAPT. S. [*Aside*] This is the hardest struggle of my life. [*Aloud*] Prisoner, here is the spot appointed for your execution.

HARRY. I am prepared. If not against your orders, captain, I would speak a word with you.

CAPT. S. With me?

HARRY. Yes, I have a father, a sister. [*Captain Singleton betrays great emotion*] You seem agitated—perhaps unwilling to—

CAPT. S. [*Aside*] O villain! [*Aloud*] Go on, go on.

HARRY. [*Takes a locket from his bosom*] I would request you to send to them this locket—the gift of my dear sister, Julia.

CAPT. S. Blast me not with that name. Let me not see it—you do not know. Oh! Agony! I—I am not used to this duty—I—

HARRY. Sir, you are a soldier and must perform your duty. You will, I know. Aid me in this last request. Say to them I died with their names on my lips and true to my country. [*Looks at the locket. Kisses it*] I trust, sweet Julia, you are happy. [*Gives locket to Captain Singleton, who betrays great agitation*]

CAPT. S. [*Overcome*] By heavens, I cannot, will not, give the signal for your death!

HARRY. I do not wish it. I would, if allow'd, give the signal myself. [*Takes out a white handkerchief from his bosom. Kisses it. Aside*] My own dear Rose, little did you think, when you presented me with this small token of thy love, it would be used as the signal of my death. [*A pause, he recovers himself*] Soldiers, when I drop this handkerchief, fire at my heart! [*Musick, muffled drum, piano. He goes slowly but firmly up above set rock on R. and kneels. Captain Singleton covers his face with his hands*]

CORP. Ready—aim—[*Musick. Harry drops the handkerchief. At the same moment two only of the Soldiers fire and Julia, from the rock, rushing on, receives their balls in her bosom. Her garments are seen bloody when she takes her hands from her bosom. Harry catches her in his arms*]

CAPT. S. Powers of Heaven—[*Rushes out, followed by Soldiers. Rose enters hastily, rushes up to Julia who is supported by Harry. At same moment, Adam Cotton enters with six American Soldiers who form a cross behind. Adam comes L. of Julia*]

JULIA. [*Raising herself with difficulty on Harry's arms*] A light breaks in upon my brain. Father, do not weep for me—'tis better it should be so. I feel I am dying—I had much to say—brother—sister—I know you all—bless you— bless you. I come, my child, I come. [*Musick. Sinks gradually down, dies. Adam Cotton kneels over her; Harry on L., gets there as she dies, relinquishing her to Adam. Rose, R. Picture above. Close in quietly*]

SCENE 5: *Front wood. Drum and fife outside play a march. Enter Azariah, six Soldiers, and Silence Sampson, followed by Uzzial with his rifle and a long sort of half sword, half bayonet, to it. Canvas wallet and a very long upright feather in his hat.*

UZZ. [*Walks up and down, examines the Men, then addresses them*] Brother sojers and fellow Americans, I ain't agoing to tell you a hull heap of stuff about what you're agoing to fight for, because all on you knows it. But I guess I'll give you some idee how you are to fight. Load as fast as you can —take sure aim—and fire like Jehu! If you get wounded in one leg, you must hop along on tother. If you get wounded in one arm, you must hold on to your gun so—[*Holds it over his shoulder by barrel*] and wait till some on 'em comes nigh enough, and then give it to 'em, but send chaw-wallop! And if both arms are wounded, why, you must kind of squat down and make a rest with your shoulders, for another on you that's crippled in the legs to take aim on. You see, we're dreadful short-handed, so every one on us must count two. You must walk into 'em like a shoulder of mutton into a hungry man's mouth, or like a streak of lightning across the top pole of Lishe Coburn's cowbarn. You must fight like catamounts, and you must do as we did at Bunker Hill, by Satan!

AZAR. Nay, swear not, Uzzial. We will contend mightily and smite wrathfully.

UZZ. Swear! Ain't it enough to make a man swear the ruff off a meetin' house. Now, afore we proceed to real business, as Deacon Doughnut used to say at town meetin', brother sojers, guess we'll take a drop of suthin' that'll raise your Ebenezers. [*Gives flask to Soldiers who drink*]

AZAR. Peradventure I do bear about my person an unclean distillation called *aqua vitae,* or the water of life. Verily, it becometh us to drink deeply of that fountain, for without life, a soldier is naught. [*Drinks a swig*] Verily it comforteth. I shall smite with extreme strength.

UZZ. Now soldiers, fall in—shoulder arms—now, right face. [*Some right, some left*] Well, 'tain't no matter, only mind, don't let me find any on you wounded in the back. I shall be all pison ugly if I do, I tell ye. I don't mind which way you right face or left face, but gaul darn ye, don't none on you show any other to the enemy but a double-breasted front face! [*Drum and fife. Countermarches them and off. Before scene changes, a distant American march is heard and distant trumpet answered again, and drums roll distant. Then scene changes*]

SCENE 6: *The flats so arranged as to present the two armies in motion in perspective—infantry, cavalry, artillery, etc. The Americans on R. and the British on L. The Americans appear first; after a short time, the British troops. A distant firing is heard of musketry and cannon, with trumpets and drums. Then, more in the foreground, appear profile figures representing American soldiers; infantry and cavalry enter, firing in platoons, are met by similar figures of the British, passing each other on different grooves so arranged. As the profile figures appear, the cannonading becomes louder, and musketry, drum and trumpet. The figures in perspective kept in motion during the whole action. Foreground represents the British camp, a set tent conspicuous with English colours to pull down. Cannon set, etc. As soon as the profile figures are worked on, loud shouts, and American Soldiers rush on as flying to R. Adam Cotton follows and rallies them. Noise a little subdued but not altogether quiet.*

COTTON. Men, men—are ye men? Turn, turn for shame! What, have ye no hearts? Will ye be slain, cowardly slain! Nor make defense? By all that is dear to you—for your wives, your children's sake—defend your homes. Stand—stand like men against these tyrants. Remember Bunker Hill. [*Renew'd shout. Flourish, cannon, all as loud as possible. English Soldiers rush on, headed by Major Ackland. Soldiers engage. The stage becomes full of combatants. Major Ackland and Adam fight. Uzzial chases Serjeant Bomb across with long rifle and off. Harry meets Captain Singleton. Two or three blows are struck when Harry passes his sword thro' him. Uzzial has reentered and catches Captain Singleton as he falls, and carries him off. Reenters and pulls down British colours. At same time that Singleton is stabbed, Major Ackland is disarmed by Cotton. British Soldiers in groups overcome by the Americans.*

Adam brings from R. the American flag on a long pole, holds it C. General Burgoyne enters with British Officers, General Gates with American Officers. Burgoyne uncovers, hands his sword to Gates who receives it. All the Officers take off their hats. The genius of Liberty descends in a cloud carrying a golden eagle which she places on the American flagstaff. Musick appropriate. Then three cheers, flourish]

CURTAIN

THE USURPER;
Or, AMERICANS IN TRIPOLI

A drama altered and compressed into three acts.

By Joseph Stevens Jones

THE USURPER;
Or, AMERICANS IN TRIPOLI

THE "indefatigable Dr. Jones" presented the playgoing public with so many plays that estimates range from sixty to more than one hundred and fifty. As early as 1845, in the middle of Jones's career, Rees offered an "admittedly incomplete" list of thirty-six plays, to which a few more are added here. Whatever this list might be, as published, it must remain "admittedly incomplete," for most of Jones's plays were more than usually ephemeral. He contributed to American drama two important items, *The Silver Spoon*, and the long-popular *Solon Shingle; or, The People's Lawyer*. The former was a first-rate dramatic composition, sometimes acted even during the twentieth century. The second gave to the American theatre one of its best-loved characters, the shrewd rustic, Solon Shingle, and his famed "bar'l of apple-sass."

Jones began his theatrical career in 1827 as an actor, when at the age of eighteen, he appeared in Providence as Crack, a low comedy part in Knight's *The Turnpike Gate*. His first permanent acting engagement began in Boston in the rôle of Old Norval in *Douglas* (the play which also marked the débuts of both John Howard Payne and John Augustus Stone!). A dramatization of *Eugene Aram* introduced Jones as a playwright. For at least ten years, his career was centered in Boston, and included three theatres, the National, the Warren, and the Tremont.

In 1839 Jones leased the Tremont for an annual rental of $8000, but gave up his managership after two years. Meanwhile, as playwright his reputation had increased sufficiently that Hamblin, manager of New York's Bowery Theatre, opened on August 16, 1841, with the proud declaration that he had engaged as dramatist, "J. S. Jones, late of the Boston theatres." With Hamblin and subsequently others, Jones continued his busy career, but also found time to complete his study of medicine, begun privately some years earlier. In 1843, Harvard made him a Doctor of Medicine, and, until his death in 1877, he practised occasionally, delivered lectures on anatomy and physiology, and continued to be widely advertised in the theatre as "the celebrated Dr. Jones."

Apparently, any theme or style would provide inspiration for his pen. His dramatic work is a medley of farce, burletta, comedy, spectacle, revisions, adaptations, anything with plenty of action and show. Rival theatres outmaneuvred each other in presenting contemporaneous productions of his latest hit. London, like New York, rushed to see his newest effort. Some of his plays, such as *The Green Mountain Boy, The Carpenter of Rouen, The Surgeon of Paris,* and *The Shoemaker of Toulouse,* had a sustained popularity. Others, revised, reduced to afterpieces, or occasionally reappearing simply under new titles, held the stage for brief periods of contemporary reputation.

The Silver Spoon, The People's Lawyer, and some few other Jones plays have been printed, the first two being easily available. Typical of its author's melodramatic style, patriotic enthusiasm, and love of display is *The Usurper; or, Americans in Tripoli,* appearing in this volume. The title should not be confused with *The Adventure; or, The Yankee in Tripoli,* nor with *The American Captives; or, The Siege of Tripoli.* The *Adventure* seems to be Jones's revision of the Elliston play, *The American Captives,* originally produced in 1812. The manuscript of *The Usurper,* however, bears the statement that the play is "altered and compressed into three acts" from some earlier play. Philadelphia saw a *Usurper* on December 26, 1827 (far too early for Jones). We may only conclude, as these and other titles suggest, that the siege of Tripoli and the American part in that siege constituted a tempting challenge to a wide variety of theatrical efforts. The names of characters may differ, but the central idea, of the bravery and patriotism of American soldiers in the face of bewildering African situations, is good for sentimental and humorous effects.

The Usurper is printed from a New York Public Library manuscript, originally the copy of J. B. Wright, prompter at the National Theatre, Boston, and dated 1842. It had been produced at the National, with the popular W. G. Jones in the leading rôle, during the season of 1840-41. Similarity of titles makes the record of any other productions hopelessly confused. Quinn, for example, dates the *Usurper* November 27, 1835, at the Park, but Odell says the play that night at the Park was *Kaspar Hauser* (also probably by Jones). Quinn and Odell also differ on the dates of *The Adventure.* From the manuscript, and from the variety of plays on the same theme, I am inclined to suspect that the version printed here was first played in the year 1840-41.

An accurate list of Jones's plays is impossible, and some of those included below are doubtful:

The Adventure; or, The Yankee in Tripoli. Park (N.Y.), 1835.
Almanen. (?)
Andek the Arab.
Battle of Lake Erie. (?) Tremont (Boston), November 2, 1842.
The Brazier of Naples. Tremont (Boston), December 19, 1842.

Captain Kyd; or, The Wizard of the Sea. National (Boston), 1830.

Carpenter of Rouen; or, The Massacre of St. Bartholomew (or, *The Confrerie of Bartholomew*). Chatham (N.Y.), November 16, 1840, or Bowery (N.Y.), August 30, 1841. (Odell says only the latter was by Jones.)

Custom. (?)

Diamond Cut Diamond. (?)

Eugene Aram. (?)

Factory Girl. (?)

Fire Warrior. (?)

The Green Mountain Boy. Chestnut (Phila.), February 25, 1833.

Hawks of Hawk Hollow. Arch (Phila.), August 1841, or Bowery (N.Y.), April 5, 1848. (Two different plays?)

Horse Hunters. (?)

Hunter of the West (or *Tippecanoe?*). Bowery (N.Y.), May 8, 1840.

The Ice Queen (or *The Ice Witch?*). 1832.

The Indian Horde. (?)

The Infernal Machine. (?)

Jonah; or, a Trip to Whales. Bowery (N.Y.), August 23, 1841.

Kaspar Hauser. Park (N.Y.), November 27, 1835.

The Last Days of Pompeii (a revision?).

The Liberty Tree; or, Boston Boys in '76. Warren (Boston), June 17, 1832.

Moll Pitcher; or, The Fortune Teller of Lynn (or *The Pirate Priest*). National (Boston), 1839.

Morton's Hope; or, Scenes of the Revolution. (?) Tremont (Boston), December 9, 1839.

Paul Revere, and the Sons of Liberty. 1875.

The People's Lawyer (afterwards *Solon Shingle; or, The People's Lawyer*). National (Boston), 1839.

Plymouth Rock. (?)

The Quadroone. (?) Chatham (N.Y.), April 12, 1841.

The Shoemaker of Toulouse. Chatham (N.Y.), April 4, 1842.

The Siege of Boston; or, The Spirit of 1776 (or *The Sons of the Soil*). (Phila.), and Tremont (Boston), 1841.

The Silver Spoon. Boston Museum, February 16, 1852.

The Surgeon of Paris; or, The Massacre of the Huguenots. National (Boston), January 8, 1838.

Tam O'Shanter. (?) 1838.

Ten Thousand a Year. (?)

Three Experiments in Banking. (?)

Three Experiments of Living. (?)
Two London Locksmiths. (?) Chatham (N.Y.), June 16, 1842.
The Usurper; or, Americans in Tripoli. 1835 (?) or 1841.
Venison Preserved; or, A Pot Uncovered. (?)
The Wheelwright; or, Boston Pride. Boston Museum, January 13, 1845.
Witches of New England. (?)

CHARACTERS

EDWARD ANDERSON, *an American captive in Algiers*	MURDOCH
ABDEL MAHADI, *the usurper*	MARSHALL
ALI-BEN-MAHADI, *his brother*	TAYLOR
HACCHAM ⎫ *Turkish officers*	J. JONES
ABDALLAH ⎭	MC FARLAND
SULIEMAN, *a young officer in love with Immorina*	BOOTH
EL HASSAN, *an old slave merchant*	CARTLITCH
KALED	GERMONE
ZEPHNA, *a slave driver*	HUNT
JACK BINNACLE, *a young American sailor, captive in Algiers*	W. G. JONES
CLEMENT, *lieutenant of Marines*	KEACH
SAILORS, GUARDS, SLAVES, ETC.	
FIRST OFFICER	CURTIS
SECOND OFFICER	MILOT
HERALD	WHITE
IMMORINA, *daughter of Ali-ben-Mahadi*	MISS ANDERSON
CLOTHINE, *her attendant*	MISS BOOTH
FEMALE SLAVES, DANCING GIRLS, ETC.	

SCENE: ALGIERS.

TIME: 1800.

ACT I.

SCENE 1: *A splendid garden in the suburbs of Tripoli. Flowers, trees, etc., in different parts of the stage. Fountain. Male and female Slaves discovered gathering flowers, etc. Music at rising of curtain.*

Chorus

> Hail to the god of rosy wine;
> We proclaim his power divine.
> Slaves we are but merry, merry be;
> Hail to the god of jollity,
> Music, dance and revelry. [*All dance and sing*]
> Fal-lal-la-la—Fal-lal-la-la,
> Music, dance and revelry. [*They all dance off at different entrances, singing the last part of the chorus. El Hassan enters, conducting Kaled*]

KALED. How say you—driven from his country to wander an exile in a desert land by his own brother?

EL HASS. Even so! The proud and haughty Abdel Mahadi who now sits on the throne he has usurped, revelling in the wealth he forces from the good people of Tripoli, who dare not murmur at the extortion. Why, the very streets groan at the deeds of the usurper.

KALED. How did this happen?

EL HASS. Abdel Mahadi, by foul reports and slanderous accusations, banished his brother from Tripoli, and then with the aid of those he had bribed to assist him, seized upon the throne, where he now sits dealing forth oppression and death to all who dare to thwart his will. But a day of retribution is at hand. I am an old man, but this arm shall help to restore the best of masters to his throne and his people.

KALED. Are you not afraid to express yourself thus? If the usurper should know of this—

EL HASS. He would add one more crime to his already overflowing measure. But let him do his worst—I care not—but come in. You need refreshment. Enter my dwelling and you shall eat in plenty.

KALED. Many thanks for your hospitality. I have travelled far and will accept your invitation.

EL HASS. This way. Enter and be welcome. [*Kaled enters house. Zephna speaks outside*]

ZEPH. The insolent Christian dog! [*Enters with a whip in his hand and crosses the stage passionately*] I'll cool down his spirits. I'll teach him to insult a person of my high standing.

EL HASS. High standing! You appear fallen, fellow, and into a violent passion, too.

ZEPH. But I'll be revenged, by the beard of Mahomet, I will.

EL HASS. Nay, my honest fellow, tell me what mighty occurrence has ruffled that sweet disposition of yours.

ZEPH. Ruffled! There it is again. First to be made a whirligig of and then very modestly to be asked why I am thus ruffled. Zounds, 'tis past all endurance.

EL HASS. Explain yourself.

ZEPH. I will. You must know that in removing the rubbish of the old castle we fell in with one of the stone pillars. To be sure, it wasn't so light that a gentle puff of the Sirocco would have blown it away. It weighed—let me see—perhaps six of you. That, you know, is a small lift for a sturdy slave.

EL HASS. Oh, very small indeed! Three of me were nothing! Well—

ZEPH. So I call'd on a lusty Irishman—plague take him—bid him take it on his shoulder and carry it down to the great pier, a distance of about—about—

EL HASS. A mile.

ZEPH. Aye, a mile.

EL HASS. Well, what said the slave?

ZEPH. What said the slave! A surly dog! He began to mutter about his blessed land, of parartees [*sic*] and called on St. Patrick to deliver him from the disgrace it would cast on his own dear Ireland. So says I to him, "None of your lingo here," at the same time raising my whip to give him a gentle touch or two. "By St. Patrick," said he, "you had better not be after that kind of play." "By Mahomet, I will," said I, and suiting the action to the word, I gave him a twinging clip or two across the back.

EL HASS. Well, my life on't, he quick went to work.

ZEPH. Yes, faith, he did go to work, and with a witness too, as my poor body can testify. Oh, the dog, he had no sooner felt the lash than he seized me by the throat and gave me such a trouncing that I really thought all my bones were disjointed, and that my soul was about taking a last farewell of my poor body. [*Rubbing himself*]

EL HASS. Ha, ha, ha! Well might you think yourself a whirligig.

ZEPH. Don't laugh now. It's no laughing matter—at least, I found it so. But he shall pay dear for it—the bastinado shall cool down his turbulent spirit. I'll to my mistress and have it done immediately. Zounds, I never was so roughly handled in my life. I'll be revenged, aye, I'll be revenged.

EL HASS. Why to your mistress?

ZEPH. My master's in the regions above, or in the regions below, and, as the distance between the two places is not inconsiderable, I e'en would save time and go to my mistress. My master's dead, good sir.

EL HASS. Oh, oh, if he resembled thee, there can be no great doubt which region he's gone to. But tell me who is your mistress.

ZEPH. As great a prattler as e'er drew breath. Her name is Belinda! [*Aside*] Curse on that Irish dog—my poor bones!

EL HASS. An old favourite of Ali-ben-Mahadi. Does she know anything of his daughter? [*Sulieman enters, stops, hearing the name of Ali-ben-Mahadi, and listens*]

ZEPH. What, the young princess?

EL HASS. The same.

ZEPH. Indeed she does. She has the charge of the young princess—oh, that Irish dog! The princess is with Belinda—lives with her—but I can't stay here any longer. I must go and prepare the bastinado for the slave. Oh, my poor bones. I'm all pap-mummy, but I'll be revenged. By Mahomet, I will. [*Exit*]

EL HASS. Ha, ha, ha! He'll be revenged—because the poor devil couldn't take a mountain on his back, he must be bastinadoed—ha, ha, ha! [*Exit into house. Sulieman comes forward*]

SULIE. What did I hear? The daughter of my much wronged monarch so near at hand. Let me fly to expose the wronger of her father's honour! O my liege, though base disloyalty and fiend-like slander have forced thee from thy throne, thou still enjoyest what Abdel ne'er can feel—a mind unsullied, tranquil and serene! But thy false brother, what torments twine about his heart! O base usurper, while my heart bleeds for him thou hast wronged, methinks I see from Heaven's high arch the bolt of vengeance, winging its rapid course to crush thy impious head. Tremble! Thou tyrant! Tremble! [*Exit*]

SCENE 2: *An apartment in the palace, first groove. Enter Abdel Mahadi.*

MAHADI. My brother banished! And Abdel Mahadi seated on his throne. O rapturous thought! I, who for years have pined in blank obscurity, have, like the ravenous tiger, o'erleaped the ignominious bound and pour'd destruction on the wretch who rashly dared to check my will. Now shall the darling passion of my soul be glutted. Plunder! Aye, plunder alone can raise our sinking realm. Peace has no charms for me; her train is misery and want. Plunder shall fill our coffers and once more give to Tripoli happiness and fame. Already do my corsairs, manned with brave and flinty hearts, beset the coast around. Soon shall the waves which lash my circling shores bear to my port the rich and ponderous prize. [*Enter Abdallah*] How now—speak Abdallah.

ABDAL. One of your gallant corsairs, my liege, has returned with a prize of no mean value.

MAHADI. Say you so! A prize, ha! It fills my heart with joy. This is the morning of my reign; its noontide blaze shall fill the earth with admiration. Speak on, Abdallah. What is the prize?

ABDAL. A ship deeply laden from America.

MAHADI. Is the cargo valuable?

ABDAL. So 'tis reported, my liege.

MAHADI. Let the slaves be taken from the prize and safely lodged within the castle. Straightway my council must convene, and ere tomorrow's sun has half performed his round, these Christian dogs shall feel my deadly hate. Away and see my orders executed. [*Exit Abdallah*] 'Tis well. This day, auspicious to my reign, with pomp and show shall mark the epoch of my grand career. Music shall waft her loftiest strains, whilst joy—ecstatic joy—beams forth from every eye. Thus, fortune, I'll repay thy gracious boon and, by my gratitude, deserve thy future favour. [*Exit*]

SCENE 3: *A room in Belinda's house. Immorina discovered seated at table viewing her father's miniature, Clothine attending.*

CLO. Ah! There she is—still in tears. Oh, it was a cruel thing to tear her father from her. I'll speak to her. Madam—

IMMO. Ha! Is it you, Clothine? See what a placid brow [*Showing a miniature*], a countenance, how serene! Those eyes, too—do they not beam with tenderness and love? Oh! he was the best of fathers.

CLO. That indeed he was, and the best of masters, too. Why, I remember how he used to call on my poor dear dead and gone mother, and would sit down and talk so socially and tell so many wonderful stories that I thought him the finest man in all Tripoli—indeed I did. Now, great men, you know madam, don't commonly do so. 'Tis very seldom they call on an old woman to prattle with her unless she has by the bye a pretty pair of young, sparkling eyes in the same roof. That, indeed, alters the case amazingly. Now I don't mean to say that your father, madam, used to visit my mother on that account. Oh, no, I was only going—

IMMO. Peace—peace, Clothine. You distract me. Leave me—I would be alone.

CLO. Oh, dear—I'm very sorry, I'm sure, madam. I came here to chase away your melancholy. I didn't mean to distract you. Indeed I'm very sorry, but if I must go, I must. [*Aside*] Her dear father wouldn't have treated me so. [*Exit*]

IMMO. Alas! Alas! Here am I doomed to linger out the remainder of my life. Well, 'tis the will of Allah! What are riches? In the world's estimation, they may purchase friends and esteem, but can they soothe one agonizing pang or shed one ray of comfort here? [*Enter Sulieman, preceded by a Slave who salaams, and exit*] Ha! Sulieman, my friend, welcome, thrice welcome. Inexpressible is the joy I feel in beholding him who shared so bountifully in my father's esteem, and yet it seems to occasion sorrow in this afflicted heart of mine. Yes, Sulieman, it brings to my recollection past scenes of enjoyment, when a stranger to the vicissitudes of life, I knew none of its wretchedness and misery.

SULIE. Great minds, Immorina, rise above the evils of this world, and look down upon affliction as productive of the greatest good. Bear up then, Immorina, nor sink beneath the weight of thy sorrows. Who can tell but that thy father may yet return to save his country and bless his Immorina.

IMMO. My father return. Oh, never, never!

SULIE. The people may relent. But whatever may be decreed, behold in me, Immorina, one whose life is devoted to thy service. Believe me, princess, for I am bound to thy father by the most sacred tie, and how can I evince my loyalty to him better than in aiding his child in the hour of danger and distress.

IMMO. Generous Sulieman, he was a tender father. Seated on his throne, it was his constant prayer that Heaven would so direct his course that every act might prove a blessing to his country. I thought him, too, beloved by all his subjects.

SULIE. And so he was till cursed ambition "infused its poison" into the heart of Abdel Mahadi. To him must be assigned the cause that wrench'd the sceptre from thy father's hands.

IMMO. What! To Abdel Mahadi—my father's brother—my uncle?

SULIE. Yes, 'twas he who stirr'd the soldiery to point their sabres at his guiltless breast, reported lies of foulest import, charged him with treason and every damned deed that malice could invent, till by his accursed art he raised the storm which pour'd its vengeance on thy father's head.

IMMO. Ah, impious fiend! Thou tyrant most accursed! Henceforth in me behold thy deadliest foe. Now sorrow, get thee hence. I feel infused within my veins a manly courage. My father's fall shall be avenged. Traitor, look to thyself. Beware a woman's vengeance. [*Exit*]

SULIE. What matchless excellence! But 'tis no time for love, oh, heart, heart. [*Exit*] *[[*Clothine enters*]

CLO. Bless me, what can be the matter with the lady Immorina? First she bids me hold my peace when she used to be glad to have me with her and would listen for hours to the songs I'd sing to her. Just now she passed me, calling for revenge on somebody, I don't know who, but it's very strange. I declare, it's quite upset me. I shan't get over it for some time. Well, never mind. I'll sing one of my favourite songs to keep off the blue devils, for I'm getting terrible melancholy. [*Music. Song introduced, and Exit*]]

SCENE 4: *Grand Hall in the palace, splendidly illuminated. Abdel Mahadi discovered seated on a throne surrounded by Officers, Guards, Slaves, male and female Dancers, etc. Banners.*

Chorus

[*At the end of chorus, a fancy dance by one of the slaves. Turkish dance. At the end, Mahadi speaks*]

MAHADI. Cease, cease your merriment! Abdallah, are the slaves at hand?

ABDAL. They are, my liege.

MAHADI. Conduct them to our presence. [*Girls dance off. Music. Abdallah goes off and reenters with Guards conducting Anderson, Jack Binnacle, and several sailors as prisoners. Guards form at back*] Speak, slaves, what country gave ye birth?

JACK. [*Aside to Anderson*] You be our spokesman, Master Anderson. They're too ceremonious for me, curse 'em.

ANDER. [*Boldly*] America.

MAHADI. By your deportment, slave, conjecture would have me think you of noble extraction, sprung from some renowned ancestor. Is it so?

ANDER. If to be the son of him who served his country in the time of peril be that which you call noble, I am of most noble extraction; but if from pampered lords and vicious princes alone descend this gift, then I am not.

MAHADI. Does your father live?

ANDER. When I left home he did.

MAHADI. What title bore he?

ANDER. An honest man, the proudest title man can have.

MAHADI. Boasts he no other?

ANDER. He needs no other.

* Bracketed lines indicate parts of the play apparently cut out of the production.

MAHADI. Have you friends?

ANDER. In my native country, many; here, alas! but few.

MAHADI. Are they rich?

JACK. [*Aside*] Well, damn his imperence! [*sic*]

ANDER. Richer than all the treasures of the east in my esteem.

MAHADI. In your esteem—ha, ha, ha! Poor indeed if that is all their treasure—ha, ha, ha!

JACK. I say, Master Anderson, that fellow with the long beard is laughing at us. Shiver my mizzen, if I shouldn't like to board him on his quarter-deck there. If you only say the word, Master Anderson, I'll—

ANDER. Nay, Jack, it will avail us nothing. We are completely in their power and 'twere useless to thwart his will.

MAHADI. Speak, slave, are you rich?

ANDER. That rests with you. You have the power to make me rich or poor.

MAHADI. Will not your country ransom you?

ANDER. Will not my property suffice?

MAHADI. Nay, that is mine already. Say, will not your country ransom you and your comrades there?

JACK. I beg your pardon, Master Anderson, but I'll answer that question, if you've no objection. [*To Mahadi*] Your mightiness wants to know, I believe, if our country will ransom us. Now, I don't want to make you uneasy, but all I've got to say is this—that the only ransom you'll get from America for us will be in iron balls in the shape of forty-two pounders. That'll make your deyship [*sic*] tremble.

MAHADI. Insolent slave—do you threaten—peace, I say—

JACK. You'll find it'll be war if you don't set us at liberty without much more delay. But crow on, old Bluebeard. Every cock on his own dunghill.

MAHADI. Guards, hence with these slaves to the fortress; there in close confinement shall they wait the issue of their country's boasted vengeance. By Allah, to be bearded in the very precincts of our mighty palace by Christian dogs. To a dungeon with them. Away—away—[*Guards advance*]

JACK. Avast then a bit. [*To Anderson*] I say, Master Anderson, we ain't agoing to surrender to these copper-coloured swabs without firing a shot, eh! No, shiver my timbers if we do. So stand by, my hearties, and we'll pour in a broadside for the honour of our country and ourselves.

MAHADI. Ah! Dare ye resist my will? Guards, upon 'em—secure the slaves. [*Music. The Guards rush upon Jack, Anderson, and Sailors, who defend themselves, but are overpowered by numbers and secured. Picture formed at end of Act*]

ACT II.

Scene i: *A room in house. Enter Immorina and Clothine.*

[[Clo. What did Sulieman say? Your uncle, Abdel Mahadi, the sole cause of your father's banishment and consequently, the cause of all your sorrows, and mine, too? Yes, indeed, mine, too! For whenever I think of your dear good father, I always sob and cry so that I disturb the whole neighbourhood with my lamentations! Well, I always thought your uncle the most ill-natured, malicious, good-for-nothing creature that ever I had seen. Why now, I remember about four years ago he came up to me and, without any provocation, gave me such a monstrous twitch by the ear that it has been about dead ever since! And on my asking him what he did that for, why said he, "To hear you squeal, you ninny!" Oh, he's a cruel dog. He banished your father, did he?

Immo. Yes, Clothine, he did so; but his treachery shall not go long unpunished. I'll to—

Clo. Why, what will you do, miss? Twitch his ear off, hey? Oh, dear, I should like to hear him squeal, that I should. [*Exit*]] [*Enter Sulieman*]

Immo. Welcome, Sulieman. Say, has my uncle yet passed sentence on these unhappy captives?

Sulie. Yes, Immorina.

Immo. Poor souls! A sentence untempered with the touch of mercy, was't not so?

Sulie. To be exposed in the market place and sold to the highest bidder.

Immo. Just Heaven!

Sulie. Why thus moved, fair Immorina? It has ever been the usage here for all Christian captives to be sold for slaves. Of this thou canst not be ignorant. Why then this emotion at the sentence of these captives?

Immo. [[No, Sulieman, I am not indeed a stranger to that custom which, in my mind, is so repugnant to that pure spirit of moral obligation, which binds man to man and teaches him to soften by his compassion instead of aggravating by new tortures, the sufferings of an unhappy fellow mortal.]] But with a monster on the throne what have they to hope? What scheme will be left unaccomplished that hatred can devise to torture these unhappy victims? Cruelty is the darling passion of his soul. O Sulieman, cruelty such as inhabits this tyrant's breast, can never be satiated till life itself expires.

[[Sulie. [*Aside*] Adorable creature! [*Aloud*] Yes, too true, lovely Immorina.]]

Immo. Hast thou seen the prisoners?

SULIE.   Yes. [[When conducted from the castle to the palace, curiosity led me with the multitude to witness a scene, which, for many years, had not occurred in this place.]] Among the captives, I observed one whose amiable deportment and fair complexion ranked him far above his fellow sufferers. Grief was strongly depicted in his countenance; his whole soul seemed wrapt in sorrow and in thought! Still there was a character of courage on his brow which marked him to be unsubdued, though a prisoner. On inquiry, I learned that this person was the owner of the vessel and cargo, the prize, on board of which he was taken, and in her condemnation, he lost his all.

IMMO.   His all! did'st thou say? Has he not a father? Oh! But away, away, 'tis womanish to weep. I will assume the man, and a man thou know'st, though afflicted with the severest trials, should not despond.

[[SULIE.   He should endeavour not to.

IMMO.   Endeavour! He should not! Misfortunes should be borne with a manly courage, and the buffetings of fate be met with that heroic fortitude which exalts human nature and places man among the blest.]]

SULIE.   I would to Mahomet that I possessed this virtue.

IMMO.   You, Sulieman! Why you?

SULIE.   That it might fortify my heart!

IMMO.   Your heart! Is then your heart in danger?

SULIE.   Hast thou not read it in my looks? O princess, there is a flame within me which burns with unabating fury, which at this ill-suited time I would suppress, at least would check its progress; but vain are all my efforts. [[I might as well bound the impetuous torrent, burst from the fetters of the mountain's sides, or stop in its diurnal course, the orb of day and turn it to my will!]]

IMMO.   In love then! May I dare ask with whom?

SULIE.   With an angel, Immorina! Fairer than she who set all Greece in arms! "Whene'er she speaks, what music fills the air! Where'er she looks, surrounding nature smiles!"

IMMO.   What if she frown'd?

SULIE.   The world would be in tears!

IMMO.   Indeed! In whom are such rare qualities combined?

SULIE.   [*Discovers much emotion*]   In—pardon me, Immorina—but—but my heart will force it out—in [*Bowing respectfully*] thyself.

IMMO.   You trifle, Sulieman!

SULIE.   Nay, by Mahomet, 'tis true. Thy matchless charms have set my soul on fire. Thy—

IMMO.   Hold! This is no time for love. My mind on higher views is bent— my father! Sulieman—my father! where is he? [*Enter Clothine abruptly*]

CLO. O princess! princess! Lord! Lord! What a perturbation I am in! Dear—dear—these slaves—

IMMO. What of these slaves, Clothine?

CLO. Why, they are all Americans! And do you know what Americans are?

IMMO. Men—are they not like other men?

CLO. Pshaw! Not they, indeed! That's just what I supposed. [*Aside*] She thinks she knows everything because she's a princess, and forsooth, she knows nothing at all! Well, 'tis the way of the world.

IMMO. Frankness appears to be your characteristic, Clothine, but pray inform me what are these Americans if they are not men?

CLO. Indians! Yes indeed, Indians! That they are. They used to tell me that these Americans, that is, Indians, if they caught a man or woman, no matter which (and I'm sure this proves them not to be men) would take off the top part of his or her head in the twinkling of an eye! Oh, dear! dear! We shall all be scalped, that we shall.

IMMO. Nay, nay, you mistake, Clothine; these Indians of whom you speak are the natives of America. They inhabit the western regions of that vast country, and are savage and barbarous like our wild Arabs. But those whom we denominate Americans are a civilized and polished people, enterprising, brave and hospitable.

CLO. Oh, dear! If this be the case, then, why you see my mistress is in want of one more slave, and if you think I shan't have the top of my head taken off, I should like to purchase one of these Americans, as you call 'em, for her.

SULIE. [*To Immorina*] Advise her to the step. Let me be her agent. I'll purchase the American before spoken of, and you will then have it in your power to alleviate the afflictions of an unhappy man.

IMMO. [*To Sulieman*] Admirable thoughts! [*To Clothine*] Well, Clothine, I think you cannot make a better choice; but you will not attend the sale yourself, sure?

CLO. Oh, no—Now if I could find some friend to?

SULIE. To do an act of kindness for you, good Clothine, be assured, would be attended with much pleasure. If you will confide in my judgment, I will do my best to procure your mistress a good and worthy slave.

CLO. Oh, that I will, indeed I will, and thank you, too. But don't give too much for him. When is the sale to commence?

SULIE. Immediately. I must away. [*Going*]

CLO. [*Calls him back*] Sulieman! Examine him well before you buy him. See that he's of a good temper! Try to find out if he ever scalped anyone. If he has, don't touch him. I had rather have a Thaibanne in my house!

SULIE. Trust to me, my good girl. [*Looks at Immorina*] Immorina—adieu. [*Exit*]

IMMO. Farewell, Sulieman. Clothine, follow me. [*Exit*]

SCENE 2: *A garden, set trees, etc. Anderson is seen with a spade in his hand. Jack and several slaves at work in the background.*

ANDER. Must I then with this menial implement toil in base servility? And this, too, without the hope of becoming one day free? Never, never. [*Throwing down the spade*] Away, away. [*Comes to the front of the stage*] Oh, what a change is here! Yesterday! What was I yesterday? Opulent and free. Today! today! A beggar and a slave! O my countrymen! Where now that Roman pride, that Spartan valour, that enthusiastic zeal, which led you on to freedom and to glory, that here, in this vile nest of pirates, beneath a sun whose pestilential rays spread death around, thy fellow countrymen must bend, like overburdened beasts, with slavery and shame. O ye spirits of their ascended chiefs, look from your blest abodes, rekindle in our hearts, that god-like flame, which marked your glorious course, to avenge our country's wrongs.

JACK. Our country's wrongs—why don't our country rescue us?

ANDER. Rescue us? She does not know as yet our fate.

JACK. She knows the fate of hundreds in Algiers. Why not rescue them? Why not blow Algiers to the devil, and put an end to this nest of pirates?

ANDER. That were impossible, so numerous are these people. We may destroy their seaboard towns but cannot do them further harm. Thus maritime nations have ever found it best to buy their favour with an annual tribute.

JACK. Well, Master Anderson, you know best about it, but shiver my mizzen, if I hadn't rather fight till my heartstrings snap than be tributary to any nation. [*Enter Zephna with a whip*]

ZEPH. What, fellow! Left your task?

JACK. [*Looks contemptuously at him*] Fellow, hey! Here's a mushroom. [*Goes up*]

ZEPH. [*To Anderson*] To your task, slave!

ANDER. Never.

ZEPH. Then you most assuredly will starve.

ANDER. Rather so, than earning my pittance thus. [*Pointing at Slaves at their work*]

ZEPH. Faith! Let me tell you, slave, you must and shall work.

ANDER. Peace, fellow! "Must and shall!" I understand you not.

ZEPH. [*Holding up his whip*] This shall then explain!

ANDER. Miscreant! I fear it not, nor the base arm that waves it o'er my head. Come not too near, fellow, or—

ZEPH. Why! What will you do?

ANDER. Grind thee to a powder, incorporate thee with Lybian sands and whirl thee to the moon, thou copper-coloured owl!

ZEPH. Ohoa! A second Irishmen, by Mahomet! Here's pretty work. Faith! I'll try your courage though. [*Lifts up his whip and is in the act of striking*]

ANDER. [*Seizes him by the throat*] Base wretch!

ZEPH. Help! Help! Murder! Murder!

ANDER. [*Rushes him with such violence that Zephna falls*] This for thy insolence! [*Enter Immorina*]

IMMO. Hold! Hold! Who calls for help?

ZEPH. The slave has nearly broke my limbs. [*Rises*]

IMMO. [*To Anderson*] Why this rash treatment, sir?

ANDER. I am thy prisoner, lady; but dost thou think me destitute of feeling that I must bear with insult from a knave like that? [*To Zephna*]

IMMO. Did he then insult thee?

ANDER. Yes, lady and basely so; and had I not laid him prostrate at my feet, he e'en had struck me.

ZEPH. Yes, most mighty princess, he laid me flat upon the ground—

ANDER. [*Aside*] The princess, ha! 'Tis she! Hope darts across my brain.

ZEPH. The slave refused to toil.

IMMO. [*To Zephna*] You may retire awhile. I'll answer for thy absence. [*Exeunt Zephna and all the Slaves. To Anderson*] I pity thy misfortunes, stranger, with all my heart, I do. But thou know'st the custom of our country—Christians here are slaves.

ANDER. Yes, well I know it, lady, yet never can submit. These hands, unused to toil, the spade would ill become. Besides, what hope have I to toil? Shall I thereby gain my freedom? No. Then I had rather meet my fate at once; e'en death, grim death with all his ghastly horrors, is preferable to slavery. But tell me, lady, is not the reigning prince thy uncle?

IMMO. Ha! Who told thee this?

ANDER. I heard thy story while a prisoner at the castle—from my guard I heard it. Thy father banished, thy uncle on his throne?

IMMO. Yes! Well—speak!

ANDER. Hast thou no brother to—

IMMO. None. [*Looks steadfastly on Anderson*] Stranger, thy looks bespeak some bold adventure, some daring enterprise, yes? My uncle, my base, perfidious uncle, usurps my father's throne! Speak, good stranger, speak!

ANDER. Dost thou love thy father?

IMMO. Love him!

ANDER. Would'st thou risk thy life to serve him?

IMMO. Would that I had ten thousand lives. I'd risk them all, nor think my duty half performed.

ANDER. Then hear me, princess. Give me my freedom, and, in exchange, I'll give thee back thy father! [*Haccham is at this moment seen listening at the back of the stage and retires*]

IMMO. Oh, torture me not thus! My father, didst thou say?

ANDER. Thy father. Convey me beyond the power of thy uncle and hold me to my word.

IMMO. Oh, 'twere impossible!

ANDER. Rather say 'twere certain. Conduct me to some private place, for here we might be overheard. My plan I'll then unfold and make it easy to thy comprehension.

IMMO. We will retire, nor lose a moment's time—but, ah! 'tis vain illusion! [*Exeunt Immorina and Anderson. Haccham advances*]

HAC. So, so treason on foot. 'Tis well for Abdel he hath a friend—one whose eye can pierce the vest of treachery and whose arm will not fail to strike his weapon deep into the traitor's heart. [*Exit*]

SCENE 3: *A room in El Hassan's house. El Hassan discovered.*

EL HASS. 'Tis near the time. At length I see the glimmering star that shall light my injured sovereign to his throne; I have pledged myself to accomplish the escape of this young American, and I will do it though my own life should pay the forfeit. But soft—he comes. [*Enter Anderson*]

ANDER. Is everything prepared, good Hassan—the disguises—

EL HASS. Are ready. The caravan waits your coming—the leader alone is acquainted with the secret. Should you be questioned by any other, say you belong to Mecca, a merchant there, that business brought you here; and that as no opportunity presented by which you might return by water, you sought protection from the caravan. But mention not my name. Mark this, for perchance it might reach Abdel's ears and so defeat your plan.

ANDER. Generous man, fear not. No act of mine shall endanger your life or my cause! And now, Heaven! infuse within me that heroic courage, the energy of soul which so distinguished the father of my country, the matchless hero of the western world, that, when returned in arms, like him, I may pursue one firm and steady course till victory perch'd upon my brow proclaims destruction to the base usurper, and vengeance, like swiftest lightning hurls him from the throne! Oh, 'twere a god-like deed! Who falls to gain so rich a prize, meets with a glorious death! [*Exit, followed by El Hassan*]

SCENE 4: *Garden in second grooves. Enter Mahadi and Haccham.*

MAHADI.   Insolent dog! Give her back her father, ha, ha, ha! It is the working of a wild, distempered mind. What said my niece—did she listen to the slave?

HAC.   She did, my liege, and with a greedy ear. He told her all his sufferings. She seem'd affected at the recital and when her father's name was mentioned, at first she grieved, then joy succeeded, as if she thought it possible the slave could keep his word.

MAHADI.   [*Sarcastically*]   Say, did he tell the course by which he would effect this grand achievement?

HAC.   No! Being in the open garden, 'twas thought he might be overheard, and hence they both withdrew.

MAHADI.   What, left the slave his task?

HAC.   Yes, my liege, he would not toil, but cast the implements of labour from him with scorn and indignation.

MAHADI.   A stubborn dog. [*Enter Abdallah hastily*]

ABDAL.   Most potent prince, thy niece conspires against thee! Anderson, the slave, has fled—thy niece—look to her well, my liege.

MAHADI.   'Sdeath! I have traitors round—my vengeance foiled. Haccham, lead forth thy troop, scour every avenue of the city, let no spot remain unsearched. Double my guards, and when you have caught the Christian dog, lead him to instant death—away—away—[*Music. Exit Mahadi, Haccham and Abdallah. Zephna enters conducting Slaves, Jack Binnacle, etc.*]

ZEPH.   There, you slaves, sit down and rest your unfortunate bones a little while. So far, you have done well.

JACK.   Thank you for nothing, but I say, my hearty, bear up alongside. I've got a word or two to say to you. You seem to be a tolerable good sort of a fellow. Why the devil don't you go to sea?

ZEPH.   Oh! bless you, I do. I go to see my pretty little black-eyed Clothine.

JACK.   Avast there, my hearty, you're steering on the wrong tack. I don't mean to go to see anybody—

ZEPH.   Why, you wouldn't have me go to see nobody, would you?

JACK. You don't understand my signals. Now, what I meant was this—why do you (such a good-looking fellow) lead such a lazy life—why not go on board a ship—plenty of work there. You'd make an excellent bo'san's mate. Besides, you'd have a chance of seeing the world. Aye, and all the tight little crafts in it, too. Oh, the delectable creatures—it makes my mouth water to think of them.

ZEPH. There you and I differ, for my mouth never waters till I see them. Do you know, the other day, I met Clothine in the garden. "Oh," says I, "my little tulip. How my mouth waters for a taste of the nectar of those sweet lips." "Does it?" says she—"Yes," says I. And with that I placed my arm round her waist and was about to try the flavour of a kiss, when she gave me such a smack in the face, that it started all the water from my mouth to my eyes, from whence it pour'd in streams.

JACK. Ha, ha, ha! Well if my Sue—

ZEPH. What sue?

JACK. Why Sue Morris! Ah, she's a tight little pinnace, that she is—I wonder where she thinks I am—gone to Davy Jones's locker, I'll be bound. Perhaps she has grappled with some other tar. If she has, and I live to get home again, I'll bear down upon him and pour in such a broadside that—

ZEPH. That what!

JACK. Why, that he'll be devilish glad to cut and run—oh, she's fairly conquered me. And I'm no coward for all that, for you must know that the heart of a sailor, though invincible when attacked by his country's foes, is at once overcome when assailed by the sparkling eye of a pretty girl! What say you, Mr. Whip?

ZEPH. Come, I say, don't you take any liberties with me—my name is Zephna, not Whip, if you please; but however, I say in answer to you that you talk pretty brave, but you may be a coward for all that. Are the American girls handsome?

JACK. Handsome, handsome, hey. Why, if you were only to see one under full sail, your poor heart—that is, if you have one—would pop out of your head's portage.

ZEPH. Excuse me for interrupting you, but you will do me a particular favour by telling me what you mean by my head portage.

JACK. Why your mouth, you lubber. Well, as I was saying, your heart would pop out in such a devil of a hurry that shiver me if I think you'd ever find it again—handsome girls in America. Only you take a trip with us there and I'll show you as fine a crew of blooming young lassies as—as—Oh, finer than you ever saw—Aye, I'll carry you to the theatre, cast anchor in the centre of the pit and charm you with the lustre of the circling boxes. You'd think yourself in Paradise, that you would.

ZEPH. You don't say so. Then I'll tell you what I'll do—only find an opportunity and I'll go with you.

JACK. You will—tip us your fin. [*Shakes hands*] There, that's settled, and now lads, heave a head. In my hammock, I've stowed away a jug of the real stuff—something that'll make your heart warm. So hurrah my lads—heave a head and I'll follow in your wake in the turning of a handspike. [*Music. Zephna, Jack, and Slaves exeunt*]

SCENE 5: *The courtyard of the castle. Walls across stage practicable. Set tower R., set dungeon L. First and Second Officers marching before the gate in wall. Enter from tower Mahadi and Immorina.*

MAHADI. Tell me! Where's the slave?

IMMO. Tell me where's my father.

MAHADI. Pitiful evasion! The niece of Abdel Mahadi to plot with slaves! I disclaim the tie which should bind me to thy care.

IMMO. Thy care! Rather say thy hate! O base deceiver, who tore my father from these tender arms? Who stirred the people to revolt? Who turned the sabres of his guards to pierce his guiltless heart? Answer me, thou perfidious monster! Thy care—O insolent!

MAHADI. Hold—who told thee this? The slave, no doubt.

IMMO. 'Twas not the slave. But I had rather call him by the endearing name of friend and all that bend beneath thy servile yoke than thee.

MAHADI. Thy father's weakness turn'd the public will against him. He was too mild to reign. He courted peace, not as I am wont to do, the crimson hand of war. To gain the friendship of each petty prince, thy father stoop'd to deeds degrading to his realm. But tell me, I command thee, who is the base slanderer of my honour? Tell me, that he may meet the fate to which my vengeance justly dooms him.

IMMO. Outrageous arrogance! My father's reign, though mild, was just. He had the people's love till thou, thou fiend, with deadly shafts assailed him. The people were deceived—by thee deceived—and dread their kindling vengeance, base usurper.

MAHADI. Usurper! Another word and—

IMMO. The rack! A noble action worthy thy great self.

MAHADI. Answer me, where's the slave?

IMMO. Free! Beyond thy reach.

MAHADI. Who aided his escape?

IMMO. I! thy niece.

MAHADI. Whither has he fled?

IMMO. That, time will unfold—but tremble, tyrant, tremble.

MAHADI. [*Disdainfully*] My guards have caught the slave and sent him headless to his grave.

IMMO. 'Tis false.

MAHADI. 'Tis true—the slave is dead!

IMMO. [*Aside*] Should it be—[*Draws a dagger. Aloud*] Thy life then for his. 'Tis Immorina strikes. [*Music. Attempts to stab Mahadi. He wrests the dagger from her*]

MAHADI. Ho there, guards! Guards! [*Music. During this scene it has been getting gradually darker. Abdallah and Guards enter*] Abdallah, take this wretch away and let her be confined in the strongest dungeon. Away with her! [*Two Guards seize her*]

IMMO. Unhand me, ruffians—I am the princess, the Princess Immorina. [*Struggling*]

MAHADI. Nay, heed her not. Away with her, guards, to a dungeon. Away —away. [*Music. Mahadi exit. Immorina is dragged into dungeon. Abdallah and Soldiers return, secure the gate and exeunt into tower. Stage dark, music continues. The Sentinel goes off. Jack enters cautiously and comes down, groping about*]

JACK. So, the coast is clear at last. Now then, to mount the wall, and then huzza for liberty. [*This is spoken through the music. Jack goes up. At the same time, Haccham enters from tower. Comes, starts, listens, indicates that he hears footsteps. Gropes about. By this time, Jack has reached the wall, when he is seized by Haccham. They struggle to front. Combat, Haccham is disarmed*]

HAC. Ho there! Treachery—guards, guards. [*Music. Sentinel reenters. Jack knocks him down, seizes his gun and mounts the wall as Abdallah, followed by Soldiers, reenters. They thrust at Jack with their spears. He keeps them down with the gun as the Act drop descends*]

ACT III.

SCENE 1: *An apartment in the palace. Enter Mahadi and Haccham.*

MAHADI. Could you get no account of the slaves?

HAC. None, my liege.

MAHADI. Has there been any opportunity by water by which they may have escaped?

HAC. None that I can learn, my lord.

MAHADI. Did you offer a reward for them, dead or alive?

HAC. Yes, my liege, a large one.

MAHADI. 'Sdeath! It staggers me; and yet it seems they must be concealed within the city walls. If so, destruction light upon the wretch that dares to shelter them! These limbs shall know no rest till, tiger-like, they hunt the traitor out, and make him feel my vengeance. Haccham, my friend, renew thy search, let not a vessel from my port depart without my special order.

HAC. Your orders shall be strictly follow'd. But, where's your niece? Perhaps 'twere well to question her about the slave; some inadvertent word may fall, by which you'll gain a clue.

MAHADI. I've seen her, questioned, and found her false—she feels my power and if she reveals not the hiding place of these Christian dogs, the rack shall force the secret from her. [*Enter Abdallah, hastily*]

ABDAL. My liege, one of the corsairs has returned, and brings intelligence of the greatest moment. She was chased within reach of the outer bastion by a frigate bearing the American flag.

MAHADI. Ha! Say you so! Haste thee, Haccham, and see my troops in readiness to meet the foe. [*Exit Haccham*] By a frigate bearing the American flag, say you?

ABDAL. Yes, my liege, and it is moreover reported that several other large vessels of war were seen standing in for Tripoli.

MAHADI. What reason is assigned for their coming?

ABDAL. It is in consequence of the intelligence communicated to the commander by the American who escaped from here; and their object to demand of you the release of all the American prisoners here.

MAHADI. Demand! He may demand, but rather than submit to this demand without a ransom, by Allah, I'd see the city laid in ruins. Oh, could I meet them on the ocean with half their force I'd make these Christians rue their rashness. [*Reenter Haccham*]

HAC. My liege, a caravan has reach'd the city and brings accounts most strange and fearful.

MAHADI. Out with it at once—speak on.

HAC. The leader of the caravan reports he passed an army in the desert bound hither to reinstate your brother.

MAHADI. My brother! Does he head the army?

HAC. So 'tis reported.

MAHADI. [*Aside*] Why had I not ere this employed some trusty hand to stop the milky current of his veins—but no, 'tis spared for me! I'll meet him face to face, and with my well-taught steel, pluck from its seat his coward heart. [*Aloud*] Say, is there no other leader?

HAC. Yes, my liege, an American, once your slave.

MAHADI. Indeed! Then we must be stirring. Is his army well equipped and numerous?

HAC. I could not learn its number or its power. 'Twas said some thousands more would join it ere it reached these walls.

MAHADI. 'Sdeath! 'Tis too true. We must away and meet my brother's force ere a junction can be form'd with the fleet. Time is now precious: it calls for blood—Immorina—Yes, death shall be the forfeit of her treachery. See to it, Abdallah. Away, Haccham, parade my troops within the public square. Lose not a moment. Away—I'll be there anon! [*Music. Exeunt Haccham, Abdallah and Mahadi*]

SCENE 2: *A plain without the walls. Enter Ali-ben-Mahadi's troops and form down on R., followed by Ali.*

ALI. My friends and fellow soldiers, under the protecting arm of the great Allah we have thus far advanced in safety. From yonder height Tripoli appears in view. In addition to our force, we are promised the cooperation of the navy already drawn up in front of the city. And I momentarily expect the return of our intrepid ally with a band of freemen who have effected a landing from the fleet. With this powerful assistance, we cannot fail of success. Victory will be ours, and my vanquished brother must sue to me for pardon—but hark [*Drums without*], they come. [*Music. Enter a party of American Marines led by Clement and followed by Jack and Sailors*] Where is my friend, the valiant Anderson?

JACK. He'll be at his post, your honour. I left him consulting with the commodore on the method of attack. [*Flourish without*] Ah! that's him. [*Enter Anderson in American uniform, military*]

ALI. Give me your hand, my friend—my preserver.

ANDER. Call me not the latter, Ali, till, with the aid of our brave comrades here, I've humbled your perfidious brother, and amid the acclamations of an injured people, led you in triumph to the throne.

ALI. Generous Christian!

ANDER. We must lose no time in words; the attack must be commenced with all possible speed. The commodore has everything in readiness and will begin the bombardment of the city on our arrival at the gates.

JACK. That's right, your honour—that's just what I was going to propose when I saw you and the commodore holding out signals, only I thought as how you wouldn't altogether like my idea. So I didn't say it, but since you're on the same wake, why I say let's heave ahead at once, and if we don't tickle that old turkey buzzard's whiskers, why, may I never see another bit of baccy, that's all.

ANDER. Let us away then, but [*To Ali*] let it be understood that the condition on which these brave men are sent your aid is, that when reinstated on the throne of Tripoli, my fellow countrymen be immediately released and their plundered property restored.

ALI. Most willingly do I accede.

ANDER. Then, my brave comrades, let's on to meet the vile usurper in the field.

JACK. Aye, shiver my timbers, Master Anderson [*Avast Jack*] I should say general now, aye and a first rater, too. Columbians, still let this your glorious motto be: "Liberty or Death." [*Trumpet without*]

ALI. Our herald comes. [*Enter Herald*]

ANDER. What says the tyrant?

HER. He defies your united powers and dares you to the fight.

ANDER. Then haste thee to the shore. A boat is waiting and will bear thee to the fleet. Say to the commodore we are prepared for battle and his first gun shall be the signal for the attack. Away. [*Exit Herald*] Now, my brave soldiers, 'tis vengeance bids us on. The foe is near at hand and dares you to the attack. He proudly boasts the day is his, but with such brave hearts as now surround me, I would dispute the prize though his numbers treble ours. Let each man think of his native land and remember he fights against tyranny and oppression. Strike up—march! [*Music. Grand march and exeunt*]

SCENE 3: *A dungeon. Immorina discovered.*

IMMO. I heard a noise! The guilty step of murder—[*Enter Abdallah and a Soldier*] Ha! Is it thou? Alas! I see my fate—'tis written in your looks. What, is not my uncle satisfied in having me immured in this dungeon's dismal gloom, but I must be placed upon the torturing rack. Speak! Is't not so?

ABDAL. Too well thou know'st the purpose of our coming.

IMMO. Well, death to me is welcome. But, O my father, my injured father!

ABDAL. Thy father did'st thou say—hast thou not heard—

IMMO. Heard—heard what?

ABDAL. Thy father's at the city gates and will be here anon.

IMMO. What say'st thou? My father at the city gates! Oh, then I will not die!

ABDAL. It is our orders, princess, that we lose no time in executing thy uncle's commands.

IMMO. Inhuman monsters, you would not tear me from a father's arms, and he so near at hand?

ABDAL. Pardon us, lady, 'tis our orders to lead thee to instant death.

IMMO. [*Frantic*] Then tell my uncle, thy master, I will not go.

ABDAL. [*Seizing her*] Force then must be used.

IMMO. Help—help! Oh, help! Unhand me, ruffians. I am the princess. [*Music*]

SULIE. [*Without*] Who calls for help? Speed, speed, my friends. [*Rushes in*] Ha! 'tis Immorina calls. Villains, stand off. Away, ye hireling slaves or feel the vengeance of this single arm when injured innocence bids it strike. [*Exeunt Abdallah and Soldier*]

IMMO. Ha! Sulieman! My friend, or do my eyes deceive me, that from this trance of ecstasy I wake to tenfold misery.

SULIE. Nay, thou art not deceived—'tis Sulieman. He comes to rescue thee. The guards who watch'd thy prison are marching to the southern gates. The city is besieged. Hence, with a chosen band of friends, I found an easy entrance.

IMMO. O my friend, my preserver! Thou hast snatch'd me from the scaffold! The grave already open'd to my view. How can I repay thee, Sulieman?

SULIE. Thy heart! Say 'tis Sulieman's.

IMMO. My heart! O Sulieman, ungrateful indeed would Immorina be did she deny thee this.

SULIE. Then Sulieman is bless'd! This is the happiest moment of his life.

IMMO. What, and in a prison, too.

SULIE. Yes, Immorina, with her I love.

IMMO. Come, let us leave this horrid place. My soul sickens at the sight of it. Lead me to my father.

SULIE. He is near at hand with the intrepid Anderson, who, like some skillful pilot, leads his forces and smiles at each danger as the source whence springs his future fame. [*Cannon heard*] But hark, already has the strife begun. Let us haste to welcome thy father's return. Come, love, come. [*Music. Exeunt*]

SCENE 4: *Apartment in the palace. Enter Zephna, much alarmed. Cannon heard.*

ZEPH. Oh, holy prophet, defend us—those Christian dogs have actually dared to attack us, and their confounded cannon balls are dancing along the streets like hailstones. I saw one hit a poor fellow just now bang in the stomach, and he went off without so much as bidding me good-bye! By Mahomet, and I went off, too, for I thought that perhaps one of those said balls might mistake me for somebody else. And as I am not fond of being physic'd, I'm afraid that would be a pill too much, one that I couldn't digest very well. [*Cannon heard*] Oh, dear, there they go. Bang! Bang! What will become of me! Suppose the enemy should gain the day—oh, dear, the very thought makes me feel queer. [*Noise without*] Eh! Somebody is coming this way. If it should be any of those Christian slaves—oh, dear—I'd better get out of the way. Here's a small chamber—it's dark, too. Just the place—they won't think of looking here, so in I goes. [*Enters door as Clothine enters followed by female Slaves terribly frightened*]

CLO. Oh, dear, oh, dear, we shall all be scalped and devoured by those savage Americans. Oh, I wish I was a man—how I would fight. I should be a hero—I should. [*Cannon fired, Girls all scream and huddle together*] Oh, dear, what's that, what are you all huddled up in that way for? [*Very frightened*] Don't you see—I—an't—frighten-ed—you—cow-ards you. What's to be done? Oh, I have it. In that chamber there is a secret entrance to a suit of rooms which very few know of. You can all go in there till the battle's over and there you'll be safe. [*Opens door*] Make haste. Why don't you go—it isn't very dark. Well, I never did see such cowards—but come, I'll be your leader. [*With assumed bravado*] Follow me. [*She enters room timidly, followed by the Girls. A short pause, a scream and Clothine and the Girls hurry out confusedly and all take cover. Falling on her knees*] I felt it—I saw its eyes glaring on me like great balls of fire—oh—oh—there the door opens—it's coming—oh, mercy, good Mr. Spirit—have mercy. [*Zephna pops his head out of room. All scream*]

ZEPH. Don't, ladies—dear, good ladies—don't scream so. I ain't a spirit—[*Aside*] though I shouldn't care if I had some. [*Aloud*] Do I look like a spirit?

CLO. Oh, dear, are you sure it's you, Zephna?

ZEPH. Well, I believe it is—at least, I'm pretty sure of it—that is, I hope so.

CLO. [*Crossing timidly and pinches him*] Why, so it is—ha, ha, ha! It was a good joke, wasn't it? Ha, ha, ha!

ZEPH. Was it though—what was it? He, he, he!

CLO. Why, do you know I was only making believe that I was frightened.

ZEPH. You don't really say so in earnest. Well, it was the best make-believe I ever saw. But, I say, Clothine, what do you think of these Christian dogs that have dared to attack us—us—that is, me and the bashaw—and the people. Don't you think we had ought to make them pay dearly for their temerity?

CLO. Certainly. Now if I was a man I'd go fight against them myself. Egad—an excellent thought—I'll raise a company of women, head them in person and lead them against the enemy. But what shall I do for arms?

ZEPH. Arms—why you ain't agoing to take any without arms, are you?

CLO. Oh, you don't understand—I mean swords, pistols, guns, spears, and so forth.

ZEPH. Oh—oh—that's it. I thought you meant this kind of arms. [*Shows his*] But you needn't wait long for them for there's plenty of all kinds in that room.

CLO. In there—your hand, my noble friend. [*Takes his hand*] For that news you're worthy to be my friend. [*With mock solemnity*] Go bring them forth. We'll arm at once and on to meet the foe. [*Zephna goes into room and brings out swords and spears for the Females. Each takes one. Clothine takes a sword*] Now, my brave warriors, fall in. [*They all form a line across stage. Zephna enters from room with a large helmet on and a shield and lance in his hand*]

ZEPH. Bless me, how fierce they do look. Shew me the man that can fight against them.

CLO. Fellow soldiers, are you all ready and willing to march against the enemy?

WOMEN. We are, we are.

ZEPH. Stop, stop—I've got this iron kettle tied so tight under my chin that I can't breathe. [*Unties it*] Now then, go ahead. I'll march in the rear and if anyone of 'em attempts to run away, I'll spear 'em with this lance. [*Noise without—distant*]

CLO. Hark! The enemy is in the field. Come, let's on, and by our deeds this day, immortalize our names. Right face—march! [*She places herself at the head and leads them to wing when a heavy discharge of cannon is heard. They all scream and hurry off. Upsetting Zephna in their confusion*]

ZEPH. [*Rising*] O Mahomet, there's pretty soldiers—run away at the first sound of the cannon. [*Cannon*] I think it's time I was off, too; I'll just hang this shield upon my back, so that if any gentleman should feel inclined to take aim at me, he won't lose his ammunition. [*Hangs shield on his back*] Now I'm ballproof as I shan't show them my face, so they'll only have my back to fire at. Here goes, and let 'em catch me if they can. [*Music. Runs off*]

SCENE 5: *Bay of Tripoli. The stage to represent the fortress; ramparts cross stage with guns pointed. A set tower on which is cannon; Sentinels, Soldiers, etc., at guns. The American fleet seen. They attack the fort, a general bombardment takes place. Soldiers of both parties enter fighting. Ali and Mahadi, at the same time, meet.*

MAHADI. Now do I touch thee, rebel, to thy heart.

ALI. Usurper, I defy thee, and Heaven defend the right. [*Music. They fight. Ali is disarmed and as Mahadi is about to dispatch him, Anderson rushes on and kills Mahadi*]

ANDER. This to thy heart. 'Tis thy slave has done the deed. A slave has power to strike a tyrant dead. [*Music. The battle becomes general. Jack Binnacle fights with Haccham, Sulieman with Abdallah. The ramparts are blown up and American Sailors are seen scaling the walls. Ali's party is victorious. Immorina is brought on by Sulieman. She goes to her father who clasps her in his arms. The American flag is hoisted and the band plays "Hail Columbia." Picture formed*]

CURTAIN

THE CROCK OF GOLD;
Or, THE TOILER'S TRIALS

Dramatized from the Popular Tale of
Martin F. Tupper, Esq., for the Boston Museum

By Silas S. Steele

THE CROCK OF GOLD;
Or, THE TOILER'S TRIALS

THE publication of *The Crock of Gold; or, The Toiler's Trials* makes available a popular play by an author hitherto represented by only one rare title. Silas S. Steele wrote more than two score acted plays and was for twenty years a popular figure, especially in the Philadelphia theatres. His *The Brazen Drum* was printed in 1841, and has remained the only evidence of his career as a dramatist.

Like most of his contemporary playwrights, Steele began as an actor, appearing first in his native Philadelphia in 1835 as Alonzo in *Pizarro*. He was not a very successful actor, but quickly won a reputation as a writer. His first play, *The Goatheads,* a burlesque melodrama, was privately performed in Philadelphia in 1836. Thereafter he turned out popular farces, burlesques, comic operas, and melodramas produced in Philadelphia, Boston, Baltimore, and London, though only occasionally in New York. His lack of fame in New York cannot be explained. Rees, in his *Dramatic Authors of America,* speaks very eulogistically of Steele, declares him the best of his kind, and sarcastically observes that "dollar-minded America" [New York?] failed to appreciate his special talents.

Steele was fond of music, of the sea, and of contemporary political and social themes. Many of his pieces are musical and operatic. In his treatment of nautical themes and characters, he won praise from the novelist Cooper. Many interesting items of history could probably be gleaned from the discovery of such lost plays of his as *Rhode Island; or, Who's the Governor?, The Battle of Tippecanoe,* and *The Lion of the Sea; or, Our Infant Navy.*

Steele's most popular plays included *The Brazen Drum, Stewart's Capture* (or *Stewart's Triumph*), and *The Crock of Gold; or, The Toiler's Trials. The Crock of Gold* differs from its author's customary type. It is a dramatization of Martin Tupper's popular tale of an "oppressed Laborer, the victim of Extortion and Temptation." The rather unusual manuscript of the play, from the Seymour Collection at Princeton University, divides the drama into four "parts," and includes a long program synopsis. The play is advertised as being made in this form especially for a Boston Museum production on June 2, 1858, "first time in 12 years." The cast printed in this volume is from the manuscript, but the original production of *The Crock of Gold* was on September 22, 1845, also at the Boston Museum. The rather heavy, sentimental plot is set in England. The most typical Steele touch seems to be the special emphasis on the "nautical" language of the comic character, Peter Perch.

A partial list of Steele's plays follows. A complete list must await the zeal of further investigators who may be able to pursue the identification of authors and titles. Steele's fate at the hands of posterity seems to have been especially severe, although it should be said that many of his less important efforts have probably reached a deserved oblivion. Some of his busiest years were spent in writing dramatic and operatic trifles for such groups as the "Ethiopian Opera" companies. He was active as a writer of operatic burlesques as late as 1857, when he wrote *Aladdin* for Buckley's Serenaders. These pieces and other burlesques are listed separately:

The Bank Monster; or, Specie vs. Shinplaster. Arch (Phila.), 1841.

The Battle of Tippecanoe. (Phila.), August 19, 1840.

The Brazen Drum; or, The Yankee in Poland. Arch (Phila.), January 27, 1841.

The Champion of Cordova. ("all the principal cities"—Rees.)

Clandare. Walnut (Phila.), March 10, 1838.

The Crock of Gold; or, The Toiler's Trials. Boston Museum, September 22, 1845.

Dandy Jim of Caroline.

The Dream; or, The Truth Unveiled. Boston Museum, November 17, 1845.

Emilie Plater, The Polish Heroine. Walnut (Phila.), May 20, 1845.

Fort La Mine; or, The Early Days of Zebulon Pike.

The Gold Bug; or, The Pirate's Treasure. Walnut (Phila.), August 8, 1843.

The Grecian Queen. (Phila.), 1844.

Kasran; or, The Crusades. Franklin (N.Y.), 1840.

Kassimbar. (Phila.), 1840.

King Henry VI; or, The Rebellion of Jack Cade. (Phila.), 1843.

The Lion of the Sea; or, Our Infant Navy. (Phila.), 1840.

The Matricide; or, The Cobbler Physician.

The Pauper's Festival. Arch (Phila.), 1843.

Philadelphia Assurance. Arch (Phila.), December 6, 1841.

The Rebellion in Canada; or, The Burning of the Caroline. National (Baltimore), 1841.

Rhode Island; or, Who's the Governor? Walnut (Phila.), 1842.

Stewart's Capture; or, The Captive's Ransom. Bowery (N.Y.), August 22, 1842 (and Philadelphia, 1842).

Truxtun's Victory; or, The Captive of the Mine. Front St. (Baltimore), November 24, 1840.
Washington and Napoleon; or, The Conqueror's Dream. 1841.
Washington's Challenge.

Some of Steele's burlesques were: *Aladdin, The Goatheads, St. Dollar and the Monster Ragon, Black Diabolo; or, The Inn at Terrapina, Post-Heel-On Ob Long Jaw Bone, Love and Hominy, Cinder-Nelly, Gazerre; or, The Doom of Shakespeare, Miss Alarmer; or, The Millerites at Darby, The Pill King, Stars and Comets, The Fawn's Leap, Spookwood, The Wench Spy,* and the extremely popular *A Night Down Town; or, De Toe Wins de Hand.*

(The following is reproduced from the playbill accompanying the manuscript.)

THIS WEDNESDAY AFTERNOON AND EVENING, JUNE 2, 1858

At 3 and 7½ o'clock
Performance will commence with the overture, Fra Diavolo
After which will be acted (1st times for 12 years),
the admirable drama in 4 parts, called the

CROCK OF GOLD; Or, THE TOILER'S TRIALS

SIR JOHN VINCENT, *heir of Hurstley Manor*	MR. F. WHITMAN
SIMON JENNINGS, *a steward, butler, bailiff and extortioner in all*	MR. J. DAVIES
JONATHAN FLOYD, *footman at Hurstley*	E. F. KEACH
M. VAUGHAN, *a magistrate*	J. H. RING
PETER PERCH, *a young fisherman*	WARREN
LORD SILLIPHANT	WALTON
HONORABLE C. SILKHAIR	J. WILSON
ROGER ACTON, *an oppressed laborer, the victim of extortion and temptation*	W. H. SMITH
BEN BURKE, *a poacher*	JOYCE
TOM ACTON, *son to Roger*	MISS M. THOMPSON
DICK, *the tanner*	WHEELOCK
OLD FLOYD	DELANO

SILAS S. STEELE

SNIP, *the landlord*	BURT
JOSEPH	NOLAN
MAYHEW	BAKER
BILLY ACTON	MISS C. THOMPSON
COUNTRYMEN, POLICE, SERVANTS, ETC.	
MRS. BRIDGET QUARLES, *housekeeper at Hurstley*	MRS. J. R. VINCENT
MARY ACTON, *Acton's second wife*	MISS ANDERSON
GRACE ACTON, *his daughter*	MISS R. SKERETT
SARAH SLACK	MRS. H. ECKHARDT
KITTY ACTON	LA PETITITE ANGELINA
ELLEN GRAY	MISS FREDRICKS
POLLY WHITE	MISS MASON
JUNE GOSSIP	MISS E. WRIGHT
VILLAGERS	MRS. WRIGHT MISS TURNER MISS EVANS, ETC.

NOTE: This cast is inaccurate in several respects. Ellen Gray and Polly White do not appear in the play as here given. Mayhew is apparently Mynton, M. Vaughan apparently the judge, and June Gossip is actually Jane Gossip.

PROGRAMME OF SCENERY AND INCIDENTS

PART I, SCENE I: Room at Hurstley Hall. Love and gossip. The aunt and nephew. Secret receptacle of ill-gotten wealth. Novel money safe. Charity versus selfishness. The honey crock. Secret design of the cunning steward. Beware, man, beware—Crime leads to crime. SCENE 2: Interior of cottage. The toiler's home. The cotter's return from labor. The wife's ill temper. Reproaches of the sorrowful husband. Poverty and despair. The ray of light! Religious feeling of poor Grace. The thirst for gold. The divine commandment, "Thou shalt not steal." SCENE 3: Room at Hurstley. Darkness visible; the missing bailiff; "My nephew, my poor child." The alarm! The search! The scandal! SCENE 4: Housekeeper's bedchamber; concealment of the villainous steward. The thief betrayed; what's to be done? Awful alternative! Mammon leads to murder! Struggle for life. Loss of the "Crock of Gold"—the murderer escapes! PART 2,* SCENE I: The toiler's home. Departure for labor. The daughter's consolation; the father's misery. The toil is grievous, and the peace long a coming. SCENE 2: Exterior of cottage. The honest fisherman. 'Tis a holiday, they're drinking like fish, swimming in a sea of good things. "Come, there might be hope yet in my dream of the crock of gold." SCENE 3: Exterior of Hurstley Hall. Gentlemen carousing; the drinking bout. The gamblers! The fight! The temptation. THE FIRST THEFT! SCENE 4: Landscape. Conscience and the last guinea. "I thought it were that plaguing gold, and it's only a button!" The baronet's gift. The bailiff's theft. "Rob not the poor." The denouncement; the discharge. SCENE 5: The cottage. The toiler's second trial; the poacher's story; the housekeeper's shawl. The dream of temptation! The finding of the crock of gold.

PART 3, SCENE I: The cottage. Does money confer happiness? Dissipation and its consequence. "Where shall I hide my money?" The daughter's grief. Woe in the crock of gold. SCENE 2: Chamber in Hurstley Hall. The steward and his pursuing fiend; conscience! conscience! The lover's quarrel and reconciliation. The calumny! SCENE 3: The toiler's attic. The bailiff on the scent of his blood-bought horde. Jennings's demand of restitution. The struggle

* The division of scenes in "Part 2" above does not correspond to the actual division of scenes in the play itself. "Scene 4" above approximates the fourth and fifth scenes of the play; "Scene 5" above includes approximately the material of Scene 7, while Scene 6 in the play is not described above.

with the finder; discovery of the crock of gold! "Grace was right, it was a friend after all." The charge of murder! The arrest! Tableau.

PART 4, SCENE 1: Landscape. Consultation of the village wiseacres; the arrest for poaching; the license. Peter Perch on the right side. "Where were you on the night of Mrs. Quarles's death?" Rage and fear of Jennings. SCENE 2: The prison. Acton confined on the charge of murder. The comfort of the BOOK. Woman's love! REPENTANCE AND HOPE. "Remember the words that were not written in vain." SCENE 3: Country view near Hurstley. The hypocrite and his intended prey. Crime still engenders crime. She is never helpless who trusts in Heaven. The plot! The surprise! The capture! SCENE 4: Chamber at Hurstley. The true and false gentleman. Discharge of Jennings. His insolence. The imprecation and departure. SCENE 5: Hurstley Court House. The examination. The defense. The doubt! The timely witness! Power of conscience! The innocent free. Death of the murderer. Tableau.

ACT I.

SCENE I: *A plain antique chamber in Hurstley Hall. In C. a tea table, set for two persons. An old-fashioned chair beside table. Sarah Slack discovered at table looking over articles.*

SARAH. Yes, all's right, all's ready but the punch. That they won't want till after tea, or they might get tea'd before supper. Bless me! I do wonder what this private party of two, Aunt Bridget Quarles and her nephew, Mr. Simon Jennings the butler, can all mean? Can't be anything wrong about Hurstley—I'm all right—little Peter Perch, the young fisherman, got in and out without being seen. [*Seats herself in chair*] Oh! Sweet little Perch! Now how much nicer it would be, if instead of this fretful, fidgety faultfinding couple, little Peter and *me* were going to be this private tea party of two! When we could sit, and talk to each other—drink to each other—look in our cups—[*During this, Peter Perch enters, and steals into the chair opposite*] Look into our lots—and then look into each other's eyes. [*Here she looks up, sees Peter, jumps up, and screams*]

PETER. [*Imitating her*] Sa-a-arah!

SARAH. Why, what in the world brings you here at this time, mister fisherman?

PETER. Why, business in my line, to be sure. I've just brought some fish to the mansion, for young Sir John; and thought mayhap you'd like some for your tea—there they be, Sally, fresh as the rain, bouncing about for their nat'ral element, like that little heart o' yourn for its dear Peter Perch—their gills as red as your own sweet lips, and—

SARAH. There, there, please to take up that long line o' your tongue. I've other fish to fry just now. Aunt Bridget and her nephew, Mr. Jennings, are coming to take tea in this room, and talk together, and so you must be off, Mr. Perch, or the butler will have us both in his net, as you say.

PETER. What! Jennings! That black fish, with the very red and blue gills?

SARAH. Why Peter! Peter Perch! Shame on you, Peter! How dare you give the pious Mr. Simon such scaly names! You see then, I'm watching all your queer fish talk. Bless me! After a bit I shall be taken for a fisheress!

PETER. Well, you see that this Mr. Simon Jennings, butler—bailiff—bulldog—and everything, with the impudence of a sturgeon wanted to make me pay him a license for the liberty of fishing in the free streams of the country.

SARAH. Did you pay him, Peter?

PETER. For fishing? Yes, with a hook! He next threatened to fine me for selling my fish to my own customers, instead of letting him have 'em for half price, or no price, for his all-supplying—all-cheating—extortion shop here in the village.

SARAH. Did you pay the fine, Peter?

PETER. Yes, with a rod! Well, he next threatened to bring an action against me for promoting "wagrancy" as I think he called it—for sending honest Roger Acton a free bait, or a mess, I should say, of fresh fish for his family.

SARAH. What! Steady Acton, as they call him across the lawn here.

PETER. The same; poor, pious, and industrious Roger Acton—a fry as far above the pike Jennings, as the sky's above water—a little rough about the scales, but a pure goldfish within.

SARAH. And you *did* send 'em the fish, Peter?

PETER. I did—two messes, and I fairly mesmerized all the little Actons with fresh perch, in spite of the angry pike; and I'll do it again as often as I like.

SARAH. No doubt they'll like it often, and so shall I, and like you all the better. Oh! What a dear-hearted little Perch you are! The very prince of fishermen, walking right in the footsteps of Peter, the fisherman of old.

PETER. Thank ye, Sally, but you haven't got the length o' my line yet.

SARAH. Well, make haste, there's a dear little perch!

PETER. Well, you must know that just afore honest Roger caught his second wife, who I am sorry to tell seems a little touch of the carp, he, poor man having no one to take care of his two little children while at work and rather than let 'em wear the pauper's scales, used to carry 'em in his arms to the field with him—and one day I saw the poor half-naked little minnows shivering on a bank in Sir John's meadow, while poor Roger sat feeding 'em with a few crusts softened only by the raindrops from his eyes, and I tell you, Sally, I felt like a choking trout with a hook, and a chunk of bait in its throat—eh? what's the matter, Sally?

SARAH. [*Rubbing her neck*] Oh! I've got the cramp in my windpipe— what a strong line that is, Peter!

BRIDG. [*Within*] Sarah!

PETER. A catfish!

SARAH. There! There! Go—go—or we're caught!

PETER. But there's more line, Sally.

SARAH. Cut it short, and run out—and come again, Peter!

BRIDG. Sarah, is the tea ready?

SARAH. Yes, ma'am—go!

BRIDG. Is the punch ready?

SARAH. Yes, ma'am. [*Pounding Peter*]

PETER. Punch! I think it is. [*Rubbing his side*]

BRIDG. Sarah, is the rock fish ready?

SARAH. Yes, ma'am, it's coming—now, Perch, go—or we're hooked!

PETER. [*Attempting to kiss her*] One nibble.

SARAH. [*Pushing him off*] With a hook!

PETER. [*Kissing her*] Yes, well baited.

SARAH. Oh! That was a whole bite. [*Exit Peter*] Ha! Here they come! Bless me! Who'd 'a thought all this wickedness of Mr. Simon Jennings? Well, I'll mark, and be mum, or I might stir up a fire to burn my own bread. It's better to keep a still tongue than to go with an empty stomach. [*Exit. Enter Bridget, neatly dressed, followed by Simon Jennings bowing to her, with a sanctimonious air; he places chair for her*]

BRIDG. Thanky nephy. [*Aside*] Dear soul it is! [*Aloud*] Take a seat.

JEN. [*Sitting*] Ha! Thank you, Aunt Bridget. Ah! Dearest aunt, how kind you have been to me—nay, how kind you still are, the image of my poor mother. [*Gazing in her face and taking out pocket handkerchief*] You have proved a second mother to me, and let me ever pay true reverence to her memory in my filial duty to you.

BRIDG. Dear, obedient child! This affection quite flusters my narvous sensibiliousness. Sarah! Bring up the rock fish and the punch, child. [*She pours out the tea*] Yes, nephy, weak woman as I am, I take the honor to myself of having made a man of you. [*They commence drinking tea*]

JEN. True generous aunt, you have raised me from a servant at Hurstley to be butler—bailiff—overseer of the estate, and chief officer of the household, while you have profitably managed as chief housekeeper, governess, and— [*Enter Sarah with the plate and punch, which she places on table*]

BRIDG. That's right, Sarah, the punch, eh? You may recreate yourself for the balance of the evening in purifying the coolenaries of the kitchen.

SARAH. [*Aside*] "The coolenaries of the kitchen." Oh, dear! Aunt Bridget's been spelling in the Jonsonary again. [*Exit Sarah. Jennings helps Bridget to fish, etc.*]

BRIDG. Yes, nephy, we are indeed in comfortable and lucre-tive quarters, with a few nest eggs put by, as the saying is.

JEN. Yes, aunt, and a pretty golden nest you have made and feathered, all this while—five hundred at least, I'll wager. Come, aunt—done for a shilling!

BRIDG. Ha! Get along, you sly one, you! Ain't you one of the tribe of Sodom to think of this. Ha, ha, ha!

JEN. No, aunt, nor of Solomon either.

BRIDG. Sodomon! Ah! 'Twas him I meant. I won't say my nest has not a feather, nephy—nor that there's not a golden egg in it—ha, ha, ha! It is easy work for us, nephy—we shave, we bleed, in couples—you the men, and I the maids, eh? Ha, ha, ha!

JEN. I get the start of you, though you were born a week beforehand. Talk of parsons, look at me! A regular grand pluralist, monopolist, and miscellaneous extortioner—butler indoors, bailiff out-of-doors, land steward, house steward, cellar man, and paymaster—and I am not all these for naught, Aunt Quarles. If so much goes through my fingers, it is but fair and natural that something should stick, eh?

BRIDG. If you come to boasting, my boy, [*Showing large bunch of keys and shaking them*] I don't carry this bunch of keys for quite nothing, neither —lord love you! Why merely for cribbing in the linen line; in one month John Draper swopped me this here costly shawl—none of my clothes have cost me one penny, and I'm not as bare as a newborn goose egg, neither— look at them trunks, [*Pointing L.*] will you, nephy. Ha, ha, ha! [*Both drink*]

JEN. Aye, aye, I'll be bound that the printer of your prayerbook left out the word *not* before steal in the Ten Commandments.

BRIDG. What? Nephy! *Steal!* Why, Simon, that's a most libelious word— fie, Simon! Them's not stealing, them's only perquisites. Where's the honesty of living in a great house, and seeing so much go to waste and run the risk of coming to want. It would be sinful proudigality but haven't struck out *not* from steal—to steal for naught, nephy?

JEN. Me steal? Not I, not I, aunt—all sheer honesty.

BRIDG. Or honesty with the shears, eh?

JEN. No, honesty and industry, aunt. Look at my little truck shop down in the village—woe betide the laborer who leaves off dealing there. Not one that works at Hurstley but eats my bacon and barley however mouldy, and they must pay my price for it, too, or quit eating. [*Both drink again and laugh. Aside*] Now then, to find out where the old gal keeps her money. [*Aloud*] My only trouble, aunt, is where to keep my gains, or what to do with them. [*Eagerly*] Now, aunt, merely for the sake of instruction, where do you really keep all your money, eh?

BRIDG. Ha, ha, ha! I know a trifle better than that, a hand to get, and a head to keep, nephy.

JEN. Now I daresay you keep it in your workbox or sew it up in your stays, or perhaps hided in your teapot—[*Eyeing her very closely*] or perhaps—

BRIDG. Oh! You wise sarpent! You little rogue, when you have money to put by, come to Aunt Bridget for a crock to hide it in, a honey crock for a hive of gold! Ha, ha, ha!

JEN. [*Aside*] My golden stars! Is it possible? [*Aloud*] And so, my mentor of an aunt, you—[*Looking and pointing L.*] you hoard up and hide your gold there with the preserves, in a honey crock, do you? Precious preserves indeed!

BRIDG. Ha, ha! Well, nephy, we'll see, we'll see. Not that the money's to be yours—you're rich enough and don't want it—I have always remembered the poor a little, and I won't forget 'em when I die. And there's your poor sister Scott, with her fourteen children, and Aunt Bridget must take care of them, must give her a trifle to help her along in life. She was a good niece to me, Simon, and she never left my side before she married. And she shall have cause to bless the dead. A charitable name is better than a rich coffin, nephy. [*Rising*]

JEN. What! Give it all *her*—[*Aside*] first—I'll—

BRIDG. There, nephy, we'll talk of this another time. Bless me, it's almost night, and I must look to the house, and the maids. So finish the punch, Simon, and look to your men. Ha, ha, ha! Remember the honey crock, nephy —ah! Ha, ha! [*Exit chuckling*]

JEN. [*After seeing her to wing and bowing*] The honey crock! Yes, I *will* remember it. And so, Aunt Bridget, after all my cares, my feigned and affectionate attentions, my smiles of congratulation at the success of your dark schemes—are all rewarded with, "You are rich enough and do not want it." All my decoys, my toils and aid, go to reward my Methodistic sister, Scott. So vast a sum, too—the earnings and extortions of at least fifty years. But how can I possess this glorious hoard and no thanks to the old witch yonder? Steal it? Good! I can—I will—I'll conceal myself in her room. There's a shower bath there which has not been used for years. It merely contains a few cloaks and may easily hold me. Blessed stars! It locks inside, too. There can I hide, and watch the old cat to sleep, take the keys of her cupboard, and bear off the hoard—the precious gold. No one will see—no one suspect me. Ha, ha, ha! Glorious thought! [*Pacing stage*] I move, I breathe in an ecstasy of hope! 'Tis mine! This night, the honey crock—the precious crock of gold! [*Exit hastily. Clear stage*]

SCENE 2: *Interior of Acton's cottage. In R. front a shattered casement partially shrouded with vine, or liverwort. At L. of window, a ladder-like staircase leading to an upper apartment. On L. of stage a rude cupboard, on shelves of which are articles of unmatched crockery, some of which are broken, and a few tins. On the lower shelf is an unshapely loaf of brown bread and some country cheese, etc. On R. of stage a rude fireplace and mantelpiece, over which is a print of "The Prodigal Son," and the Christmas Carol, busts of Albert and Victoria. A large black boiler is hanging in the fireplace over a dim peat fire. On the window sill is an old Bible, a few tracts, and a loaf of white bread. Near the ceiling is hooked an old fowling piece, by which a rope of onions is suspended. The walls of cottage are decorated with rude prints, "The Sailor's Return," "Death of Nelson," "May Fair," etc. The furniture consists of an old triangular tri-legged table and two old rush bottom chairs, a small bench by window, and an old stool by fire. On the floor a few yards of matting. Music. Mary Acton enters. She stirs up the fire. Her manner is restless and disconsolate.*

MARY. Heigho! Three years of marriage and three years of misery, and with little prospect save for the worse. 'Twas well enough to marry Roger—for though poor and an ill provider, he has a good heart—but to be tied to his impudent, unruly children is too much. [*Calls*] Grace! Off again and without asking me. [*Goes to door*] You Grace! Where are you?

GRACE. [*Without*] Here, mother! [*She enters*] Do you want me, mother?

MARY. Want you? To be sure I want you! And that's the very time you're not near me.

GRACE. Why, bless you, mother, I had done all the work, put the little children to bed, kissed them to sleep, and stepped out but for a moment to see if father was returning from work. See, it's past his usual hour.

MARY. Always after your father, Miss Grace. You think a great deal more of him than of me, girl—when he does so poorly, too—for all my talking to him. It's no wonder I'm neglected, so it aint. [*Sobbing*]

GRACE. Ah, now, dear mother, such talk is really cruel, when you know that I would willingly do anything in the world for you. I am sure that I have never given you a harsh or irreverent word. I have never refused to assist or to obey you in every duty due from a child to its parent, and yet you accuse me of neglect. [*Half sobbing*] Well, although you may still reproach me, mother, you shall never have cause to say that I ever omitted any act of affection or consolation to relieve and cheer your hard and lowly lot. [*A sound of implements is heard at door. It opens. Roger Acton places his spade and mattock at door and enters. Grace runs up and embraces him, with the fondest affection. Mary keeps her position rather sullenly*] Dear father!

ACTON. Ha! Grace! My young rosebush. [*Kissing her*]

GRACE. Why, the sun has set this hour, father.

ACTON. Aye, but he shines still in your face, my girl. [*Kissing her again. He gives her his hat, and provision wallet. She hangs them up at the side of cupboard. He is speaking as he takes them off*] Where's Tom, Grace?

Tom. [*At door*]   Here I am, father! [*Enter Tom with a basket of peat on his shoulder. Roger lifts it off*] See father, what a load of peat I've brought.

Acton. [*Kissing and patting him*]   Ha, ha! A good boy! A man! [*Tom takes basket to fireside and empties it. Grace commences setting the table. Roger, with an air of suppressed melancholy, crosses to Mary and touches her on the shoulder*]

Mary. [*Sullenly*]   I hope you have brought something, too, Roger, instead of bad luck and hard times.

Acton.   What! Moll Acton, girl—is this a poor husband's cheer after twelve hours of hard labor and two miles' travel? A bad balsam for wearied limbs and blistered hands I trow! Dang it wench, isn't there deep water enough in our big sea of poverty, but you must still be dropping into it, from eyes, too, that used to be all sunny. Well, well, I know your lot is a hard one, but the sweat of the eye is a poor reward for the sweat of the brow. [*Sits down, L. of table*]

Mary.   True, Roger Acton, but it is time you were doing a little better, so it is.

Acton. [*Springing up suddenly*]   Why, you are right, Moll, it *is* time. These toil-worn hands, these roan locks, and bending shoulders tell as plainly as yourself it is time. And I will do something better than toil for misery, but how? [*Sinks into chair again*] Fool! Fool! Impious fool, Acton! The laborer cannot make his tools; he can only use 'em. Man can't make means, he can only use such as be given him. Mary Acton, you reproach me, and make me reproach providence. Till late, poor Roger Acton, mid all his toils and trials, was a patient, pious man, still hoping for the reward promised by his divine employer. I said to myself, "Well, if things don't go right here, why, they'll all come right hereafter." If poor in purse, I was rich in hope. What if poverty did pinch me, I was still a great heir. [*Looking up*] What if extortion robbed me? *There* said I, would I be repaid with interest, and while this hope smiled upon my sunburnt brow, and peace welcomed me home, I cared not for backbreaking toil, for I felt that I worked for another master, whose reward was bounty without end. But, after all—[*Looks at Mary and leans on back of chair*]

Grace. [*Quickly*]   "Buts" are doubts. Hope still, and pray. Remember, father, the Scriptures say, "The effectual fervent prayer of the righteous man availeth much." Elias prayed, and the Heavens gave rain and earth brought forth her fruit.

Acton.   But it's hard, very hard that—

Mary.   Hush, unless you can pray us gold! We can't feed our children on hopes and prayers.

ACTON. But there's something in kind words and looks, Mary, that sweeten a child's crust if it be ever so hard—something that makes a morsel to it better than a feast, gives comfort to his little heart. Why look you, woman, when poor Anne Acton—Heaven be her home—died and left me a breaking heart, and these two children, then infants like your own, I was their only mother, only nurse—and little time for such soft cares has he whose toil is the field from light to dark, but when rich neighbors, with a chilly air of charity, came to feast them with their luxuries, they followed me like little lambs into the fields, and preferred sharing my cold and scanty meal, from nature's stony table, to all the tempting dainties of a castle. My girl, as if a tender word, or a look, or smile—or playful pat o' the hand were a feast of feeling that came to their motherless hearts—[*They cling to him, and kneel*] like rain on wilted roses. Remember, Mary, these cheering feasts of tenderness cost no toil nor money. They're free as Heaven's air if the heart be right, and yet you cannot spare them; but you cry "Food, food!" while your little children cry only for a mother's looks, and a mother's soothing smile.

MARY. [*Stamping and endeavoring to turn a natural burst of feeling into that of rage*] Roger Acton! You'd—you'd break my heart—so you would!

ACTON. No, no, I'd only *open* it, my girl.

GRACE. There, there, father and mother, peace, I implore you! Peace can make wealth of poverty. Come, sit down and share our homely meal, and Heaven will bless it!

ACTON. It's hard that an honest and industrious man cannot pick a living out of this rich earth that Heaven made for him. And, after all is said, let the parson preach as he will, it's a fine thing to have money, or he would not look so closely after his dues. [*He droops disconsolately*] Ah! Without gold in the pocket, the heart's lead!

GRACE. O father, look up! Look upon us!

ACTON. [*Starting up*] Look upon you! No! I must look for gold—gold—see there—a dark and greedy spirit rises and cries "Bring me gold! There's no peace, nor rest, nor home without it!" She turns my little children into hungry imps, that scream in my ears for gold! Yes! I will have it! I'll rob from the robber! You, master Jennings! You! [*Catching at vacancy, then starts suddenly back*] No! No! A solemn voice, more piercing than the rest, cries out "Thou shalt not steal!" [*Drops on his knees*] Forgive me, Heaven, forgive me! [*Grace and Tom kneel beside him as scene closes*]

SCENE 3: *An entry, or a narrow passage in Hurstley Hall. Lights down. Music. Enter Jennings cautiously and very pale, with his neckcloth off, and in his stocking feet.*

JEN. Now's the only time—the old hag is scolding in the kitchen. Now then, to get into her bedroom unperceived—then to feel my way into the shower bath, and hide till she sleeps. This way [*Going to L. Enter Sarah Slack*] Confusion! Who's that coming? Down! Down! or I am discovered! [*He stoops very low, and gropes along*]

SARAH. Bless me! How very dark this entry is! Who'd a thought it was so late? I just slipped upstairs to get rid of Mrs. Quarles's evening scold, and ugly Simon Jennings's horrid civilities, and—

JEN. [*Aside*] Ha! Jade! [*Stifling his rage*]

SARAH. Oh, what's that? I really saw a voice!

JEN. [*Aside*] Perdition! How shall I escape her. Down! Down!

SARAH. I'm sure I did, and 'twas like Mr. Simon's. I almost believe he has a double, for the nasty cur is everywhere. Oh! Let me get out of this. [*They grope their way toward each other*] I hope the little wretch won't come near me again. [*They come close together. He dodges under arm which she holds out to feel her way, and exit*] Bless my heart! What a strong breeze runs through this entry. It fairly tickled my arm like a sweeping brush. Ha! Now I'm safe. There's the kitchen stairway. I thought I heard a ghost but I didn't. I wasn't going to get frightened and raise the whole house for nothing, and be called a cowardess forever after—not I. [*Runs out quickly, after looking behind her*]

BRIDG. [*Within*] Come along, Sarah, come everybody! [*Enter sobbing, followed by Jonathan Floyd and Servants, male and female, with lights*] Poor nephy! My poor dear Simon! Where can he be? Search the house from top to bottom—parlor, kitchen, pantry, buttery—look in the garden. [*To Coachman*] Joseph, return to the coach house, dear child.

JOS. Yes, ma'am. [*Aside*] Wish I mayn't find him though. [*Exit*]

BRIDG. [*To Ostler*] Dick, you look in the stables.

DICK. Yes, ma'am. [*Aside*] Hope he's kicked to death! [*Exit*]

BRIDG. And girls, you look everywhere. Poor boy!

GIRLS. Yes, ma'am. [*They run off L. Lights down*]

BRIDG. And Jonathan Floyd! Oh, dear!

JONA. Madam, don't fret yourself so much, he may possibly be near us all the while, but I will make every search, madam. I wouldn't lose Mr. Jennings for the world!

BRIDG. Nor I, for he's a world of a boy to me, Jonathan. Fly, Jonathan! Fly! [*Exit Jonathan*] Poor—[*Sobbing*] little nephy! Oh, dear! My sensibilious state is coming on again. I am not long for this world! [*Exit, sobbing*]

SCENE 4: *Bridget's bedroom. Bedsteps, R. Toilette table, R. of bed. A neatly made bed, on a low and old-fashioned bedstead at C. On L. of bed a shower bath, with a door, lock and key, etc. A cloak and one or two articles of apparel hung up in bath. On R. of bed, a narrow cupboard with doors and key. On the upper shelf are six small honey jars or stone crocks, the mouth of each secured by a bladder tied over it. In the middle crock a number of gold pieces, covered with buckskin, à la button. On middle shelf is a tin money box with a hole in the top, and marked "Savings Bank," a few pieces of metal in it, sufficient to make a rattle. At L., a door, leading to an apartment. On R., opposite, a high-set door, and a window looking upon the lawn. In C. of room, a small table, a couple of chairs, washstand, etc., near the bed. Lights down. Music. Jennings is discovered L., grasping the door of the shower bath and listening, and watching L. door with intense anxiety.*

JEN. So far, safe—so far sure—here's the old shower bath in which I can safely watch all of her movements and learn where the precious crock is hidden. How cold it is! Cannot the heat of hope and impatience keep off these shaking chills? How long must I remain here before she sleeps? Ha! I see a light. Blessed stars! She comes! [*Enter Bridget with candle, sobbing and wringing her hands. Lights up*]

BRIDG. Oh, Simon! Simon! Dear boy! Gone—nowhere to be found! Oh! He was, I fear, too smart and useful to live long—just forty tomorrow—to die before he lived to see that day, poor boy! I thought he was ill at tea. He stared and questioned so wildly—seemed consarned for the safety of his money, and even for mine, too. Ah! Well, his father died in the lunacy 'sylum. Well, my only comfort now is in my poor niece Scott and her little ones. My dear, dear crock! [*Goes toward closet*] Yes, I must—

JEN. [*Eagerly*] Ha! The closet, eh?

BRIDG. Eh? Bless me, what's that? [*She shuts the door, looks about, under bed, etc.*] I really heard a—a—something—it's in the shower bath. [*Goes to it and turns the handle*] Oh, drat it! That Sarah has taken away the key. Well, can't be anything in there, a mouse maybe has pulled one of the cloaks down. Now, then, to look at my darling, my crock. [*Gets on chair at closet, unlocks and opens the door. Jennings peeps out with tremulous eagerness from bath*] Ha! Ha! Come down, my dear Narbonne! Come down, my honey. How near the boy guessed, poor child! If he don't come, I must hunt up *his* bank tomorrow. [*Gets down and goes to table with the middle crock, cuts up a piece of glove, takes off cover of crock*] Ha! ha! There you are. [*Hugs it*] Beauties, all safe!

JEN. [*Aside*] Ha! The glorious prize—the crock. Oh! Tortuous suspense. I've a mind to seize upon the hoard, and fly straight to America. But, no, no, couldn't leave my heavy box behind—my hat, my shoes. Besides, I might alarm and raise the house. Quick, quick! Old hen, to your roost! [*Slight rain and thunder at intervals. Bridget takes out a piece of gold from her pocket, and commences sewing it in the buckskin or gloved finger*]

BRIDG. Ah, Mr. Scrub, you thought to put me off with a crown piece, but this had to come, or you would have dealt no more at Hurstley. There! [*Throws it into the crock*] Join your brother yellow boys! Ha! Sweet dumbies! [*Covering the crock*] No sound! [*Going to closet*] Oh, Bridget knows how to keep money. [*Putting it on shelf*] No telltale jingling, no wearing away the precious stuff.

JEN. [*Aside*] Glorious thought! Thank you, old girl, for that. [*She drops a piece of copper in the "Savings Bank"*]

BRIDG. There, that's to cheat thieves if they should come. They'll take the tin and copper, and never think o' the crocks. Ha, ha, ha! [*Having locked the closet, she goes to head of bed, and commences undressing. She places her shawl on table and then returns*] Ha, ha, ha! Simon was right—that punch was putting in a good night's rest. My head feels as heavy as a water bucket, and my eyes are beginning to glue themselves already. [*Nodding*] I shall be asleep before I can get into bed—if I'm not quick—now then [*Gets in*], goo-good—n-night, my crock, and my gold—[*Falls over, and snores loudly. Jennings peeps and gradually comes from bath. Blows out candle. Lights down*]

JEN. She's gone at last. Now then—luckily she left the key in the closet door. [*Goes to closet on tiptoe, unlocks cupboard, feels on shelf*] Ha! Here they are! Like the jars of the "Forty Thieves" but the thief's without instead of within. One, two, six of them—but which contains the hoard? All alike— confusion! I shall have to take all, a load, a sackful! Well, it's worth a tug to be certain of the store. [*Takes crocks and puts them on the table*] Stop. There's something more—the savings bank she spoke of. [*Goes back to cupboard*] Ha! Here it is! A tin—no doubt half full of silver—precious prize! Joyous moment! But how to carry them all? [*His hand accidentally touches shawl*] Ha! Lucky chance, this shawl! The shawl! Quick, quick! She moves —[*The money in the box is heard to rattle in his agitation*] and may awaken! She stirs—quick! [*Rain and thunder. Trembling*] Perdition! How weak I grow. It's growling conscience crying "Restore! Fly! Save yourself ere 'tis too late!" What! And lose the crock of gold? Never. [*Biting his nails nervously. He has reached the door. Bridget, having been aroused by the last and emphatic exclamation, springs from her bed as a flash of lightning betrays him to her*]

BRIDG. Murder! Thieves! Fire! My gold! Nephew Jennings, is that you with my honey pots? Help! Help! Murder! [*Seizes him*]

JEN. Death! She'll alarm the house and ruin me. Hang me! *She* shall choke first, then! [*Seizes her by the throat. She screams and fights furiously, clutching him also by the throat. He endeavors to choke her and stop her mouth with his fist, etc. They struggle about the stage with desperation. In the course of the strife, Jennings gets hold of the shawl, and backing her against the bedpost, winds it around her neck and over her face, and finally stops her utterance. She ceases struggling, and being apparently strangled, he makes an effort to throw her on the bed. She falls, her hand striking on one of the crocks. She grasps it convulsively, and makes an effort to speak. He again chokes her. She makes an audible gasp or gurgle and drops prostrate by the bed. Jennings ties up the crocks in the shawl in tremulous haste, and rushes to the R. door*] Fly! Quick! To the lake! The punt! Stop! If any should wake, and enter the room? Aunt Bridget's dead! How did she die? In a fit. I have it! Glorious thought! I'm saved! [*He puts down bundle, raises the body, and with a desperate effort places it in the bed*] Death's a heavy weight to the murderer's arms, but what to his soul! No matter now—there! [*Composing her limbs and smoothing the bedclothes*] No marks. A fit has killed her. [*Picking up bundle*] Now then, the pond hide the crock of gold! [*Rain and thunder. At door*] Confusion. The day I fear is breaking! Quick! Now to hide my prize, then back again to bed, and I'm safe! [*Music. He looks back an instant. Hurstley clock commences striking four. At the first stroke he rushes wildly out as the drop falls slowly at the stroke of the bell*]

ACT II.

SCENE 1: *The cottage of Acton as before. Table, C., with wallet on it with some provision in it. Slight rain heard. Acton is seen, slowly descending the stairs with an air and look of extreme despondency. He puts on his hat, frock, etc. during speech.*

ACTON. Yes, day is breaking, and I must be gone. Sir John's meadow lies two long miles off, and Master Jennings shows no favor to a man that's late. The loss of a quarter of a day is a heavy paring from my poor pittance. Poor flock! They're all asleep. I took my morning's cup o' comfort in a kiss, all round, and my heart feels a little lighter. I had a dream, too—a dream of luck and a crock of gold—a morning dream. But habit, that's everybody's master, waked me up betimes to toil and disappointment. Well, well, maybe it will come out. [*Going to door*] I nearly forgot my wallet. [*Goes to table and takes it*] Yes, here's my little fare put in overnight by careful Grace— poor, dear little heart. But I'm glad she sleeps after her last night's trouble.

Well, well, when I look at her and think of her, I sometimes fancy there are more angels than what are blessed in Heaven. [*Goes to door. Grace descends staircase hastily with a prayer book in her hand*]

GRACE. A happy morning, father.

ACTON. [*Kissing her*] Ah, I wish it were, good Grace. I wish that— [*Pauses and places his hand to his brow, then turns to door*]

GRACE. But must you go so soon, dear father.

ACTON. Aye, *must*, Grace. That's the only word with the poor toiler. [*Seizes his spade*]

GRACE. But there's still comfort here, father. [*Reads*] "The sufferings of the present time are not worthy to be compared with the glory of—"

ACTON. Enough, enough, my girl. Heaven wot but the sufferings are grievous, and the glory long, long a coming. [*Rushes out of door*]

GRACE. [*Bursting into tears and turning toward the table*] Heaven! Heaven help him. [*Sinks into chair, her face in her hands, sobbing violently as scene closes*]

SCENE 2: *Exterior of Acton's cottage. A low and dark thatched tenement. The time is in the month of March, and the dwelling partially covered with dead vines and creeping plants of summer. In the near distance, a small lake and island, near which on a smooth eminence, studded with trees, walks, statues, etc., sloping to the water's edge, stands Hurstley Hall, a large Elizabethan mansion with mullioned windows, pinnacles, high-peaked roof, etc. The back surrounding grounds consist of clipped hedges, terraced gardens, etc. Acton enters with his spade on his shoulder, and provision wallet slung to his side.*

ACTON. Fool! Wretch! To leave her so. I have no time to listen to her now. [*Looks at cottage*] Ah, what a dreary bed for such a flower to bloom in. And yonder, as if smiling at our wretched hovel, stands young Sir John's rich mansion. Yet I don't covet its wealth. I want no castle—all I want is comfort. That I toiled for, prayed for, but all in vain. And what more can I do than toil and pray? Nothing. 'Tis all that an honest man should do. [*Musing in a state of abstraction. Enter Peter Perch, with a fishing rod and basket*]

PETER. Hook me, if there isn't Steady Acton ready for his hard daily toil, but with his head hanging like a dipsy. Ha! Mr. Acton—a good morning to you, and all your sweet little fishes, heads, bones, fins and all.

ACTON. Ah, Peter, my noble lad, good day. But we are before you— gratitude is an early riser, and, my friend, an angel's prayer went up for you before the day broke.

PETER. Eh? Prayers for me? How? Untangle that line.

ACTON. Why, you'll think, I hope, Peter, that the needy have hearts as well as wants; and no one has a more grateful one than poor Roger Acton, or his daughter Grace.

PETER. Oh! Odds bites and nibbles! You doesn't mean to say that that little sunfish prayed for poor Perch and all on account o' them few—oh, bless her sweet little gills. I'm just on my way to the pond for my morning's fishing. If she has prayed for me, won't I have luck! I'll catch such a mess for her, and you, and all. [*Going*] Come, Mr. Acton, down with that worm-cuttin', back-breakin' spade and along with me to see how I'll hook 'em out.

ACTON. Ah! If we could but fish up a little o' this world's blessings—this world's idol—gold—gold—I would go with you.

PETER. Gold, Mr. Acton?

ACTON. Yes, Peter, money! That's what all fish for. The old saying's true —"*Money makes the mare go.*"

PETER. Yes, but it often makes her carry her rider to the old boy. But come, I'll give you all a nice bite o' fry. Come!

ACTON. No, no, I must to the meadow, to my hard task—dig—dig—[*Aside*] in despair.

PETER. What! Leads and dipsies, man! Break the earth before you break your fast? Nonsense—come, come. [*Pulling him*] Why, this is a holiday this morning. His worship's clock struck twenty-one, and last night at his little private mansion, he and some of the goldfish, or rather frog fish, o' the city, began a jolli-grogification. I passed along there last night on my way to the "Great Grey Tug" yonder. [*Pointing to castle*] I took a peep in, and saw 'em drinking like fish and swimming in a sea of good things. I tell you, man, it is a holiday.

ACTON. Aye, but there's no holiday with Master Jennings. Besides, there's no holiday for a heart laboring with pain and oppression.

PETER. Hang oppression, and that black beetle, Jennings, and he's not about, I know. He was missing last night from the castle like a shark from a shoal; and my line against a pin hook, he's at the private mansion looking out for the picking; and precious pickings there be, too—for I saw the gold lying about the tables as thick as minnows in a basket.

ACTON. [*Suddenly*] Gold! Say you gold!

PETER. Yes, gold! Real rich rhino—shining about like fish scales in the sun.

ACTON. [*Aside*] Gold. Maybe—[*Aloud*] I'll go Peter—I'll go with you! [*Pauses, aside*] Yet why should I go to look on and covet what can't be mine? Besides, the sight of gold is dangerous to the needy—yet it can't be so to him that's *honest*. I'll go—my dream may come—Sir John might see—

Peter, I'll go that way unto my work. Quick, lad, a morning's wages will be
a heavy loss to poor Acton.

PETER.   Yes, and my fish will all be on a frolic.

ACTON.   Come, there's some hope yet in my dream of the crock of gold!
[*Exeunt Acton and Peter*]

SCENE 3: *The antique apartment in the private mansion of Sir John Vincent
seen through two large casement windows extending to the floor and
occupying the entire front flat. The windows hung with rich scarlet and gold
draperies, the back flat decorated with costly framed portraits, prints, hangings, etc. The windows or casements are partly open and discover a splendid
banqueting room; a superb chandelier hanging from C.; a number of richly
covered tables on which are costly glasses, fruits, wines. Wax candles lighted,
cards, dice, etc. A table at L. casement covered with green cloth, on which
are large heaps of gold and silver coins, cards, dice, etc. At R. casement,
another table set similarly, at which are three or four fashionably-dressed
persons playing at dice. At L. table, Lord Silliphant, Henry Mynton, Caesar
Silkhair, playing cards. A dice box also on table. At a table, C., Sir John
Vincent and others are drinking and watching the gamesters. Candles nearly
burnt out.*

SIR JOHN.   Bravo, gentlemen, bravo! Keep it up! Though age may come,
we never again come to age. So keep all your hearts warm, old classmates!
I'll give the next toast. Here's "Dulcit unos et viginti!"

SILK.   Deuced bad Latin for sweet one and twenty! By my suavity! But
I suppose it will go down with the aid of a little liquor. Tilt, boys—or
gentlemen, I should say—tilt your fingers, curl up your moustaches, expand
your lips, and kip [*sic*] my translation. Here's sweet one and twenty.

OMNES.   [*Drinking*]   Here's sweet twenty-one.

SILLI.   Now, gentlemen, in honor of our worthy host, I'll give a toast to
keep that down. Here's long life to Sir John Vincent, the heir of Hurstley!
[*All repeat toast and drink, with shouts of "Bravo! Bravo!" The gamesters
proceed vigorously on both sides. Sir John and his friends converse*]

SIR JOHN.   Keep up the siege, friends. Old Hurstley is well stocked. Keep
open the casements and let the dawn and the air of my blest majority enter
—join in our revels and outface our mimic light. [*Loud shouts and cries of
"Bravo! Bravo!" The windows are thrown further open. Roger Acton enters,
R. The music continues piano*]

ACTON.   [*Starts suddenly and then gazes on the scene in utter amazement.
On tiptoe, pushing window, aside*] Great powers. *This* is no dream. It is gold
—pure shining gold, heaped up like cakes o' clay. I've known and felt how

poor a mortal can be, but never thought one could be so rich. What a treasure would but one bright piece be to me, and yet no loss to him. What comforts it would bring to my poor home. Oh, heavens! Can this be right, that one can have so much and another so little. Nay, nothing! [*Turns*] I turn my eyes from it, and see my own wretched hovel—the pale, lank faces of my little children—and I've only to lift my hand, and—no one will see—no one will feel—nor ever care—no, no, to work, Acton, to work! [*He is crossing as the parties at the L. table spring up suddenly, dashing down their cards*]

MYNT. Silliphant, you're a scoundrel, a villain, a *cheat,* and to comprehend all, a robber!

SILLI. [*Dashing a dice box at his head*] Liar! That's no cheating!

MYNT. Ha! [*Strikes at him. Silliphant returns blow*]

SIR JOHN. Hold, gentlemen! Peace, I say! Forbear! [*They push him away and fight*]

SILK. [*Lifting up a chair*] Fie, gentlemen, allow me to take the chair and knock down order and suavity! [*Striking at them; the party at the R. table interferes, general fight ensues. Boxes and decanters are thrown. The table is upset and the money scattered about the room. Silliphant is knocked down by Mynton, who holds a chair over him. Sir John rushes between and holds up his hands in menacing attitude. Candlesticks are thrown, swords and canes are drawn, a few pieces of gold roll outside of casement. Acton picks one up nervously and rushes out, L., as the scene closes*]

SCENE 4: *A view on the estate of Hurstley. Acton runs in clutching his gold piece with a momentary look of rapture.*

ACTON. Mine! mine! A bright gold guinea! Luck at last has found poor Roger out. But, yet, is it luck or is it wicked theft—*theft!* Honest Acton, what have you done? You have leaped the fence of honesty. What! Am I no longer *Honest* Acton? Back, back with the glittering tempter [*Going R.*] to its den again! [*Pauses*] Yet, what be they that own it? A throng of noisy gamesters, profaning the Lord's name over His very bounty. Not one of them can need this single little piece—so large to me—not one of them would make it a blessing as I can. 'Twill help to stop my wife's heart-rending slurs. And poor Grace, too—oh, what would poor Grace say? But is it a theft? No, no, it rolled upon the ground, and anybody else would have picked it up as I did. I'll keep it. [*Puts it in his pocket*] Mayhap it is my bright dream coming out. I'll get it changed slyly and take it home as extra pay for extra labor. Dear Grace shall have a ribbon—Moll a cotton kerchief—the babes a doll, a rattle. Tom shall have a book, a knife, or any trifle he may like. I'll have a holiday. We'll all dress neat and go to church Sunday. Oh, what happiness a bit of gold can buy! [*Runs out. Enter Jennings, pale and agitated*]

JEN. [*He moves hurriedly to R., and starts suddenly back. Trembles*] Ha, a footstep! Misery! The falling of a leaf unnerves me. [*Looks off*] Pshaw! 'Tis but Acton going to his work. [*Looks at watch*] He's an hour late. [*Takes out memo book and writes*] I'll dock him, and his loss shall be my gain. I must follow and reprimand the wretch. The tenantry grows bold, and I somewhat fear suspicious. I must therefore assume more stern authority. Yet at present I have but little nerve to bear me out. Aunt Quarles is still before me. I feel her hot fingers still pressing on my throat. But what have I now to fear? The inquest traced her death as I had planned they should, to apoplexy, with scarce a murmur of suspicion. Yet who could he have been, whom I met across the lake, and whose hollow shout so startled me, that in my horror I dashed down the precious store, and fled to the boat. [*Sees Jonathan enter and starts tremulously*] Eh? Jonathan, is it you, boy?

JONA. Me! That's rather an odd question for you to ask, Master Jennings!

JEN. Not at all. Bless you, my sight is a little dull this morning.

JONA. But that was rather an odd kind of a start you made, too.

JEN. [*Aside*] Confusion! What can he—[*Aloud*] Well, I'm rather nervous this morning, Jonathan.

JONA. So am I, Master Jennings. In truth, we are all nervous. I can't keep poor Mrs. Quarles out of my mind for the life of me, Mr. Steward.

JEN. Nor I either, boy—nor I either—nor I—[*Unconsciously dwelling on the words*] Yet she—yet we all have to die, Jonathan.

JONA. It's very hard to be hurried off in that way.

JEN. Hurried, eh? In what way, boy?

JONA. Like poor Mrs. Quarles—without a friend to close her eyes— without even a prayer, or word of consolation—a poor minute's warning at such a time may save an eternity of torment.

JEN. Jonathan, this is irreverence to the memory as well as to the character of my poor aunt. Did you think her so wicked, boy?

JONA. I am not her judge, Master Jennings, but who is *perfect*? It is no disrespect to say she needed the last comforts of the dying, for often when a little boy, and even later, when I have sat near her reading my Bible, I have seen the quick tears rolling down her cheeks till my heart seemed to be in my very eyes. Oh, I would give the world, had I seen those tears in her dying hour!

JEN. Why—why—Jonathan—you—are growing sentimental, truly! [*Aside*] But there were tears though, tears of blood! [*Aloud*] But come, lad, sorrow must not interfere with duty. No more of poor aunt, but peace to her. I must look to the tenantry, you to—

JONA. To my master, Sir John, who is going to drive up this way for a morning's airing, and I am to attend him here.

JEN. How! His worship coming this way? Then I must be stirring. Good morning! [*Going*]

JONA. And I'll walk with you till he arrives.

JEN. [*Aside*] 'Sdeath! [*Aloud*] Hadn't you better stay and meet him, lad? I have some business with a tenant or two—that—that—might detain you too long. [*Aside*] I'll have no witness to my secret operation, none!

JONA. But, Master Jennings, do you not think that was rather a suspicious and unnatural mark upon the neck of Mrs. Quarles?

JEN. [*Aside*] Perdition! [*Aloud*] Why, a little strange, but nothing but what she could have done in the struggles of an apoplectic fit.

JONA. Very like—but she couldn't have struggled much either.

JEN. [*Forgetting himself*] Not struggle, man! But she *did* struggle. [*Recovering*] I mean she *must* have struggled to have produced such a mark as that—poor aunt!

JONA. But what I mean to say is, that if she had struggled as folks struggle in a fit, the bedclothes could hardly have been so smooth and unrumpled.

JEN. Well, well, the jury—the coroner—they are more able to judge of that than you or me, boy. No more of my poor aunt, but rest to her in a better world.

JONA. Amen! [*Exeunt*]

SCENE 5: *The meadow. The dropping well of Knarsborough in the distance. In the front view, a few drains and ditches cut. A set ground piece at the fourth entrance, behind which is sod and earth thrown up, with set pieces representing a drain half dug, the whole picturesquely filled up with set banks, trees, etc. Enter Acton.*

ACTON. Here at last, but an hour late though, and all through a sinful coveting of gold. Money that was not mine—I couldn't keep the guinea—something here kept saying "Roger, that be theft, be ill-got gold!" I took it back and laid it with the heap upon the table. I've lost a quarter of a day though. Well, well, better lose a whole day than lose a pure conscience. My heart feels heavy, but my soul feels lighter. [*Unconsciously placing hand in pocket, and trembles*] Bless my queer brains—I thought it were my guinea there again. Ha, ha, ha! It's a button. A button's better than a pilfered guinea—couldn't work well wi' a snake in one's pocket. I feel as light as a haycock—I may ha' some luck yet. To work, to work again. I'm Honest

Acton! [*Goes up and commences digging*] Ill-got money never comes to good, though a little honestly got would make a man of me after all. [*Enter Jennings. He starts a little back and recovers himself*]

JEN. 'Sdeath! Must I always start in this way? I can't bear this, everybody will notice it. [*Goes up to Roger pompously*] How's this, Acton? Isn't this drain finished yet? You have been too long about it, and I shall be compelled to fine you.

ACTON. Please you, Master Jennings, I have stuck to it steadily and toiled hardly. But it's heavy clay, you see, wet above and iron hard below. It shall be done by tomorrow, Master Jennings.

JEN. See that it is done, and done well; and now I have just another word to say to you. His honor, Sir John, is coming round this way, and if he should make any inquiries concerning your condition, *mind* that you tell him this and no more—you have a comfortable cottage, you want for nothing and are earning twelve shillings a week. Do ye hear?

ACTON. Heaven help me, Master Jennings, why, you know, my wages are but eight shillings, and my house lets in the wind and the rain, and is little better than a pigsty. [*Digging*]

JEN. Look you, Steady Acton, dare to tell Sir John what you've told me, and you are a ruined man! Make it twelve shillings to Sir John and who knows—eh, Roger, perhaps his honor may make it twelve instead of eight!

ACTON. Then I suppose *you* are to keep the other four, Master Jennings. [*Eyeing him closely*]

JEN. How, man! Do you dare ask me that? Remember, sir, at your peril, that you and all the rest *have had* twelve shillings a week since you have worked upon this estate, and that if you dare to hint, speak or think to the contrary, you never earn a penny here again. Here comes Sir John, my master, as I am yours. Now mind what I have said, or you're a beggar. [*Comes down*]

ACTON. Tell a lie, or starve! Heaven's wot, but it is a trying choice. [*Gives a heavy sigh and resumes work. Enter Sir John, Silliphant, and Silkhair, followed by Jonathan*]

SIR JOHN. [*Speaking as he enters*] Let our horses wait by yonder hedge.

JONA. [*Bowing*] Yes, your honor. [*Exit*]

JEN. [*Makes the usual tremulous start, then bows*]

SIR JOHN. Hello, Jennings! What the devil made you give that mysterious start? Why, man, you couldn't look more horrified if twenty ghosts were at your elbow. Why, bless my soul, your face is like a skull done in plaster of Paris. Look another way, man, or my mare yonder will get skittish.

SILK. Yes, do, fellow, oblige me, or you'll give my horse the nightmare or the blind staggers, you will, by my suavity.

SILLI. Perhaps, like some of us, he's been squeezing the neck of—[*Wiping mouth with handkerchief*]

JEN. [*Forgetting himself*] The neck—my lord!

SILLI. Yes—of a decanter!

OMNES. Ha, ha, ha!

JEN. Your pardon, Sir John, it's but a spasmodic infirmity—forgive it. This meadow, Sir John—

SIR JOHN. Well, is it bewitched, is it quaking, that you must shake so?

SILLI. I see, he's caught the intermittent fever from the marsh.

JEN. This meadow, you perceive, requires draining, after which I propose dressing it with free chalk to sweeten the grass, your honor. But if you will just go to the next field, you will take notice the Guano—

SIR JOHN. Very well. Who is that poor fellow yonder, toiling up to his knees in mud, eh?

JEN. Why, that, sir, is Roger Acton, of the handsome cottage below him.

SIR JOHN. Oh, yes, my father used to call him Steady Acton. Well, have you taken good care of him—is he pretty well off now?

JEN. Oh, yes, your honor. I only wish half of the little farmers were so well to live—a handsome cottage, an acre of garden, and twelve shillings a week is quite a comfortable condition for a *single* man, your honor!

SIR JOHN. [*Looks earnestly at Roger*]

SILK. Bless me! Twelve shillings a week? Why, Silliphant, that would starve one of our poodle dogs, by my suavity.

SIR JOHN. Twelve shillings. Very well! But the poor fellow looks very wretched. Stay! I'll just step and ask him if he's in want of anything. [*Starts to go*]

JEN. [*Stopping him quickly*] Don't, Sir John, I pray don't. Allow me to advise your honor. These men are always wanting, if you'd believe them; and would impose upon your honor's generosity. Acton can't want for anything, but to save your honor trouble, if you have anything you wish to bestow by way of—I'll deliver it with punctuality and pleasure.

SIR JOHN. Certainly! Thank you, Jennings. So, just to make a beginning, as we are all merry at the hall, and the poor man is up to his neck—[*Takes out a green silk purse*] Why do you start? Up to his neck in mud—give him this from me, to drink my health! [*Tosses a gold piece to him*]

ACTON. [*Has been listening; aside*] Ha! By all my troubles, a piece of gold, a bright glittering sovereign for poor Roger! Blest powers! At last a bit of gold will *honestly* be mine.

JEN. [*Puts the gold piece in his pocket, and fumbling about for a shilling, which he pulls out. Meanwhile Sir John joins his companions*]

SILK. Come, Sir John, you are too rustic—too agricultural this morning —you are, by my suavity! You've brought us out here, up to our knees in mud when we should be up to our noses in liquor. It is too *terra aqueous*, it is, by my suavity.

SIR JOHN. Ha, ha, ha! Never mind, my boy, a little mud will do us some good. It will remind us that we are nothing but clay after all.

SILK. A dirty idea, by my suavity!

SIR JOHN. Good-bye, Jennings. Confound him, how he starts—you'll find me at Knarsborough shower bath! [*Exeunt Sir John, Silkhair and Silliphant*]

JEN. [*Aside*] Shower bath! Malediction! Is there no word any more, but what must strike through like an electric shock? [*Aloud*] Roger Acton! [*Pompously*]

ACTON. Well, Master Jennings?

JEN. Roger, his honor has been so liberal as to give you a shilling to drink his health with.

ACTON. [*Starting with astonishment*] A shilling, Master Jennings! Why, I'll make oath it was a pound. I saw it, as clear as the sun. Come now, master, don't be cruel—don't break jokes on the back of a poor man.

JEN. Jokes! Roger Acton—sir—if you say another word—here, take Sir John's shilling!

ACTON. Come now, for pity's sake, Master Jennings. Be just—be generous —give me my gold, my own bit of gold. I swear that his honor gave it— blessing on his head—you know he did, Master Jennings—don't play upon me. Give me my gold, if not for me, let me have it for the sake of my poor family, my little suffering children. [*Imploringly*]

JEN. "Play upon!" Your gold—why what is it you mean? The man's delirious. Come, we'll have no madmen about us, I assure you. Take your gift—your shilling—or else—

ACTON. "Rob not the poor, because he's poor, for the Lord shall plead his cause."

JEN. Roger Acton—

ACTON. "Masters, give unto your servants that which is just and equal, knowing that ye also have a master in heaven."

JEN. Roger, you have dared to quote the Bible against me—but dearly, deeply shall you rue it.

ACTON. Shall I? Then you shall hear more. [*Seizes him by the arm*] Hear, villain, that the sacred truths may sink deep into your black heart. "Your gold and silver is cankered and the rust of them shall be a witness against you, and shall eat your flesh as it were fire!" [*Pushes him off*] Remember this when you lock away the poor man's rights. Remember it and tremble.

JEN. Roger Acton, you work on this place no more. [*Aside*] Perdition! His words ring like a death knell in my ears—[*Aloud*] Wretch, you shall pay for it in beggary and starvation! [*Exit*]

ACTON. Spurned like a poor weed to the earth at last—ruined, crushed and heartbroken—my wife, children—all—all—a helpless prey to want, misery, and madness. [*Goes upstage, and closed in*]

SCENE 6: *The back gardens and walks at Hurstley. Enter Sarah Slack, followed by Peter Perch with rod, basket, etc.*

SARAH. There, now, Peter, you needn't 'scot me any further. Sir John and all the rest about him have heard of Mrs. Quarles's doleful death, and there'll be so many there, and they'll all of them ask so many hard questions, and give a body so much trouble. I answered more questions already than I knowed the meaning of—and I know you don't want to be pumped when you know nothing.

PETER. Not I. I don't know anything at all about the dead. I've no acquaintance among 'em. I don't fish in that stream at all. But I say, Sally, the poor old gal went off suddenly queer.

SARAH. Yes, and queerly sudden, too, without sign or sickness, so quiet. And then she was found so nat'ral and straight, just as if she could have prepared herself for the undertaker—that's so strange. I have heard of people laying out to die, but never of their dying and laying themselves out. I first went to her room to wake her, because we all thought she slept very late—so late that she would hardly have time to give us the reg'lar morning scold. So in I went—up to the bed I went, an'—an' then—

PETER. What?

SARAH. Then I went back, for she laid as still as a stone—and I'd never seen anybody sleep with their eyes so staring wide open afore—so then I screamed to wake her—and—

PETER. Well?

SARAH. And then I screamed because she wouldn't wake.

PETER. That was enough to wake her, I'll be hooked! Well?

SARAH. Then I got on the bed alongside of her, and—and called her three or four times, and she looked as if she was going to speak, an' I thought she would speak—but—

PETER. Well?

SARAH. But she *didn't* speak, an' she'll never speak any more. [*Sobbing violently*] I put my hand on her cheek and it felt as cold as the wall.

PETER. And it was about as white, I s'pose!

SARAH. No, it was as red as the bedstead.

PETER. Red—what, the old woman's gills red?

SARAH. Yes—rederer an' more nat'ral than life—an' she had a big mark on her neck.

PETER. The old fish was scalen a little I s'pose? What color was it?

SARAH. Oh, black an' blue, an' red and yellow.

PETER. Black, blue, red an'—can't tell, but if you'd mix all them together I should say it would make a very suspicious looking mark. And they say she died of the nat'ral 'plexy. Well, if it wasn't an old woman, I'd declare that was a fish story.

SARAH. No, they said she died "Found dead!"

PETER. Hem! [*Aside*] Bait for gudgeon!

SARAH. But bless me, I should have been in the hall before this. That's always the way whenever you come to help me over the lake, or the fences. You always take so much time to it.

PETER. Yes, and now I'll take toll. [*Tries to kiss her. She avoids him*]

SARAH. No! This time I go free. [*Runs off laughing*]

PETER. Hem! Slipped the hook that time. Well, I don't know, but I think there's some iniquity at the bottom of this deep pool of death here, if one could but fish it out. Hollo! Who's this? [*Tom Acton runs in with a small piece of fence rail in his hand*]

TOM. Hurrah! Hurrah! I beat him! I beat him!

PETER. Hollo! Tom Acton, my little sprat, what have you been doing, boy?

TOM. Why, Master Simon Jennings saw me pick up this little piece of fence rail that I was going to carry home to help make a supper fire, and he galloped after me with his old pony to take me up. But I took to my heels, and away we went through the mud and marshes like a cony chase. So I thought I would give 'em a swim for it. So I flew down the bank to the lake, jumped into a dory, and poled across. Old Gray wouldn't follow—he throwed his ears back—Simon throwed his head back, and called the dogs at me, but I'll be dogged if I was going to be caught and caged for nothing, so I shot off like a bullet and left 'em sticking in the mud, like bugs in a tar pot.

PETER. Well done, my gay little gudgeon. You did right to slip the old pike. I wish he may stick there till the crows eat him.

Tom. I'm sure, Mr. Perch, that this bit of half rotten wood is no loss to Sir John, and of no use to anybody but poor folks in need of fuel.

Peter. Of use, no! Or the little old shark would have picked it up long ago and put it in his extortion shop in the village, and made some of the tenants pay half a day's wages for it. I tell you what, my little roach, I only wish for your father's sake, my own sake, and the old boy, his namesake, that I had this hook in his gills. I'd pull him up and down Hurstley pond, till I had washed some of the villain out of him, or I'm no judge of foul fish.

Tom. Never mind, he'll get trapped one of these days when he's full and ripe. There never was a troublesome rat that didn't meet his cat, or his death cheese. But, good day, Mr. Perch. I'm going up to the eel pond to meet Ben Burke. We've something up there—hooks, bait, and dipsys, Mr. Perch.

Peter. I see, going to fish for fowl instead of foul fish! Ha, ha, ha! Ben Burke's a true rock fish—but I'm afeard them 'ere poppin' rods of his may shoot a little too far—and take care, lad, that he doesn't pop both of you into the ugly net of the law. It's a little ticklish, lad, to go about so much with—

Tom. Hang it, Mr. Perch. A poor boy must go somewhere for a bit of comfort when there be none at home. It's very hard to do the best one can, and get nothing but raps and snaps for it. Ah, Mr. Perch, folks may talk as they will about getting second mothers to take care of the first mother's children, but the first be the best. [*With emotion*] But there is but one mother, after all.

Peter. [*Aside*] That's natur's gospel. [*Aloud*] Well, well, only take care, lad. Old Jennings has them cats about you talk of [*Enter Jennings with Men. Jennings is bespattered with mud*]

Jen. Aye, and here they are, too. Seize that young pilferer! [*To Men, who advance. Tom raises his piece of rail fence. Peter throws down his rod and strikes an attitude*]

Tom. Pilferer! They'll have to get over this bit of fence first.

Jen. Quick, I say!

Peter. Hark ye, Mr. Jennings—you shark—you dogfish—just one of you lay a fin upon that little sprat, an' I'll scale you to the very bone.

Jen. What! Dare you assault a bailiff?

Peter. 'Salt! Aye, and pepper you, too!

Jen. Men, do you hear this? Seize the poaching scoundrel instantly! [*The Men advance upon Peter, they fight. Jennings attempts to seize Tom, who keeps him off with the stake, he striking with his cane. Peter finally beats the Men and throws his fish at them as they run off. He immediately gets a thick line from his basket, gets behind Jennings and fastens the hook of it in the back of his cravat, pulls him suddenly round and commences to*

*drag him off backwards. Tom gets before him, striking him with the stake,
while Jennings parries with his cane, in great fury*]

PETER.   Yeo ho! A double haul—a prize—a shark!

TOM.   Huzza! The great poacher poached! Ha, ha, ha!

JEN.   Villains! Murderers! You shall hang for this! Hang! Be gibbeted—
no mercy—

PETER.   Where was *your* mercy? [*Till all off*]

SCENE 7: *Interior of Acton's cottage as before. Acton is discovered upon a
chair beside the table, C., with his hands in his hair. Grace and Mary are
bending over him with tender anxiety.*

GRACE.   Nay, dear father, look up. Speak, that we may comfort you.

ACTON. [*Wildly*] Who'll comfort me?

MARY.   We will. *I* will, Roger! Yes, bear up, arouse you, man. Bear up,
dear Roger. We have heard all. Jonathan has told us. Jennings has discharged
you—but never mind—come what may, Roger, I will share your cares, and
we'll fight it out together and you shall still have a place in my poor heart
forever. [*Roger, hearing her voice, looks up with astonishment*]

ACTON. [*Springing up*]   Mary, my girl, my kind wife again—bless you,
bless you. [*Embraces her*]

GRACE.   Ah! Mother! [*Kisses her*] Blessings, blessings on you for that dear
look, for those kind words, the rainbow of hope in our storm of sorrow—
a dove bringing the olive branch of peace to our little ark, tossed on troubled
waters.

MARY.   Grace dear, you are a sensible girl, with a feeling heart. Do now,
try—say something to cheer your poor father. There, get your prayer book,
and read something for him. It will do us all good.

GRACE.   I will most gladly, mother. [*Gets book*]

ACTON.   Ah, Mary! This is a balm for the many wounds o' my wronged
heart. There's hope yet for honest Roger Acton. But these troubles, girl, are
hard to bear, and a little lot of gold would save us from them all.

GRACE.   Gold! No, no, not gold! Religion! Faith!

ACTON.   Well, well! Anyhow I wish that a dream of mine might come
true.

MARY.   Eh! Dream, husband, what dream?

GRACE.   Tell us, father.

ACTON.   Why I dreamed I was working in my garden, by the celery
trenches in the hedge. I was moaning over my lot, as well I may, and a sort
of angel came to me—only he looked dark and sorrowful—and kindly said,
"What would you have, Roger?" I, nothing fearful in my dream, for all

his strange unearthly face and dark broad wings, answered boldly, "Money!" He pointed with his long thin fingers to the hedge, then laughed aloud and vanished away. I thought a moment wonderingly—turned to look where he pointed, and, oh, the blessing, Moll—I found—

MARY. What?

ACTON. A crock of gold!

MARY. A crock of gold! Heavens, if it only would come true.

GRACE. That was an *evil spirit,* father!

ACTON. No, an angel, girl, an angel!

GRACE. No, it was the Fiend of Temptation! And that loud laugh was his laugh of triumph. He has dropped evil thoughts upon your heart. O father, for the love of peace and Heaven, think no more of it, or 'twill tempt you to your ruin here and hereafter.

ACTON. Whoever he were—if he brought me gold, he would bring me blessing—there's meat and drink and warmth and shelter in yellow gold. Aye, and rest from labor, child, and independence from oppression. I wish I had found the crock the dev—I mean the angel brought me! [*A knock is heard at door*] Ha! See who's there, Moll!

GRACE. [*Aside*] Oh! Perhaps dear Jonathan, with—[*Mary opens door, Grace lights candle. Enter Tom Acton with a gun upon his shoulder and a couple of pheasants under his smocked frock, followed by Ben Burke with a large stuffed club*]

ACTON. Ah, Tom, that you—out rather late—been a good boy, I hope? Ha! Bold Ben Burke! How de do, lad?

BURKE. Well, I always does well, bless your honest heart, Roger, an' all your hearts at the same time. What makes you look so sodden. I'm a lord, if your eyes aren't all as red as hedgehogs, and you seems to be all as merry as mutes. [*Grace gives Burke a stool*]

ACTON. It be'an't the best o' luck with us, Ben.

BURKE. Oh, traps and snares! But don't I see what it is? Be sure I does— it's that 'ere precious porridge that's given you all the influenzy. Now, I'll tell you what, jist tip it down the sink, dame, an' trust to me for better!

ACTON. Better!

TOM. Yes—I've got the eyes can fetch down what'll make the mouth water, hasn't I, Ben?

BURKE. Yes, your Tom here's a lad o' stuff, that he is, an' that old rusty iron o' yourn be as true as a compass, and pepper me, if the pheasants wouldn't *come* to it, all the same as if it had been a lode stone. Here, dame, pluck the angel's will—Tommy, drop 'em out.

Toм. There they be, warm and fresh as nater! [*Takes two pheasants from under his frock and lays them on table*]

Acton. [*Looks at Tom and draws a heavy sigh*] My dear, brave boy at such a trade! Oh, this is too much! [*Sinking into chair*] What will not hunger and neglect bring? Well, well, it cannot be the child's fault—nor mine—poor boy! [*Weeping*]

Toм. What! Eh? What's the matter, father? You look so mournfully upon me. I've done no harm—no wrong—indeed I've not!

Grace. Oh, Burke! Burke! Why will you lead the boy astray? Thomas, brother, what have you done? [*Weeping*]

Mary. Well, it's no use grieving now, or we'll spoil our appetite for a supper for once—and they were made to eat, I'm sure. [*Commences to pick*]

Burke. [*To Roger, not hearing Grace*] Why, what *is* the matter now, Steady Acton? One would think we was Jennings come to raise the rent, instead of son Tom, an' friend Burke. Hang it, man, we wouldn't fill your stomachs by hurting your minds. So if you doesn't like luck when it does come to you, why burn the fowls, or bury 'em, and let brave Tom and me risk limbs for nothing!

Grace. We cannot enjoy with a clear conscience what is not either earned or given, Ben.

Burke. Miss Grace—[*Bowing awkwardly; aside*] Bless her purty white bill, she makes me so narvous all over that I couldn't shoot an ox. [*Aloud*] Miss Grace, I wish I was as good as you, but I isn't, nor can't be. But don't condemn us. Hear and say where's the sin. Bless your sweet mouth, it ought to feed more sweetener an' wholesome—and there's brave Tom—isn't he as lean as a lizard. What were fowl made for, but for us to eat, I'd like to know?

Grace. It is not ours, Ben, and I cannot touch it. A hungry sleep is better than a guilty one—and so Heaven be with you. [*Exit upstairs*]

Burke. Here, Acton, here's the great lasses drop for sorrer. [*Pulls out flask*] Here, this will make the birds go down without stickin' in your throat!

Acton. [*Hesitating*] No, thank you, Ben, but I feel no thirst that way! I'm too hot within—too hot already, Ben.

Burke. Why, there you be again—you wants for everything, an' won't take nothing. Come, this 'ere won't burn you; it's summat short o' the right stuff—stingo that hasn't seen the face of a wishy-washy 'cise man—so just tip it for trial.

Acton. [*Drinking*] Hem! It's scaldin' hot, man, for all that. Moll, we'll save the birds for breakfast?

Mary. Yes, it's a pity to wake the babes now.

BURKE. 'Cause you be'nt use to it! [*Drinks heavily*] It's a black and burnin' shame, Honest Acton, that you are so badly treated, so it is. But you shan't want while Ben has a heart in the right place, and a hand to help his friend. [*Striking his breast furiously*] And more than that, Roger, hark to that, man! [*Strikes his pockets and money rattles*] And more than hark— here, good wife, hold your apron. [*Mary holds her apron, Burke throws a handful of silver into it. Roger and Tom stare in amazement*]

ACTON. Money! Blessed money, as I live, Moll! [*With avaricious joy*]

MARY. All big bright silver!

TOM. Bless me—is all that for us, Ben?

BURKE. Be sure!

ACTON. [*Whose manner and countenance is entirely changed*] Hush! Ben! Put it up! It's blood money, and—Tom, my poor boy, Tom, with— with—heavens, man! How came you by it? Speak, man, or—

BURKE. Honestly, neighbor. Leastways middlin' honest—don't—dang it, man—don't damp a poor fellow when he means to save you.

TOM. Why, bless you, dear father, and mother, too. [*Crosses to Mary*] I *am* innocent. I never knowed till this minute that Ben had any blunt at all, did I, Ben?

ACTON. Is it true, Ben, that my boy isn't—isn't—a thief? Oh, heavens, Ben, tell me the truth.

BURKE. Blockhead, man! What, not believe your own son? Be sure—why look you, neighbor—do you think as your dove-face, open-hearted boy, would do worse than Ben Burke? And do you think that I would turn the bloody villain to take a man's life? No, I kills game, not keepers. All that's wrong in me the wrong game laws put there. But I should be a fool if I didn't stoop to pick up money that a madman flings away.

ACTON. Madman! What mean you, Burke?

MARY. Yes, tell us about it, Ben.

BURKE. Well then, listen. I was setting my night lines around Pike Island, just here, just in the middle—and after that thunderstorm 'tween three and four o'clock, all at once a boat—no, a dory—came across and quietly up. I creeps a little down, and a mad chap, with never a tile on his head, nor a shoe to his foot, creeps out from the punt, and when I bawls out to ax his business, the lunatic sprang at me like a tiger. I didn't wish to hurt a poor little piece of insanity, so I just grabbed him by the throat in this 'ere vice, and shook him off. He shook like a dying pheasant in a snare, and when I peeped close into his face, blow me if it didn't look like a white devil. What are you for, man? says I. With that the frightened fool flings something at my head, gives a shivering howl, and jumped into the punt and off he went.

ACTON and MARY. Well! [*Very eagerly*]

BURKE. Well, if I had any doubts of his being mad they all vanished. Now to think that a man should come out to Pike Island at that time to count out a little lot of silver, and guzzle down six pots of honey! There it was all tied up in a shawl. So by his throwing it at me, thinks I he means to give it to me in course. So I began 'xamine and found among the pots a little box marked "Savings Bank" rattling with chink. So I chucked the bank into the pond, emptied the till, pocketed the silver, and there it is in your good wife's apron.

ACTON. But this is strange—wonderful!

MARY. But what did you do with the honey, Ben?

BURKE. [*Takes a long drink*] Oh! Burn the 'lasses stuff! I warn't going to spoil the 'bacca in my mouth for it. So having no stones by me to stir up the pike with, I chucked the gallipots into the shallows, and that druv 'em right up on my hooks. So, neighbors, I didn't make a bad night's work— forty pounds of pike—twelve of eels—and a savings bank wa'n't bad pickings. [*Ben drinks. Acton thinking of pots*]

MARY. Dear, it was a pity though, to have throwed away all that honey! But what became of the shawl, Ben?

BURKE. Oh, after being sorry afterward for not saving the honey for your little ones, I thought I'd be 'conomical for once. So I dipped into the pond, squeezed it out like any washerwoman, and here I'd had it about my waist ever since. P'r'aps you or Miss Grace would like to have it, but 'taint fashion though. [*Pulls it off and shows it*]

MARY. [*Taking it*] Why, Ben, husband, this is old Mrs. Quarles's shawl. I'd know it among a hundred. Sarah Slack used to wear it sometimes. I saw it on her one day at church, with Peter Perch. Green-edged yellow—B. Q. for Bridget Quarles on the corner. Oh, if they'd only heard of this at the inquest!

ACTON. I tell you what, Ben—it's kindly meant, I know, but you'd best keep it, or take it to Hurstley—it might bring us into trouble.

BURKE. Take it to—I don't know about that, Roger Acton. P'r'aps they might ask me for the "Savings Bank," too. [*Here Tom is seen nodding on a stool*]

ACTON. I see. No, no, it'll never do to lose the money. Let a bygone be a bygone, and don't disturb the old woman, now she's dead. So if the shawl is like to be a telltale—in my mind, the hearth's the safest place for it. [*He takes the shawl and throws it in fire. It makes a large blaze. Mary and Acton gaze in a kind of superstitious fear. Tom is asleep. Burke flings himself down by fire*] Ben, isn't that a strange blaze for a thing like that to make?

BURKE. Why no, it's only the color of the shawl—red, green, and yellow. Why, what's the matter, man?

ACTON. Nothing—only I thought—

BURKE. Ha! There, I told you the boy wasn't guilty. He wouldn't roll over to sleep that way if he was. He's like me, got too sensible a conscience —so we'll just take a snooze together for company's sake. [*Stretches himself out alongside Tom*]

MARY. Why, bless me, if the two creatures ain't fast dead asleep. [*She throws a matting over them. Acton is walking the stage in front, ruminating*]

ACTON. [*Aside*] Yes, he pointed to that very spot, or near it, but then these are all nothing but honey. Well, it will do for the children's bread. If I can but find the pots—I'll try—I'll try! [*Exit hurriedly*]

MARY. [*Seated at fire*] Well, this is all as strange as a story book. That shawl isn't all burnt up yet and the letters seem to be shining right at me. Something wrong—the honey pots gone from Mrs. Quarles's cupboard— keys were in the door—Jonathan Floyd saw something on the lake when he called the dog—Ben saw a white-faced dev—O Heaven, pardon me—Simon Jennings is a *little white-faced man.* How wrong it was of Roger to burn that shawl. It was a shame for him. Oh, if I could only have had it to take to the hall, what a stir I would have made. Everybody would have come to me—the doctors—the inquest—the—oh, I'll go right and tell Sir John all about the shawl in the morning, and the savings bank and the money, and the galli—[*Enter Acton with a crock in his hand*]

ACTON. Here, Moll, here's one of the pots that Ben Burke throwed away. When I pulled it out my heart was in my mouth it was so surprising heavy. I thought—I was fool enough to ha' thought that—but see—it's no crock of gold, Moll—look it's marked "Honey." Luck isn't in't for such as me—but the babes may like it on their bread! [*Sorrowfully*] Moll, I hope the water hasn't spoiled it. [*Music. Mary takes a pair of scissors and cuts the string that hold the bladder on it and removes the cover*]

MARY. Why it's *bran,* Acton. There's no honey here. Look, man.

ACTON. [*Looking*] Alas! No—no—not even a drop of honey for my poor babes—every little honest hope is mocked.

MARY. See, it's only bran—I'll empty the gallipots and—[*She half turns the pot, a little bran or sawdust runs out on the table, then a few pieces of coin sewed in leather; this is immediately followed by a vast lot of gold pieces rolling in profusion on the table and floor. In amazement*] Mercy! Heavens! What is all this?

ACTON. [*In wild ecstasy*] 'Tis gold! Bright gold! Hurrah! My dream is out! The crock of gold is mine! Hurrah! [*He seizes his hands full in frantic *joy. Mary stands in fearful wonder. Ben and Tom start and put their heads up, half asleep, from the matting, not seeing the gold. Grace, with a light in her hand, runs a few steps down the ladder in her nightdress, looks on in ignorant terror with her hand and eyes upturned, invoking Heaven's aid for her father's madness, as quick drop falls on the picture]*

ACT III.

SCENE 1: *Interior of Acton's cottage as before. Enter Grace hurriedly downstairs, her cloak and bonnet off.*

GRACE.   Home—and before mother is awake, thank Heaven! Now then, to look at dear Jonathan's keepsake. Noble lad, what a generous heart he has. [*Takes paper from her bosom, tremulously opens it, and starts in astonishment*] Ha! Heavens, what's here? Two gold pieces—two sovereigns along with the half crown! Oh, how sly, how delicate, and yet how generous. [*Kisses the paper*] Yet what shall I do with them? Keep them? No, I cannot. No, Jonathan, dearly as they bespeak thy heart's true affection, I dare not keep them! Yes, I will insist on his receiving them back and taking care of them if it's only for me. [*Mary comes downstairs dejectedly*] Ha! There's mother! [*Hides the money in her bosom*]

MARY.   Ha! Grace, girl, are you there? Have you seen your father?

GRACE.   Seen him? Why surely he has not remained out all night. I thought I heard him in your room as I came up—I mean as I came down from my chamber.

MARY.   Alas, no, girl. [*Sorrowfully*]

GRACE.   Merciful providence. [*Going to door hastily. Acton pitches in door much intoxicated, with jug under his arm*]

ACTON.   Hoorah! Moll, hooray! Here's the stingo, girl. Little long coming, it's true, but it'll taste all the sweeter for't. Hooray! Here I be again—a gentle folk—a lord, a king, Moll. Hollo, daughter Grace, what's come over you, girl? [*Taking hold of her rather roughly; she weeps*]

MARY.   Why, bless me, Acton—Roger—husband—where have you been? You'll fright the poor girl, man.

ACTON.   Come, come, won't have any dull looks about today! [*Takes the crock of gold from chimney*] Look here, girl—isn't this enough to make a poor man merry? No more toil! Ha, ha, ha! No more troubles! I'll drain the jug now instead of Jennings's meadow. Here, girls, kiss me! [*Kisses both*] Ha, ha, ha! Isn't *this* enough to make a man sing out. Ha, ha, ha! Thank the crock for this—the blessed crock of gold! [*Shaking it in ecstasy. Mary goes mournfully to the fire*]

GRACE. Hush! Hush! Be not deceived, father. That gold will be no blessing to you! Heaven grant that it does not bring a curse. It will be a sore temptation. It is not—it cannot be ours.

ACTON. Not ours, girl? Now, Grace, you're a sensible girl—how—how—the dev—the mischief can you talk so foolish as that? Whose is it I'd like to know? Didn't I fish it up? Who finds, owns, girl! You are a good girl, Grace, but don't talk to me in that way, if you *please!*

MARY. [*Coming down, aside*] It's too horrible to have a murdered body's things about, it is! [*Aloud*] Roger, that gold belonged to Mrs. Quarles. I'm morally sure of it, and it now must belong to Simon Jennings, her heir!

ACTON. What, he? [*Furiously*] What, dame, shall that white—no, that black-hearted villain rob me again? No, no, Moll—I'll hang first. The crock I found and the crock I'll keep. [*Takes cup and fills from jug*] But come, girls, and help me, down with your mugs and help me to get through with this jug. Bless you, I never felt so husky and dry in all my life! Here! Here's blessings on him as sent it, and on him as has it, and on him as means to keep it. Come, drink, drink. [*Sings "We'll conquer or die," etc. Both gaze on him in mute horror*] But where's Tom, eh? Where's my brave Tom!

GRACE. He went out at daylight, to hunt for Ben Burke! [*Acton makes a sudden start at the name of Ben Burke. Grace continues aside*] Alas! That I should live to see a beloved brother with such a companion or a dear parent sunk from honest poverty to vice and perhaps crime. [*Goes up weeping. Mary leads her to fire, where they both sit sorrowfully, Mary occasionally watching Acton who is seated near jug, and has been ruminating during the last speech in alarm*]

ACTON. Yes—he may—I didn't think of that—Ben Burke's for going halves in everything. True, I managed to let him slip out last night without knowing anything of the crock—or the gold—but he may come back—find it out, and then want the half of it. I couldn't spare any part of the precious gold. Let me think—con—consider how—how I shall continue to keep it from him. Ah! I must take another drink to brighten up my thoughts. [*Drinks*] Ah! How quick a little bit of liquor sharpens one's ideas—it's the very guano to manure the mind! Ha, ha, ha! I've got it already. I'll hide it. I hide the crock and take out a guinea at a time and get it changed secretly. But stop—speaking of change—there's little Snip at the Bacchuses owes me—oh, I must go back while I think of it. [*Puts crock on cupboard and covers it with the tins*] There, nobody'll think o' looking there till I come back. [*Goes to door*]

MARY. [*Starting up*] Why, mercy, Roger, you are not going out again?

ACTON. Yes, Moll, you and Grace make yourself ha-a-appy. I'm only going back to the village to get my change.

GRACE. My dear father, do not go. Get the money tomorrow. Father, remember you were out all last night. O father, it wrings my very heart to think—

ACTON. Think, girl—why what the deuce have you to think about? I'll do all the thinking now. I've plenty of time. Catch me working now—catch me a calling at Hurstley Hall unless it be to arrest that robber Jennings, or invite Sir John to dine with me! Ha, ha, ha! Good day till I come back. Hooray! I'm a lord! An archbishop!

MARY. [*Holding on to him*] Nay, not today, dear husband. Not today, again I pray you! [*Weeping*]

GRACE. Let me beg of you, father, to stay with us today. [*Earnestly*]

ACTON. Now, now, Grace—you're a good girl—only you will preach too much. There's a time for all things. So just you be quiet, keep yourself snug, and don't tease one, and you shall have a church Bible big enough to eat breakfast off of, and all bound in *gold*, too. That'll make the book o' some real value, too, Grace. Good-bye, girl, good-bye, Moll—be merry, wench, and you shall dress like a lady. I'll jump out of the old smock, too, as a snake jumps out of his hide, and we'll all look like somebody—be as great as anybody, and care for nobody! Hooray! for the crock of gold! [*Exit. Speaks outside*] I'll come back as soon as I get my change.

GRACE. [*Following him*] Father, father—he's gone. Heaven knows how or when he'll come home. Oh! There's endless misery in the fatal crock of gold! [*Weeping; goes to fire*]

MARY. Ah! There was a time when Roger Acton couldn't ha' left me in that way—when I could hold him like a child, and stay him with my words if not with my hands. But the thought of that crock and o' that shawl and the marks of blood upon it have made me as weak an' cowardly as a lamb. Every little cup in my cupboard seems now a fearful gallipot spotted with blood and gold—and the hateful *crock* itself—I dread the sight of it, as if it contained—a frightful fiend—the fire, too—I can sit there no more to hear my children prattle—for it smells of the mur—of the burnt and bloodstained shawl. Besides, it may all come out—and that gold may buy a halter for us all. Oh, I can't stay here, I feel—I feel as cold as if I was at the bottom of the well. [*Fainting*] Grace, help—me—girl—help! [*Music*]

GRACE. [*Screams and runs down*] Mother! [*Mary faints in Grace's arms*] Oh! There's more woe in that crock of gold! [*Closed in*]

SCENE 2: *The steward's hall in Hurstley Hall. Enter Jennings, pale and nervous as usual.*

JEN. Acton I hear has money. He has presented pieces of gold for change and it has become the gossip of the village. Yet he never could have found the crock without blabbing it. No, no, the fool's too honest, and had he found it, would have been glad to have given all up to me in order to obtain his place again. And yet a more fearful suspicion strikes me. He may have exposed me to Sir John, and have received a few pieces from him. 'Sdeath, there I am wracked again—I must see—[*Enter Sarah Slack*]

SARAH. [*Starting back*] Oh, dear, Mr. Simon—I'm glad—[*Aside*] No, I'm sorry—[*Aloud*] Yes, I'm glad it's you. I was afraid it was Mrs. Quarles's ghost, I was.

JEN. [*Panting*] Ghost! Why, Sarah, who would have thought that you were such a coward.

SARAH. I'm no coward, Mr. Simon. Why, I'm as bold as a lion in the kitchen, but somehow every time I come apast Mrs. Quarles's room, I feel as cold as though I had been in the shower bath.

JEN. [*Aside*] Confusion! [*Aloud*] To fear the dead is a proof that you did them some injury while alive!

SARAH. La, is it? Oh, bless me, then that's the reason why you start and shiver whenever you go that way!

JEN. [*Furiously*] Sarah Slack!

SARAH. [*Loudly*] Mr. Simon Jennings! Why, what ails you, Mr. Simon? You look like a starched *blue rag!* But I must go to my work. [*Going*]

JEN. No, stay, Sarah. I've something to say to you.

SARAH. Oh, what do you want, Master Simon?

JEN. You've heard some of this talk about Roger Acton having money—having gold?

SARAH. Oh, yes! Well?

JEN. Do you know how much he got?

SARAH. No, but I hope it's a crockful.

JEN. Has Roger or any of the family been here since yesterday? [*Greatly agitated*]

SARAH. Oh, yes! Grace—sweet Grace—was here early in the morning asking to see his lordship. Don't squeeze my pulse out!

JEN. And did she see—

SIR JOHN. [*Outside*] Jennings! Jennings!

SARAH. Go and ask him, Mr. Simon!

JEN. [*Aside*] Furies! It must be so—exposed—blasted! Ruined! [*Runs off*]

SARAH. [*Imitating him*] Ruined! Blasted! I'll tell you what, Mr. Simon, it wouldn't be well if Sir John heard you call him such names—a ruined! a blast—what else I wonder. There is something the matter but it is no matter to me. Oh, bless me, I forgot. I must run down to Acton's and wish them joy of their good luck, wherever it comes from. Oh, who's that? [*Enter Peter Perch on tiptoe*] Oh, Peter, I'm glad you've come.

PETER. So am I! Is pike—dogfish about?

SARAH. Hush!

PETER. Hush! Corks and dipsys! What are you hushing about, and you told me that I had his lordship's permission to fish about these waters now and then.

SARAH. Aye, but you mustn't throw your bait out too hard or you might fall into trouble, but I'm glad you've come, though. I want you to 'scot me down to Roger Acton's to give 'em all a kiss and joy of their good fortune.

PETER. I'll save you all that trouble. Give me the kiss and I'll tell you all about their fortune. Just one—that'll do for the whole family! [*Kisses her*] There!

SARAH. And there! [*Slaps his face*]

PETER. Oh! You strike like a catfish!

SARAH. You bite like one.

PETER. I've a mind not to see you down there.

SARAH. [*Indignantly*] You *won't?* Thank ye, I'll go by myself. [*Crosses with dignity*] Hem! Won't see me down. [*Walking about*]

PETER. There, don't get up about it, and I'll tell you the reason. [*Following her*]

SARAH. Don't want any reasons.

PETER. I've an awful line to throw out.

SARAH. Don't want any lines. You may throw yourself out along with it.

PETER. [*Turning about quickly and going*] Hem! There's as good fish as ever were caught down in the village.

SARAH. [*She turns and catches him*] No, I won't either. [*Turns and struts to L.*] There's as good fisherman as ever fished in the hall here from Lun'nun. Good-bye! [*Sobbing*]

PETER. Good-bye. You've broken the line and lost your poor Perch. [*Sobbing and going out*]

SARAH. [*Aside*] Oh, he's throwing out. [*Aloud*] Peter! [*Extending her arms*] Here be the hooks yet.

PETER. Are they? Oh, then here's tie up again. [*Embrace*] There, that's right. You were the first to throw out and the first to haul up, and now you shall hear—

SARAH. Yes, make haste, my Perch—

PETER. You see, I can't take you down to Acton's. There's been a terrible stir-up in the pond, and they're fighting like catfish.

SARAH. Fighting! Who's fighting?

PETER. Well, you must know that Roger Acton by some means or other contrived to make a great haul of money.

SARAH. Yes. Set a beggar on horseback, Peter, an'—an'

PETER. Yes. We all know where he'll ride to. But he shouldn't get on the horse without someone to hold the reins awhile. Gold is like physic, Sally, and should be taken in small doses at first.

SARAH. Oh, poor Grace—the poor babes—what will come of them? O Peter, Peter, of all your fishing, never fish for gold.

PETER. No, goldfish is near enough, but the trouble at home isn't half so bad as the stories abroad, Sally—

SARAH. What stories?

PETER. Oh, some say that Roger must have killed someone. Some say that little Tom, his son, stole somewhere, because he's always in the company of Ben Burke, the poacher, and—[*In a somewhat subdued tone*] and others say the pretty Grace—

SARAH. Eh, what! Dare anybody say anything against Grace? Why, I'll, I'll—what do they say of Grace?

PETER. Something very grace*less*—something about her and my lord, the baronet—and all this gold—

SARAH. It's—it's—oh, I could bite every tongue off that dared to hint such things o' sweet Grace Acton. It's the biggest scandal that ever—[*Enter Jonathan Floyd and Jane Gossip, disputing*]

JONA. I say it is false, and the poor girl shall come in—

JANE. Then his worship may let her in at his *own* door. The proud hussy shan't pass through where I am.

PETER. Hollo! Another stir-up in the pond!

SARAH. Why, Jane—Jonathan—what is all this row about?

JONA. Why, poor Grace Acton, heart-deep in trouble, comes here and begs permission to see his lordship and this precious compound of envy and malice, very coolly shuts the door in her face without even informing his honor of her wish. [*Jonathan and Peter converse apart*]

JANE. Yes, and I'll do it again, too. And if Sir John is going to admit such a character every day in the mansion, I will leave his wicked service, so I will! Oh! Oh! I've heard it all.

SARAH. I don't care what you've heard, Miss Longears, but if I catch you spreading any of your spider webs o' scandal about Grace Acton I'll make onions of your eyes, so I will.

JANE. What all people say must be true.

SARAH. *I'm* a people—and I say it's false! Oh, I'll—[*Rushes at her*]

PETER. There, there, ladies—haul in your hooks or you may spoil your eyes. [*Coming in between them; they try to get at each other*]

JANE. And as for you, Mr. Jonathan, a pretty family you're likely to get into. What'll your poor father and mother say!

JONA. I can't help what they say—what you or the whole tribe of heartless gossips say. I will not stand tamely and see suffering innocence insulted. I'll this instant to Sir John—for while I hold my humble station in his mansion, Grace Acton shall have an entrance, if she has to find a doorway through my heart! [*Exit*]

PETER. Swallow that hook, will you?

SARAH. There, now, Miss Jane, if you'd mind your work and be a good girl instead of trying to make poor Grace a bad one, it would become you much better.

PETER. Yes, Jane, and when you marry the groom, I'll be groomsman.

JANE. Thank ye—he wouldn't have a *fish-poacher*.

SARAH. [*Flying at her*] You jade—how dare you to slander the purity of my Perch—my Grace.

JANE. Touch me and I'll call Master Jennings.

SARAH. [*Slapping her*] There!

JANE. [*Slapping back*] There! [*They attack each other. Peter tries to get between them*]

PETER. There, ladies—peace—shame—wind up! I'll bear the scaly reflection. Peace—you'll spoil your pretty gills. I'll have to string you both. [*He throws his arms about them both and pulls them off in confusion*]

SCENE 3: *The dormitory, or upper chamber in the Acton cottage. Steps leading up from trap, or by a rude lattice door up front. A small truckle bed on L. A rude, low post bed on R. Each with scanty and ragged coverlids. A few old chairs, and a small broken table near bed. A portion of thatched roof visible to the audience and so arranged as to admit the crock of gold. Music hurried. Acton comes hurriedly but still inebriated up the steps with the crock under his arm. He pulls off his coat and takes off the wallet quickly.*

ACTON. Ha, ha, ha! I gave them a drink and then the slip. It wouldn't have **done** to ha' stayed there with my heart thumping at this gold, till one of them heard it jingle. Now then, go back to your honey pot. [*Pours it into* *crock*] It's dangerous to carry so much gold about one—a fight and it would have been gone. Phew! I'm as dry as dust again. [*Takes flask from coat pocket and drinks*] Now then, to put the crock in a sure place of safety. I've already hid it everywhere and thought it safe nowhere. Let's see—in the bed? No, it might work through and drop out. Where? Where? [*Drinks*] Ha! In the thatch here. Ha, ha, ha! Who'll think o' looking there? [*Takes out a few pieces and puts them in his pocket*] There's enough for a month, if I don't spend it afore. [*Puts crock in the thatch*] Now, then, in you go—there, safe and smooth. Haven't had a good nap since my good luck. Have everything handy—[*Puts the table at the head of the bed and the flask upon it*] all safe! [*Gets into bed. Gets out again and examines thatch*] Yes, smooth as a sovereign. [*Gets in bed*] Now then, for a dream of gold, gold! Moll's gone out to walk with the children, so I'm cozy for the day. [*Noise heard*] Here she comes back. I'll go to sleep before she—she has time to sco-o-old. [*Enter Jennings. Starting up*] Hollo! Jennings, what the deuce brings *you* here?

JEN. Acton, man—that crock of gold is mine! I've paid for it—aye, paid its price in—come, come give me the honey pot.

ACTON. Ten thousand plagues to you. [*Softened*] I—I—Master Jennings, I've no pot o' gold. Maybe you'll have a little stingo. [*Offering bottle*] I've got no *gold!*

JEN. Man, you lie! You have got the money—the crock of gold—give it me at once. [*In a low hoarse voice*] And we'll say nothing of the *murder!*

ACTON. [*Springing up*] Murder! Mur—[*In astonishment*]

JEN. Aye, murder! [*Aside, as if something haunted him; looking about*] Away, I say, old—[*Trembling, aloud*] Aye, murder for the gold!

ACTON. I—I—I—did no murder, Master Jennings!

JEN. Roger, you are the murderer of Bridget Quarles. [*Acton stares at him as if totally stupefied*] Yet notwithstanding your guilt, give me the gold, Acton, and none shall know about the murder. We'll keep it all quiet and snug, you know, Roger. Only give me the crock of gold. Come! [*Determinedly*]

ACTON. [*Springing to the ground, proudly and emphatically*] Never, you cursed imp of darkness—never—by all my hatred!

JEN. Roger Acton, give it up—give me my crock or else—

ACTON. Or else what? You infernal whitened villain!

JEN. Or else I'll serve you as I—[*In great desperation*] give it to me! [*Seizes Acton by the throat*]

ACTON. Ha! You're a choker, be you! [*Seizes him*] Let go o' me, Jennings, or by the land, I'll leave no work for the hangman.

JEN. Never! Give me the crock!

ACTON. Dog! Thief! You have robbed me—trampled upon me—starved me—made my once happy home a howling den of misery, an' now you want more of me, and I'll *pay* you. Now then, for justice and a dog's reward. [*They struggle about violently. Acton finally throws him to the floor, drags him to the steps and hurls him down*] There's gold for you—that's the coin to pay such a villain in. [*Panting*] Now then, for my nap. He'll hardly come up here again after that fun, and he may take all the gold he can get downstairs, and Moll's tongue on him in the bargain. By the land, how quick that was. It seems like a dream already. [*Noise and talking heard below*]

JEN. [*Outside*] Search the ash pit!

MARY. [*Outside*] You shan't go up. There's nothing there.

GRACE. [*Outside*] Oh, heavens! What new terrors await us! [*Enter Jennings up steps, with a few empty leather bags, and a fragment of the burnt shawl, and followed by two Constables, Mary, Grace, Children, Tom, Snip, Dick, the tanner, Neighbors, male and female. Acton springs out of bed*]

JEN. [*Looking at Acton and showing articles*] Look here, villain—no gold —no murder! What do you call these, sir? My Aunt Bridget's shawl, here torn and burnt, and fragments scattered about your hearth.

ACTON. [*Aside*] Ben Burke's fault—plague upon him. [*He looks very earnestly towards the thatch*] Be still, Moll—not a word—the crock is safe. They shall never have the gold. [*Watching the thatch. Here Jennings, following Acton's eyes, runs his cane into the thatch and the crock falls out, scattering the gold upon the floor. Roger, Grace and Mary all start in terror. Jennings seizes and hugs the crock*]

JEN. 'Tis mine, mine, my crock of gold!

ACTON. Ah! Grace was right—it was a fiend!

JEN. 'Tis mine, 'tis mine—don't touch a coin of it. My aunt's dear crock. Arrest her murderer! [*Pointing to Acton. Officers advance and seize Acton, who seems stupefied at the word* murder]

OMNES. A murderer! [*Acton clasps his hands and sinks across foot of bed. Picture and curtain*]

ACT IV.

SCENE 1: *A street in the village near Hurstley. Enter Peter Perch, Old Floyd, Dick, the tanner, Snip, the landlord.*

PETER. But after all, neighbors, they may have hauled up the wrong fish. Roger Acton couldn't be such a pike as to pick the life out of an old carp like Bridget Quarles merely for the sake of a few golden scales. *I* think so—*Sarah Slack* thinks so—we both think so, and good Mr. Floyd, your sharp-eyed perch of a son, Jonathan, would take his oath on't.

FLOYD. Well, well, tomorrow the man's trial comes, and after that you'll all think differently. I wish for my own part, for my son's part, as well as the prisoner and his bereaved family that he may be able to prove his innocence, but—

DICK. His innocence—with Mrs. Quarles's gold in his pocket—with Mrs. Quarles's burnt shawl in his fireplace—with the whole history of the murder wrote on the corner of it in letters of blood—her honey pot hid in the thatch of his hovel—a queer place to put presarves truly. Innocent! Why, Peter Perch, you're a roach to think so.

PETER. A roach, am I—thank ye—you're a sucker.

DICK. A sucker?

PETER. Yes, a sucker. You were glad enough to swim in liquor bought by Acton's gold, that you say was bloody money. I tell you what, Mr. Dick Swipes, you must ha' had a strong stomach, and a conscience as big as one of your tan vats. Before you show such delicate nerves about the guilty, you'd better grind yourself over in your bark mill.

FLOYD. There, Peter, don't defend the guilty too far; it's a dangerous charity.

DICK. Yes, particularly in one as fishes in forbidden waters. The law calls that poaching, and a poacher is nothing better than—[*Enter Jennings quickly*]

JEN. Than *stealing!*

DICK. That's the word, Master Jennings.

SNIP. That's hard stingo to swaller.

JEN. Peter Perch, I arrest you for poaching upon Sir John's manor. [*Snip and Dick exult apart, rubbing their hands*]

PETER. Queer manner of arrest, but as you may have come without a warrant, as you very often do—I'll furnish you with one ready filled up. There! [*Gives paper*]

JEN. [*Reads*] Confusion! A free license for fishing in Hurstley ponds, and signed by Sir John. 'Sdeath.

DICK. The mischief!

PETER. Ha, ha, ha! Master Simon, don't that hook kind a sort o' throttle you!

JEN. [*Aside, starting*] Throttle—[*Aloud*] Peter, you're a—

PETER. You can't *out*warrant that, I'll warrant you! [*Snatches paper from Jennings who was about to tear it*] No, you don't—you are good at clawing neck or nothing—but you can't come your dragnet over me. I say, little bailiff, meet me at Pike Pond in an hour an'—[*Holding up paper*] I'll treat you to such a mess of crock—or rock, I mean—can't get that crock out of my throat —such a mess of rock, as sweet as Mrs. Quarles's honey. [*Exit*]

JEN. [*Gazes after him as if every word had a double meaning. Aside*] Death on his stinging tongue.

FLOYD. You seem disturbed, Mr. Simon.

JEN. Farmer, I am disturbed, and well I may be. The painful duty I have had to perform in bringing the murderer of my dear Aunt Bridget to justice may well disturb a tender mind like mine. But half of the dreadful task is over, and Roger Acton stands his trial for robbery and murder.

FLOYD. It appears certain, I believe, that a full conviction must follow?

JEN. As certain as the trial shall come. Never was proof so unanswerable and crushing. The jury will but echo tomorrow what his own conscience and public opinion declared today. [*Enter Jonathan Floyd*]

JONA. [*Aside*] Ha! Jennings here!

FLOYD. Ha, son, I was just waiting to see you. Where have you been all the morning?

JONA. Attending poor Grace Acton and her mother to Roger Acton's prison.

JEN. I could have wished you a worthier office, Jonathan.

FLOYD. [*Sternly*] And I, too, sir.

DICK and SNIP. And everybody.

JONA. [*To Dick and Snip*] Peace, vile scandal makers—there's more murder in your vile breath than would fill a prison. To you, father, I am and will be accountable, but for you, Master Simon, who so kindly wish me a better office, I can assure you I know of none nobler than that of giving my humble solace to persecuted innocence—and I only hope that your own conscience may be as free from blood as that of Roger Acton.

JEN. [*Starting*] From blood—man—bloo—

FLOYD. Jonathan, forebear, for—

JONA. Father, I will speak out—it is here—[*Touching his heart*] and it will come out. Pray, mister butler, [*Crosses*] where were you on the night of Mrs. Quarles's death?

JEN. [*Aside, trembling*] Death and torture. [*Aloud*] Jonathan Floyd—but I will not humble or degrade you before your father. You have dared to hint —[*Rushing at him*] No, no, I'll seek a fitter, a more proper time—and you shall rue—[*To Dick and Snip*] neighbors follow me. *You* shall hear what I cannot descend to relate unto a boy—a servant—a lover of a—

JONA. What? [*Enraged*]

JEN. [*Aside*] I'll be hanged but I'll be revenged on him—and Grace Acton shall be my instrument of vengeance! [*Exit with Snip and Dick*]

FLOYD. Jonathan, you have risked your place, your name and character by implicating the respected Simon Jennings! Renounce the abandoned girl, or—

JONA. Never, father, never! Granting poor Acton the wretch you think—but I do not believe one word of it—does his crime make his daughter wicked, too? No! She is an angel, a pure, a blessed soul, too good for such as I. And happy is the man who has gained her love. No, dear Grace, we will go down to the grave together. Come weal, or woe—let malice do its worst, man vent his hate—Heaven is above all, and that Heaven will bless us. Remember, father, "Judge not." Come with me, see Acton in his penitential cell, humbled in heart, but free in *soul,* as if the Great Searcher had been there, and found no stain of crime. [*Exeunt*]

SCENE 2: *The prison. A table and a couple of stools and stone jug near table. Music. Roger Acton discovered seated at table with a Bible in his hand. Mary near him.*

ACTON. [*Pressing the Bible*] *There's* comfort, Mary, and *here's* comfort. [*Embracing her*] And there's comfort everywhere for the truly penitent and humble—yet, my kind and faithful girl, I can't but feel myself unworthy of it all—wretch, brute, monster, that I have been to you—to Heaven—to myself —to all. And yet to find the word of Heaven speaking sweet music in my far deep prison cell. To find you leaving our helpless babes and trudging this long and weary way to cheer me with love, comfort, and every hope. And poor Grace, too—oh, no—this is too much kindness—reproaches and despair should visit me alone.

MARY. Nay, do not talk so, husband. This true contrition deserves every-thing. I am your partner for life, Roger, not only in its pleasures but in its pains. I have shared the one with you, and I will bear the other with you, and though you were fallen thrice as far—aye—even at the world's end—my feet would trace you out, my hands would succor you, my voice and love would cheer and console you! [*Falls upon his neck*]

ACTON. Ah, bless you, Moll, bless you! These tears are like the rainy balsam to the cracked soil. Oh, when I compare my forty years of peaceful poverty and Christian-like course with my wicked and blasphemous career for one bad week of wealth, I feel nothing but my own reproaches and ab-horrence. My children, too, heirs to a felon's shame—poor orphans—their father doomed and broken-hearted.

MARY. Doomed! O Acton, think not so, while there is one on earth whose voice can clear. Heaven will send that one, though ever so far away. Ben Burke can save you, and he may yet be found. Aye, Heaven will send Ben Burke to free you, Roger!

ACTON. No, no, Mary, I cannot hope aid from kind-hearted Ben Burke, you know! Oh, why didn't I think on't that fatal night! You know that

Burke's way of living is not clearly lawful, and my naming him as a witness might bring him into trouble by putting him into the hands of the law. No, no, Mary, I would not endanger another's life to save my own.

MARY. Nay, but it is our duty, Acton, to Heaven—to ourselves, and to the state, to call up anyone whose oath can save an innocent man, and prevent justice from committing a murder. But alas! I must leave you for a while—'tis nearly night, and our babes will need me.

ACTON. Ah, then, go dear—give the dear little ones my poor blessing, and Heaven bless you.

MARY. You'll not be long alone. Grace will soon be here. Farewell till I return, and Heaven be with you.

ACTON. Farewell, my girl. [*With feeling*] God bless you. [*They embrace and Mary exit*] Oh, what blessings are in that ever growing treasure—*wife!* Man's second self—his other heart, that, when his own does fail him, she comes in like a sturdy staff, to bear him up in sorrow and affliction. [*Takes up jug*] Come, one kiss from thee, the pure companion of my lonely home, nature's pure crock of health, and peace of mind. If a thousand crocks of earth's seducing ore were placed before me now, I'd shun them all, as a deadly poison, and cling, old jug, to you! [*Drinks. Noise of chains. Door opens, and Grace enters. She rushes into her father's arms*] Grace, my angel.

GRACE. Ah, my dear father, how have you fared? Have you been lonely?

ACTON. No, my child! My conscience has been with me—besides, you left Heaven's word with me—[*Pointing to Bible*] I trust in deep remorse and penitence for my deliverance. But yet, Grace, my remorse cannot be punishment equal to my sins—my wicked thirst for gold! The gibbet—the hangman should be my retribution here, and for the next—

GRACE. Nay, father, let not the penitent bow himself too low. Be humbled as you may before Heaven, father, but stand boldly up before *man!* For in his sight, and in his laws you are sinful, but not criminal. Money was your temptation—its love, your fault—its possession, your misfortune. If you do feel yourself too guilty in the sight of Heaven, it must not harm your cause before man. Though weary of life, you must not be doomed innocently to death. Manfully confront your false accuser—tell openly the truth—plead your own cause firmly—and Heaven defend the right.

ACTON. Oh, blessings on you, my brave girl, blessings. [*Sobbing*] I'll try to do all you tell, Grace; but it is a hard thing to feel myself so wicked, and to speak so boldly, like a Christian man. What has made me live like a beast —sin like a heathen—and lie down here like a felon? Gold! The crock of gold! And, oh, my Grace—my hope—think that its curses touched *thee,* too —and branded thee with infamy—placed scorn's hissing serpents in thy path,

that should have been all flowers. Oh, dear Grace, dear, pure, and patient child
—here upon my knees I—I beg—I pray you to forgive that wrong!

GRACE. [*Kissing his forehead and raising him*] Up, dear father. When
they whispered so against me, I would have borne all—all in silence, and let
them believe me bad, could I have thought that by uttering the truth I should
have seen thee here in this dungeon and treated as a murderer. Oh, forgive
me, too, this wrong, my father.

ACTON. From my heart, I do, my child. [*They embrace with great emotion*] Now, my child, the night draws on, and your way is long and lonely.
Leave me, my girl, to prayer and penitence. I shall be happy.

GRACE. So shall a blessing come upon it at last. Remember the words that
were not written in vain. Farewell, dear father! Heaven will defend the right!

ACTON. [*Embracing and kissing her*] Farewell, my child, my guardian
angel. I'm happy, my Grace—happy—I shall die happy. [*He sinks down in
chair, with tears of penitence and affectionate emotion, his hands upon the
Bible, as Grace exits through door*]

SCENE 3: *An ordinary country view. Dark stage. Enter Jennings.*

JEN. The outcry against Acton grows stronger. There's not a living voice
or witness in his favor, and he must hang! Ha, ha, ha! Revenge and the
wealth are mine—the precious crock of gold I have secured along with my
own private gains in the great iron safe within my chamber. Now then, to
secure the favor of Sir John, and revenge myself from that stinging serpent,
Jonathan Floyd. That curst Peter Perch, too, is full of harrowing innuendoes.
And yet what clue can they have to suspect? No matter now—let my vengeance come singly. Sir John is young—Grace Acton's young and beautiful—
I have it—first to triumph myself, and then to dispose of the fair spoil to Sir
John; and thus revenge myself on bold young Floyd. This way she always
passes from the prison! I have contrived to detain Jonathan at the hall, and
she will be alone and at my mercy. [*Looks off*] Ha! By all my aims, she comes
here. [*Hides. Enter Grace Acton*]

GRACE. 'Tis very strange; he always met me at the gates to attend me
home, but now I see him nowhere. Oh, heavens, can it be that threatened by
his parents for my father's misfortunes, he has forsaken me! And after all his
vows—his constant cares and noble generosity—our hands and hearts betrothed? O Jonathan! The thought would kill me. Yet, no, I will not doubt
his true unselfish honor. Something must have happened at the hall. Yes, yes
—I'll on alone. Heaven be my light and my companion.

JEN. [*Comes down, bowing*] Suffer me to be the latter, fair Miss Grace.

GRACE. [*Starting*] How! Master Jennings!

JEN. Yes, Miss Acton, my walk is in your way—I'll see you home.

GRACE. You are very kind, Mr. Jennings—but—

JEN. Pray, Miss Grace, I assure you, this reserve is ill-timed. Besides, I have an important word to say to you touching your father's inno—I mean the safety of his life.

GRACE. The safety of his life—my dear father's life? Oh, speak, Mr. Simon, speak—is there a hope?

JEN. Hope and safety. You bear both hope and freedom in yourself.

GRACE. In myself—how—where?

JEN. [*Taking hold of her*] In your sweet charms, Miss Grace. I, you know, am your father's prosecutor for the murder of my aunt. His life is in my hands, to give or take. [*Pressing her rudely*] Now make me *blessed,* and set your father free.

GRACE. [*Throwing him off furiously*] Begone, thou lurking fiend!

JEN. [*Aside*] Perdition! [*Aloud*] Fool, dare you spurn me?

GRACE. Aye, Condemned of Heaven! I spurn you as I would a viper! Coward! Had I a thousand parents at your mercy, they'd smile in death to see me scorn your polluted grasp! Away! [*He seizes her*] Off, villain, off!

JEN. Ha! then I will take the jewel without the price. Come this way— nay, your cries and struggles won't avail. You're here alone and helpless!

GRACE. She's never helpless that trusts in Heaven!

JEN. Will Heaven hear a felon's daughter? Ha, ha, ha!

GRACE. Help me, Heaven! Jonathan, save me! Save me!

JONA. [*Outside*] Here, Grace! [*Jonathan rushes in, followed by Peter Perch. He throws Jennings off, and Grace falls in his arms. Peter gets behind Jennings*]

GRACE. Heaven be praised!

JEN. Malediction! [*Turns to go, Peter seizes him*]

PETER. No, you're hooked, mister devilfish!

JONA. So, Mr. Simon, you couldn't quite stifle the cries this time!

PETER. No, nor mesmerize the dog!

JEN. [*Furiously*] Rascals, this is no talk to me—I understand it not, but perhaps your chaste fair one's father may.

JONA. We understand you, though, Mr. Simon, and so shall his worship. Drag him along, Peter. Come, dear Grace, his honor shall hear your story.

GRACE. Yes, dear Jonathan, you shall hear all!

JONA. Come, my love, look up. You've naught to fear. Drag him along, Peter, the bailiff shall have justice! [*Exit, leading Grace*]

PETER. Come along, black fish! You're in a *pickle*—for all the *honey!* [*Pulling him*]

JEN. Villain! Stand! I'll go, but I'll not be dragged. I am steward of Hurstley, and your master. Beware how you insult my office.

PETER. [*Holding on to him*] I know that it's tough swimming against tide, so I'll just tow you along gently. [*Pulls him by the collar*] Come, swim along!

JEN. [*Catching at the air*] Take your cold hands from my throat, I'll strangle.

PETER. I don't touch your throat—you must have swallowed a poisoned toad, old pike—let me unchoke you. [*Takes hold of his cravat, shaking him as he pulls him off*]

JEN. [*Wildly*] Away, old hag—away! [*Exeunt*]

SCENE 4: *A chamber in Hurstley Hall. Enter Silliphant, Silkhair, and Sir John.*

SILK. Ha, ha, ha! Foine, chawming! Chawming! A most ravishing idea— a bailiff turning poacher on the grounds of Cupid—surprised and kicked by the boot of a Mercury of a footman—Venus rescued—Mars floored—most mythologically romantic, it is, by my suavity!

SILLI. Good! Capital! A relief to the monotony of cards, cribbage, and brandy.

SIR JOHN. Ha, ha! This is a surprising adventure indeed. I never thought that Jennings had the least turn *that* way. The fellow is for monopolizing everything on my estate.

SILK. I say, Sir John, it's devilish unfortunate that the parties are of such shocking vulgar grade—or in fashionable words—that they are nobody. We might get up a sociable little duel on the strength of the adventure—we might, by my suavity!

SIR JOHN. You will excuse me, sir, when I tell you that the injured party in this affair has rights and feelings like other people—aye, sir, like the best, and such as should ever command respect in court, hall, and cottage.

SILK. Oh, shocking! I admire your appreciation of cornfed flesh—I do, by my suavity!

SIR JOHN. And as their lives are too useful and valuable to be lost in the *"social sport,"* or rather, the murder that you speak of, we'll leave such as you for its sacrifices, being fit for nothing else.

SILLI. Ha, ha, ha! Silky, a shot for you already!

SILK. Foil—foil! Don't even penetrate my Clarence [*sic*] belt! [*Enter Jonathan, leading Grace, who follows very timidly. They are followed by Perch dragging in Jennings. Sarah Slack on*]

SILLI. I say, Silkhair—devilish pretty—fine creature—[*Sarah goes to Grace, consoling her*]

SILK. [*Looking through glass and crossing*] Yaas, very fine article of the sort, by my suavity!

SIR JOHN. Well, Jonathan lad, how's all this?

JONA. Why, in a word, my honored master, this scoundrel here has been wickedly insulting the honor of my Grace—my own poor, suffering Grace— by promising to save her father, on such foul terms as your worship may conceive, and need not shock all here by naming.

SIR JOHN. Jennings, is it possible, sir, that you were brute enough, to attempt the ruin of the poor man Acton's daughter, just as he is about to be tried for his life? [*Jennings stands guiltstricken, but silent and sullen. Grace bows to Sir John as acknowledging the truth of the charge, and bursts into tears*]

SARAH. Oh, don't cry, Miss Grace dear. We'll make him grin for this, like a red-hot gridiron.

PETER. It'll be the old boy's then—won't he have a mess o' foul fish!

SILK. Why, bless me, Silliphant, her cheeks positively bear the fluid from her eyes without losing—without changing—color—waterproof vermillion, by my suavity!

SIR JOHN. Simon Jennings, I have paused for your defense. 'Tis clear you have none. Now, sir, listen—

JEN. Your worship—

SIR JOHN. Silence, sir. I have been gradually finding out your dark rascality for some days past. I have learnt much more than you imagine and now this foul, this crowning villainy gives me just occasion to say—begone forever from my service.

JEN. [*Drawing himself up proudly*] Sir John Vincent, I am proud to leave your service. And know, if you please, sir, that I can afford to live without it —aye, and richly, too.

SIR JOHN. Perhaps, sir, you are not aware that your systematic thievings and extortions have justified me in detaining your iron chest and other valuables till I find out how you came by them!

PETER. [*Aside*] A pike in salt water!

JEN. [*Aside*] What, gone! My store—my gold—my blood-bought crock of gold! My hope—my only solace—gone! [*Grasps his hair in desperation*]

SIR JOHN. Away, away with him! [*To Jonathan*] And if you'll kick the villain downstairs on your private account, I'll forgive you for it.

JONA. Say no more, your worship. [*Seizing Jennings*]

PETER. Let me have a hook in! [*Seizes Jennings also*]

JEN. [*Trying to throw them off, proudly*] Sir John, if you dare to rob me of my rights, my blood, my wealth, may a pestilence light upon your estate— may the ghost of my strangled—my murdered aunt haunt you by day and night, and choke you as she—as rage and hate now choke me. [*They drag him out, all following and enjoying the scene. Grace bows to Sir John and is going out, as Silkhair attempts to kiss her. She shrinks from him, and pushes him off with a look of insulted modesty, and rushes out. Silliphant laughing at Silkhair*]

SILK. Come, Silliphant, that's a horrible and excruciating laugh of yours —a vulgar laugh it is, by my suavity!

SIR JOHN. Silkhair, if ever again you repeat a rudeness of the kind upon anyone under my protection, I'll compliment your suavity with a cane.

SILK. Aw! Aw! Very foine—Oi comprehend distinctly—Sir John wants her all to himself—foine, by my suavity!

SIR JOHN. [*Quickly*] Say that again, sir, and you follow Jennings instanter. [*Going towards him, Silkhair stops him*]

SILK. There, there, my boy, I wouldn't trouble you in the least—I wouldn't 'pon honor, for any civility of the kind, and to bring your super, superlative sensibilities to a state of equilibrium—I apologize—I do, by my suavity!

SIR JOHN. Enough, sir! But you must also tender an apology to the young lady.

SILK. Aw! I shall do it with pleasure, and shall do you and myself the honor of accommodating her young Apollo in blue livery one also. 'Pologizing's no trouble to me, whatever, Sir John—like assurance, I always keep a good stock on hand—I do, by my suavity! [*Sarah Slack is heard sobbing. She enters*]

SARAH. O Sir John, my good, kind master, Sir John—

SIR JOHN. Why, bless me, Sarah! What in the world is the matter—have they broken Jennings's neck?

SARAH. No—o—o, your worship, but they're going to break poor Roger Acton's neck—so they are—going to hang him; it's a choking shame, so it is.

SIR JOHN. Well, I'm very sorry, but I can't help it, girl—if the poor man's guilty. But why do you come to me?

SARAH. Why, why—you've got a fast horse, your worship, and I want you to send after Ben Burke.

SIR JOHN. Send for Ben Burke. Why who the deuce is Ben Burke?

SARAH. Why, Ben Burke, your worship—Grace Acton says that he knows all about the crock of gold—who it belonged to—who stole it—and he can save poor Acton's life—only—only—

SIR JOHN. [*Quickly*] What?

SARAH. He aint jist here!

SIR JOHN. Well, where is he then?

SARAH. They say he's at London, or Liverpool—or—or—somewhere else.

SILK. Explicit, by my suavity.

SIR JOHN. And you wish me to send after him, to London, to Liverpool, or somewhere else—eh?

SARAH. Ye—ye—yes, your worship, right away!

SIR JOHN. Nonsense, girl! The poor man might be tried and hanged before I could send to London, or Liverpool—and as for the somewhere else—

SARAH. Maybe that isn't so far, your worship.

SIR JOHN. And as for this knowing individual, Burke, as you call him, one might as well think of looking for a particular straw in a stack. Nonsense, girl! [Goes up]

SARAH. Your worship, there's no nonsense in being hanged, and partic'lar when one haint been doing nothing nohow to nobody. Oh, dear, there's Master Jennings as white as an egg—telling a long, crooked story. There's the jurymen, chokin' for fear they'll have to hang Roger! But I'll be hanged if they shall. I'll go after Ben Burke myself—so I will! [Exit sobbing]

SILK. Foine! She'll travel to London—Liverpool—or anywhere else—sympathetic creature, by my suavity.

SIR JOHN. Come, gentlemen! I feel much interested in the result of this seemingly mysterious affair. Let's on to the court!

SILK. I'd much rather it were the court of Cupid than of John Flitch, Esq., by my suavity. [Exeunt]

SCENE 5: *A court of justice, whole stage. Judge, Jury, Counsels, Spectators, Acton, Mary, Grace, Jennings, very pale, Floyd, Perch, Dick, Snip, Sir John, Silliphant, Silkhair, etc., all discovered looking upon Acton with attention and sympathy. Mary and Grace are both weeping.*

JUDGE. [*Is concluding a few words to Acton*] The crock—the shawl—aye —I grieve to add—the robbery and the *murder* being so clearly traced to you, Acton—before I recommit you, what can you say in your defense?

ACTON. Wi' your worship's leave, if my tongue was as free as my heart be I could say sommat—say much in proof o' my innocence—but a poor, plain laborer is brought to listen more than to speak. But, good countrymen, hearken. Of late I knows I ha' done many evils against Heaven and against my neighbor. I have sworn and drank and wickedly coveted. Nevertheless, countrymen, wicked though I be in sight of Him that judges all—yet, 'cording to man's innocence, an' man's judgment, I had lived a blameless life among you all till I found the crock of gold. I did find it, countrymen, as

Heaven be my witness—I found it in the hedge that skirts my garden—aye, in my own celery trench. I did wickedly and foolishly hide my find—did worse to deny it, and worse than all to spend it. But of robbery I am as guiltless as any man here. And as for this black charge of murder—till Master Jennings there spoke the word, I never knew a murder had been done. Folk of Hurstley, man an' woman, dame and daughter, neighbors and friends— you all know Roger Acton, the old time Honest Roger, before the evil 'un made him mad by giving him gold. Did he ever do intended wrong to man or woman—to child or poor dumb brute? No, countrymen, I'm no murderer. That seemings be against me, well I wot—they may excuse your judgment in condemning me to death, an' the good gentle there that took my part— Heaven bless you, sir—cannot go against the facts, however much they belie me—for they do speak falsely—and I *truly*, countrymen. For I still do declare afore my maker—Roger Acton be an innocent man, as may Heaven defend the right.

GRACE. [*Aside*] Amen! And Heaven *will* defend the right! [*The jury consult. Jennings watches them in great agitation*]

JUDGE. Prisoner, you seem to speak like an innocent man—but you said truly, we cannot go against facts, and these facts must inevitably—[*A loud noise is heard at the door, and Ben Burke speaks outside*]

BURKE. I'se a witness, an' I will come in.

JEN. [Aside] That voice—the fiend upon the lake that—[*All rise as Ben Burke breaks through them, throwing up his cap and flourishing his club, followed by Tom Acton*]

GRACE. Heaven is just.

ACTON. An' will defend the right! [*Jennings trembles violently*]

BURKE. Swear me. I'm a witness. There's the white devil that fetched the crocks to the lake to bury 'em. Here's where he grabbed [*Showing a mark on his own neck*], an' here's the snare hook that caught in his coat—[*Pulls a small hook from the collar of his coat and flourishing* [*sic*] *it about. Tom Acton embraces his father, and all eyes are turned upon Jennings, who is struggling at the air violently*]

JEN. Let go my throat, old woman! Let go and I'll tell all! See there. [*Gazes at Acton*]

ACTON. What be the matter, Master Jennings? Untie his kerchief.

BURKE. No, hang him by it!

JEN. Let go, I say, old hag—why do you strangle me now? I have lost the crock, lost all, my gains—my soul—my victims! All, all! Ah! The bedroom— the strangled corse—the form upon the lake—it's there again—but is no spectre—it breathes—it speaks to damn me. I confess I am guilty! Guilty!

ACTON. Look up, Master Simon, and pray for—

JEN. I can't—she chokes—she strangles me. [*Pulls at his throat furiously*] Let go, Aunt Quarles, let go, I say. Ha! She masters me—I'll not die! One effort more—[*He springs to his feet wildly. Stands erect, gazing an instant around in horror and falls dead*]

JUDGE. [*Bending over him*] Ah, Heaven has spoken. Roger Acton, you are an innocent man—you are free!

ACTON. Free! Grace, Mary—kneel with me. [*They kneel*] Father of Mercy, receive an old man's thanks! [*General shout and a quick curtain*]

JOB AND HIS CHILDREN

A Domestic Drama in Two Acts

By J. M. Field

JOB AND HIS CHILDREN

JOSEPH M. FIELD, playwright, actor, manager, reporter, editor, "colyumist," packed into the forty-six years of his life a variety of theatrical experience. Born in Dublin in 1810, Field came from an old Warwickshire ancestry, of which the Elizabethan playwright, Nathaniel Field, was the most famous member. Brought to the United States at the age of two, Joseph Field began his theatrical career at seventeen, on the stage of Boston's Tremont Theatre in November 1827. In the ensuing twenty-nine years he wrote or adapted a score of plays, appeared as an actor in many different cities, owned and managed a theatre in Saint Louis, operated a newspaper there, and gained temporary fame as a writer of humorous stories and articles for the New Orleans *Picayune*.

Field's career coincides with the rapid westward movement of the theatre in his generation. As early as 1830 he spent at least part of the summer on the stage of the old Salt House in Saint Louis. Audiences in Saint Louis, New Orleans, Mobile, Montgomery, Cincinnati, Baltimore, Philadelphia, New York, and Boston saw his performances, and gave him a contemporary reputation especially in eccentric comedy rôles. His own comedies and farces were closely associated with his career as an actor.

The practice of employing guest stars for short engagements kept Field traveling much of the time. In the years 1835 and 1836, for example, he acted first at Montgomery, Ala., then went to Saint Louis for six weeks, returning, with stops in Cincinnati and Baltimore, to New York. After a brief appearance at the Park Theatre in September, he went to New Orleans for the winter. Within less than a year he had again spent a brief season in Saint Louis, and had returned to Mrs. Hamblin's Theatre in New York by early August 1836.

If there is any one place especially to be associated with the name of J. M. Field, it is Saint Louis. In cooperation with those two pioneers of the western theatre, Sol Smith and Noah M. Ludlow, Field contributed some of his best efforts. Several of his plays were first produced at the Saint Louis theatre. With his brother Matthew (also, for a brief time, an actor) and Mr. Charles Keemle, he published a paper, *The Reveille,* in Saint Louis, beginning in May 1844. Important in Saint Louis theatrical history is Field's Varieties Theatre, operated from May 1852 to the end of the year 1853.

But through these same years Field spent occasional seasons in Mobile, New Orleans, Philadelphia, and New York. He wrote poems and humorous articles for a New Orleans *Picayune* column, over the signature, "Straws," in 1839 and 1840. The *Picayune* sent him abroad as a foreign correspondent the next year. Upon his return, he spent several months at a time as a member of the company at Mitchell's Olympic Theatre (New York), at the Chatham, the Park, the Walnut Street Theatre (Philadelphia), and later at the Chestnut Street Theatre (Philadelphia), and at Burton's and the Metropolitan (New York). At Mitchell's Olympic in 1842 he received the top salary of twenty-five dollars a week, plus one-third of the receipts of one benefit, on the condition that Mitchell have title to any new plays Field might write.

Early in his career he tried almost any rôle. In one season (1837) he played Richard III, Macbeth, Lear, Othello, Hamlet, Iago, Prince Hal, Orlando, Benedick, Sir Giles Overreach, and Hastings (*Jane Shore*). These rôles were played in Saint Louis and other provincial theatres, where Field was a star. He established his reputation as an actor, particularly in the East, not with these rôles, but upon his interpretation of comic characters, to which he soon gave his full attention. Most of these comic parts were in ephemeral farces and comedies, but he was especially admired in the rôle of Sir Benjamin Backbite.

Except for the *Picayune* articles and *The Reveille,* Field's only published works were two volumes of prose sketches, *The Drama in Pokerville,* and *The Bench and Bar of Jurytown and Other Stories* (1847). None of his plays was ever published, and the only one known to be in existence is the recently discovered *Job and His Children,* appearing in this volume. The following list supplies, in order of original production, all the plays that may safely be assigned to Field. Authorship of the first play in the list is the most doubtful, for if both Odell and Carson (*The Theatre on the Frontier*) are to be accepted, Field acted at the Park Theatre in New York and at the Salt House in Saint Louis at the same time.

Down South; or, a Militia Training. Park (N.Y.), July 5, 1830.

Amalgamation; or, Southern Visitors, "a new Satirical farce." Saint Louis, October 10, 1838.

Victoria; or, The Lion and the Kiss. Saint Louis, October 1838. New Bowery (N.Y.), June 12, 1839.

The Tourists (or, Tourists in America). Walnut (Phila.), October 31, 1839. Chatham (N.Y.), March 19, 1840.

Such As It Is. Park (N.Y.), September 4, 1842.

Nervo Vitalics; or, The March of Science (or, What Next?). Mitchell's Olympic (N.Y.), September 19, 1842. Walnut (Phila.), September 21, 1843.

Antony and Cleopatra, "a dramatic eccentricity" (burletta). Olympic (N.Y.),
    March 1, 1843. Walnut (Phila.), September 26, 1843.
The Artful Dodger. Bowery (N.Y.), September 4, 1843.
Gabrielle; or, A Night's Hazard (or, The Fatal Hazard). (Probably from
    Dumas' *Mademoiselle de Belle-Isle.*) Walnut (Phila.), September 16, 1843.
Life in China. New Orleans, April 2, 1844.
Belle Isle. (Perhaps the same play as *Gabrielle.*) New Orleans, January 12,
    1846.
Oregon; or, The Disputed Territory. Mobile, January 26, 1846.
Foreign and Native. Mobile, January 26, 1846.
Family Ties; or, The Will of Uncle Josh (written with J. S. Robb). Park
    (N.Y.), June 19, 1846. Arch (Phila.), July 24, 1851.
Married an Actress. Burton's (N.Y.), December 19, 1850.
Doctor Bilboquet (a translation from the French). Saint Louis, 1851.
Job and His Children. Saint Louis, August 25, 1852.
Griselda; or, The Patient Woman (from a German play by Waldauer).
    Chestnut (Phila.), October 23, 1854. Metropolitan (N.Y.), November 27,
    1854.

Ludlow says that Field wrote the successful burlesque of the popular *La
Bayadere, The Maid of Casimere,* entitled *Buy It, Dear! Tis Made of Cash-
mere,* first produced on March 16, 1843; but Odell assigns this play to Horn-
castle, and its first production to November 2, 1840. Although Ludlow appears
to be in error in this instance, there are probably many more plays which
might be assigned to Field, could their authorship be determined.

Of the plays listed, *The Artful Dodger* was the most popular. *Family Ties*
won a five-hundred dollar prize given by Danforth Marble for the best
Yankee play, but it was none the less a failure. The plays perhaps averaged
ten to fifteen performances each. For the curious reader, the most regrettable
loss is *Victoria,* in which the Queen and James Gordon Bennett were the
chief characters, supported by the Duke of Wellington, the Duchess of Kent,
and *Prince* John Van Buren!

It seems safe to say that Field was a better actor than playwright or
theatrical manager. His managerial career included the seasons of 1850 and
1851 at Mobile, after which he ventured on his own responsibility in opening
Field's Varieties Theatre in Saint Louis, on May 10, 1852. This theatre,
accommodating nearly twelve hundred people, was located on the south side
of Market Street, between Fifth and Sixth Streets. It survived less than two
years, for (according to Ludlow) Field was not a shrewd manager.

After abandoning his experiment in December 1853, Field spent the fall
season of 1854 in the East, and then went to the theatre in Mobile, where he

remained until his death, on January 28, 1856. He was survived by his wife, Eliza Riddle, a popular actress whom he had married in Saint Louis in November 1837, and by a daughter, Mary Katherine Keemle Field. In later years, under the name of Kate Field, his daughter became a well-known lecturer-entertainer, and the editor of a political paper, *Kate Field's Washington*.

From accounts of Field's plays, it seems pretty certain that *Job and His Children* was one of its author's rare attempts at serious drama. It involves a sentimental plot of the stern parent and the disobedient daughter, whose reconciliation occurs after a series of complications and misunderstandings. *Job and His Children* was first produced by Field at his own Varieties Theatre, and was later produced in Mobile. The manuscript seems to have been owned by the popular actor, W. H. Chippendale (whose autograph it bears), and it was he who played the part of Job. It was discovered in the possession of a book dealer in New Brunswick, New Jersey, from whom it was purchased by Mr. Barrett H. Clark.

For additional information concerning Field, see especially N. M. Ludlow's *Dramatic Life As I Found It*, W. G. B. Carson's *The Theatre on the Frontier*, and Lilian Whiting's *Kate Field, A Record*. A portrait of J. M. Field appears on page 438 of the third volume of Odell's *Annals of the New York Stage*.

CAST OF CHARACTERS

JOB DAY	MR. W. H. CHIPPENDALE
HAMPDEN DAY	MR. A. WELSH
MILTON TRICE	MR. WRIGHT
OBY OILSTONE	MR. M. SMITH
ABEL	MR. SCHOOLCRAFT
FIRST VISITOR	MR. DUFFIELD
SECOND VISITOR	MR. DUNCAN
THIRD VISITOR	MR. LEAMAN
CHILD	MASTER G. CAULFIELD
FAITH DAY	MRS. J. M. FIELD
MELISSA	MISS HILL
SARAH	MRS. MELVILLE
RACHEL	MRS. CAULFIELD

VISITORS, PEASANTS, ETC.

(This is the original cast of characters at Field's Varieties, St. Louis, Mo., Aug. 25, 1852.)

ACT I.

SCENE: *An apartment in a New England farmhouse. Enter Milton Trice and Faith Day.*

FAITH. Not love you, Milton!

MILT. Oh, I know you exclaim at that; just as if I'd said you were not a Christian, or not a good girl. But if you *do* love me, marry me, marry me now. I tell you that the sickness of the supercargo forbids his going, and that the house, knowing my ability as a former clerk with them, offers me every inducement to give up my berth as Chief Mate, and to take care of their interests in the disposal of the cargo. Come, love, as we've exchanged hearts, now clasp hands. The ship sets sail from the dock, in the city, this evening, and the cabin is at your service.

FAITH. Oh, Milton! to disobey my old, dear father! He regards you as reckless and profane.

MILT. Let him give his farm to your pious brother, Hampden, who will make much of him in his old age, no doubt. My songs against his psalms, tho', any day. [*About to kiss her. Enter Oby Oilstone*]

OBY. Oh, ho! say nothing!

MILT. Oh, Oby, come here; you're my friend at any rate. Where is the old gentleman now?

OBY. Why, layin' out his things to go to meetin'. All the farm'll be here bimeby; Sunday mornin's a great time, you know.

MILT. Faith, walk with me across the meadow. We must be firm. [*Aside*] Oby, go in half an hour to the livery stable in the village; get my buggy and bring it to me at the bridge. [*Gives him a gold piece*]

OBY. Say nothin'—that's the way to get along.

MILT. Come, Faith, take your sunbonnet. [*Exeunt Milton and Faith*]

OBY. He'll never be anything but a sailor—shellin' out his money this way! It takes some people all their lives to learn anything when it's just as easy. All you've got to do is just 'gree with people and think just as they do, and that ain't any trouble. There's Hampden Day, now, that's married to my sister Sally. What's he been doin' all his life but humourin' old Daddy Day, and getting what he pleased out of him. Well, if a feller can git along by humourin' one, oughtent he to get along faster by humourin' everybody? That's my plan. [*Melissa speaks without*] Ah, there's Melissay, Faith Day's cousin. No use of humourin' her. Softest horn she's got, I ever did see! I'll marry that gal. One must have someone to make fly 'round. [*Enter Melissa*]

MELIS. Well, Oby, how you always do look Sunday mornings.

OBY. [*Patronizingly*] Ahem! I don't see that I look anything extra! [*Tossing gold piece*]

MELIS. Why, how can you say that, with all that there vest, and that there stiffener 'round your neck! What's that you're a'flippin', a button?

OBY. I should like to find holes for all them buttons, *I* should.

MELIS. It's a span new half-cent.

OBY. [*Disdainfully*] Pearls to swine! Why it's real gold. Feel the heft on't.

MELIS. Creation! How you do git along, Oby.

OBY. Ahem! You ain't all-killin' pooty, and you don't know much, but then, you've com—com—combustibility of character—putty in the hands of the artist, you know! How much have you got in that there money box I gin you?

MELIS. Why, them first ten cents that you put in and all that I got at the factory, and what Aunty White paid me for sewin', and Granddaddy Day's dollar a month, and a power of cents besides, for chores, and it's chuckful a'most.

OBY. Whew! She's a perfect institootion! Won't she save up for a feller! Well, ahem! Melissa, there's that span new gold half-cent, as you call it, right now; and you put it right up in that box, and lock it right up in my drawer, and we'll count it up, the whole on't, after meetin'. Melissa, you've got quite a responsible look about you this morning.

MELIS. [*Coquetting*] I swan I won't go to meetin' with you—I won't.

OBY. You won't, won't you? Now I say you shill!

MELIS. I won't take your old gold piece.

OBY. Now I say you *shill!* And tha's what I'll always say when you go to kick up! I don't go in for humourin' women, I don't. That ain't the way to git along. [*Sarah calls Oby. Aside*] Hello! here's sister Sally comin' to order me about. [*Aloud*] You, Melissy, you go and stir up all the farm folks for meetin', and be quick about it. Old Job Day will head the procession— [*Aside*] as he will at his own funeral soon, I hope. [*Aloud*] Jump! [*Exit Melissa. Laughing, aside*] Sally's got her shirt collar up; had a spat on the sly with her husband, I guess; else the baby's got the cholic! If she makes me take it, won't I stick pins in it. [*Enter Sarah Day*]

SARAH. Obediah, where are the people?

OBY. Ready and waitin', and only to think what a blessed mess of piety one's got into, and 'bleeged to keep it up until Daddy Day pegs out—

SARAH. Pegs out! the venerable patriarch!

OBY. In course he is. Only what dreadful long wind he's got over his blessin's!

SARAH. Fool! Have discretion, if nothing else.

OBY. Why, it's all I've got yet! Don't I 'gree with everyone? Have I said my soul's my own since I've been in the family? Don't I go 'round sayin' your husband, Hampden Day, is a saint when he's so mean the fleas won't bite him. And there's where you took yourself in—

SARAH. Silence, you empty-headed—Place the chairs in order.

OBY. Like a blessed young firewarden of the temple, as Elder Slack calls me! Don't git mad now. How's baby and the skeeter bites? [*Aside*] The pinholes. [*Sets the stage in order, tables, chairs, etc. The people of the farm, all neatly dressed, enter and range themselves*] It's time for me to take Milton Trice his buggy. Here they come, like the beasts to the Ark. I'll be off like the pidgeon. [*Exit. Enter Job Day, very patriarchial in appearance and scrupulously dressed in the old fashion. Hampden Day supports him, affecting great plainness and austerity in manner*]

JOB. All the folks, eh? Ah, well, children, another summons to be grateful. For me, Old Job, I've reached the allotted age; Heaven be praised that I have lived without an enemy, that I shall die among kind friends. Heaven be praised, that has crowned my industry, and that renders my means a refuge. Hampden!

HAMP. Father?

JOB. [*After putting on specs and looking around*] I don't see Faith.

HAMP. Shall Sarah look for her?

JOB. You, Sarah. You are a woman to win happiness. Faith is not so confirmed in the path as you. I fear for her. The Sabbath meeting, too! Yes, you may seek her. [*Exit Sarah*] Where is Obediah?

HAMP. Something unavoidable, surely—

JOB. Unavoidable! Woe to the Sabbath breaker! Yes, even as unto the blasphemer!

HAMP. I'm not sure but I think Milton Trice is about the village, and he generally entices Obediah away.

JOB. [*Shuddering*] Yes—yes—but he's about to sail away again soon on a long voyage, is he not? Heaven go with him but I wish he was gone. He—he—has not ceased to speak to Faith. He—well, in all cases, I will do my duty. I don't see Melissa. There is—but that presently. Old Abel has promised to join us this morning—first time in a year.

ABEL. Here I am, Job.

JOB. [*Shaking hands*] Ah, so—so, you came instead of your crutch; your old wound is healing still once more then. These are not the weapons we handled at Breed's Hill and Bunker's! We escaped then and you lived to spill your blood in a second war of independence, far from me. Well, well, in the sunshine of our country's glory, we can look out over calm graves, Abel.

ABEL. [*Shaking hands again*] I received my pension from Washington yesterday, Job, and here is the money you used for me in the winter.

JOB. No—no—I mean—Pooh! Business on the Sabbath. True, it was to be returned—for you have no family and don't need it but, pooh—pooh. Where is Aunt Rachel?

RACHEL. Agh—Uncle Job, I'm here, in course.

JOB. Why—why—now just look here, Abel! Just now you look here at this old fool—Stop, that is wrong. But what on airth has rigged *you* out in *ribbons?*

RACHEL. There now! When I'm ten years younger than 'fore I was sick; and Oby swapped 'em off to me for Nathan's vest that's never bin on him or never will be.

JOB. Ninepence worth of ribbons for a new vest like that! Why you old —well—well—That fellow, Obediah, would cheat his own mother in a swap! Your runaway son, then, is not likely to return the little store he took away from you?

RACHEL. No; all saved up, too, for Jemminy's darter's schoolin'.

JOB. Well, Abel, you just buy, with the money you want to pay me, Aunt Rachel's ribbons, will you? A better bargain, Rachel, than you made with Obediah, ha, ha! Go, do now, and take them off for Abel. [*The old couple retire up, Rachel grumbling*] Abram's foot that was cut with the scythe is well, eh? And Samuel finds relief from the blackberry cordial? [*They assent*] Ah, now let Melissa stand forth among her family.

MELIS. Why, what's a comin' now?

JOB. Melissa! before meeting let us purge ourselves of folly. You—you can't cherish the flesh and feel the spirit. Stand right out there now before me. Now: a young man was seen to kiss you on this—the Sabbath morning while coming through the apple orchard.

MELIS. [*Crying*] There now, just what I said—and such a fool, too, not to have slapped his face. On'y I was just laughin' in my sleeve at him and didn't think he'd 'a had the spunk to dare to, nuther. But if I don't pay him off when we're married—Oh, massy me! [*Crying violently*] And Aunt Rachel's bin and told this, with her nasty red ribbons—

JOB. You, Melissa, be silent. Repentings and not revilings become you. Who was your companion?

MELIS. Why, it was Oby, there now, and he'd been at Sam's blackberry cordial or he couldn't 'a bucked up to me in that way, I know.

Job. Bad example! Bad example! Milton Trice has been in the village and that's enough. Where is Obediah? [*Oby, partially intoxicated, rushes in, overturning Rachel, chairs, etc.*]

Oby. Run down to the meadow, all of you; git in the hay—just saved my new vest. There's the devil coming over the hill, riding a hailstorm!

Job. [*With all his force*] Seize that mocker and blasphemer, and force him on his knees.

Oby. Want to spoil the crop?

Job. Shall we prize the gems in the earth before him who planteth life in it? What means this riot? [*Hampden slings him around*]

Hamp. Has Milton Trice made you drunk?

Oby. No, but when I shook hands and bade good-bye to Faith, I was taken with such a weakness of the heart—all about here—that I stepped into Sam's room by the barn, where the blackberry cordial—

Job. Good-bye to Faith! O Heaven, strengthen its servant. You mean that they—they—

Oby. Have go off? Yes, I do, to the city, to set sail tonight. [*Job staggers back into a chair. At the same moment, Faith rushes in, followed by Milton*]

Faith. Father! Father! I have not left you. I could not leave you without your blessing.

Milt. Your daughter will obey the dictates of her heart, Mr. Day. She will be my wife.

Faith. Only your blessing, father!

Job. [*Recovering*] He who strengthens for the sacrifice, who hath promised chastening to those who serve Him, nerve now the heart of old Job Day. [*Severely*] Faith, you have been reared in the path of soberness, piety guided thy steps, and love and hope sprang up in thy footprint.

Faith. Can I forget your affection, father?

Job. Can you forget this bad youth who clouds thy path, who turns these flowers to weeds of sin and bitterness.

Faith. He is good and generous, father, and respects you truly.

Job. And steals into my house to lay stain upon my hearthstone.

Milt. Stain, old man! Peace, probity, and honour are my kinsmen. Truth and sweetness, with your daughter, are to be my helpmates, and if a stain gather upon your hearth, see that it be placed there, not by me, but by the avarice and hypocrisy [*Pointing to Hampden*] which have filled your ears with lies, and your heart with hate against me.

Hamp. Dare you to charge me—

Milt. Peace, hypocrite. [*The storm is heard distinctly, stage darkened*]

Job. Peace all! The heavens rebuke—Is this a day of praise! Hampden, stand forward with Sarah your wife. [*Milton draws Faith close to him, confronting Hampden*] Listen to me, all! I thought to have had *two* homes—no tears, old Job! "In all this Job repined not, neither did he sin against the Lord." Hampden, from this moment, this farm and all that I possess is yours. You, with your wife, are my only children and my sole care on earth will be to leave it.

Milt. Sad infatuation!

Faith. Father, give away your farm but not your heart from me! Let me still call that my home! Say not your *only* children! Do not hate me!

Job. Hate you, Faith? You are no longer my child, but I hate none of Heaven's creatures.

Faith. Forgive me, then!

Job. Plead where you have offended, Faith, there! [*Music commences piano*]

Faith. Say but that you bless our union.

Job. When Heaven shall bless it, I will bless it! [*The peasantry open on each side to make room for Job, etc. All have their backs to the audience except Faith and Milton. Hampden stands, C., with folded arms, looking exultantly at Milton. During the last few moments the clouds have passed and the stage is light again. With Job's last words, is heard the distant toll of the church bell. He signs for his hat and stick. All prepare to go. The orchestra plays pianissimo a strain of sacred music. Tableau*]

A lapse of five years between Acts I and II.

ACT II.

Scene 1: "*Cove Hotel," kept by Oby Oilstone, near the farm of Hampden Day. View through the open windows and doors of the beach, with fishing boats, ocean, horizon, etc. A crowd from the city waiting to go upon the fishing grounds.*

First Vis. Oby! Oby Oilstone! Where the deuce is the fellow? We want to push off.

Second Vis. He's getting to be a greater fool every day.

Third Vis. His wife is boss! He's Oby, but she's Mr. Oilstone! She'd better mince him up and sell him for bait.

All. Oby! [*Enter Melissa*] O Mr. Oilstone! Where's Oby? How d'ye do? [*They crowd around her*]

MELIS. Do stand off, you people! Oby's some place between this and Egg Rock. Some of you nice young men sent a boat adrift.

FIRST VIS. And you sent Oby adrift after it. That's right.

SECOND VIS. The sailboat wants baiting—

THIRD VIS. Somebody's been cutting the fishing lines.

FIRST VIS. Suppose we consider ourselves caught and all remain? [*Takes hold of her*]

MELIS. Don't bite at the bare hook, if you're sensible.

FIRST VIS. If I can be made use of in a friendly chowder—

SECOND VIS. Or I—[*Enter Oby*]

MELIS. Chowder! No, we use *Sheepshead* as a panfish.

OBY. [*Coming forward*] Yes, and out of the pan into the fire! What kinder gettin' along d'ye call this?

ALL. Why Oby! Ha, ha, ha!

MELIS. You, Oby! Don't you trouble your weak head, if you please, but bail out the boat for these gentlemen.

FIRST VIS. And we'll bail you out, Oby, when we catch you in town! Ha, ha, ha! [*As they banter him, he retreats, falling into a cradle, in which are a hen and chickens. A great laugh*] Hollo, Oby, you've got a family?

OBY. All my fault, I suppose! Everything's all my fault since I got married.

MELIS. Do get up. What are you settin' there for?

OBY. Settin'! Are you speakin' to me or the hen? [*Melissa drives him off. Visitors following*]

MELIS. Well, I didn't marry Oby for his head, at any rate, so I've no right to complain; but if I took him for a fool, he's as good as I took him for, that's all! Five years without a family and yet he *will* keep a cradle about. He *is* a fool. [*Hums a song. Air, "I would I were a boy again"*] I would I were a *gal* again.

OBY. [*Reentering*] Well, I guess if you *was* a gal again, you'd spite the whole village. Singing on Sunday.

MELIS. Have you sent off that party?

OBY. Yes, they pushed off with me in the boat and if I hadn't jumped like a sturgeon, I'd a had to swim like a flatfish. Hotel life's hard gettin' along, after all.

MELIS. How should we have got along without it? When old Job gave up his property, we all had to give up eating, Hampden Day turned you out, though his wife was your sister. And me, though I was his own cousin. As for poor old Job, between abuse and starvation, no wonder he's lost his senses.

OBY. Hampden Day has got along, amazin', and all in five years! He's rich as a Jew.

MELIS. And heartless as a heathen. He gave you a lease of this old house at the Cove here and now that it's got to be a place and folks come to it from town and people want to buy it, he's fit to set fire to it over our heads to git rid of us.

OBY. He does git along 'stonishin'!

MELIS. Come now, *fly 'round,* as you say. There'll be a good many people down today and you've ice to get, and mint to cull, and lemons to cut, and bait to catch, and boats to look after, and nets to mend, and fish to fry. [*Steamboat whistle*] And only look! The steamboat's landed, and here come the passengers! Fly 'round! [*Exit Melissa*]

OBY. Ain't she destructive on linen, though! Don't she git along! And just to think that I used to take her for a softee! Why she married me when I hadn't a red cent, got a lease out of Hampden Day, managed to git the Cove here into the newspapers, and hang me if I don't think she'll, next season, make a reg'lar engagement with the Sea-Sarpint! [*In running to meet the company, he stumbles against the cradle*] Consarn that empty cradle! [*People from steamboat cross the stage, Oby attending them. Reenter Melissa, conducting Milton and Faith, poorly clad, apparently, and further disguised*]

MELIS. If you want to enquire about Mr. Day's family, you'd better walk in, I guess.

MILT. Milton Trice lost at sea, you say?

MELIS. Yes, with his wife, poor Faith, three years ago. Poor creatures!

OBY. [*Coming forward*] Yes, drownded! The ship and all aboard—never was heard of after leaving the Philippina Islands!

MELIS. Poor Faith! Poor Milton!

OBY. Both in Heaven! *You* know nothing about 'em, do you?

MILT. And the family in this neighbourhood?

MELIS. We're all the family that's left—as far as feeling goes. [*Faith droops; runs to her*] What's the matter, ma'am? You're faint, ain't you? Take off your veil—eh—why—Oby!

OBY. Eh—why—Melissy!

MELIS. As sure as the world—my heart—not *Faith?*

FAITH. Yes, Melissa! [*They embrace*]

OBY. And you—if you'd on'y shave and take your hat off! Ain't you—eh, Milton!

MILT. Your old friend, Oby.

OBY. Not drownded—nor chawed up! nor a ghost either? What a devil of a cruise—ha, ha, ha! How have you been gettin' along. [*Shaking hands*]

FAITH. My poor old father then, Melissa?

MELIS. He's alive, Faith, but not happy.

OBY. Pretty near starved all the feelin' out of him, I reckon.

MILT. Speak Melissa, how fares it with the old man?

MELIS. Well, after you left and Hampden got the farm, with Grandfather Job it was neglect on neglect, yet he never uttered a word of complaint. At last, news came of your loss, and then the old man never spoke at all. He didn't weep or complain, but seemed to go about in a dream, and then they treated him worse and worse, and now they say he's crazy, and if Heaven is merciful, he is so, for who can speak his misery if he's not? [*Faith weeps on Milton's breast*]

MILT. Poor Faith, be calm. And this unnatural Hampden.

OBY. Oh, you never *did* see! Why the farm's worth three times what it was, besides this landin' at the Cove. And then he's an elder and a selectman. And if the devil don't select him also, there's no truth in the doctrine of pre-discrimination!

MELIS. But little need to ask the question, Faith; you have not returned rich?

OBY. Nothin' to brag of, I suppose?

MILT. We have at least retained youth and health and Job shall find that we can toil for him.

OBY. He gits no sign of love or labour now, except from little Job—the baby that I used to stick pins into and call it the Cholic.

FAITH. I cannot resist, Melissa. I must see my father.

OBY. Hush. Wait a little, till Hampden and sister Sal's gone to meetin'—poor Job is too weak to leave the house. He takes the Good Book, tho', when the bell rings. I'll go with you to the farm, and see the coast clear.

MELIS. Run, Oby. Take Milton and Faith the short way through the road that's been opened.

OBY. Come along! We'll be there directly—[*Stumbles against cradle*] Devil take that cradle! Always flying up in my face! All my fault, though! [*Exeunt Milton, Faith and Oby*]

SCENE 2: *The farm. Table set. Hampden and Sarah discovered at breakfast. Fireplace, second wing, R., and beside it an old-fashioned chest and chair used by Job Day. A desk. Child discovered on one side scooping a gourd.*

HAMP. [*Angrily*] I tell you I shall die poor. I feel it—I know it! When you are a beggar, you will mourn past extravagances. [*Coming forward*] You but live to rival the peacock!

SARAH. [*Coming forward*] As you do to resemble the owl. You should know well enough by this time that I sympathise as little in your schemes as I share in their profits.

HAMP. Fiends! Woman, do not make me swear on this day.

SARAH. Less sin than in your prayers. When you curse, you are sincere.

HAMP. [*Groaning*] If I were alone I could be happy! This devil of a woman—and yet I must endure her. That child, too, will be like her.

CHILD. Father, may old grannypa have his breakfast? I know he's hungry.

HAMP. The old man, too, a burthen and vexation. He can't live much longer.

SARAH. Call him in off the steps. [*Exit Child*] No wonder he's grown dumb and an idiot; he ought never to speak after fooling himself as he did with you.

HAMP. Each in his turn. He had his enjoyment. [*Reenter Child, leading Job, who is miserably clad, and decrepit with age and neglect. Child seats him in the corner, then brings him from table, a wooden bowl and spoon. The old man eats*]

SARAH. You must make up the old man some place in the barn; since his room has been taken from him he coils himself up on that old chest, and plenty of straw would be better than that.

HAMP. Anywhere, for he don't seem to mind it.

SARAH. He must surely be getting dumb.

HAMP. He has never complained at anytime; not much trouble that way.

SARAH. Ha, ha, ha! If I were only as tractable, eh? I wonder if that child will ever become like you? [*The Child is waiting on and fondling about Job*]

HAMP. Heaven grant it!

SARAH. And *you* like *your* father, eh? [*Points to Job*]

HAMP. Devil! Ha, ha, ha! I shall be too sharp for you and your imp, too! [*Enter Oby*]

OBY. Sis, have you taken to lay abed Sunday mornin's? The bells will soon be ringing. Good morning, brother Hampden. Good morning, granddaddy. [*Job recognizes him and takes his hand. The Child also expresses gladness*] You, young Job, how you do grow. [*Aside*] Filled up all the pinholes long ago. Spoon victuals for granddaddy always, eh? But then, he ain't got no teeth for *beefsteak,* I suppose.

CHILD. I always give grannypa some of my meat.

OBY. That's right, like a fiery young phoenix, feeding its—granddaddy! What are you scooping out that for?

CHILD. Grannypa never has anything to eat from but a bowl.

OBY. Well, what are you makin' another for?

CHILD. Oh, for my father, when he gets old, like grannypa. [*The old man, unnoticed, pauses, lays aside his bowl and droops his head. Hampden turns, exchanging angry glances with his wife. Oby gives a low whistle aside. Sarah and Child clear the table*]

OBY. [*Aside*] That young idea made a mighty close shot, that time, I calculate.

HAMP. What's your business with me, Obediah?

OBY. Oh, not much—besides, as it's Sunday—

HAMP. True, ahem! Are you prepared to pay double rent at the Cove? Your lease expires with the season.

OBY. Why, Melissy says that as we've built a barn and a stable and had hard work to get along—

HAMP. Double the rent is offered. Pay or quit—no discussions on the Sabbath!

OBY. Well, there don't appear to me much room for argument, certainly! I'll tell Melissy. I say, sis, that there benefit tea party comes off tomorrow night for the poor. You and Melissy's among the manageres-es-es, you know.

SARAH. Well?

OBY. Well, it's always the rule to divide duplicate contributions, as you call them, among the managers. You took home that second box of raisins, you know, and d'ye think that Melissy won't touch a morsel! Is that the way git along, with her sense, too?

SARAH. You're a fool!

OBY. Well, she's another. You're baking the big tea-party cake, ain't you? What are you going to do about the jewelry?

SARAH. What do you mean?

OBY. Why the diamond ring, and the brooch, and the breastpin—dollar a chance you know—baked up into the numbered slices? Melissy told me how it's fixed, generally.

SARAH. You're a pair of mischief-makers.

OBY. Oh, I think it's all right! Just tell me under which numbers you put 'em, and go snacks, and I'll locate my sections in that gingerbread easy, I tell you. [*Distant toll of the church bell. Job listens, then takes out his old Bible from the chest*]

HAMP. A morning wasted! We shall be too late. Elder Slack there to remark upon it, too!

SARAH. And his wife to flaunt along and telling me at every step that she's better than I am. [*Putting on a bonnet*]

HAMP. No discussion! Humility becomes us. Make haste. Look at that old man there. Is not his presence a rebuke to extravagance? Luxury and fine raiment retard not age. Obediah, give me an answer about the Cove by Wednesday. Double rent or quit. Come, come. [*Exeunt Hampden, Sarah, and Child. Oby pretends to follow them out, but returns. Job, supposing himself alone, repeats with great feeling*]

JOB. "In all this Job sinned not nor charged Heaven foolishly." [*Lays aside book and weeps*]

OBY. They're off. Now's the time for Milton and Faith. [*Makes a signal. They enter*] He always reads of a Sunday, but it's by rote, I reckon, for he's almost blind and little Job broke his specs more than a year ago, and Hampden has never got him a new pair.

MILT. Speak to him, Oby.

OBY. Granddaddy Job!

JOB. Eh? Why—why I thought all had gone but me! That's you, Obediah, isn't it?

OBY. Yes, granddaddy, here's a pot of jelly Melissy has made for you, by way of a change. [*Job rises, assisted by Oby*]

JOB. Eh? Oh, yes—something nice for little Job. Yes—yes.

OBY. No, for you, granddaddy.

JOB. No, no, no. She's a good girl, but I have enough, quite enough. It will be nice for little Job.

OBY. [*Aside*] Always the way, never complaint, never lets on that his son's starvin' him. Granddaddy, here's a gentleman just come from a long way off —at sea, the Philippina Islands. He says Milton Trice and poor Faith— before—[*Job trembles*]

MILT. Hush! We must be careful. I saw your daughter, sir, who sent a message to you.

JOB. [*Wanderingly*] Aye, aye, aye, poor Faith! "And behold, there came a great wind from the wilderness, and smote the four corners of the house and it fell upon the young, and they are dead, and I only am escaped alone."

MILT. She spoke of the time when she should again see you, with her husband and her child, to once more crave forgiveness for having grieved you.

JOB. [*Weeping*] I—I—cannot well see you, young man. Your voice is kind and good, yet you say sore things to me. But go on, go on. Faith was happy with her husband?

MILT. Most happy, sir, and—*is so still*. And dearly does he love her.

JOB. [*In great astonishment*] *Still!* loves her!

MILT. Yes. You've heard, I see, of their terrible shipwreck.

JOB. Yes, yes, and of—

MILT. Be calm, sir. Yes, their sufferings were terrible, but their escape—

JOB. Ah!

MILT. Your poor children are still alive! [*Job falls on his knees, raising his hands to Heaven*]

JOB. "At destruction and famine thou shalt laugh; neither shalt thou fear the beast of the earth!" [*Gradually works himself into a paroxysm*] Ha, ha, ha! "By the blast of him they perish and by the breath of his nostril are they consumed." Make me not a mockery!

MILT. Dear sir, be calm. [*Raises him up*]

JOB. Your voice is not strange to me, but my eyes—[*Faith advances and stretches forth her arms*] "A spirit passeth before my face"—

FAITH. Father!

JOB. My child—Faith! [*Staggers into her arms. They place him in a chair*]

FAITH. Oh, will not joy destroy him?

MILT. Let him see your face; keep close to him.

JOB. [*Wandering*] Hampden—Hampden—you did not strike me, did you? Eh! No—no one to talk to since old Abel died. My poor Faith—and she's dead, too—down in the sea—and only asking of me not to hate her! Hampden does right! He's kinder to me than I was to Faith. He'll give me a grave—where is hers? [*Faith, weeping, throws her arms 'round his neck*] What face is this so near me?—Little Job broke my—Heaven's mercy! Faith! I remember now—[*Sobs upon her neck*]

MILT. The paroxysm is past. Good old man, you have kind children yet.

JOB. Old Job has children yet! Ha, ha, ha! "And Job's daughters were the fairest of the land." But you—you have lost all. And I—I gave away unwisely.

FAITH. Think of nothing, father, save that we shall be happy again together.

JOB. [*With sudden fervor*] If I have withheld the poor from their desire or have caused the eyes of the widow to fail, if I have lifted my arm against the fatherless, or made gold my hope, then let me still sow and another eat. Yea—let my offspring be rooted out!

FAITH. We have heard of your cruel treatment, father; but Milton is not altogether poor, neither, and all will be well.

MILT. In truth, father Job, spite of appearances, assumed for effect, we're pretty well off. Though ruined by our wreck, I've since had luck in the Far East, and have remitted to an agent, from time to time, who has invested in your name. Forgive me; and here, let these papers, and this bag of yellow boys, square off the debt—of revenge, if you will, between us. They have been earned, and they are registered in your name.

JOB. [*Musing*] Wealth—wealth! and ready gold!

MILT. It is a debt, I insist, and you must take it.

JOB. Hard, glistening gold! And—and I cannot well read—little Job broke my glasses—these are—

MILT. The best stocks in Boston, father Job, to the tune of ten thousand.

JOB. [*Eagerly*] And in *my name?* My name?—

MILT. Your name. What the deuce—do you want to be off to State Street among the brokers?

OBY. Well, I swan! After all that parson talk—see how he hugs the money!

JOB. You—you shall leave this with me, Milton. Ha, ha, ha! old Job, the idiot! Blind and dumb! Ha, ha, no feeling! Sleep in the barn—all the same. Ha, ha, ha! [*Totters about eagerly, goes to door and looks out*]

FAITH. Merciful powers! Can his brain be turned?

MILT. He acts most strangely!

OBY. Why, I couldn't 'a cut up more, if you'd made a small investment in my name.

JOB. [*Returning*] Hush—you must not stay here—hide, hide—in here—out of sight, but be witnesses. You will know when to come out again.

MILT. What can he mean?

JOB. Bless you, Faith. Good young man, Milton! Oby is kind, too, ha, ha, ha! Used to be cunning at a swap—ha, ha, ha! Go—go in all! [*Hurrying them off*]

OBY. Well, I believe the devil does lurk in a bag of gold. He's generally more economical in his temptations with me, though! [*They go off. Job spreads his handkerchief on table, and pours the gold into it. He then opens the chest, places the papers in it, takes his seat by it, holds the handkerchief of gold open on his knees, and pretends to sleep. Enter Child*]

CHILD. O grannypa, I've brought you a nice cake before father comes. My grannypa's asleep! And, oh, such bright pennies! [*The Child busies himself about the old man. Hampden and Sarah enter*]

HAMP. I have an object to gain with neighbour Slack, and that's why I asked him to dinner.

SARAH. And his wife, your object to spite me, I suppose. Why look at the old man—asleep. You'll send him into the kitchen, I hope?

HAMP. Anywhere.

CHILD. Father, just look at all grannypa's beautiful pennies!

HAMP. What is this! It can't be possible! Gold! gold—a flood of gold!

SARAH. Hush! don't wake him. Yes, real gold! The old miser. Like father, like son, after all.

HAMP. He did not part with all his wealth, then; and I thought so at the time! Why, this sum alone would more than purchase Slack's acres. What are these in the chest? Scrip—bank insurance—gas—and bearing date the present year. The sly old speculator, worth a fortune still! And none but me to possess it! Ha! Caution, I've been too careless. He still has his wits about him, it seems. Hush. [*They steal off with the Child as Job stirs*]

JOB. Aye, aye, aye, the idiot has his wits about him! He will not dine in the kitchen, this day! [*Shuts up money and papers, and takes his seat and book, as usual, after a pause. Reenter Hampden*]

HAMP. [*Aside*] All hid away again, the old fox! A miracle that I made the discovery at all. Ahem! [*Draws chair. Aloud*] Father! [*Job turns, scarcely hearing*] Ahem, that reminds me of your spectacles. I've thought recently of asking them from you to get them mended. Little Job's work, the monkey.

JOB. Ah, no matter. Poor little Job.

HAMP. But if your sight should be injured—

JOB. No, I see more clearly *now* than when I was *younger!*

HAMP. [*Aside*] Misses nothing as long as he has his gold to hug! [*Aloud*] Well, father, Elder Slack is coming to dinner, and—

JOB. Aye, aye, I'll take my bowl into the kitchen.

HAMP. No, no, you must no longer be so—so eccentric; you must sit with us. It *looks* so strange.

JOB. Oh, *looks* are nothing, son, if one does not *feel*.

HAMP. Exactly! And so I'm going to complain of you! If you feel affection for me, father, you would not keep money locked up idle, when I'm so much in want of it to extend the farm by purchase from neighbour Slack.

JOB. Ah, ha! Aye, aye, what, you've found out—

HAMP. That you have ready money and stocks! Pooh, pooh, I've known it all along. I've heard of operations of yours lately.

JOB. Ah, ha, ha, ha! Yes, son, my last, now, was a mighty happy one!

HAMP. Ha, ha! We grow *keen* as we grow old, father, eh?

JOB. Yes, yes, never too late to learn.

HAMP. Or to give a lesson either, father. Come, you've something you can teach me yet.

JOB. Why, yes, Hampden, I can yet give you a lesson to remember.

HAMP. My dear old father, I knew you would. Well, and your reserved wealth, it shall be employed, eh?

JOB. All's arranged. There is but one alive to trust my money to.

HAMP. I could almost shed tears, indeed I could!

JOB. Don't do it, Hampden—not just yet. You don't know the lesson yet. [*Enter Sarah*]

SARAH. [*Aside*] He thinks to grasp the whole of the new windfall to himself. [*Aloud*] My dear father Job, I've just had your bed made up in your old room again. Astonishing you ever left it!

JOB. I *did* feel a little astonished, child, at first. I soon got used to it.

HAMP. [*Aside*] Hush! Leave him to me. Go! [*Aloud*] Ahem! Your ready gold, father, will secure Slack's farm, a great bargain. The rest, you must let me employ for you in this neighbourhood. Stocks fluctuate. There's Watson's water power, now, will be a mint, if—

JOB. I've said, Hampden, there is but one to inherit what I have, and to that one I shall resign all, at any moment.

SARAH. Father Job—

HAMP. [*Aside*] I'll strangle you if—

JOB. Let me see the contents of that chest, added to the homestead, deeded long ago—doubtless never even yet recorded, eh? [*Hampden assents*] Ha, ha! So much the better! They would look well reconveyed, eh? All together in a new instrument?

HAMP. [*Aside*] He's doting! Now or never is the moment! [*Goes to desk and brings deeds*] Here is the old deed, father. By all means, make a new one; put all together.

JOB. Yes, that's the plan. [*Looks around and sees Milton, etc., watching*] Let me see. Yes, my signature and seal. Ha, ha! I don't think I shall need spectacles again. But—

HAMP. [*Eagerly*] Don't stand on forms, father. The papers can be made out—but we can't execute 'till Monday.

JOB. Well, well. There, Hampden! [*Tears off name and seal*] You are *without the farm again, son!*

HAMP. A dependent on my dear old father Job once more. [*Milton and Faith, having thrown off their disguises, now advance*]

MILT. You are indeed. We are here to witness it!

HAMP. Ah! [*Job tears the deed, and totters up and down, in tearful triumph. Neighbours and people of the farm enter*]

JOB. Who ever perished, being innocent? They who plough iniquity and sow wickedness, reap the same!

HAMP. What—what is all this?

JOB. Your desired *last lesson,* Hampden; though a deed do come from a dotard, never fail to have it recorded. [*Embraces Neighbours*]

HAMP. Perdition!

SARAH. You'll be too sharp for your own son! Ha, ha! Wise man in your blind confidence.

HAMP. If Faith and her husband are alive—

Oby. Alive! Yes. Just up from the Philippina Islands! Wonderful recovery from drowning. If you can only have the same luck when it comes to hanging!

Hamp. Though the lost be found, am I not still your son?

Job. Witness my straw within the barn, Hampden—my starved frame—wrung heart—and pauper garments! Go!

Hamp. Ruined! Outwitted!

Job. The hypocrite's hope shall perish, his trust shall be a spider's web. You have had your lesson. I, too, have learned that one father can better take care of ten children, than ten children can take care of one father!

Oby. Sis, guess you've cut the cake in the wrong place, this time! Brother Hampden—when you're ready to renew the Cove—you know. You can bring along the papers!

Job. [*Between Milton and Faith*] My dear children, Heaven hath indeed blessed your union. For me, it hath rebuked my over wisdom. It hath brought down the wicked, too, that men might know them. [*Advancing*] If there be here a head bowed down or turned grey with sorrow, still let him remember that the captivity of Job was turned, when he prayed for his friends. Let him not repine; so shall he come to his grave in a full age, like as a shock of corn cometh in his season.

SLOW CURTAIN

SIGNOR MARC

A Play in Five Acts

By John H. Wilkins

SIGNOR MARC

OF John H. Wilkins there is little to say. He was a citizen of England, a journalist, and an actor in the company at Sadler's Wells Theatre, who apparently came to America to seek success as a dramatist, only to be cut short by early death. Allibone (*A Dictionary of the Drama*) says that Wilkins died on August 29, 1853, which would mean that the American productions of all but one of his plays were posthumous.

None the less, the American theatre saw six Wilkins plays between 1853 and 1857, two or three of which were very successful. His *Civilization; or, The Huron Chief*, a comedy based on Voltaire's romance of *Le Huron*, had a number of performances in New York and Philadelphia. Both this play and *The Egyptian; or, The Fall of Palmyra* were printed in French's Acting Drama. Of more interest is the fact that Wilkins at least had something to do with the first American *Camille*. In the autumn of 1853 both Philadelphia and New York patronized the adaptation of the younger Dumas's *La Dame aux Camélias*, with Miss Jean Margaret Davenport in the starring rôle. Durang, reporting the first Philadelphia performance, assigns the play first to Wilkins and later to Miss Davenport herself. Many years later, William Winter referred to the play as an adaptation by Miss Davenport, "edited" by Wilkins. This seems a rather subtle distinction, but at least indicates some contribution by Wilkins.

Equally as successful as *Camille* and the two printed plays was Wilkins's popular melodrama, *Signor Marc*, which, as far as can be discovered, has always been referred to with the curious misnomer of *Saint Marc*. Playbills and advertisements so identify it, and historians of the drama have accepted this title. From the following pages it will be obvious that the proper title is *Signor Marc*. The manuscript copy labels the hero "Sr. Marc," a "soldier of fortune," in no way to be confused with a saint. At one line in the play, the hero is doubly saluted, ". . . to you, the Sr. Signor Marc. . . ." The whole pattern of the plot necessitates the title of "Signor," not "Saint," for the hero.

Signor Marc is a melodramatic tragedy in a foreign "historical" setting. It has a complicated plot, providing opportunity for spectacle and for effective acting. The play was first produced at the Broadway Theatre in New York on September 13, 1854, and was successfully revived many times. It was presented also at the Walnut Street Theatre in Philadelphia on September 26, 1854, and thereafter. For at least fifteen years, the leading rôle was a favorite of its original interpreter, E. L. Davenport. The manuscript, which comes from the Seymour Collection at Princeton University, through the courtesy of Dr. Robert H. Ball, is a poor copy, showing many signs of revision. Changes or faults in the copy are indicated or explained in bracketed lines. The cast listed for the play is that given by Odell for the initial production.

A chronological record of American productions of Wilkins's plays follows:

Civilization; or, The Huron Chief: a Play in Five Acts. Burton's (N.Y.), April 18, 1853.

Camille (adaptation of *La Dame aux Camélias*). Walnut St. (Phila.), September 23, 1853.

Signor Marc. Broadway (N.Y.), September 13, 1854.

The Egyptian; or, The Fall of Palmyra. Broadway (N.Y.), February 28, 1855.

The Scalp Hunters. American (N.Y.), March 12, 1857.

The Green Hills of the West. American (N.Y.), March 20, 1857.

DRAMATIS PERSONAE*

LORENZO, *Prince of Modena*	MR. GALLEGHER
COUNT ROSARIO	MR. GROSVENOR
BELCASTRO, *minister of finance*	MR. LEFFINGWELL
PAUL VULCANI, *judge of law*	MR. HENRY
PETRONIO, *councillor of state*	MR. CUTTER
STEFANO LODORI, *controller of the army*	MR. CROCKER
SR. MARC, *a soldier of fortune*	MR. E. L. DAVENPORT
GISMONDO, *his friend, captain of a disbanded regiment, and a fanatic*	MR. CONWAY
BELLAFIORE, *a gentleman of court*	MR. WALTERS
COROLLA, *page to Prince Lorenzo*	
PIETRO, *a servant*	
SERVANT TO SR. MARC	
DUC LIONI, *a friend to the prince*	
GAOLER	
DIANORA, *a rich Modenese lady, married to Sr. Marc*	MME. PONISI
THERESA, *her friend*	MRS. ABBOTT

TIME: ABOUT 1528

PLACE: MODENA

* *The parts listed are those given by Odell.*

(Parts of this play which appear to attempt at least an approximation of blank verse form are reprinted in this copy according to the line pattern of the original manuscript.)

ACT I.

SCENE 1: *Garden at the palace of the Prince Lorenzo of Modena. Steps and portico of the palace at an upper entrance. Gismondo leaning moodily against a tree. Several nobles in the garden about the steps of the palace awaiting audience, among whom are Petronio, of the State Council, Paul Vulcani, a judge, Belcastro, chief [sic] of finance, and Stefano Lodori, controller of the army. A servant enters from the palace.*

PETRO. Now, fellow, what says the discourteous prince
        To our request for audience?

SERV. Not today
        He's sick—and pre-engaged: another time—
        Say a week hence, he'll entertain you.

PETRO. But
        Did you not tell him that his ministers
        Would wait upon him? I come to speak
        Of perils to the State.

PAUL. I from the court of justice.

STEF. I am Stefano, controller of his armies.
        Take him my name again.

BEL. And mine, and tell him
        This waste of hours drains gold as well as time.
        His treasury will pine for't.

SERV. Pardon me—
        He will not be disturbed—nor dare I peril
        My place by disobedience. [*Servant exits*]

BEL. Who would serve
        So vain and frail a prince!

PAUL. This is the mood
        He wastes the golden hours of the day,
        And solemn darkness in. No care for state—

BEL. Wisdom will come with beggar'd pouches!

PETRO. Wisdom!
        Yes, when neglect steals like a rotting damp
        'Neath the foundations of the State.

PAUL. His ears
        Are closed to the great cry of justice!

GIS. At back, justice!
Ho, ho! Ask justice of Lorenzo!
Ask pity of the rav'nous tiger! Life
To light its fires in the eyes of Death!
The whirlwind to forbear when in its wrath
It tears the bedded ocean up in fury!
These are as kindred to their natures as
Justice to proud Modena's prince.

STEF. I bear
Your claim in mine, for services forgotten
In the rewards for nobleness of arms.

PETRO. Yes, 'tis Gismondo: here's your last petition
Wherein you speak of one Lodovico—

GIS. Yes, yes, my father—

PETRO. Somewhat too hurriedly
Punished with death on sentence of the prince.
But he died under error.

PAUL. It was proved so
Upon the trial.

GIS. Trial! Yes, you tried
His crime in court after the man was dead!
A worthy code of laws! I claim redress!
I'll have it. I have visions night by night—
A specter of a bleeding man whose face
Is twined with childhood's silver memories—
Whose lips although they speak not, move like words,
And in that silence have an eloquence
Louder than thunder—once the word was justice,
But it has changed of late.

PAUL. To what?

GIS. Revenge.
One day 'twill come, one day 'twill come! [Goes]

BEL. Poor fellow!
His father's death has struck him to the brain—
That, and a wound in battle, it is said,
Hath made him gloomy and fanatical;
A man may see it. Madness glides on him
Like the red twilight of a coming storm.

PAUL. Thus will he linger day by day before
The palace portal watching for the prince,
To ask him justice—a frail hope indeed.

STEF. See, who comes here, the Count Rosario—
The scented fopling of a gilded court!
The prince's jackal!

PETRO. But will *he* make way
Into the presence *we* have sought in vain?

PAUL. Stay, and you'll see how easily!
[*Enter the Count Rosario*]

ROS. Signors, your slave. Hath the sun shone today?
Hath the prince glittered forth like Mars in glory?

BEL. He is denied to us.

ROS. No doubt to *you*—
You who come full of musty business
To shadow hours that love the summer shine.
His highness is all light—all spirit—fire
Yet when he snatches up the cup of life
To drink existence in a nectar draught,
You'd fill it full of sand.

PETRO. Your councils smack
Of a thick-blood debauchery that sluggards
The healthy stream of life.

ROS. Psha. Life's our day.
Death comes tomorrow. Let's be gay by daylight.
'Tis time enough to think of sadder things
I' the cool of the evening. [*Enter Servant*]
Well, Pietro, well?

SERV. His highness has expected you.

PAUL. I said so.
Did I not say so; and this butterfly
Makes way where we, the more industrious ants
Of the great social fabric
Are shut out from an audience. [*Exeunt the four Councillors, Nobles,
etc. Manent Servant, Rosario, and Gismondo*]

SERV. [*Pointing to Gismondo*]
Get *him* hence.
He's ever pestering the prince with claims.
Get him away, my lord will join you there. [*Points within*]

Ros.   What, surly bulldog, black Gismondo—
Something about a father, was it not?
A father killed by accident which he
Construed by his sad dictionary, the mind,
Into a murder. I remember! Psha.
What an unseemly pother for a father,
Who, as I take it, should be looked upon
As a mere watch key, just to wind one up
And set one going—there's an end of him!
Well, I'll get rid of the pale-faced fanatic—
Hie to the prince.

Serv.   If he should ask the nature
Of your affair—

Ros.   Why, tell him, "Dianora!"
That's answer for him. That will set his heart
Leaping within him like a wave at play.
The rest I'll keep for him.
[*Exit Servant. Aside*]
And now with all
Courtier civility and courtly courtesy
To kick this sluggish, obstinate Gismondo
Out in the street, for words when rightly used,
Make themselves toes, to kick as lustily
As ever an uncourtly foot that tags
The nether end of rural-born mortality! [*Aloud*]
Captain Gismondo—
You hang about these gardens like a spider,
A huge unsightly insect that turns cold
High blood at sight of you.

Gis.   And you like—what?

Ros.   Like what? Aye. Come, let's have it.

Gis.   Like a toad—
No, that's got something valuable in its head
And you've got nothing there.

Ros.   Some similes
Are cursedly unpleasant, and what's more,
As cursedly personal—but there—he's mad!
I'll put his wit down to his ignorance.
He knows no better.

Gis.   Like a worm that leaves
      Its track behind it, yea, a track of slime,
      You're a contagion, poisoning as you walk.

Ros.   You soldiers have strange fashions. Flattery
      And candor in a breath.

Gis.   I heard you speak
      A name but now—the name of a good man's wife—
      Have you cast lures about *her* innocence?
      Heaven help her then!

Ros.   The prince admired her,
      Loved her before she married out of pique
      This nameless man, Sr. Marc. And she loved him
      The world could see't. Modena rang with it.
      But Lord Lorenzo and fair Dianora,
      Whose rank and beauty equalized the match,
      Must needs fall squabbling like young brothers and sisters.
      And boiling with her passion, in the heat on't,
      She flung her hand away.

Gis.   She wedded one
      Who hung upon her footsteps like their echo.
           Yes, Sr. Marc
      Is what the world calls a good man.

Ros.   What's that?
      A good man! Why the breed's extinct, Gismondo.
      We've brave men, rich men, poor men, and what not
      Dropping sometimes across the hemisphere,
      Called great men—but *good* men—God bless the fellow!
      We've many rare and curious fossils today
      From musty, rusty, dark antiquity,
      And there may something yet be found called *good,*
      Among the mummies in the tomb of Cheops.
      But nowadays men must be good for something,
      Like places, rewards, or titles—I alone
      Among the disinterested class myself
      As good for nothing—and I *think* I *am.*
      Sr. Marc, he—loves his wife.

Gis.   And trusts the world about her,
      Because he would not stand in the full gleam
      Of the false glare in which she finds her turn,

And deems it *happiness*. Shame sees your prince,
Who feeds the fire of a love his honor
Should crush forever out.

Ros.   [*Aside*] This fellow
Is not one half as mad as is believed.
He sees through both of us. [*Aloud*] You know, Gismondo,
Women and weathercocks are synonyms.
The lady soon must weary of her husband,
With his coarse soldier ruggedness and pine
After the prince's coronet. That's natural.

Gis.   Ho, ho! Yes, natural! But now the prince
Worships a shadow. They cannot wed.

Ros.   You have two eyes with only sight in one.
You cannot look two ways at once. The lady
Would not say nay to a divorce.

Gis.   Divorce!
Sr. Marc would ne'er consent.

Ros.   That's to be seen.
Go—meditate in gloom, and visions—read
The stars and destiny—we are content
To take the world for granted, as it wags—
Men for things human only, to be blinded—
And women for true women, to be bought. [*Exit*]

Gis.   He's right. The world is but a work day world.
The true romance is t'other side of it—
Above it—*there*—I'll linger here no more—
Tomorrow I may see him—yes, tomorrow—
Hush, what is that? I heard a footstep sure.
There is no one near, yet there it is again.
I hear it as though close beside me pressing
The grass blades 'neath its ghostly tread! 'Tis there!
And now the wind is sighing 'round my ears,
Shaping its unsubstantial tongue to sound,
Voicing the word revenge! And there's the shadow
Stalking before me with an upraised arm
In readiness to strike—and now it falls—
Fool, 'tis mine own!—I'll seek Sr. Marc—my home
Is full of spectral forms—I'll seek Sr. Marc! [*Exit*]

Scene 2: *An elegant apartment in the villa of Sr. Marc. Enter Dianora and Theresa.*

DIAN. Such themes cease to be pleasantries, Theresa, when stretched beyond the limit of modesty. I'll grant the prince's claims upon the female heart to be both just and irresistible. I'll grant that love held little sway over the impetuous action that made me bride to Sr. Marc. I'll grant, too, that Sr. Marc is little skilled in the courtly modes of winning female hearts—that he is rude, rugged, soldier-like, and better fitted to companion the rough natures that inhabit camps than the softer beings that bronze life's autumn with their golden glance—but, Theresa, he is a man worth any woman—and this answers all, he is my husband!

THER. But the prince, Dianora, the prince! To rule the heart that rules Modena! To be the monarch's monarch—the prince's prince! Oh, you were silly—very silly—what won't women do in a passion? And the prince! When he heard that you were married—mercy on us!

DIAN. I think Lorenzo loved me.

THER. My dear, he went mad—positively mad. Now, like a good girl, listen to the advice of a sister in misfortune, who, born poor, married a rich tradesman who is a mere sleeping partner in the Firm Matrimony. If I were you—and I wish I was—and your husband my husband—which I wish he was—and the prince in love with me—which I wish he was—I'd be divorced tonight and marry the prince tomorrow!

DIAN. But if Sr. Marc loves me—

THER. I should not entertain such a supposition.

DIAN. And if I love Sr. Marc—

THER. So extremely unlikely that it sounds ridiculous. Come, let your heart be judge between them.

DIAN. Too partial a judge to be a just one, I fear, Theresa.

THER. Lorenzo, whose every word is spoken music, whose every glance kills as it falls, whose ancestry dates back to the fossil frogs, whose honors even in recitation would make a herald gasp for breath, whose grace, dignity, stature—

DIAN. No more, Theresa, no more.

THER. Compare these with your blunt, bluff, blusterous soldier husband! And for you! For Dianora, the planet of Modena! The galaxy—the constellation—the cynosure! She who once loved to build such visions of future splendor as a prince's bride, degenerated to a mere camp follower, or a suttler!

DIAN. Be silent, Theresa. I cannot deny that there are moments now in which I sigh at the mental review of what I might have been.

THER. Sigh! It would have made me cry.

DIAN. And, perhaps, there is mingled with the thought something of self-reproof.

THER. Yes, my dear, a sort of inward-spirit-voice, whispering to you, "Dianora, what a fool you've been!"

DIAN. And when I turn from the sadness of these thought-dispelling visions that fade slowly into the arc of Heaven, like a wreathed column of bright vapor, I meet my husband—

THER. Yes, with a gruff "Dianora, my boots"—or else, "Dianora, buckle my sword on"—or, "Dianora, take the child—he's growing troublesome."

DIAN. And that's the one thought that masters me. Yes, Theresa, that love of motherhood that is a covenant to woman of the Creator's pardon and pity for her fall! That love of my infant boy that clothes the heart with a gay garb of flowers, and studs the cold bonds of worldly dispensations with stars that glitter like bright jewels! No, I have put on a new heart with my new estate—fresh hopes with my fresh station.

THER. A hum-drum jog-trot nameless soldier's lady wife.

DIAN. Yes, and forgotten my past folly and past love for Modena's prince.

THER. [Archly] Really?

DIAN. Yes—or if not—yes, yes. Besides, Theresa, would you counsel your friend to a dishonorable step?

THER. [Honestly] No, as I'm a woman. But the Count Rosario suggests, and you know he's both lungs and mouthpiece of the prince—he suggests—

DIAN. What?

THER. A divorce.

DIAN. Theresa! I shall hate—detest the Count Rosario. [Enter Sr. Marc, Gismondo, and Corolla]

MARC. There's the lady Dianora, my little Mercury—do your errand like a precocious young courtier, henceforward to become a skilled breaker of hearts and worrier of jealous husbands. Dianora, he brings you a missive from the prince, embossed, painted, and perfumed bravely. Give it her.

DIAN. Have you not read it, sir?

MARC. I read it? Is it not sealed—and moreover, superscribed to you only? What, my girl, do you take me for—one of your jealous-pated Italian tyrant-husbands, that make the marriage bed one of thorns, and feed a vulture at their thoughts more insatiable than the fabled one that gnawed Prometheus? One day you will know me better!

COR. [Gives packet to Dianora] From my princely master, to the love-light of Modena.

Marc. [*Crossing to Theresa*] So, signora, you can steal a few spare moments from the gay round of fashion to visit my little prisoner. I say "prisoner" for I believe when I walk forth with her, the people of Modena look upon me and my rough bearing as on a gaoler with his dog, and she as a poor timid victim and passive thrall. I thank you for your thought for both of us!

Dian. [*Who has opened the packet and taken out a gold bracelet*] A jeweled bracelet!

Ther. A princely present.

Dian. Too princely for the wear of a soldier's wife! Take it back, sir.

Cor. With no message to my master?

Marc. [*Taking it*] Aye, that would be discourteous. Tell him the signor —Sr. Marc acknowledges his princely liberality in behalf of the signora— perceives the gentle reproof he therein gives him for his neglect in not himself thus decorating her—thanks him alike for the honor and hint, and will not fail to take it.

Cor. No other answer?

Marc. Nothing's needed more. Good day. [*Exit Corolla*] Well, brother soldier, so Modena is half mad with anticipation of the coming splendor of the masque at the palace.

Gis. Yes, it's the theme and din of the city.

Ther. Of course, Dianora will go.

Dian. Indeed she will not.

Marc. And why not? It is in these scenes you shine. It is amid luster and loveliness like this you gleam forth a meteor among stars. I'd have you go— I'd have you plunge among happiness and pleasure that my thick-sided plain bluntness would never have devised for you; not because it cannot trust you there—for faith is the bulwark of love, but because I am myself born without a taste for them, or a genius to invent them. To you they are as habits; therefore I'd have you share them. To you they are life's charms; therefore I'd see you glittering among them. To you they are both dear and pleasant; therefore I'd have them make you happy for in *your* happiness is mine! [*Goes up with Gismondo*]

Ther. Oh, the fellow will drive me out of patience! What could nature have been thinking about when she shut up such a chestnut of a heart in such a coarse and prickly shell. This man's a misfit of Providence and nothing less.

Dian. He has a *royal* heart and that heart loves me.

Ther. And a most desirable investment, next to the prince.

Dian. Don't pester so, Theresa, I'm weary of the prince's very name.

THER. You'd not have been so weary of his title. Farewell, signori. [*Gismondo bows*]

MARC. A bright day for your pleasures, capital lady.

DIAN. What think you now of my coarse husband?

THER. Oh, he'll do, my love. But you were very foolish. Rub as hard as you like, you can't polish him up into a prince; he's only silver gilt.

DIAN. He is a brave, good, honest man—and he's my husband! If I do not love, he has taught me something better—to esteem and honor him. [*Exits with Theresa*]

GIS.   Yes, thus the world talks. [*Coming down*]

MARC. Why, the world will talk—
Will have its jest—will fling its arrowy hail
And wound, if faith hath not its armor on,
To turn the drift aside. The world, Gismondo,
Would make me jealous; man, I love my wife—
There's the world's answer!

GIS.   You may trust too much.
Friends glittering like an adder in the sun
May be as false and venomous.

MARC. The man
Himself deceived, believes deceit to dwell
In every other man. I'm no such being.
And if it were so—no—I tell you, friend,
To worship Dianora has become
An attribute of nature. Do I breathe,
It is to pray for her, or coin such words
As fit the timid ear on which they fall;
My blood runs through me only to be shed
In her protection; pride is born in me
That she and honor are my richest gifts.
And when I think of that, I feel my foot
Beat firmer, and my inward spirit swell
As proudly as a prince.

GIS.   Whom did you wed?
A girl on fire with wounded pride—her heart
Was many miles away.

MARC. And were it so,
I'd make a home for the returning wanderer,
That it might out of love remain with me.
But it is something new indeed, Gismondo,

That you should hang about the skirts of courts
Picking up castaway reports; or worse,
Believing in the idle tales bred out of nothing
Among the feather-brained courtiers, who wage war
'Gainst virtue, and kill characters! To love
Is something so akin to Heaven, to doubt
Were paganism in its face.

GIS.   They say at court
I'm mad, and do not hesitate to speak
Their thoughts before me.

MARC.   And what say they?

GIS.   This:
The prince is a good huntsman when the chase
Is loveliness like Dianora's.

MARC.   Well?

GIS.   That your wife's *duty* holds her to your side—
And not her love.

MARC.   That love's the oak that grows
The surer from its slow and gradual progress.
It is the tender, delicate exotic
That lives a mere ephemeral life! What more?

GIS.   That Dianora charms the prince, and he
Unused to thwart his will for common lets,
Will push on a divorce.

MARC.   Divorce! Unmarry us!
My lips should rot to dust
Before they gave consent.

GIS.   Psha! He's a prince;
And you are but—a man!

MARC.   That's all. A man!
Gismondo, there is something in that name—
That brief word full of solemn meaning like
The name of God—the name of *Man,* that hath
The voice of him that preached the great crusades,
And stirred up all the world! I am a man—
But I am one who like a bark at sea
Steers by a star—my honor—shining ever
Through night, and storm, and sunlight! To keep on
One never deviating course; to make
The right the reigning and impulsive law,

To guide and rule; to face a threatening shame
And waive it hence—but not to dream dishonor,
Till it comes on in presence palpable.
And then to rise in warrior majesty
And die before it, or else beat it back.
This is to be a man—and such am I!

GIS.   And I believe it from my soul Sr. Marc.
See who comes here. Rosario and your wife;
He is the prince's friend, and she's a woman.
I'll to my vision-haunted chamber—home!
The prince must do me right tomorrow. [*Exit*]

MARC.   Yes.
Gismondo means well, but his brain is weak.
He builds on visions, with distempered senses
Turning plain fact about till they distort
Its honest simple meaning. Gismondo's mad.
The world agrees so, and when rumor's hand
Points to a theme like this—like doubt of her—
He must be mad indeed. Doubt Dianora!
Mad as a fierce volcano!
[*Enter the Count Rosario and Dianora*]

ROS.   'Tis the hope
On which he fed—his motive, impulse, all—
'Twas to see you again, joy's central beam,
Gilding the ring of satellites with light
Ennobling where it falls, he gives this fete—
Now really you *must* come.

DIAN.   Do you forget
My husband's presence?

ROS.   Really. Pardon me,
I quite forgot to notice you! The lady
Casts such a glare about her that my eyes
Were dazzled into blindness. Sir, your *servant*.

MARC.   You wrong yourself. The prince's friends are mine—
And *friend's* a good man's title.

ROS.   True.
The Lady Dianora is resolved
To break the prince's heart!

MARC.   That's most disloyal.
What's her high treason?

Ros.   She still hesitates
        To bless the prince with sight of her tomorrow
        At the great festival.
Marc.   She'll think better, sir,
        She'll bless his eyesight and his fête besides.
        I'll promise she shall come.
Dian.   I have no wish
        To join this revelry, unless you'll go [*Crossing to Marc*],
        Yourself at once my cavalier and friend.
Marc.   You know I cannot. I must ride to Parma
        On urgent matters; but we'll find a friend
        To take the charge upon him.
Ros.   Such an office
        Might turn old age to nimble-footed youth!
        Let me be honored.
Marc.   She'll be grateful, signor.
        A word here with my valet, I'll rejoin you—
        You'll pardon me? [*Goes out, but soon returns*]
Ros.   The Cerberus is gone. [*With hasty earnestness*]
        Sweet lady, still Lorenzo is your slave,
        Still lives—still dares to hope.
Dian.   Count—
Ros.   Speak not yet.
        You've not heard all his offers—
Dian.   Offers! [*Reenter Sr. Marc at back*]
Ros.   Join
        The golden circle of this festival.
        Masques are convenient visors for sweet love
        That burns in secret. Lips can whisper—kiss—
        Under their friendly shadow—mystery
        Is love's true atmosphere—cast this husband off—
        Sign the deeds requisite to win divorce
        From these coarse twiggen bonds like those that bind
        The graves of nameless beggars—and the prince
        Will buy your loutish husband's willing hand,
        By countless honors.
Dian.   Never.
Ros.   Wealth, then?

DIAN.　Buy
　　　　The empire of the stars with mines of gold—
　　　　Then seek to buy Sr. Marc.

ROS.　If obdurate
　　　　He dares resist his prince, torture and chain
　　　　Shall force him—

MARC.　[*Advancing*]　Hold! I thank the noble prince
　　　　For his intentions towards his honored slave,
　　　　Who casts his threats back into his teeth! So tell him.
　　　　To you, my wife, I speak a few brief words,
　　　　And bid you by your honor, mark that well,
　　　　To answer justly in the sight of Heaven
　　　　And act upon the impulse of your soul.
　　　　Disdaining fear, I came to you a soldier,
　　　　With no more riches than my heart and sword,
　　　　My honor and my love. I did not say
　　　　You were an angel born, but such a creature
　　　　Sent among men to be beloved, and so—
　　　　So dearly did I love you, I laid down
　　　　An honest man's devotion at your feet—
　　　　A heart without reproach—a spirit rough,
　　　　But in your presence, tamed like a pet bird
　　　　And doating—that's the word—yes, doating on you.
　　　　You raised me to your bosom—married me!
　　　　And now this prince, who could have made you great,
　　　　But not have loved you better, sends the count—
　　　　No doubt a very warm ambassador—
　　　　With certain offers. Choose between us now—
　　　　I give you back your liberty again.
　　　　A pen's stroke does it all—a word, you're free—
　　　　If I inherit not your heart with you.
　　　　I will not be the jailor [*sic*] of your soul.

ROS.　[*To her*]　Magnificent! You're free.

DIAN.　I use it thus! [*Crossing to Sr. Marc*]
　　　　My home is with my husband!

ROS.　Folly! Madness!

MARC.　What ho! [*Calling*] Without there! Tell the Prince Lorenzo
　　　　My lady shall not fail his festival. [*Enter Servant*]
　　　　Go show the Count Rosario
　　　　The outer gate—and see it shut upon him.

Ros.   Sr. Marc!

Marc.   Shut fast, good fellow. It is wisdom, count,
To close our portals on a pestilence,
And shut a plague wind out. Shut out the count.

Ros.   The more of the world I note, the more I feel delighted
With myself and disgusted with everybody else. [*Exit Rosario*]

Dian.   You overheard the message of the prince!
How he still pesters me with his wearisome
Forgotten passion.

Marc.   It will die of age.
Let it alone.

Dian.   I will not go tomorrow.
You'd fear to trust me.

Marc.   Fear to trust thee, wife!
I'd trust thee mid a myriad such temptations,
As grow amid the atmosphere of courts.
My love is a pure worship of the soul—
Where doubt or fear is heresy; a structure
Based on a rock—tempest defying, deep
As mines of gold, and lifting to the stars
Its head of glittering glory. Fear to trust thee—
Within my heart there's no room to doubt—
'Tis too brim full of love—of love for thee! [*Exeunt*]

ACT II.

Scene 1: *A corridor or gallery in the palace. Gismondo discovered pacing to and fro. After short pause Pietro, the servant, enters.*

Pietro. In heaven's name, signor, how got you in here? The very sanctuary of the Prince Lorenzo. What want you?

Gis. A somewhat scarce commodity at courts, justice.

Pietro. You should come at proper times, signor.

Gis. And what may your wisdom call the proper times?

Pietro. The prince holds audience here at midday for two whole hours, and transacts the business of the State.

Gis. In two hours! Faith, if there's a hole in the State's fabric, it can be but meanly patched in two hours! Twenty-two hours to sin in, and two to make up for it!—That's justice in Modena! Take him my name: he knows my business, and me.

PIETRO. Not for a wardrobe of castoff apparel! Come, you must go, or I must thrust you out.

GIS. Did I hear? [*Touching sword*]

PIETRO. My orders are positive!

GIS. And so is my resolution. I stay here. Will the sunlight of Modena break here? I must salute his earliest beams, and here I'll wait, and patiently.

PIETRO. Take your own will then, with the devil's fortune. As you owe me no spite, do me no ill favor. Hide hereabout, and at the best opportunity secure the prince's ear, but don't drop a whisper of my name. In this day—the day of his grand fiesta—he has dispensed even with the usual hours of audience.

GIS. Indeed! Justice is elbowed into a lumber closet just to give more room for pleasure to revel in. I'll be wise—go.

PIETRO. [*Aside*] The world must be right when it says he's mad. Some folks seem to think the prince has nothing else to do but listen to the people, as well expect the gilt knob of the church spire to take notice of the bricks and stones set there to support it. [*Exit*]

GIS. No. I'll be fooled no longer. I will see him—
See him alone, and at his hands demand
Both right and reparation for my father.
The spirit frowned on me last night—it chides me
For negligence in being daff'd with words,
Instead of forcing that which, wanting, keeps his grave
Unhallowed and irreverend—revenge!
If he denies, I'll take. He comes—and with him
The man with all his being knit in smiles,
And all his frame a yielding complacence—
Cringing, plastic, and subservient ever—
A courtly football—when he's gone I'll speak.
These columns will conceal me. [*He retires. Enter Prince Lorenzo, in an elegant gown, and the Count Rosario*]

PRINCE. So her husband
Refused my jeweled gift with haughty scorn
And sent it back to me.

ROS. As proudfully
As though his foot was used to tread on thrones,
His head to sweep the stars! The lady, too—
As highly toned as he.

PRINCE. She, like the sea,
Takes color from the overhanging arc
Confining and commanding her. Before him

She cannot choose but be obedient.
No matter! You are sure she'll come tonight—
He promised that—alone, too?

Ros.   Quite alone—
Her husband hath some business at Parma
And will return too late.

Prince. That's well. The fête
Had been as tame and spiritless as life
Viewed by a sobering drunkard, lacking her.

Ros.   You love her.

Prince. Love her!
Rosario, she seems my life's one motive.
Pictures are fair or false as they resemble
Her golden eyes—her beauty. Would I speak
Of heavenly things and paint them by my speech,
I speak of her—and beautiful she stands
Glowing like sunset o'er a harvest field.
She must break off this match and live for me.

Ros.   What means? She's obdurate as an avalanche—
Insensible as rocks. And then 'tis meet
We steer quite clear of *him*—I mean her husband—
The man is such a blunt plain-speaking boor—
Such a determined, damned, straightforward fellow—
One must be careful. He is like a flint,
No matter how you hit him, he shows fire!
And as for wheedling him, one might as well
Just try to tickle a polar bear. If offended,
He'd strike you dead with his paw. If pleased,
He'd hug you into the next world, posthaste!

Prince. My scheme is this. You'll have to play
A part in't. Therefore learn it in reserve.
Women were ever mysteries, Rosario—
Contraries, unreconciled antagonisms;
And Dianora is—a woman.

Ros.   True!
Women are kittens, playful when they're young,
But grow up cats in time.

Prince. Her heart is mine;
And that's the helm of the frail vessel, woman.
By that I'll guide her—at this evening's fête

I'll beg her hand's subscription to divorce.
And if she hesitates—as she will do—
In all modesty of timorous nature—
I'll make a loving prisoner of herself
Among staunch friends of my high state and me
Till she consent to sign. That once obtained,
I'll hit on means to force Sr. Marc's approval
By promises to set his brain on fire
Or perils that shall shake it into fear.

Ros. And if that fail, I have a master scheme
To bend her like a reed to your desire,
And 'gainst his will make him a party to it,
A willing, coinciding party.

Prince. Faith!
A master scheme indeed to bring 'round that.
The Duke Lioni, you, Rosario,
And my own kinsman, Prince Bellafiore,
With other trusty partisans must play
The lady's gaolers.

Ros. Humph! I could have wished
Better than either—Duke Lioni fears
The glitter of the sword worse than the very devil;
And Prince Bellafiore, though he's brave,
Hath too much love for foppery.

Prince. What matters
For actual valor with a lady foe?
Her fears will win the victory for us. Come,
The daylight wears; with evening comes a light
Brighter than stars; it brings me Dianora.

Ros. Unless ill luck, her husband, snuffs our candle out. [*Exeunt*]

Gis. [*Emerging*] A cunning plot! A rare and quaint device!
Shrewd meshes to entangle in its web
A lady's honor. But I've heard men say
A fool has proved too cunning for a sage
In bygone times. Why not the brain called mad
Devise a counterplot to o'erthrow these!
No, no—mine labors like a water-logged ship
And cannot make a course. I have it now!
I'll to Sr. Marc—prevent him setting forth—
Bring him to take hand at this same game

Of honor cast into the stake with hearts.
He'll play it out and bravely! No delay—
Mad am I! It may chance, as I will work,
I shall not prove the maddest in Modena! [*Exit*]

SCENE 2: *Hall in the villa of Sr. Marc. Enter Sr. Marc, attired for riding, and his Servant.*

MARC.   What horse is saddled for me?
SERV.   Sir, the grey.
MARC.   The grey! No, surely, the Arabian. He
       Of all my stable is my favorite.
SERV.   You named the grey last night, sir.
MARC.   Did I? Well,
       I can believe it. For my mind, last night,
       Was troubled with dull thoughts that stole upon me,
       Like the gloom of a thundershower. Well, the grey
       Must suit my need then. Has your lady yet
       Departed for the masque?
SERV.   Not yet, sir, but
       The coach is waiting for her at the gate.
MARC.   What horses harnessed?
SERV.   At my lady's wish
       The roan and white, sir.
MARC.   Good. Sure-footed both,
       Gentle, and most obedient to the voice.
       Who drives them?
SERV.   Marco.
MARC.   Steady and careful, too,
       And loves his lady. She is safe with him.
       So there's no ground to fret my breast with fears;
       And yet they rise in spite of me. I saw her
       In the gay garb of the approaching masque—
       So beautiful. Through its simplicity
       Her grace outbeaming grandly and sublime
       Like ocean sleeping in the starlight! Yet
       I could not shut the thought out from my breast
       Of my unworthiness to hold a prize
       So past a mortal's valuing.
SERV.   I hear
       The distant wheels; my lady is gone.

MARC. She's gone!
      A blessing go with her, as *she* goes ever
      A blessing where she strays. See to my horse. [*Exit Servant. Enter*
      Gismondo]
      What, my sad comrade of the gloom and shadow—
      What is the news your end of the city?

GIS. News!
      That rogues will cheat, that thieves will steal, that faith
      Was meant for rascals to grow rich upon.
      That day was made for villains to plot mischief,
      And night to hide them from the consequence.
      That Heaven's a right good name to swear a lie by.
      That honest men are meant for knavish tools,
      And knaves to handle them! There's the latest news
      My end of the city. What's the news in yours?

MARC. That there's a bright side to the darkest cloud.
      Friends in the world worth prizing—faith and truth
      More than mere names, and honor more than shadow.
      The world with all its faults a pleasant world
      To him who has the tact to make it so.
      That life is gay and precious to fresh hearts
      That leap up full of confidence in nature,
      When morning like a mother lifts night's veil
      From the fair forehead of the infant day—
      And there's my news. Existence takes its hue
      From the mind's color that looks out on it.
      But come, I waste the time of pressing matters.
      Wilt ride with me?

GIS. Not I. I come to turn
      Your purpose from this journey.

MARC. What pretense?

GIS. On something more than mere pretense, Sr. Marc.
      On the authority of friendship.

MARC. That's
      A sovereign authority. Speak on.
      What must I do?

GIS. Follow your wife—nay, hear me.
      And having heard me speak, follow your wife.
      Observe her at this masque in some disguise.

MARC.   What, follow her! A mean and paltry spy,
         Dogging her footsteps like her evil spirit,
         To construe by the lexicon distrust
         Light actions into false! I follow her!
         Gismondo, when I wedded Dianora*
         I did not take a slave unto my wife,
         Whose every deed I could not answer for,
         Nor for her honor vouch! I did not make
         This jewel mine to pine in inner fear
         That shame would tarnish it, or thievish hands
         Made bold by oily tongues, purloin it from me.
         I did not risk it to be gem or glass.
         I knew it to be sterling diamond,
         The rich might envy and the poor admire;
         But no more to be sullied by their contact
         Than the calm moon by the thick smoke of Etna.
         I'd trust her—

GIS.   Aye—her honor—but her strength
         Against the plottings of a passionate man
         Horsed on the fiery courser of his will,
         Must fall resistless. I have overheard
         By merest chance a shrewd conspiracy
         To rob you of your wife.

MARC.   The means?

GIS.   At this same masque tonight.
         To make her buy the price of liberty
         From Prince Lorenzo's power, by consenting
         To a prepared legal document
         In readiness, to be divorced from you—
         Your own agreement in mere afterthought
         To be secured by force!

MARC.   The masque tonight!
         Then the prince does love her—loves her honorably—
         Would push aside by law our marriage vows,
         To wed her to himself.

GIS.   He would.

* These lines, like many others in the manuscript, have been partly crossed out. The manuscript, however, is so full of alterations and emendations that it has seemed best to include the whole copy, ignoring any evidence of rewriting or revision.

MARC. If she
       In spite of all should love him—
GIS.   What of that?
       Why ask yourself such a question?
MARC. It might be
       She really loved him—dazzled by her cage—
       As though the sun might quarrel with the earth,
       And turn its beams upon some world in shadow—
       She lit up my existence with her smile.
       And now her vision hath untranced itself,
       She looks upon her past with sorrowing
       As something full of bitterness like death.
       You know it might be so, Gismondo—might—
       I do not say it is—the hope is there,
       The small sweet hope! E'en as the prisoner thinks
       The taper light, that through the crevice gleams,
       Carried by coming liberty more bright
       Than sunrise on the mountains. But I'll *go*—
       [*Calling*] My mask and mantle, boy! I have my sword.
GIS.   Be wise, Sr. Marc, be politic.
MARC. I'll be
       What the time makes me, ice or blazing fire.
       I do not go to rave, to curse, to kill,
       Nor blindly—on misconstructions, based
       Upon surmise or hints conjectural—
       But watch, and act. Don't fear me, honest friend,
       I'll not forget I am a man, nor he
       My prince, nor she a woman and my wife!
       Here hangs my sword, here beats my heart. One side
       Holds both. But do not tremble for her sake
       On my hot wrath. My heart's above my sword! [*Exeunt*]

SCENE 3: *Magnificent ballroom in the palace. The stage crowded with charac-*
ters in masquerade. Music, dancers, etc. Enter the Count Rosario who is
masked.

ROS. Where is the lady? She's not among the maskers, and that bids fair
to spoil as pretty a plot as ever man hatched. Our lines and nets are well laid,
our anglers skillful, our baits unexceptionable, but either there's no fish in the
pond, or she's too cunning to bite.

THER. [*Without*] I shall remember, signora.

Ros. Who's that? No, 'tis not her—the lady Theresa!

THER. [*Entering*] Count! Count—I'm delighted to have encountered you. I'm on tenterhooks, with laudable curiosity. What mystery is this on foot to-night? There's the prince seeking for someone everywhere and the lords whispering and nodding to each other as if each was loaded to the brim with wonderment. What is the matter?

Ros. Guess.

THER. What?

Ros. A riddle.

THER. I dote on them—let's have it.

Ros. What is that that wants, might have, would have, can and won't have? There 'tis for you.

THER. A woman.

Ros. Right. Nothing else could create such a contrarity. In the world's grammar she's a sort of affirmative, made by two negatives. In life's chemistry, the acid which, thrown on a man's carbonate, raises his effervescence. A jumble of flints which, shaken together in a bag, rub down each other's sharp edges, and that's a woman. Now, Theresa, you are very pretty.

THER. Do you think so?

Ros. [*Aside*] She does, or there's rank treachery in her looking-glass. [*Aloud*] Were you in Dianora's place, would you not break down the barrier between a throne and yourself, and marry our sovereign, Lord Lorenzo?

THER. I would.

Ros. If you loved him.

THER. Without. But she does love him.

Ros. Did! It's almost a doubt, so let's put it in the most perfect participle tense of *did*. Now the prince is still perfectly rabid in his passion. A title—love—power are at her beck—

THER. But she won't marry him.

Ros. Of course she won't! She'd be renegade to her sex if she did what she was wanted to do! Theresa, you must aid us for the prince's sake—he often admires your figure.

THER. The prince is very kind, and very clear-sighted, but I'll join in no plots against her.

Ros. Plots! Theresa, plots are for assassins and conspirators—we call it finesse; but if you could just hold the trap open while the mouse walked in—

THER. Catch your own mice, signor. Plot your own schemes; I'm no decoy duck!

Ros. But the prince requests—and you *are* handsome.

THER. I can't help it, signor.

Ros. How could you? If the prince could now look at your nose—of course, I mean in the abstract, not in the actual, which would necessitate a squint—if the prince has a weakness, it's noses. He's a judge of them, and when he fairly lays hold of yours, well, I'll not tell you all he says of it! But I'll venture this much on my own responsibility—if with your womanly art you'd aid him to win the lady, there's a title somewhere or other lying in his highness's gift, which would suit a strongly developed woman. Well, well, still tongues make wise heads.

THER. Signor, it is not the title affects me, but my friend's welfare. I will aid you with all my power. It is a pity a good title should grow rusty for a wearer. If the lady's here, I'll find her! [*Exit*]

Ros. O woman, woman! Truly you are the cyphers of our being—the noughts of life's arithmetic—strung together by yourselves meaning nothing, but appended to a substantial figure called man, increasing his value ten- or a hundredfold! For this poor creature, one must give her a subterfuge to sin under. So, *for her friend's* sake, she'll labor to deserve the prince's favors. Yes, money and patronage, backed by fashion, can do everything in this world, and in the next—but I believe fashion's out of fashion there! [*Enter Prince, in red mask and white mantle*]

PRINCE. Strange, she is not here. Without her, all is but a sunless summer. Joy a mere name, a vision.

Ros. I do not recognize her among the dancers. Can her churlish husband have turned mastiff at the eleventh hour, and put the chain of his iron will on her freedom?

PRINCE. I know not. [*Loud and joyous laughter, and cries of "Brava! Brava!"*] What's that? Have we some famed improvisatore among us? Such laughter follows not the stale worn jests that are the usual themes of courtly company.

Ros. The gayest of the city are gathered in a cluster around some popular mask. See, the Prince Bellafiore sees your highness, and breaking through the throng, hurries this way, all red, like the sun in a thick fog, or an effigy wrought in sealing wax. We shall soon solve this riddle. [*Enter the Prince Bellafiore wearing a red domino and a red mask*]

BELLA. My noble kinsman, this gay masque hath set the hearts of every noble glowing like a furnace. She's beautiful, spite of the envious mask, which only plays the part of trumpeter to her charms, and aids her spell. Her wit flashes like a spark by night—jests on her lips touch and fly off lighter than thistledown, yet sparkling like the facets of a gem! Who can she be?

Ros. What mask? She in the Spanish garb?

BELLA. The same—a seraph—a siren—an enchantress!

PRINCE. [*Looking off*] 'Tis she! The form—the stately motion that is the true bearing of nobility, and betrays her secret through her masquerade. Yes, it is Dianora!

BELLA. Dianora, and is such an angel wife to a poor, rough soldier? O Mercury, what profanation!

PRINCE. And now to sow the seeds of my adventure. Play your parts cautiously and the harvest cannot fail to be a golden one. [*Enter several masks, surrounding Dianora, who is masked, and wearing a picturesque Spanish costume. Among her followers is the Duke Lioni, who alone, with the exception of the Prince, wears a white domino and white mask*]

ALL. [*Entering*] Excellent! Charming!

LIONI. Declare yourself! Let men know if you are mortal or a coruscation of loveliness, which it is not heresy to worship. Your name?

DIAN. In that the secret lies. In the *mystery* exists the magic. Is it not the fickle nature of mankind to make a god of novelty, which though it precede a common good to the world, decking and adorning it, becomes a mere household name when the strangeness is worn off. Keep the mask on the face and we believe the virtue. Remove it, and the virtue is a mere commodity, and nothing more.

LIONI. This is satire. Those who look to praise, can find themes that deserve it!

DIAN. And while they look, how much more will they find to scorn? Could the false world gaze in a mirror on itself, would it recognize the picture, or rather, would it acknowledge the fidelity?

ROS. Is the world false when it calls you charming?

DIAN. Is he a true man who judgeth by the show? Can your eyes pierce my mask?

ROS. Yes.

DIAN. And what see they beneath it?

ROS. A sweet face the index of a sweet mind, the symbol of a bright heart.

DIAN. Shall I read yours? Some faces are no more than masks—the stuccoed front of an ill-built dwelling, the flowery surface of a concealed morass, the wrecker's fire by night, not to succor but betray—the outer film of a diseased conscience! Such a face is yours!

ROS. Lady, really—upon my word—do you know me?

DIAN. Do I not? Have I not told you yourself?

ROS. I am a nobleman of Modena.

DIAN. That's a name; wise eyes look lower for the man himself. A Roman emperor once deified his horse, but the god ate oats. Princes and lineage make men noble, but they do not make them honest.

LIONI. Honesty *is* nobleness.

DIAN. Yes, but nobleness is not honesty. The world has changed it to a mere puppet name.

BELLA. You've a sharp tongue, lady.

DIAN. Yes, when folly whets it.

BELLA. But your graces are your shield.

DIAN. As your high descent is yours; else, raillery would launch a shaft that would strike home.

LIONI. Beauty is a good armor.

DIAN. Vanity is a better, for it numbs the sensibilities, that otherwise would feel and wince at the attacks of truth.

Ros. [*Aside*] She has a tongue like a cat, that rasps while it licks. Perhaps she'll purr more pleasantly to his highness—if not, his highness will get gloriously maul'd. [*All retire up but Dianora and Prince, and gradually disperse, leaving the stage clear to them*]

PRINCE. You have scared the gaiety of half Modena.

DIAN. Let the chaff fly off—the grain's beneath.

PRINCE. Life's golden grain—beauty! And I pity you.

DIAN. Pity me! You know me not. [*Going*]

PRINCE. Dianora! [*She stops, after a pause*] Dianora!

DIAN. You name the name of a dear friend!

PRINCE. As dear to you as your own self! 'Tis well you know her, for you shall be love's ambassador to tell her of a great man's passion.

DIAN. I know her answer ere you speak. Nay, I could play the part of both, the great man who loves, and the lady who would listen.

PRINCE. Go on, then! So she *would* listen—wins him half the victory. He says he loves.

DIAN. How says it? Why as a schoolboy deserving to be chid, with his tongue quivering in his choked throat! Thus would he woo: "Dianora, I am a prince, and—nothing more! Having no need of work, I am as useless in the world as a drone. With no necessity to beg, I lack the endurance of the beggar—I pant beneath the heat—I shiver in the cold. I have no virtue but my rank, and that I'd sell for a cork, were I drowning at sea! I have no accomplishments but riches, and were I drouthy in the desert I'd exchange them for a cup of water! I'm brave, but I have braver men for scullions. I dance, but make a miserable figure beside my buffoon. I sing, but my feathered prisoner shames me. To be brief, were I a boy I'd tremble—were I a woman I'd blush—were I an honest man I'd repent—but not having grace to repent nor spirit to be honest I'll tell you, Dianora, that I love you—out of an old love that hangs about me, like the tatters of an old robe, worth little when 'twas new."

PRINCE. A novel mode of pressing suit to beauty! Well, for the lady's answer.

DIAN. A while she wouldn't speak for laughing.

PRINCE. At her own inward joy?

DIAN. For mocking him! "Tell the prince," she'd say, "I've listened to him fairly through, and were I free—"

PRINCE. She'd wed him!

DIAN. She'd make him keeper of her squirrel and her monkey, which would have the merit of giving him usefulness at least. She'd mock him—

PRINCE. As a prelude to marrying him! She'd turn from the passing world and, glancing back upon the sweetness of times bygone, find in their memories a resistless spell that would incline her to his passion and, yielding to those tender records all the tribute of her woman's nature, she'd consent—

DIAN. To what?

PRINCE. To break this marriage knot, to sign the scroll of liberty, to be free, and wed him! Ponder upon it in the solitude of your own sweet thoughts, gentle Dianora—for now our hearts cast off this masking foppery— let your prince leave his image to plead for him in your bosom, and be the past—the bright precious past—his warmest pleader! For a time—only for a time, farewell! [Exit]

DIAN.   I dare not—dare not! In my solitude
      I'm forced to crush his rising image down,
      As something sacrilegious and unholy,
      Defiling the mind temple of a wife!
      My heart cleaves to him like the moss on ruins,
      His memory a verdure ever green,
      And ever beautiful! My heart shall speak—
      I'll write to him—I dare not trust my tongue—
      I will not lest it play the traitor to me,
      And utter thoughts that only lie between
      My soul and it. I'll write—that done, depart—
      Steal from this sickening and infecting air,
      This scene of foppery and shallow pleasure,
      And look on him no more. I'll rend the love
      Out from my bosom as I would an adder.
      I'll tear up heart and all, but it shall go,

Although the torture kill me. I will soar
Above dishonor—and above myself! [*Exit. Enter Sr. Marc, at back,
in a black mask and domino*]

MARC. One half's achieved: I'm here. A golden bribe
Bought the o'erzealous janitor, and now
I vainly seek for her. On every side
I hear her name, and note on every lip
A smile of meaning and of triumph there,
As though the victory were one half sure!
The plot's progressing then—not with *her* will!
I'll gage my soul she is no party to it—
Everywhere is joy! Everywhere gaiety! And thus
Is revelry the loom and mirth the shuttle
Weaving a thread of silk among the web
Of pleasure's shining garb! How shall I act?
I must remove her from this Fair of Foppery,
This Carnival of Vanity—the means?
Aye, there we stumble—softly—who's here. [*Retires. Reenter Rosario,
Bellafiore and Lioni*]

Ros. Remember, signors, it is the prince's hope! She's writing in yon alcove a love missive, for a thousand ducats! A love missive to the prince.

Lioni. Corolla says her carriage has been ordered. She means to lurch Lorenzo and the fête—quit it in its brightest hours.

Bella. Well, we understand the rest: keep her a prisoner—of course, with all the honors of beauty—till she bows to the prince's will.

Ros. Resigning her only to the prince's care—whom you cannot fail to know by his white mantle and red mask.

MARC. [*At back*] White mantle and red mask!

Ros. Unto all who question the will of the Prince Lorenzo you have one answer only, your swords. Now to set spies upon the actions of the lady. Come, my lord duke, come, Prince Bellafiore.

Bella. I follow! [*Exeunt Rosario and Lioni*]

MARC. [*Coming down*] I'll play Gismondo's game! Yes, policy and caution may win me more than passion.

Bella. I like not this business! It's not honorable for one of high blood to stir in—yet to offend Lorenzo!

MARC. [*Advancing*] Your servant, signor.

Bella. A strange mask.

MARC. A poor artist of Modena, basking in the smile of our right noble and generous prince. Reckoned, too, a not indifferent judge of colors, and their lights and shades. Your mask's a red one, so is your domino, hat—feather! The monotony spoils all—the color kills itself.

BELLA. I think he's right. I do look all afire. But how to remedy the evil now—

MARC. A simple remedy: change but the mask, 'twill serve. Mine's at your service.

BELLA. A bargain! [*Exchanging*] Thou'rt an honest fellow. Call on me in the morning—you shall take my picture. I love to honor men of merit. [*Exit*]

MARC. That's a first step. Here comes, as if upon my wish, a mantle of the livery of the lilies! Yes, 'tis the patrician Lioni, a man who trembles at his shadow on the hedge. For him I'll change my tactics. Yes, more policy! [*Enter Lioni*]

LIONI. Where loiters Bellafiore—the lady will be gone!

MARC. [*As if cautiously*] Signor! Signor!

LIONI. Mercy, what now?

MARC. Murder. Secret assassins—in the room disguised!

LIONI. Holy St. Gregory!

MARC. They have their orders—to strike at a white mantle such as yours.

LIONI. As mine! The prince wears such another!

MARC. Yes, but his red mask distinguishes his highness. Thwart them—defeat them.

LIONI. I shall be most happy. How?

MARC. Give me your mantle and take mine!

LIONI. Upon the instant! This generosity is touching, for you to be so good as to be killed instead of me! [*Exchanging mantles*] An interposition of providence—a most miraculous escape! [*Exit*]

MARC. She comes! I have learned well this novel principle of policy—now for the master stroke! [*Retires. Reenter Dianora and the three Nobles*]

DIAN. This is discourteous, unmanly, signors! A prisoner! The prince will punish this presumption.

BELLA. We are the prince's slaves.

LIONI. And your adorers!

ROS. You would be free, beautiful Dianora. Shall the prince vainly sue, and your eyes wilfully blind themselves to fortune and to love!

DIAN. Insolent! I demand my freedom! [*They oppose her*]

ROS. It is here! Under the legal captivity of Sr. Marc you're a poor lark in a cage, with enough turf beneath you to remind you of free fields, enough view of Heaven above to remind you of liberty. What you desire is yours, on signing this! [*Shows a scroll*]

DIAN. To quit my husband! To give consent to a divorce and break a good man's heart! I will not do it! I'll call for help! Even in this haunt there must beat a few honest hearts. [*All draw swords*]

Ros. We do not fear resistance! Think—a sighing prince! Rank—dazzling equipage—and splendor! On the other hand, a fortuneless, nameless beggary!

DIAN. O Heaven! Hear me—aid me!

Ros. You will sign!

DIAN. To my death warrant sooner! Let me pass. [*Enter Sr. Marc, wearing a red mask and a white mantle. Believing him to be the prince, all bow and give way. To him*] O prince, if in your bosom dwells the olden chivalry of your ancient house, by that and by your honor as a man, I implore you to restore me to my husband and to my home!

MARC. [*In an undertone*]   Both, Dianora. Home and husband!

DIAN. Ha, that voice!

MARC. Hush! [*Going up. As they reach C., the Prince Lorenzo enters*]

PRINCE. Gone! Has she signed the paper?

BELLA. [*Astounded*]   The prince!

Ros. And multiplied by two! [*All point to Sr. Marc*]

PRINCE. Stay! Impostor! Villain!

MARC. [*Unmasking*]   A little late, my lord, that's all. [*All start*] Keep your friends back, my lord, and let them learn *my* lesson if they value their poor lives. [*Draws*] And not to stir one step. It's *policy,* and worthy their attention.

PRINCE. Insolent and nameless villain—but my sword—

MARC. Proud lord,
　　　　Take heed I do not win myself a name
　　　　For slaying of a prince! My sword is out,
　　　　Grasped in a hand that's grown into the hilt,
　　　　And wielded, too, by one whom people say
　　　　Knows something of his trade! Let him who dares
　　　　To tempt the adder, tremble for the sting.
　　　　[*Tableau. Exeunt*]

ACT III.

SCENE 1: *A private walk in the palace gardens. Enter Prince Lorenzo and Bellafiore. A month has elapsed.*

BELLA. If only practicable, a good device,
　　　　And judging by the flower, promising

The best of fruit. Far better than the scheme
That failed so signally a month ago
To win the lady, though the scheme was yours.

PRINCE. It cannot fail to prove
A good one, for a woman's at the root on't.
Rosario hath a master mind for plots,
And for Theresa, when did female tact
Handle the rudder, but the ship made harbor,
In spite of storms or quicksands.

BELLA. Doth Theresa
Take share in this plot on your side? I deemed her
The friend of Dianora.

PRINCE. Is she not?
Would she not aid her to throw off this churl—
This husband madly chosen from the camp—
To share a golden destiny? She aids us
To see her friend grow great, as she grew rich,
Not caring for the means, so honest ones.
Bellafiore, since my last repulse
There's something more than love mixed up in this.

BELLA. Revenge on him!

PRINCE. And triumph over her!
She spurned my offers, *he* refused my bribes—
Nay, cast them back as though I'd proffered dross,
And in the face of justice in Modena,
I'd dare not give full swing to my authority,
Or else a prison—no: let this plot hold,
I'm master o'er them both!

BELLA. The night has come
To bring the plot to issue.

PRINCE. Yes. The day
Following the masque wherein Sr. Marc o'erturned
My half won project, I received a letter
From Dianora, bidding me farewell,
Yet breathing tones of memoried love that told me
The fire was not dead, but dormant merely.
Armed with this instrument, this night Theresa
Will with it start the husband's jealousy.

BELLA. In her own writing! A resistless aid!

PRINCE. And while the ferment tingles in his breast,
      Come I to proffer friendly aid, and tell him
      My love has worn itself to sleep, admiring
      His manly spirit—its *first* lullaby,
      And *secondary,* the proofs that meet my ear
      Of Dianora's falsehood!
BELLA. Fortunate
      You are the prince that tell him so, or else
      He'd strike the teller with no velvet hand,
      And fling the lie in his teeth!
PRINCE. I'll offer proof—
      Refer him to the chamber of his wife—
      And there he'll find Rosario, conveyed
      Into the sacred temple of his honor,
      By a well-given bribe, and artifice!
BELLA. And on this proof, he cannot fail to fling her
      To the world's mercy!
PRINCE. Then she falls on mine!
      You and your friends must bear me company.
      Go summon them—'tis on the hour—here
      I'll wait your coming back! [*Exit Bellafiore*]
      Love scorned, creates
      A restless chiding pride—an inward shame
      Like that which follows the defeated host
      'Gainst whom the tide of battle has been turned
      By a mere chance of fortune! [*Enter Gismondo, observing*]
      The desire
      Burning to combat in the cause again—
      A mental confidence in victory—
      A resolution, and—
GIS. The Prince Lorenzo. [*Advances*]
PRINCE. Who speaks?
GIS. A beggar, yet a strange one, too—
      A man who comes to ask his own.
PRINCE. The hours
      Of public justice are—
GIS. I know—asleep—
      Tucked in their beds ere this—but I must wake them.
      They must please think their dwelling is afire
      And turn them out in their night clothes!

PRINCE. You've a name:
    Let me hear that, and I may answer you.
GIS.   Gismondo.
PRINCE. Called the Mad!
GIS.   By fools. I've heard
    A story in the history of Rome
    Of one man called the Brutish and the Mad,
    Who when the time arrived to prove him so,
    Turned out no fool indeed.
PRINCE. I cannot waste
    Time upon you—[*About to pass on*]
GIS.   [*Opposing him and drawing sword*]   You can, my lord,
    You must!
    My claims unto Modena's gratitude
    In her great hour of peril, you've neglected;
    Let them go whistle. But you slew my father—
    Yes, I say slew him, for, on mere pretense—
    An error open as the light of day—
    You gave him to the block!
PRINCE. Ho, there! Friends! Guards! [*As the Prince turns to summon the Guard, Gismondo seizes him by the arm and throws him over to the other side of the stage*]
GIS.   I'll speak, though round my forehead gleamed a forest
    Of deathly weapons! You *must* hear me now!
    The grass grows not upon my father's grave;
    The twigs that bind it burst like thread and up
    His restless spirit through the marshy earth
    Rises to haunt me, and to point to you
    To do his murder justice! No proud tombs—
    Huge monuments of stone to press dead men
    Down in their graves, can satisfy *him*.
PRINCE. Peace!
    You shall not be my jailor.
GIS.   I'll be worse—
    Your doomsman! [*Attacks him. Prince defends himself. Gismondo beats the Prince to the ground and is about to dispatch him when the Guards enter and secure him. Reenter Bellafiore, followed by Lioni and several Nobles*]
PRINCE. Timely service, by the Mass.
    The fellow's wrist is iron.

LIONI. Hold him tight!
　　　Is your grace hurt?
PRINCE. Not I. Away with him.
　　　Tomorrow shall the law avenge—but no,
　　　The man is mad! A prisoner till death,
　　　He shall repent at leisure, and oft bless
　　　The mercy that restores to him his life,
　　　At cost of freedom only!
GIS. Only freedom!
　　　And he must wander unrevenged! [*Exit guarded*]
PRINCE. Come, signors!
　　　This little interlude has given a spur
　　　To our adventure, firing up the passion
　　　Of knightly errantry! And that combines
　　　Love's silken dalliance with the clash of steel!
　　　And now to teach this queen of beauty, matchless
　　　Save by her obduracy, to do herself
　　　A justice; take a palace for a camp,
　　　A prince—*her* prince—for a poor nameless soldier!
ALL. Success go with our scheme!
PRINCE. Who fears it? None!
　　　We'll teach the soldier something of his trade.
　　　When outwardly the citadel's impregnable,
　　　We undermine the structure. Valor then
　　　Avails but nothing—it must fall—must yield! [*Exeunt*]

SCENE 2: *An apartment in the villa of Sr. Marc. On one side, folding doors leading to an inner chamber. A window in C., opening on a terrace and garden. Theresa and Sr. Marc discovered, seated.*

MARC. I think our worthy prince at last has grown wearied of schemes to part me from my wife. He has let us rest a clear moon.

THER. Yes, his highness has pocketed up his misery, and luxuriates privately in unlimited wretchedness! Shame on you to stand between two hearts full to the brim with love for each other, like the wall twixt Pyramus and Thisbe. To shut the very door on her glorious destiny, and yet declare you love her!

MARC. [*Smiling*] Well, I dare say it does seem a strange way of showing it, to keep my wife to myself; but I am a man of singular notions, and that's one of them!

THER. You can't want for precedent! Didn't the young Count de Trevorsa divorce his wife to marry the prince's great aunt!

MARC. So I have heard.

THER. Did not the Marchesa Luiza divorce her husband to marry the Duc Limona? Did not the prince command both the marriages, and they were too well bred to disobey.

MARC. But I am not well bred, and so—I do.

THER. Captain Sr. Marc, you are a riddle to me.

MARC. Indeed!

THER. I can't read you at all! You are a soldier, bred from the ranks of the people, familiar with hardships, and aware of the enormous gulf that gapes like a drowsy whale between your name and rank—yet you've no ambition— no love of ease—no desire to take friendly advice which would bridge you over the chasm, and set you down titled and noble! Are you a man?

MARC. I am whatever you please.

THER. Then you're a fool! A deaf, dumb, and blind fool! Deaf to your own interest, dumb to the offers of fortune, blind to the road to riches. Pardon me, I'm one who always speaks my mind.

MARC. And by so speaking show the littleness of it, as those who take the verdict of their own opinion, and too readily speak upon it, generally do. You ask me if I am a man? Well, that's a question that puzzles me to reply to— I am a captain in the Italian Army, and one who earned his commission by desert, not purchase. I never wronged my fellow in my life. I pay my debts, and help the needy. I love my wife, I honor my prince, and I worship Heaven. What do you call me now?

THER. A plebeian! One of the indefinite body who always break out in revolutions when they think themselves burdened with a grief, like that great sneeze of nature, a volcano, sets its whole frame in motion to throw off some trifling irritation in the shape of an earthquake or two! Now, shall I be candid with you?

MARC. Do. It's a favorite habit of mine and a novelty to you. What would you speak of?

THER. Your wife!

MARC. Then I'll listen on that theme until the stars wax old.

THER. Well then, she's an angel! And you, not to disparage your qualifications as a man and a soldier, you are not.

MARC. No. I believe that, according to poets, painters, and romanticists— no doubt excellent authorities for the domestic economy of the heavens— angels are mostly of the opposite sex.

THER. *She* has graces, accomplishments, fascinations.

Marc. Granted.

Ther. *You* are a soldier; *she* is the object of a prince's adoration. *You* are a soldier only! *She* is highly born. *You* are—

Marc. Her husband. Signora, I know the value at which hearts are rated in the world of fashion. I know that there men are weighed less by their actions than their fortune; that the neck is bowed to family and rank—chimeras both, taken against the true aristocracy of worth and genius—but no law binds me to make one among those title-panders, those homagers of the Golden Calf whose friendship gained is but a bubble caught, which in the grasping perishes. I honor rank as I adore the sun, not for its splendor or its glitter but the warmth and light it spreads on all within its beams; and that, signora, is, as I read it, the true mission of the highborn upon earth.

Ther. Heterodox principles, tolerated but not established. Now you are brave, I've heard men say—honor your guiding star—I fling defiance in the face of the assertion.

Marc. Upon what ground?

Ther. Dianora. You know that in a pique she wedded you—flung away a destiny bright as an Aurora! No heart—no love to give—merely a hand. And you were coward enough to take advantage of her rash blindness, and dishonorable enough to satisfy your love at the price of your conviction!

Marc. No. I *did* believe she loved me—*did* believe that what was lacked would grow, and I have hoped for it—watched for it—prayed for it! Sometimes I have thought she pined in secret for proud honors, to be the worshipped and the homaged of beauty's pilgrims, and lady of a principality! But then she's looked into my face and smiled, and away the doubt fled like a cloud in June, and I felt sure she loved me.

Ther. If I could prove the contrary?

Marc. Then—then I should have a stern duty to perform, and sternly should that duty *be* performed.

Ther. Then read that letter! [*Gives it*] The letter that she sent the prince the day following the festival. Read it, I say—and if you are content to sit down lord of the mere shell of a wife, then say I that soldiers are only soldiers! [*Aside*] If that moves him not, he's granite inside and out. [*Exit*]

Marc. It is her hand, and sent to him, and yet
          I lack the strength to read the characters
          As though I'd find there death of someone dear,
          As dear as Dianora! What is here
          Worse than the enemy's shot—more terrible
          Than the battalia of an armed host,
          That thus I quail before it as a child—

I who have looked on slaughter and on death
And never shed one tear. The worst is better
Than this eternal torture of suspense!

[*Reads*] "My Lord—My Prince—I dare not say my love—let me
speak honestly the thoughts that rise within the heart once yours, and still a
silent worshipper!"

Yes, yes, she loves him still!

"Let me still love you, prince, as the jealous guardian of my honor as a wife,
and not its fiercest foe! Make me your sister in your heart—let me feel that
you are my prince, my sovereign, and that to look to you for justice and protection is my right as a subject, my charter as a woman! Forgive the past—
forget me! For I am now one whose memory is sacred. But let me honor you
in place of loving you with the holy fire of old, though that fire will never
cease to burn like the heart's lava till the heart itself be dead.

Dianora."

There cannot be a doubt! The veil is torn
That shut the image from my sight. I see it
And stand a beggared bankrupt in my heart—
A driveling dotard in my eyes! Go, tears!
I will not play the boy till I have swelled
Above the man! I'll question her once more,
And if it be so, I will set her free—
Free as the birds! It is a heavy thing
To say the word, but that word *shall* be said
Although it kill me in the utterance.
She comes—and with her, ever on her steps,
The Count Rosario. Days past he hath been
Her shadow and her echo. Were it not
That he's too good a jackal for the prince,
There might be ground for jealousy—for what!
For laughter, when the jealousy's of her. [*Retires. Enter Dianora
and Rosario*]

DIAN.   It is a great resolve, a grand resolve;
Worthy of blood that claims its ancestry
In a clear stream through thrice four hundred years.
Lorenzo will depart from here, and join
The martial glory whose far-sounding fame
Rings like a peal that makes the world its bell.
Yes, there he'll win honor!

Ros.   And oblivion, too—
        Oblivion from the memories that gnaw
        His heart like inward wolves. Nothing's left him
        But smoke, and blood, and fire and battle glory—
        To put a name down on the page of fame,
        And write "Here fought Lorenzo. Here he charged
        A mounted squadron. Here he ran away—
        Just to take breath, and back to it again!
        Here he fought three six-foot-high dragoons—
        For three good mortal hours—how they swore,
        And lunged—and lunged and swore—how valiantly he
        Killed two—and how the t'other one killed him!"
        Then tombs and trumpets, catacombs and cannons—
        And glory weeps and says, "Good night, Lorenzo!"
        Ah! Battle's very beautiful! Ere he departs—
        And dawn will find him on the march—he prays
        Some token to remind him of the love
        Once his soul-worship.

DIAN.   He shall have it—all
        That honor has to grant, that honor can
        In the like spirit take. [*Detaches a jewel from her dress*]

Ros.   [*Aside*] He's close at hand.
        Now to feed up the fire. [*Kneels. Aloud*] On my knee,
        I take the sacred embassy. My prince
        Bends in the spirit, too. [*Reenter Sr. Marc at back*]

DIAN.   Let the gift raise
        High aspirations even with the prayer
        That would endow it as an amulet.

Ros.   And nothing more?

DIAN.   A blessing, and farewell! [*Rosario, going up and seeing Sr. Marc, feigns a desire to avoid him, and goes out through the folding door at the side*]

Ros.   [*Going*] Now for my lady's chamber. Alas!
        Poor devil! He little guesses what's in store for him.

MARC. A strange departure! But he's gone—that's well,
        As I would speak to her alone. [*Aloud*] The count
        Has grown a very clock in constancy.
        He and the day keep time together.

DIAN. First
He came ambassador from Prince Lorenzo,
To ask his pardon for what happ'd the night
Of the grand masque; then to entreat me visit
The routs and levees at the palace; lastly,
To ask a token that the prince might wear,
A glittering talisman to guard his helm
Amid the carnage of the battle!

MARC. Battle!
Hath he turned warrior o' the sudden?

DIAN. Yes—
Fitting his race and blood illustrious,
Yearning for glorious enterprise.

MARC. Some men
Are built of restless aspirations; some
Contented to be humbled and unknown.
The eagles some, some moles! And women, too—
Some born with simple thoughts, that lift their heads
No higher than the hedge—some that leap up
Above the mountains and their crown of clouds
As high as Heaven itself!

DIAN. And what has woman
Left her but love and pride? In silent hours
When solitude and fancy, like twin genii
Give life to the ideal, and to dreams.
The charm of that ideal realized,
What has she to build up her future on
But thoughts that take reality from hope
And then become ambition?

MARC. True—as you
Have sometimes done.

DIAN. As I did once—but now
Have grown more wise.

MARC. More politic perhaps.
You've learned the art of masking in your mind,
And showing a more smooth and calm outside,
While there's an ebullition just beneath,
Might make the gazer hold his breath could he
But break the surface through.

DIAN.   What should I fear
        To open all my heart within to you?
        You are no tyrant. In your darkest mood
        Your frown has more the aspect of a smile,
        And let me cast my arms about your neck,
        The sun comes out again!

MARC.   Well then, we'll talk
        About this Prince Lorenzo and his love.

DIAN.   Another theme!

MARC.   No, that! You loved him once.

DIAN.   Yes, once, for nature made him to be loved,
        So noble—gentle—such a heart of fire—
        Such tones that while they spoke the listener's spirit
        Flew back unto enchanted realms, and left
        The cold dull earth beyond! Let's change the theme.

MARC.   Go on.

DIAN.   To speak of such a lover thus
        Will anger you.

MARC.   'Twill please me.

DIAN.   You will mock
        The empty head that dwells so idly on
        A retrospect of vanity.

MARC.   Go on!
        I'll tell you when to stop. He spoke to you
        Of a throne's splendor?

DIAN.   Yes—not dazzlingly
        With its proud rays, but telling me the great
        Could pour down fortune on the lowly born
        As mountain streams that irrigate the vales,
        And make them rich with verdure. Then I'd listen,
        Turning the luxury of doing good,
        And its attendant blessings in my thoughts
        To raise the humble from their lowliness;
        To be presiding spirit—not of charity,
        For that betokens beggary beneath it—
        But of a great genial and pervading love
        Like that which draws the brood about the hen,
        And all-instructive worship—looking up,
        Out of my dreams, I'd meet his eyes of fire,
        And smiles that seemed alive with love for me,

And forth outpoured the torrent of *my* heart
In a wild deathless adoration.

MARC. [*Anxiously*] Aye,
But this was fascination merely; scarce
More lasting than a name writ on the sands.
Was yours no firmer rooted?

DIAN. Memnon-like,
Defying time and storm! When he was far
Away from me, the days crawled tortoise-pace—
Each hour a week, each week appeared a year.
I grew impatient—music, pictures, books
Seemed a dull round of trifles seen before,
Soon wearied of—and while this sickly calm
Hung o'er my spirit like a blighting air,
I'd hear *his* voice or footstep—see his plume
Nodding above the terraced wall beyond—
For I could pick them from surrounding throngs.
Oh, such a gush of sunshine filled my heart!
I found my feet obeying my hot will,
And hurrying to meet him—I was not
Upon the earth or of it—in his arms
I grasped the world—its pleasures were all new,
Its evening daylight, and its season summer!
My soul was not my own; my being, heart
Lay at his feet, his worshipper and slave!
[*Sr. Marc is sitting, his head sunk in his hands*]
Sr. Marc! See now, my giddy tongue has run
Too freely with its fraught—I was to blame.
But yet you would not let me change the theme.

MARC. [*Cheerfully*] No, Dianora, no, I am but a man,
And men are vain as well as women—proud
To think that I had won you for my wife,
Through such a love as this. [*Bell without*]
What, visitors?
At such an hour—rejoin me when they're gone,
Then we'll speak further.

DIAN. You'll not nurse at heart
What I have said. It was a pent up stream
Bursting its dam, now overflowed and gone.
You will not heed it.

MARC.   No, Dianora, no. [*Exit Dianora*]
    This was her love! The name belies it—love—
    'Twas what she called it—adoration! Nay,
    A solemn spirit-deep religion. Well—
    She shall be happy—happy in the right
    To call him husband. Happy in his love!
    I'd stand between her and her love
    No longer like an envious night cloud! No.
    [*Sitting at a table and writing*]
    My better nature now shall speak to her
    Smiling through all my spirit agony! [*Speaks as he writes*]
    "Heaven's blessing go with you. Marry him you love.
    I hereby give my hand to your—divorce. [*With agony*]
    My soul is with you still."
    [*Folds the letter, given him by Theresa, in the packet*]
    And that will tell her all better than words,
    Rooting the heart up as it strives to speak them. [*Enter Servant*]

SERV.   The prince, with many nobles of the court
    And who have ridden hard, beg audience of you.

MARC.   The prince!

SERV.   They're here, sir. [*Enter Prince Lorenzo, Lioni, Bellafiore, and the Nobles of the Court*]

MARC.   They're welcome all! [*Gives packet to Servant*]
    This to your lady—in the anteroom
    Give it, and leave her; do you understand?

SERV.   Most perfectly. [*Exit*]

MARC.   Now, may I ask this honor—

PRINCE. Sr. Marc, the prince who was your jealous foe
    In envy of your wife, becomes your friend
    Discovering the cause to be unworthy
    A noble lover, or an honest husband.

MARC.   Right, sire, 'tis a most unworthy cause
    For greatness to be jealous of the honor
    Of a good man's good wife!

PRINCE. You misconceive me.
    I cannot see you duped and fooled besides
    By an unworthy woman!

MARC.   Prince! [*Fiercely*] But stay—you *do* fight—so do I.

PRINCE. The Lady Dianora, sir, your wife—
  Has tricked us both! Made us believe she loved,
  While in her secret heart she bent her ear
  To a soft-tongued and silken liveried lover,
  The Count Rosario!
MARC. Oh, good, good, good!
  I'll trust my honor and my lady, too,
  In such a keeping! Each bird to his mate.
  The peacock will not humble to the dove,
  Nor doth the dove desire it.
PRINCE. You think so:
  You will be blind until the shame shall bite you,
  And then you'll burn and shudder. They've been watched—
  His nightly roost her chamber. Nay, to prove
  I speak on strata-grafted truth—go seek
  That chamber now—he's there!
MARC. Awaiting her?
PRINCE. Go let your eyes convince you; if I speak
  Falsehood, condemn and blazon me a liar!
MARC. I *will* go—in *her* chamber! [*Exit*]
PRINCE. She is won!
  The fool convinced! [*Reenter Dianora, with open packet*]
DIAN. What means this writing? Gentlemen! The prince!
  You're welcome all!
BELLA. To what? A home made hateful
  By shameless practices, good lady!
DIAN. Sir!
LIONI. All's known—the secret meetings with the count!
  The lover in your chamber!
DIAN. Speak, sir, speak.
  I will not be insulted by a breath
  Of slander from the proudest head that wears
  A coronet to gild its worthlessness!
PRINCE. Your husband has discovered all—fear naught—
  Our swords shall champion you!
DIAN. And you, prince, you!
PRINCE. Bear it out bravely—do not shrink before him.
  He's but a man!
DIAN. He's then what not a creature
  Is that stands now before me, being man!

Whatever this stain be, sprung of your malice,
Whatever your quick mischief-breeding brains
Have raised against me, tremble for it, lords—
There is an arm shall battle for my cause
And sweep ye on before his wrath like weeds
Borne by the rising tide!

LIONI.   As I'm alive
She beats the husband for a fiend let loose! [*Reenter Sr. Marc*]

PRINCE. Didst find the man?

MARC.   Oh, yes, I found the man!

DIAN.   What slanderous calumny is raised against me?

PRINCE. Are you convinced?

MARC.   I am [*To her*]. You've read that paper—
It cannot tell the husband's inward war,
The combat twixt his love for you, and wish
To see you seated on the throne of pride.
It cannot breathe the bitterness, the pang
With which he tore your image from his breast,
Nor of the quivering lip—the tearful eye—
The parched and choking throat with which the words
Were penned upon the paper! But it tells you
That he is all content to suffer—ready
To face the world a broken, homeless man,
So you are happy. Bless him in your prayers,
And all his pangs are paid a thousand times—
It tells you you are free! [*Turns away*]

DIAN.   Sr. Marc! My husband!

PRINCE. Hear, lady, at your feet a husband kneels,
Your prince—your subject! [*Kneels*]

MARC.   [*Placing his hand on the Prince's shoulder*]
Hear me, Prince Lorenzo!
Now you are kneeling there, kneeling before
The shrine of virtue you have basely outraged—
Branding her honor with a wanton's name,
Her soul's integrity with blistering shame—
Like a detected villain at an altar,
Avow your lie!

PRINCE. Sr. Marc!

MARC. [*Passionately, keeping him to his knee. Draws sword*]
Avow your lie!
Before the face and in the ears of these
High nobles of your court, you cast a slur
Upon my wife—the shadow falls on me
And on my house—so all of us endure
The damning stigma! Now then, take it back.
Recall it, by confessing the black fraud,
Before their ears and eyes!

PRINCE. [*Appealing*] My lords—

MARC. The man
That lifts a weapon slays his prince—the hand
Raised in his rescue strikes him dead! Confess!
Or with the falsehood flapping on your lips
Perish a liar's death!

PRINCE. I do confess—[*Rises*]
It was a fabrication merely.

MARC. There,
Your honor, Dianora, is declared
Spotless and bright as ever! [*She throws herself weeping on a couch.
To them*] You'll find your friend the Count Rosario within.
To every noble feeling—honor—truth—
Faith—sanctity—the courage of a man—
I found him dead, and so I left him!

BELLA. Dead!
You have not slain the Count Rosario?

PRINCE. Mad man!
What have you done?

MARC. What should a husband do
Who finds a lover in his lady's chamber? [*With energy*]
I slew him like a reptile! And for you—
[*Striking the Prince with sword*]
Thus do I pay you back your shame!

[*The Prince seizes sword from Noble next him. Strikes at Sr. Marc
who disarms and throws him around to L. Is about to strike when
Dianora pushes between them exclaiming, "Husband! Husband!"
Dianora falls senseless. Marc backs away to C. door. Curtain*]

ACT IV.

Scene 1: *Six years have elapsed. A corridor in a prison. Paul Vulcani and Petronio discovered.*

PAUL.   We cannot choose a better man, Petronio.
        'Tis now six years of hopeless, rayless thralldom
        Gismondo has within these walls endured,
        For his attack upon the prince's life.
        And where so good a man to carry out
        The measures of our secret enterprise,
        Who, knitting his own vengeance to our wrongs
        Is a fit instrument to wreak the rage
        Of plotting schemers on their tyrant ruler.

PETRO. Modena cannot longer bear the spur
        Of her impatient and despotic prince.
        All thrives, and our conspiracy tomorrow,
        Treading like sorrow on the heels of joy,
        Shall bring its death veil o'er the hope-bright life
        He looks for in his marriage, long delayed,
        With Lady Dianora. Yes, tomorrow
        Will crown all with the downfall of Lorenzo,
        Struck by a trusty hand.

PAUL.   And such a hand
        I take it is Gismondo's in whose breast
        A double fire of rebellion burns,
        Both for his father's wrongs, and for his own.
        [*Enter a Gaoler*]

GAOL.   Please you, signors,
        Here is the man you seek. See! [*Enter Gismondo, his face bearing the marks of confirmed lunacy*]

PAUL.   Gaoler, we'd be alone with him.

GAOL.   Fear nothing!
        Only upon one theme is he fiercely mad,
        And that's his father's name.

PAUL.   We shall observe. [*Exit Gaoler*]

GIS.   [*Restlessly swaying to and fro*]
        I'm here! What would you have of me? I'm here!
        Good company is somewhat novel grown
        To me of late—I who have only one

That's ever constant to my solitude.
But one—
PAUL. Your gaoler?
GIS. He! Another kind
Of friend—a speechless friend—my gaoler comes
A distance, too, from Sicily—but he
Comes further far than that.
PAUL. From whence?
GIS. Aye, that
Is a rare question for philosophers!
Where do the dead reside? It cannot be
In Heaven, for they'd stay there. Nor in hell—
The devil holds his own too tightly clawed
To let them go astraying! The specter
Is sleepless—death and sleep are not twin angels!
For the dead sleep not—he is ever with me,
A visible but noiseless presence here—
Then there—behind me; then before me, stalking—
I talk with him by day, and he replies
With the same voiceless lips—I understand him—
And if I wake at midnight and should turn,
His face is on my straw by my side,
With the dull eyes wide open, and about him
A cold phosphoric glare, enough to light him
As if he were a fungus of the gloom,
Its natural offspring—so, I'm not alone,
Not even in my dungeon.
PAUL. We are come
To set the portals of your dungeon open,
And give you liberty!
GIS. You'll let the ghost
Go with me—he'd be weary here alone,
And I should miss him, too.
PAUL. Have you no thought
Of vengeance for his death?
GIS. Of vengeance—of vengeance—
That's not the word now—for the spirit's lips
Move now another meaning—justice once,
Then vengeance! Now 'tis retribution!

PETRO.   They
        Are several names for the selfsame mind-spur,
        And mean but death.

GIS.   No, no, not all the same.
        Justice is justice in the primal claim,
        Revenge is passion—retribution, duty.

PETRO.   If you were free—the palace gates flung open—
        The Prince Lorenzo—

GIS.   [*Savagely*] I would spring upon him
        Through a surrounding forest of his friends,
        And kill—and kill—

PETRO.   And fall in the attempt.
        Were it not better to be shrewd and cautious,
        To make the vengeance sure?

GIS.   Not I! I'd dash
        Upon him like a falling star through space,
        And crush myself in the act.

PETRO.   [*To Paul*] He would mar all.
        His wild intemperate revenge would fall
        Short of the deed, and all the blood that flowed
        Would be his own.

PAUL.   Right, right, Petronio. Gaoler! [*Reenter Gaoler*]
        Tomorrow morn the Prince Lorenzo weds
        The Lady Dianora, who for years—
        Some say for love of her first lord Sr. Marc—
        Has turned an ear of deafness to his prayers
        But wearied in a heart-sorrowing widowhood,
        And legally divorced, she weds him tomorrow. He,
        To make the joy a fashion in Modena,
        Lets free all state offenders—there are your warrants—
        When the first gun proclaims the marriage o'er,
        Throw ope the prison doors. [*Gaoler bows*]
        The time grows short! [*Aside to Petronio*]
        A trusty bravo must be found tonight.

PETRO.   Yes, to strike home in his full hour of joy,
        When from the church he comes a bridegroom back!
        So must he die—Modena be enfranchised—
        And each of us made noble! [*Exeunt*]

GAOL.   Did you hear
        What said the judge? He spoke of liberty!

GIS.   I heard—and he said caution. Well, he's right—
        Caution's the true foundation for exploit—
        And I'll be cautious! I can't miss the way—
        The spirit with its emanating light
        Will guide me. Sure and cautious I'll creep on,
        As noiseless as the shadows of the evening—
        Further and further—nearer to the bound
        Of earth and night—but sure—oh, very sure!
        And when I strike—strike sure!
GAOL.   Whom, signor?
GIS.   Whom—
        Whom but—the specter's finger's on its lip.
        Yes, silence is the child of caution, too—
        And I'll be sure and silent! As I live—
        He smiles—the first for many loitering years.
        Still smiling—consecrating what I go
        To do as something holy. Smile again!
        I'll do it—there, smile on! Smile on! Smile on! [*Exeunt*]

SCENE 2: *Exterior of the villa of Sr. Marc, and its gardens by moonlight, the whole much neglected and dilapidated. Sr. Marc, rudely attired, discovered gazing at the house.*

MARC.   And thou art fallen, too! My home! My home!
        And on each other's broken front we gaze
        Like maim'd and limbless warriors! So dull!
        So heavy, with thy eyeless windows closed,
        Thy broken door, like a blind toothless mastiff,
        The only friend of ruin! Yet six years
        Have barely glided by since on thy threshold
        I turned my back in sorrow! Where's the light
        That, when two years before I'd brought my bride,
        My Dianora home, streamed forth from thee,
        As giving back the love-smile that beamed out
        A herald of my soul—that light was thine,
        Thy soul—a welcome to thy master's bride—
        And losing her, the gloom stole o'er our hearts,
        And desolation reigns o'er both of us.
        [*Belcastro passes at back with a Servant bearing a torch. He looks at Sr. Marc and goes out observing him*]
        And there's a face that knew me once, once held

The hand of friendship forth to me. Small marvel
Man should forget so easily the living,
When life can hold its revel recklessly
Within six paces of the dead!
[*Reenter Belcastro, alone, carrying torch*]

BEL.   It is
Sr. Marc! And such a man above all others
Would be the man for us. Sr. Marc!

MARC.   That name
Belonged to my bright fortunes—call me now
An humbler title.

BEL.   Friend!

MARC.   That's frank—that's honest.
Four years' captivity have done their work
Across a brow and cheek that never owed
Thanks to Dame Nature for much comeliness.
You see the gilded plating is rubbed off.
There's nothing left beneath but man, and that
Is, in the acceptation of the times,
But very sorry copper.

BEL.   Which will burnish
To look like gold, and it will pass for gold
With those who know no better.

MARC.   And is this
The modern creed of Prince Lorenzo's court!
How the world changes! In my boyhood days
They'd call it falsehood and hypocrisy,
But now they call it fashion.

BEL.   Hear me out
As one who owes the prince but little love.
I'll teach you to grow rich on one brave deed!

MARC.   Those are strange words.

BEL.   With meaning stranger still!
They who dig down for gold must bring up earth,
And through the clods of strangeness may lie meaning
As rich as gold!

MARC.   I've an old-fashioned way,
Inherited from my old-fashioned parents,
Of speaking boldly out. And what I mean
To say in just so many words as fit

The business. I don't understand these hints,
This hanging round the door of an intent,
Like a mere lounger by the way. Belcastro,
Something you mean, and by your speech obscure,
And backward glances, something you would say,
That if it's honest, is not fashionable—
And might illiberally be construed
Into a plot.

BEL. You've named it. Now, Sr. Marc,
I know you may be trusted; you are poor.

MARC. Yes, you may trust me with my poverty.
No one will filch it from me.

BEL. You've no cause
To love the prince.

MARC. Not much, i' faith.

BEL. Your wife
From your first going forth, found that her heart
Had followed you—and spurning fortune's offers,
Although they pleaded in the prince's name,
Refused his passion audience.

MARC. It was true then!

BEL. And since that day, he hath become a tyrant
O'er all his people—nay, Modena's curse!
All grades and stations feel the grinding hand
Of lustful and rapacious Lorenzo.
And lastly, Dianora—

MARC. Well? There is something
In the old name that on my spirit falls
Like rain on parched up flowers.

BEL. To indulge
A most unmanly spleen, and force her neck
Into his yoke, he hath by small degrees
Possessed himself of all her lands, and left her now
No choice twixt want and wealth by wedding him.
What's left her then to do?

MARC. To marry him!
Her heart *was* mine then! Mine, past breaking off;
And the world's waves that burst our hearts apart,
Have tried us, proved us, and in love regained

Washed all our treasures up upon the beach,
To make our lives one joy!

BEL.　And yet between
This joy and you there is a bar.

MARC.　A bar!
Call it a mountain—I would overtop it;
A sea, I'd stem it—or a gulf, I'd leap it—
Place her before me, and then talk of bars!
I'd make away to her—

BEL.　Join us—a band
Of faithful friends combine to put down tyrants
Swelled out by passions from their honest selves.
Your hand shall slay the prince!

MARC.　Milord Belcastro—[*A distant cry heard; the Duc Lioni enters*]

LIONI.　I knew it would be so. I told the prince so, but he was as head-strong and as obstinate as is compatible with his station. I said the horses would take fright, and so they have.

BEL.　What horses, my lord?

LIONI.　The horses of the Lady Dianora's carriage. I told him they would run away and break her neck, and that's what they're doing now, as sure as death!

MARC.　Dianora! [*Runs out*]

LIONI.　The wheel's broken, and nothing can save her from being killed on the spot! I did intend to get home early tonight, because of the coming wedding; but as it is, I'll stop to see the end of it, to tell the bridegroom expectant that he's a widower in advance.

BEL.　How silent all the city seems. The streets are quite deserted.

LIONI.　Yes, they've gone—that is to say, the inhabitants—to see the gala and fireworks let off by the prince in honor of his nuptials tomorrow with Dianora. Fireworks are not bad emblems of the married state. *I'm* married, Belcastro. I'm a flowerpot and my wife's a squib. She goes off with a fizz and ends with a bang.

BEL.　As I live, he's rescued her. He bears her this way. I'll let my hints sink into his mind, and return hereafter to stir up the thoughts within him that I'd have give color to the whole. [*Exit. Enter Sr. Marc, carrying Dianora senseless*]

LIONI.　Bless my soul, not killed! I need not have stopped if I'd only foreseen that. I'll take charge of the lady.

MARC.　You! There lies your way! [*Pointing*]

LIONI.　Why, you impudent varlet! Do you know what I am?

MARC. No better than all men in the dark. You must grope and stumble. Do you know what I am?

LIONI. An infernal, impertinent scoundrel.

MARC. One who has served an apprenticeship to fighting, and may try a little journeywork on his own account. Go!

LIONI. But this lady is—

MARC. In excellent keeping! Begone!

LIONI. I am the prince's dear friend and councillor.

MARC. Then tell him to choose better friends for councillors and better councillors for friends! I shall be a better protector to the lady than the Duc Lioni.

LIONI. [*Perfectly petrified*] By heaven! [*Exit*]

MARC. Alone with her! The secret-mantling night,
   A friend that aids me in my long desire
   To hear her voice unknown to her and speak
   With her upon the times—the sunny times—
   That I have hallowed in my memory,
   And in my solitude made sacred with
   An offering of tears. She knows herself—
   Her own sweet self—and I remain time's living precept,
   That love and hope lives deathless as our souls.

DIAN. What brings me here? To my old ruined home—[*Staggering; he catches her, leads her to a ruin'd garden seat*]
   The weakness of my woman's nature lingers
   Yet in my limbs, but in my heart there is strength
   Still left to thank the brave arm that was thrust
   Like a staunch wall of iron between death
   And me. Your name?

MARC. [*Roughly*] They call'd me in the ranks,
   Bluff Pedro.

DIAN. You have been a soldier then.

MARC. Yes, lady, though Italian by my birth,
   I served the German emperor, Charles V,
   For some years past against the Pope.

DIAN. Indeed.
   [*Aside*] The emperor that Sr. Marc commanded under,
   After his flight. [*Aloud*] Some echoes of those wars
   Have reached us even here, and they laud high
   For valor those who combated therein,
   The soldiers—captains—

MARC.　And with justice, lady,
　　　　For every man of those embattled hosts
　　　　Was fit to lead them, and to die among them
　　　　Was honor—glowing honor!

DIAN.　Can you call
　　　　To mind the captains serving with the king?
　　　　I mean those lowborn men who owed to naught
　　　　Their honors but their own right hands and hearts!
　　　　For those are men to speak of proudfully,
　　　　And glorify in thought.

MARC.　Some few of them
　　　　I can remember—Guelph, the Florentine—
　　　　Batista, master of the cavalry,
　　　　Gilhelm—Rodrigue—Sr. Marc—

DIAN.　Sr. Marc! Was he
　　　　One of your band?

MARC.　You mean the Modenese.
　　　　Yes, he commanded that same regiment
　　　　In which I served.

DIAN.　You often saw him?

MARC.　Often.
　　　　He soon found out that we were countrymen;
　　　　And in the bivouac upon the heath,
　　　　With nothing round us but the night and silence,
　　　　Just on the eve of battle he would come
　　　　And talk to me of home.

DIAN.　Of home? [*Aside*] Now comes the fear—the thrilling sickening fear—
　　　　The yearning like a mother's longing wish,
　　　　Yet dread to know the worst—suspense—[*Aloud*] He'd speak
　　　　To you of home then—of his wife?

MARC.　Of her
　　　　Who was presiding genius of his home!
　　　　He'd talk—you see, I'm rough, and mar, it may be,
　　　　His plain tale in the telling—but he loved her—
　　　　More than his heart would have his lip believe,
　　　　Yet it would swell up sometimes from its prison,
　　　　And burst abroad!

DIAN.　And he would tell you then
　　　　He loved her?

MARC. Lady, he would tell me then that he adored her.
       I know I speak this ruggedly, but then
       I am a churl to him! And he would say
       He looked upon the bright and summer world
       Like the blind beggar—he was dark within.
       The shade was on his spirit and his soul,
       And all his being changed within his bosom
       To rock, despair, the petrifying stream
       Wherein man plunges with his heart alive,
       And comes from it a stone!
DIAN. He little knew
       How soon his wayward wife perceived the flower
       Which she called duty was in substance love,
       And rooted in her breast.
MARC. Then he would say—
       His eyes two spouting cataracts—that I
       From mere remembrance find the waters leap
       Up bubbling into mine! He'd say he knew
       How like a selfish hawk he'd seized a dove,
       And would have had it love him—he so rough
       And rugged like the elm; he'd say he took her
       In youth that sat upon her like the dawn
       Upon some dancing shallop on the waters.
       And what high aspirations had he fed
       Upon his passion's pilgrimage while watching
       For that sweet light of love that never came,
       And then—and then—
DIAN. He did not know her heart—
       She did not know it. When she looked within
       She saw a picture shining full of colors
       Like prisms of stalactites. He went—
       Then came the gloom—the ruin'd earth-deep darkness—
       The utter loneliness—the desolation—
       The memory of the absent one that hung
       About this dwelling like a haunting ghost—
       The shuddering solitude of a vast waste
       Where one lies dying, and the night wind sings
       In mourning dirge! For he was gone! was gone!
       He'd call her heartless—cruel—
       And she deserved this!

MARC.   No. But he would chide
          Himself, and kneel and pray for her, and then
          Amid the thunder of the battle charge—
          The shriek—the yell—the upward-cleaving curse
          Drowned in the war cry and the trumpet clang,
          He'd shout her name aloud; then on he'd rush
          Amid the awful jubilee of death,
          Unharmed—a very spirit of destruction,
          Yet towering up among the carnage, like
          Death's spectral self! And men would fall before him
          As if he were a phantom warrior!

DIAN.   He left the army then, and went abroad—
          So ran the rumors, and for four years past
          I've heard no more.

MARC.   This much I know of him.
          Pursued by a relentless secret foe,
          He left the emperor's camp a wanderer—
          But one day heard his wife—his Dianora—
          His being—his existence—she was this—
          All this to him!—was still unwed—loved him
          So dearly as to dedicate her youth
          And beauty to a widowhood eternal
          But for his sake. The hope was fire within him.
          He hurried towards Modena, where the same
          Concealed and pitiless enemy found means
          To put the soldiers of the papal power—
          And had he lived—
          If he lives now—and if he came to you—
          Beaming with all the fiery, doting love—
          Came here tonight—[*Enter the Prince and Attendants*]

PRINCE. The lady's safe—she's here!
          [*Sr. Marc slouches his hat, and goes apart*]
          The careless slave that drove your chariot
          Now lingers in a prison, there to howl
          His penitence to walls of granite. Safe?
          No hurt, no scathe?

DIAN.   I am unhurt, but owe
          My life to yon brave stranger. He it was
          That checked the mad'ning steeds in their career,
          And led me into safety.

PRINCE. Hark ye, fellow—
 Call at the palace in the morn.
MARC. For what?
PRINCE. Reward.
MARC. I want none.
PRINCE. You're proud.
MARC. As Lucifer.
PRINCE. And poor.
MARC. Yes, that
 Accounts for what your highness calls my pride.
 For pride and poverty go hand in hand,
 Like lawyers and the Devil!
PRINCE. Call tomorrow,
 And you shall find reward, if money tempts you—
 If place, promotion.
MARC. Well, I'll see my humor
 When morning comes.
PRINCE. A churlish-minded boor.
DIAN. A humble soldier,
 Whose sword is ever readier than tongue
 To do his country service.
 He has served—borne
 Arms under Sr. Marc. Your pardon that his name
 Slipped from me—do not chide me.
PRINCE. [*To Servant*] See the lady
 In safety to her uncle Stefano's.
 Tomorrow we shall meet again—tomorrow—
 A blissful blest tomorrow! [*Exeunt Dianora and Servant*]
 Such a tomorrow [*To his Lords*]
 As she but little dreams of. Years of pangs
 Her pride hath caused, her heart must pay the price of.
 Wearing and agonizing day by day.
 [*Sees Sr. Marc near him. Holds out his purse to him*]
 I would owe no man gratitude or favor.
 Here's gold.
MARC. Pray keep it to buy friends with, prince,
 You'll need them some day!
PRINCE. When chance pleases so. You knew this man Sr. Marc?
MARC. I did, my lord.

PRINCE. Tell me he's dead, no matter by what means—
Secret assassination—fever—or struck down
In battle—and I'll load you with rewards—
The baton of my armies—gold to buy
The tenant-right of thrones!

MARC. The news of it
Would gladden you?

PRINCE. With the fierce joy of fiends
Triumphant over man!

MARC. If he be dead?

PRINCE. If he be dead.

MARC. Well, then—
He's *not* dead yet—there's comfort for you, prince.
Tomorrow may bring news. Wait for the day.

PRINCE. What news? Not that he's burst his prison gates—
Not that he's free?

MARC. You've heard then that he fell
Into the hands of foes?

PRINCE. The soldiers of
The unforgiving Pope! It was my care
That set the bloodhounds on his scent, for years
To groan away in bondage! Did I not
Six years ago at mercy of his sword,
Lie prostrate! Was the insult unforgotten?
Could memory play me traitor like a coward
And life beat in me still!

MARC. He owes *you* that!
For his long years of dreary bondage borne
With spirit dull and broken! I am glad
To learn thus much—'tis well I know it.

PRINCE. Wherefor?

MARC. Because I am—his friend. And it is just
That roaming in his liberty in search
Of vengeance on the heads that wrought him evil
He strike the right.

PRINCE. He must be sudden then!
For tell him, you—his *friend*—that should he dare
To face the daylight in Modena, chains
And dungeons dreary as he left in Rome,
Await him here. 'Tis well that he should know

That, too—and you're his friend!
[*Aside, as he goes*]—it *is* Sr. Marc!

MARC. Fool, I had well-nigh burst my secret out
Before it's time. But I have seen her, heard her,
Gathered the tones confessing her yet glowing
And hallowing love like manna rained from Heaven.
Yes, there's a ray of golden liveried glory
Comes glittering like sun on raindrops through
The thick opaque of my past heavy life.
Light—hope—joy—all my soul is steeped in brightness,
For in her love there is a heaven more,
A heart-enthroned Elysium! [*Reenter Belcastro*]

BEL. Are you resolved
To link yourself to us, or let tomorrow
Part you from Dianora like a sea?

MARC. What union is there twixt a name so pure
And the black deed you'd have my hand commit?
There is no kindred twixt a dove and vulture,
Nor Dianora and a damned assassin!

BEL. And you would lose her—lose her on the verge
Of winning back a wife so doted on!
The prince was here but now. Of course he told you,
Unless his modesty sealed up the words,
How that tomorrow morn he weds the lady,
Here—in this town—tomorrow!

MARC. Powers of Heaven!

BEL. And she loves not her bridegroom, but looks back
With a remembrance full of tears to one
Who made her all his idol. But she weds him
For very helplessness—no friend—protector—

MARC. I'm yours, my lord. Heart, being, spirit, brain—
All enter'd in your service! Wed tomorrow—
I'll tear her from him at the altar foot!
In face of all the thunders of the church,
And the great Pope's anathema!
[*Reenter Prince and Soldiers*]

PRINCE. He's there!
Soldiers, arrest Sr. Marc. [*They seize him*]

MARC.   My lord, if you
        Had been a man—

PRINCE. I should have bade them
        Spear you e'en where you stand like a gaunt wolf.
        I promised to Sr. Marc a prison's greeting
        By his good friend. A prince must keep his word.
        Tomorrow listen for the choral hymn
        That echoes to Modena the glad news
        Of Dianora's marriage!

MARC.   Devil!

BEL.   [*Aside to him*] Patience.
        Tomorrow you shall be free—for vengeance!

MARC.   I'll be patient then.
        Revenge will keep its color for one night—
        Lead to my prison, sirs.

PRINCE. At last, Sr. Marc,
        We shall write even!

MARC.   Yes, tomorrow, prince,
        The dead are equal!

PRINCE. Dare you brave me, dog!

MARC.   I do, for on my lips is prophecy,
        Uprising like a threatening volcano!
        Look to it, pitiless and despot prince,
        Who cannot curb the terror that's within thee
        At these my words! It is despair that speaks—
        Despair long pent—bitter—that brings forth tears,
        Foreheralds of the bursting of the heart within,
        With anguish overladen, but not one
        Flowing for fear of thee! Each one a thorn—
        A barbed sword—but not one drop of fear!
        Here in the gleaming moonlight, the revered
        And silver-haired old age of day, I tell thee
        Tomorrow shall uproot thee like a blast—
        Thy power shall be dust—thy brows be crownless—
        Thy princely robe a pall—thine empire Death!
        Look to your prince—he faints. Lead me to prison!

[*Tableau*]

ACT V.

SCENE 1: *An apartment in the house of Stefano Lodori, controller of the army. Signor Lodori discovered at a table busied with papers. Theresa lying on a sofa with a book, which she throws down.*

THER. Well, signor, the day has come.

STEF. Yes, signora, the happy day.

THER. The most miserable edition of happiness that ever mortal read. The poor Lady Dianora is breaking her heart piecemeal and the prince is as willfully blind as a Cyclops with a glass eye. I wonder that you, the only relative the poor soul has, don't do something with your authority—but no— you let it hang by the wall like old armor, too rotten to be useful and too rusty to be ornamental.

STEF. Me! What can I do in the affair? Nothing.

THER. Because you will not.

STEF. Right, because I will not. The prince—

THER. Oh, don't talk about him. I've no patience to hear his name. He's my abhorrence—my detestation!

STEF. And yet once he was your oracle—your idol!

THER. Well, but that was six years ago, signor. A woman can't be expected to keep in one mind for six years.

STEF. Her husband went away, and then, with her sex's obstinacy she resolved to keep faithful to his memory. For years the prince vainly strove to break her determination, until at last wearied with fruitless hoping, and fearing that love which she had transformed into a weapon against her, she consented.

THER. Yes, to marry the Prince Lorenzo who, determined to conquer her —the wretch! has laid the strong hand of might upon her possessions, till now she's as poor as a workman's daughter. She's literally obliged to marry him.

STEF. But tomorrow she'll be a princess!

THER. And for the prince himself! Six years ago he was a noble, chivalrous, lovable gentleman. Now he's a stern, pitiless, merciless, revengeful bear. I pity poor Dianora's life with him!

STEF. It is her own deed—even to the metamorphosis of the prince. Love unrequited sometimes reverses the virtue of the philosopher's stone, and turns honest gold to base metal. Shall you go to the wedding this morning?

THER. Yes, I've promised not to leave the poor creature till she's a happy wretch for life. Shall you?

STEF. Not I. I've weightier business at home. She comes. My lord's ambassadors will be here presently, to take his bride to him. I shall be ready to receive them. [*Exit*]

THER. There, he's like all the men. The burden's always laid upon poor weak woman. [*Enter Dianora, in bridal vestments*] Well, Dianora, you don't seem happy.

DIAN. I am a most ungrateful, worthless creature, Theresa, but I am not happy. The prince loves me—yet I do not leap forward to this step with the spring-like elasticity of hope. The weight is here—the dull, dead, lifeless weight.

THER. Ah, your heart's not at home, my girl—and it's a very bad locum tenens in possession.

DIAN. Ah—had Sr. Marc but loved me less—or known me better.

THER. He'd never have flung his sweetmeat into the road for the prince to snap up. You love him just as well as ever, I expect.

DIAN. Wrong! For what was then respect, esteem, duty, obedience—what you please—has taken a holier name—devotion! Reverence, as we reverence the memory of the dead. Yes, Theresa, I heard last night what I have so long dreaded to hear, that he was dead—had died in bonds abroad. Fie, fie! This melancholy and these thoughts are grown dishonorable now. My very soul should be another's, and he shall not find me a rebellious slave.

THER. Slave! What a name for a bride.

DIAN. It's the true one. My heart, my remembrance, my very spirit worship is in Sr. Marc's grave—what more than the mere possessions of a slave have I to give the prince.

THER. I begin to feel very wretched, too, and if you'd cry I would. I've really learned to prize my little old man a great deal more lately, and to think that the maxim of "Let well alone" sometimes applies to husbands. He's an ordinary little mortal, but I shouldn't like to change him now—I've got used to his very inconveniences.

DIAN.   Theresa, I can trust you with one secret,
        Of which the very proudful thought comes now
        Over my spirit like a perfumed breeze,
        Letting my heart within my bosom dancing,
        And strengthening me to this sacrifice.

THER.   Yes. There's a change in thee—your eye is bright
        As with the olden fire, and your voice
        Has something of its bygone music now—
        The secret then—

DIAN. Is this—unknown to him
       I was a helping angel to Sr. Marc,
       A fortune-cloud. The commandant beneath
       Whose baton he once served loved gold—and mine
       Was dross to me. I sold some lands, dispatched
       A trusty messenger to do my errand,
       And bought the service of the officer.
       For this Sr. Marc rose up from rank to rank—
       For this was set upon the road to honor—
       But yet he knew not who had helped him to it,
       Scarce thought, or if he did, but to shower blessings
       Upon his unknown friend. That's me, Theresa!
       Did I not pay back something of his nobleness
       In its own coin? His was the action of
       A god, and mine the action of a woman.
THER. Ah, could the prince but look upon you now
       He'd love indeed.
DIAN. I often wished to hear
       His fortune—follow his adventurous spirit—
       And as the petted child that flings away
       Its toy into the river, being gone,
       Its value swells up fifty fold! He's gone,
       And manliness seems gone with him. [*Enter Servant*]
SERV. Please you, signora,
       The Duc Lioni from the prince—
DIAN. I know
       His mission—I am ready. [*Exit Servant*]
       It has come!
       The bitterest parting of my life—from this—
       [*Taking a small portrait from her vest*]
       I will not sin against my honor now
       By wearing aught to link my memory
       To what it loved so well!
THER. The portrait of
       Sr. Marc. What will you do?
DIAN. My duty now!
       All duty! Sternly duty! [*Placing it on table*]
                 And I turn
       Away from it as the bereaved mother
       Turns from the grave of her last little one!

THER.   Come, Dianora—cheerly—come! [*Exeunt. Reenter Stefano*]
STEF.   Poor girl!
        I little deemed how deep the fibrous root
        Of love had struck that bound her to Sr. Marc.
        [*Enter Servant with a letter*]
SERV.   [*Gives letter*]   To be delivered with the utmost haste,
        The bearer said, who, panting out his words,
        Avowed that on my speed a life did hang,
        Most precious to Modena.
STEF.   From the prisons!
        Some wretched felon, who to gain liberty,
        Pretends discovery of some secret plot
        Against the State, no doubt. The trick's grown stale.
        [*Scanning letter*] Humph! But there seems sound sense in this.
        The names
        Of the land's highest dignitaries, too
        Mixed in the business. Who writes? Sr. Marc!
        Living! And here—I'll see him! Horses quickly! [*Exit Servant*]
        I knew that murmurs of conspiracy
        Cloaking cabals beneath the mask of night
        Were often heard abroad, and this confirms them!
        Sr. Marc of all the world returned to see
        This day of days! What will tonight bring forth?
        The threatening peril throws its shade across
        The sunlight of Modena's joy—eclipse
        Foretells destruction and sometimes the sun
        Glares lividly like blood! A prince's blood!
        To horse! to horse! The hours fly! Away! [*Exit*]

SCENE 2: *The hall of the prison. Enter Belcastro and the Gaoler.*

GAOL.   But, my good lord Belcastro, this Sr. Marc
        Was sent a prisoner here last night, my warrant
        Signed by the prince himself.
BEL.   And are not names
        Like these I show you on the order for
        Sr. Marc's release, enough to guarantee
        Your safety in the business? I tell you
        The pleasure of the ministers is as great
        As Prince Lorenzo's, and their power, too.
        Set Sr. Marc free.

GAOL. Why not prefer your quest
       Unto the governor of the prison.

BEL. You are a wise man and I'll trust you thus far.
       Modena trembles on the point of changes
       Wondrous and little dreamed of. There are reasons—
       State reasons—why Sr. Marc should break his prison.
       And here are reasons, quite as strong, why you
       Should shut your eyes and lock your tongue from wagging.
       [Gives bag of gold]

GAOL. Grave reasons—weighty reasons—yet the peril
       I run in aiding his escape—

BEL. Give me
       Your keys and show me to his dungeon door.
       Then leave all else to me.

GAOL. 'Tis yonder, signor—
       The second on the right.

BEL. Enough. *[Exit Belcastro. Enter Gismondo]*

GAOL. I give
       You joy.

GIS. Of what?

GAOL. Your liberty regained—
       The prince is merciful.

GIS. Oh, very merciful. I'll thank him in its kind.
       Yes, in his very palace!

GAOL. Madness only
       Could dream so wild a scheme. He weds today—
       Modena's all ablaze with festival
       In honor of his nuptials.

GIS. Aye, aye, aye!
       The spirit told me something of the matter
       And more, reminded me that bygone ages
       Crowned all great festivals with sacrifice!
       Some with a sacrifice of beasts—and some
       With human victims. Strange!

GAOL. What's strange?

GIS. If such
       An antique fashion of the darker times
       Should come to ours! At this feast be offered up
       A human sacrifice!

GAOL.   And round his person
The friends and relatives of his high bearing stand
In an array impregnable. Farewell!
Health and returning sanity attend you! [*Exit*]

GIS.   Yes, that's the world's way—he thinks me mad—
He that is mad himself. All men are mad,
And I alone the truly sane. The mad
Are they who live without imagination,
Without the active spirit of invention—
It teems throughout me—it is blood, breath, sense—
The active part of me. All things that seem
Great difficulties i' the way of common men,
Are to me easy, save to reach the prince—
All things but that—all things but that!
[*Retires. Enter Belcastro and Sr. Marc*]

BEL.   You're free!
Your prison gates are open. Liberty
Looks smiling in upon you in the gleam
Of daylight through yon iron door that swings
Back on its massive hinges. Say, Sr. Marc,
Have I not kept my word?

MARC.   You have.

BEL.   And now
Keep yours. The prince must never live to see
Night wrap her star-pounced mantle round the earth!
Here is your weapon! [*Gives a dagger*]
Gold has cleared the way
Into the very presence of the prince.
A private door admits you from the garden
Into the prince's chamber.

MARC.   Good.

GIS.   [*Apart*]   And so
Say I—most excellent good! [*Distant music of a march, continued
till the entrance of the Prince and Dianora in the next scene*]

BEL.   Listen, Sr. Marc.

MARC.   I hear the distant measure of a march,
And through it swells the melody of voices
Quiring [*sic*] forth joy like a sweet atmosphere
Of music reaching up from earth to Heaven!

BEL.   It is their nuptial peal.

MARC.   Theirs! It has grown
In those brief words as hateful as the hoot
Of owls, or yell of famished wolves. And yet
The noble nature of the prince cannot
Be undermined in this brief glide of time.
Some fraction of the structure must remain
At the foundation.

BEL.   What is that to us?
You stand forth, not as slayer of a prince,
But the avenger of your wrongs. If not
Your own, of Dianora's.

MARC.   True. Lead on,
I'll follow on your steps.

BEL.   Remember, he
Must perish by your hand, struck down as low
As to your feet—pierced to the very heart—
You will not tremble?

MARC.   Fear not.

BEL.   Follow me.
All smiles on us! What, shall I wake tomorrow? [*Exit*]

MARC.   Down to my feet—pierced to the very heart—
Out, out, this weapon is not sharp enough.
There is a better and a nobler one
Called gratitude! And that shall humble him
As low as this could do! My messenger
Ere this has borne the letter to Lodori,
And would he meet me here [*Sees Gismondo*] Gismondo!

GIS.   Yes, you are Sr. Marc.

MARC.   Your friend, Sr. Marc, who looks
Into your wasted features as a mirror,
And therein sees his own.
You hear that music?

GIS.   Yes, a sacrifice.
The spirit said so.

MARC.   Sacrifice indeed!
But where's your sense, Gismondo? What's become
Of the old friend I left behind six years
Ago here in Modena? These nipped features—
These wasted limbs—these bloodshot, restless eyes

Are none of his! No more a part of him
Than the parched up and crackled weeds are kindred
To the fresh flowrets opening to the sun!
What necromancer wrought about this change?
This metamorphosis of man to creature?

GIS.   The restless, sleepless spirit—this is all
A seeming only—a mere vizard worn
Masking a purpose! Or a livery
Marking me out the specter's bonded thrall!
I wear it cunningly!

MARC.   Where will you go?

GIS.   With you.

MARC.   That cannot be.
I've business, of a vital moment, too,
At Prince Lorenzo's palace.

GIS.   So have I.
Great business—pressing business—we'll go
Together to the gate—part there, and take
Our roads for Heaven. [*Touching the dagger in Sr. Marc's belt*]
Humph! That's a pretty toy!

MARC.   I wear it for fashion.
Come on, old friend. We'll see this *sacrifice*
And maybe, take a part in 't too. Come on!
You're weak—lean on my arm—'tis strong enough
To bear the burden of a friend! Come on! [*Exeunt*]

SCENE 3: *Reception room in the palace. Large massive folding doors, C. Paul Vulcani, Petronio, and others of the confederate Lords, discovered. Shouts, music, and church bells heard in the distance and gradually approaching.*

PAUL.   They are returning!

PETRO. Yet Sr. Marc comes not!
What's to be done! The golden hour lost
Returns no more.

PAUL.   Here is Belcastro. [*Enter Belcastro*]
Well? What news? What of Sr. Marc!

BEL.   Fear nothing! All
Shines gaily on our scheme! He's close at hand!
Be ready for your parts.

PETRO. That's well, but hold—
One word: The people will demand a victim
If the prince falls.
BEL. That's taken care of, too.
The deed once done, the doer dies. The weapon
Once used, the safest method's to destroy it.
[*Enter Prince, Dianora, Theresa, Nobles, Ladies, Pages, etc.*]
ALL. Greetings and congratulations, sire! [*Servilely*]
PRINCE. I thank you.
My bride would thank you, too, but that she's lost
In such a past-rich dream as to forget
The courtesy that would befit her better.
DIAN. Pardon, my duties shall not lack—
PRINCE. Oh, duties now—
An hour since 'twas love.
DIAN. Is love still with all
The resolution to fulfill her duty
E'en to the strictest letter.
PRINCE. Let it *be* so.
Your favor, signors! [*Pointing to the doors. All bow, etc., and with-
draw at different entrances*]
THER. [*Aside as she goes out*] Mercy on us! Here's a matrimonial
tête-à-tête already—one seldom comes to that under a month at least! Talk
of the sweets of the honeymoon—here they begin with the wax! [*Exit*]
PAUL. [*Aside as they go*] Sr. Marc still absent!
PETRO. There's time yet.
BEL. Courage. As yet there's naught to fear! [*Exeunt. Dianora is seated
on one side of the stage, the Prince leaning against a table on the
other*]
PRINCE. Well, Dianora,
At last you are my wife.
DIAN. Yes, yes, my lord—
A cheerful, willing, and obedient wife.
PRINCE. Obedient. Let me see a proof of that—
A smile upon your lip.
DIAN. As you command.
The smile is there!
PRINCE. The sunshine on a grave!
Where is the blush of glowing love—the streak
Of joy's inspiring roseate hue that played

In bygone times about that face at sound
Of my mere voice? I do not see it now.
And yet we are each other's!
DIAN. O prince—prince—
Love is not master of itself!
PRINCE. Am I
Changed unto *you?* Modena calls me harsh,
Tyrannical, unjust—a despot ruler,
A pitiless, revengeful, rigorous prince—
And yet to you I am the same as ever,
Patiently worshipping, with the selfsame form
That made your heart leap up to see—the same
Eyes laden with affection like the stars
With light and deathless beauty? *You* are changed,
Not I—for years I've been content to be
Your spaniel. Now, fair lady, you're my wife.
DIAN. And as your wife, devoting self to you,
Thrusting the past back into deep oblivion,
And from the present dating a new life,
And all that life your slave.
PRINCE. That's well. You're now
My subject, like the rebels of my city,
And I will have you humbled to the dust,
In an eternal penance for the past.
DIAN. [*Astounded*] My prince! My husband!
PRINCE. Oh, it's husband now.
You've learned the word at last. What made me tyrant?
You, Dianora! For my love for you
Once was my heart-breath and my adoration.
For a mere word, a straw, that like a scratch
Made the soft skin of tender vanity
In woman's weak heart bleed, you flung it off,
And wedded with Sr. Marc! It crushed me down
Beneath it like an avalanche. I rose
Changed inward to a fiend—yet calm and patient
With the deep rancor smouldering beneath,
As the scarce heaving sea appears to slumber
Beneath the moon, but murmuring in its sleep
Like as it dreamt of vengeance!

DIAN. Vengeance! Vengeance! Vengeance and the glance
Of stern and bitter resolution, too,
That looks the word twice o'er!

PRINCE. It looks my heart—
Implacable and unforgiving!

DIAN. Prince! My lord!

PRINCE. Lord of a myriad lives and destinies,
And yours!

DIAN. My husband!

PRINCE. A mere name that's lost
Its power and spell. Call me another name!

DIAN. Yes. *Coward!*

PRINCE. Ha!

DIAN. A coward baser than the wretch that strikes
His prostrate foe at his feet! Am *I* not prostrate?
A shackled prisoner, heart and will alike
Thralled to you—powerless to stir myself—
Bound like a very martyr to the rack,
Worse than a serf—a wife! O God, O God!
That the one sex that mothered men and gave
The world its human fruit and harvest grain,
Should by that selfish world's great laws, become
The slave and vassal of her bosom's offspring!
Speak out, and be my doomsman!

PRINCE. Yes, a dungeon
Rayless and gloomy as the realm of death!
Fit dwelling for despair!

DIAN. Go, lead me to it!

PRINCE. Now for your prayers; now let repentance come,
For your past sporting with a heart of fire!
While, to sink into yours, and stir within
The anguish giving charm to my revenge,
Know that Sr. Marc yet lives—is in Modena.

DIAN. Living, and here!

PRINCE. Gaol'd like a felon, deep
Within a pitiless prison! Now rave, weep!
You're woman, and have tears at your command,
And let them gush forth now!
Have you no tears to shed?

DIAN.   And if I had,
         You should not see me shed them! I would set
         My pride to battle with my sex's weakness,
         And jail [*sic*] each crystal in its mother-bed!
         I'd check the spirit-waters like a rock,
         Although the inward fever burnt me up
         Like a hot sun, and the continued drought
         Cracked my parched heart at last! A tear! a tear!
         You should not see a quiver of the lip,
         A sob, a check o' the breath! I am aroused!
         My womanhood has blushed itself to fire,
         And speaks in lightnings! O Sr. Marc! Sr. Marc!
PRINCE. Let *his* name share thy prison's sanctity!
         Ho, there! Who's nearest? [*Calling off. Enter Sr. Marc*]
MARC.   I, my lord!
PRINCE. Sr. Marc!
DIAN.   My husband—no—not my husband now—
         The blessing has gone from me—gone forever.
PRINCE. What traitor hand hath broken through the walls
         Of thy strong prison—but this intrusion, slave,
         Is coin to purchase death! Your errand here?
MARC.   To strike the blow of wrath that rises up
         From the deep heart of an o'erladen city,
         To be an instrument of retribution
         In the great hand of Heaven! Prince, the bolt
         Of death hangs o'er thy head!
PRINCE. To murder me!
         Sr. Marc, is life so bitter?
MARC.   Life! A fable!
         I might have come to give it back to thee—
         What if I come to take it!
PRINCE. Ho, without there? [*Enter the confederate Nobles, etc.*]
         Seize on that murderous blood-spiller!
         [*All draw swords and, turning suddenly, present them at the Prince's
         breast*]
PAUL.   Behold
         The retribution of Modena!
PRINCE. All!
         All traitors to their prince?

DIAN.   Sr. Marc! Sr. Marc!
        You would not turn a bravo, and sell honor
        For gold of traitors! Let me see you still
        The proud Sr. Marc who would not stoop his neck
        Down to the lowest level of dishonor's flood
        To buy a prince's favors! If these men
        Love guilt for petty self-advancing ends,
        Or for its glitter 'neath the lamp of crime—
        Be yours the soul-light and the spirit-fire
        Gleaming above their worldly earthliness
        Like a proud constellation!
MARC.   You shall judge me. Quick there! The guards!
ALL.   The guards! [*Enter Soldiery, led by Stefano Lodori, and with them
        Bellafiore and Lioni*]
MARC.   Secure your prisoners! [*The Guards seize on and arrest the Con-
        spirators; general consternation*]
PRINCE. Ha, gentlemen! The fortune of the day
        Hath turned to me! Away with them! [*They are led off*]
        See them in safety, good Bellafiore,
        Loaded with iron shackles! Go, Lioni,
        Summon the people—you alarm the palace—
        The nest holds many traitors more!
        [*All go out but Sr. Marc, Prince and Dianora*]
        She knows
        Her share of the doom! The dungeon gapes—
MARC.   A dungeon!
PRINCE. The retribution of her prince!
MARC.   For her! For Dianora!
PRINCE. Follow me!
DIAN.   Farewell, my heart! Farewell, Sr. Marc, my daylight!
        [*Gismondo is seen at C. doors, his whole appearance indicative of
        morose madness. Observing the Prince he retires*]
MARC.   My lord! My lord! You are Modena's prince,
        And with it, master of Modena's hearts.
        You have a right to break them, if you will,
        And mine is at your feet. Spare *her*! Spare *her*!
        I gave *you* life just now.
PRINCE. Ask gold! Ask lands!
        But not a fraction of revenge!

MARC.   My lord!
        You never saw me humbled to a slave,
        Even to *you* but I am humbled now. [*Kneels*]
        I came, my bosom flooded with warm hope
        To claim my wife again—I found her yours!
        If you have wrath to wreak, wreak it on me—
        Chains, dungeons, scourge—but be a friend to her.
        Forgive her! Love her! Take her to your heart,
        For she'll be worthy of it—gilding it,
        My lord, with grace and beauty—pray you, spare her!
        Dear God! I seem to have a heart that's full
        Of words that could move mountains in her cause,
        And yet their full fraught chokes my utterance up
        And makes me worse than speechless!
PRINCE. I have sworn
        An oath as deep as death! I'll keep my oath!
        Come, follow me! [*Exit*]
MARC.   My dagger! Dianora,
        It is this man's life alone that stands between
        Us and our happiness! [*Draws his dagger*]
DIAN.   What then?
MARC.   He dead,
        We'd fly together into Germany,
        The emperor would welcome us. New wed,
        The future should be Heaven!
PRINCE. [*Without*] Dianora!
DIAN.   I come, my lord! Sr. Marc, even while the thought
        Sets all my brain in one ecstatic thrill,
        I see the price you'd pay for it—your soul!
        The ransom of my freedom is his blood!
        You shall not buy it at so high a price.
PRINCE. [*Without*] Still lingering!
DIAN.   Farewell.
MARC.   I will not lose thee!
        My being is bound up in thee! My blood
        The river of my heart and thou its ocean!
DIAN.   I'll have that dagger! [*Wresting it from him, and flinging it out at
        C. doors. Gismondo picks it up*]
        Let us love apart,
        But worthy of each other even then!

Sr. Marc! My worship—homage—lover—husband!
I go from thee a wreck!

PRINCE. [*Speaking as he is entering*] Must I come back
To make my will a law—

GIS. [*Stabbing him as he passes*] Home, for my father! [*The Prince falls dead instantaneously. Dianora utters a cry of alarm and throws herself into Sr. Marc's arms. Bellafiore, Lodori, Courtiers and Guards re-enter. Great confusion*]

LORDS. Seize the assassin!

BELLA. Slay the madman! [*Killing Gismondo. Gismondo falls into the arms of the Soldiers. The Nobles close round the body of Lorenzo*]

STEF. Fear naught, Sr. Marc. This day that broke so bitterly
Shall end in gladness!

MARC. She is mine again!
Clings to me, to the breast that cannot thrall
The wild tempestuous throbbings of the heart
Ecstatic in its joy! She's mine again!
Bound closer by the deathless links of love—
And as a child, that looketh on a light
Through tears, beholds a radiance all about him,
I gaze on *her,* and all my past sorrow fades,
My future glittering like a golden sunset.
We're knit again together, heart and soul!

END

(Following the play in the manuscript a musical score of the "Grand March —Sr. Marc" is included.)

THE DUKE'S MOTTO;
Or, I AM HERE!

A Play in a Prologue and Four Acts

By John Brougham

THE DUKE'S MOTTO;
Or, I AM HERE!

IF AMERICA has ever had an Aristophanes, John Brougham was his name."[1] For nearly forty years Brougham's name as actor or playwright was a magic attraction to the American playgoer. Here was a man whose life was in and of the theatre, and whose contribution to its art was a matchless personality and a lifelong enthusiasm. "The world was waiting for John Brougham when he appeared; and richly did he reward in fun and frolic, often irrelevant but irresistible."[2]

Brougham's American career began at the Park Theatre on October 4, 1842. By that time he had already acquired a London reputation as actor, writer, and manager. Born in Dublin on May 9, 1810, Brougham left his surgical studies because of family financial difficulties, and in July 1830 made his first stage appearance at the Tottenham Street Theatre, London. On this occasion he played six different characters in Egan's *Tom and Jerry*. He joined Madame Vestris's company at Covent Garden the next year, and for the ensuing decade played in London and in the provinces. His first play, a burlesque, was written in 1835 for W. E. Burton at the Pavilion Theatre. In the summer of 1840, he became manager of the London Lyceum, and wrote several plays, including *Life in the Clouds, Love's Livery, Enthusiasm, Tom Thumb the Second,* and *The Demon Gift,* for production at that house. To this list might be added Brougham's own claim (never settled) to a considerable share in the authorship of *London Assurance* (1841).

During his first season at the Park, Brougham acted with his first wife, formerly Emma Williams, whom he had married in 1838. In the fall of 1843, he went on a starring tour of the United States, and lost all his money in a Mississippi steamboat poker game! He returned to New York, to Burton's and the Chatham Theatres, and to a career of thirty-five years of acting, managing, and playwriting, which carried him from one theatre to another, always successful and popular as an actor, and nearly always a failure in his persistent managerial attempts.

Brougham was a talented comedian, an adept at concocting farces, burlesques, melodramas, and adaptations. He was sentimental, happy-go-lucky, and full of grandiose plans. As an actor, he was most popular in Irish rôles,

[1] Hutton, *Curiosities of the American Stage,* p. 164.   [2] Odell, IV, 608.

notably the rôle of Sir Lucius O'Trigger, although it has been said that no
matter what the part, he was always just John Brougham. As an interpreter
of Irish rôles, Brougham succeeded the popular Tyrone Power, who died in
1841. His career as a playwright is almost a history of American dramatic
fashions in comedy and melodrama. He wrote at least a hundred plays, including adaptations of several Dickens novels, *Vanity Fair, Jane Eyre,* and
several other novels, and such popular burlesques as *Met-a-mora, Columbus
el Filibustero!,* and *Pocahontas,* besides melodramas like *The Duke's Motto*
and *Temptation.*

In August 1846, Brougham went to Boston, where after one season at the
Federal Street Theatre, he took over the management of the Adelphi Theatre
in April 1847. He lasted a year, returning to Burton's as "stage manager."
Here he not only wrote many identifiable plays, but probably had a hand in
nearly all the new pieces which appeared with amazing frequency. After two
more years he again tried independent management, in opening "Brougham's
Lyceum Theatre" on December 23, 1850. For various alleged reasons, this
attempt failed after a year and a half. Brougham then enjoyed one of his most
successful periods of acting, for three or four years, at Wallack's very popular
theatre. During the year 1856-57, he directed at the Bowery, and at the same
time played frequently at Burton's and Wallack's. As to this strange state of
affairs, Professor Odell can only comment, "I cannot say." There followed
two more seasons at Wallack's, and then Brougham went to London, where
he spent five years from October 1860 to October 1865.

The Winter Garden, Wallack's, Daly's, another brief managerial attempt
at "Brougham's Fifth Avenue Theatre" (1869), and several years spent in
touring the United States occupied Brougham until 1878. When his projected
tour of 1877-78 was interrupted by illness, he was left so destitute that his
friends held a testimonial benefit for him at the Academy of Music on January
17, 1878. So great was Brougham's popularity that the benefit brought the
sum of $10,278.56, which was invested in a life annuity. Brougham recovered
sufficiently to spend another season in Wallack's company, and to bring his
career to a close on October 25, 1879, at Booth's Theatre, in a performance
of Boucicault's *Rescued.* His death occurred not long afterwards, on June 7,
1880.

In addition to his popularity as playwright and actor, Brougham was socially very much liked. He was gay and witty, could make clever speeches,
was something of a scholar, and ventured for a time into the editorship of a
humorous periodical, *The Lantern.* Typical of his extravagant humor are
such items as *Pocahontas,* billed as an "Original, Aboriginal, Erratic, Operatic,
Semi-civilized, and Demi-savage Extravaganza"; and *Columbus el Filibus-*

tero, "a New and Audaciously Original, Historico-plagiaristic, Ante-national, Pre-patriotic, and Omni-local Confusion of Circumstances, Running through Two Acts and Four Centuries." At one performance of *Pocahontas,* when the leading actress failed to appear, Brougham went ahead with the play, and at every point where her lines came, he or another actor spoke up: "Now, if she were here, this is what she would say—." *Pocahontas* perhaps put an end to the long popular "Indian" plays, but Brougham had burlesqued the type earlier in *Met-a-mora; or, The Last of the Pollywogs.* With speeches in rhymed couplets, silly dialogue, and such names as Badenough, Fitzfaddle, and Tapiokee, Brougham made fun of the greatest favorite among Indian plays.

Of Brougham's many plays, a few were printed, but most of them are now very hard to find. Others must surely be discoverable, but at the present time the inclusion of *The Duke's Motto* in this volume brings Brougham into a modern collection for the first time. Although *The Duke's Motto* does not represent Brougham in his favorite field of comedy, it is typical of his interest in melodrama. This play was first performed in England under the direction of Charles Fechter, who rewarded its author with a box of cigars! The first American production, at Niblo's Garden, on June 1, 1863, equalled the great triumph of London. As Odell says, "this play was soon parodied, plagiarized, or maltreated in several theatres and minstrel halls simultaneously," but *The Duke's Device, The Duke's Signal,* and *The Duke's What Is It?* merely added to the popularity of the original. The original American cast was headed by Collins, Wheatley, Collier, and Mme. Ponisi. When Charles Fechter came to this country in 1869, he was seen here in his original rôle of Lagardere.

The Duke's Motto is printed here from a manuscript in the Seymour Collection at Princeton University, through the courtesy of Dr. Robert H. Ball. The manuscript is inscribed, "Wm. Seymour, Scribe," and was used by the company headed by Laurence Barrett for a production on January 29, 1874, the playbill for which follows.

Thursday Evening, Jan. 29th, 1874

The Thrilling and Romantic French Drama in a Prologue and Four Acts

THE DUKE'S MOTTO
"I AM HERE!"

CHARACTERS

CAPT. HENRI DE LAGARDERE, *a soldier of fortune*

LAWRENCE BARRETT

CARRICKFERGUS, *his friend*   Mr. JOHN W. NORTON

PRINCE DE GONZAGUES	HARRY MEREDITH
PRINCE REGENT	GEORGE MORTON
AESOP, *a hunchback*	WILLIAM SEYMOUR
HECTOR PEYROLLES, *steward to the prince*	J. P. KILBOURNE
DUC DE NEVERS	MR. FOREST
LEMUEL, *chief of the zingari*	JOHN E. SUTTON
NAVAILLES } *courtiers*	FRANCIS O. ROSE
CHAVERNEY }	W. F. EDWARDS
MALICOME }	JOHN H. DAVIS
BANNERMAN } *ruffians*	C. B. MARCUS
TONIO }	W. MANTON
DIEGO, *an innkeeper*	R. J. BROWNE
TRUMPETER, *page to Lagardere*	R. O. FRANCIS
NOTARY	H. P. JOHNSON

RUFFIANS, SOLDIERS, GYPSIES, ETC.

BLANCHE DE NEVERS   Miss LOUISE HAWTHORNE

ZILLAH, *a gitana*   Miss M. E. GORDON

PRINCESS DE NEVERS, *afterwards wedded to Gonzagues*   ISABEL PRESTON

MADELON, *a maid*   MISS MAY

Following this list of characters (which saves four parts by doubling), the playbill includes a synopsis of scenes. Included in the manuscript are elaborate stage directions, prompter's notes, lists of properties needed, and diagrams of stage settings.

The manuscript itself is a curiosity. Almost all of the speeches of the hero, Lagardere, are represented only by cue lines. It seems likely that the manuscript represents a copy used by all the cast except Mr. Barrett, who played Lagardere. Inasmuch as Lagardere is a blunt fellow apparently not given to long speeches, very little sense of the play is lost. In fact, in only two or three cases is there any confusion or difficulty for the reader. The incompleteness of Lagardere's speeches will be seen easily in those lines which do not begin with a capital letter. As this is the only extant manuscript of *The Duke's Motto,* the omissions are regrettable, though they may intrigue the reader as an indication of theatrical practices.

The following alphabetical list of Brougham plays with dates of first production is undoubtedly incomplete, but is much more nearly adequate than any other now in print:

The Actress of Padua. Brougham's Lyceum (N.Y.), September 29, 1851. (Probably a revision of the play by R. Penn Smith, again revised by Brougham, 1854.)

All's Fair in Love. Bowery (N.Y.), 1856.

Ambrose Germaine. Niblo's Garden (N.Y.), 1850.

The Arcade. Chestnut (Phila.), January 5, 1846.

Art and Artifice. Burton's (N.Y.), June 20, 1859.

Atherley Court. Union Square (N.Y.), January 6, 1873.

Bachelor of Arts. Chestnut (Phila.), August 15, 1854.

Bel Demonio. Niblo's Garden (N.Y.), May 16, 1864. (Previously produced in London.)

Better Late Than Never. Brougham's Fifth Ave. (N.Y.), January 25, 1869.

The Birth of Freedom. Bowery (N.Y.), July 4, 1856.

Bleak House. Wallack's Lyceum (N.Y.), October 13, 1853.

The Capture of Captain Cuttle, and Bunsby's Wedding. Burton's Chambers St. (N.Y.), September 7, 1848. (A joint piece, obviously indebted to Dickens.)

The Cataract of the Ganges. Grand Opera House (N.Y.), January 20, 1873. (An alteration.)

Cher Ryan Dfairs Tar. Chatham (N.Y.), August 9, 1847. (Burlesque of *Cherry and Fair Star.*)

Christian Martyrs under Constantine and Maxantius. Barnum's Museum (N.Y.), February 4, 1867.

Columbus el Filibustero! Burton's (N.Y.), December 31, 1857.

The Confidence Man. Burton's Chambers St. (N.Y.), July 23, 1849.

The Dark Hour Before Dawn (with F. B. Goodrich). Amateur production, Academy of Music (N.Y.), April 28, 1859.

David Copperfield. Brougham's Lyceum (N.Y.), January 6, 1851.

A Decided Case. Wallack's (N.Y.), April 30, 1857.

The Declaration of Independence. Mobile, February 27, 1844.

The Demon Gift. London, 1840.

The Demon Lover; or, My Cousin German. Wallack's (N.Y.), September 21, 1854.

The Devil's Horse; or, The Curse of Ambition. Bowery (N.Y.), May 11, 1857.

Dombey and Son. Burton's (N.Y.), July 24, 1848. (Revised August 16, 1848; and again October 21, 1850, the last time at the Brooklyn Museum.)

Don Keyser (or *Caesar*) *de Bassoon.* Burton's Chambers St. (N.Y.), October 24, 1848.

Dred; or, The Dismal Swamp. Bowery (N.Y.), September 29, 1856. (One of several current versions.)

The Duke's Motto. London Lyceum, 1862, Niblo's Garden (N.Y.), June 1, 1863.

The Emerald Ring. Broadway (N.Y.), December 7, 1868.

Enthusiasm. London, 1840.

Flies in the Web. Winter Garden (N.Y.), November 13, 1865. (Altered from *The Game of Love.*)

Franklin. Chestnut (Phila.), January 17, 1846.

The Game of Life. Wallack's (N.Y.), December 12, 1853.

The Game of Love. Wallack's (N.Y.), September 12, 1855. (Plot adapted from Dickens's *Bleak House.*)

Gold Dust. Brooklyn Theatre, December 3, 1871. (Adaptation from Dickens.)

The Golden Dream. Manchester, England, 1864.

Goodbye. 1877. (?)

The Great Tragic Revival. Burton's (N.Y.), April 17, 1858.

The Gun Maker of Moscow. Bowery (N.Y.), January 24, 1857.

Hamlet Travestie. Burton's (N.Y.), December 2, 1857. (Not the first of this title.)

The Haunted Man and the Ghost's Bargain. Burton's Chambers St. (N.Y.), January 10, 1849. (From Dickens.)

Hearts; or, The Serpents of Society. Walnut (Phila.), 1868.

Home. Niblo's Garden (N.Y.), May 13, 1850.

Home Rule. 1879. (?)

The Irish Emigrant. Burton's (N.Y.), June 8, 1857.

The Irish Fortune Hunter; or, Gold versus Love. Broadway (N.Y.), September 16, 1850.

Irish Stew; or, The Mysterious Widow of Long Branch. Brougham's (N.Y.), February 8, 1869.

The Irish Yankee; or, The Birthday of Freedom. Broadway (N.Y.), June 19, 1854.

Jane Eyre. Bowery (N.Y.), March 26, 1849.

John Garth. Wallack's (N.Y.), December 12, 1871.

Jupiter Jealous; or, Life in the Clouds. Mitchell's Olympic (N.Y.), October 3, 1842.

Karmel the Scout; or, The Rebel of the Jerseys (with J. B. Howe). Bowery (N.Y.), March 2, 1857.

Lady Audley's Secret. Winter Garden (N.Y.), September 1, 1863. (Originally *The Mystery of Audley Court.*)

Life in the Clouds. [see *Jupiter Jealous*] London, 1840.

Life in the Clouds; or, Olympus in an Uproar. Chatham (N.Y.), August 2, 1847. (A different piece.)

Life in New York. Chatham (N.Y.), November 30, 1844. (Not the first of this title.)

Life in New York; or, Tom and Jerry on a Visit. Bowery (N.Y.), 1856. (Probably a revision.)

The Lily of France. Booth's (N.Y.), December 16, 1872.

Little Nell and the Marchioness. Wallack's (N.Y.), August 14, 1867. (From Dickens.)

The Lottery of Life. Wallack's (N.Y.), June 8, 1868.

Love and Murder (with Baker). Olympic (N.Y.), April 17, 1848.

Love in Livery. Winter Garden (N.Y.), December 21, 1865. (Perhaps the same play as below.)

Love's Livery. London, 1841. Mitchell's Olympic (N.Y.), December 6, 1841.

Met-a-mora; or, The Last of the Pollywogs. Adelphi (Boston), December 9, 1847.

The Might of Right. Astley's (London), 1865.

The Miller of New Jersey; or, The Prison Hulk. Bowery (N.Y.), March 21, 1859.

Minnie's Luck; or, Ups and Downs of City Life. Wallack's (N.Y.), June 27, 1870.

The Money Market. Brougham's Lyceum (N.Y.), November 10, 1851.

Much Ado About a Merchant of Venice. Brougham's (N.Y.), March 8, 1869. ("From the original text—a long way.")

The Musard Ball; or, Love at the Academy. Burton's (N.Y.), May 1, 1858.

My Cousin German. [see *Demon Lover*]

Neptune's Defeat; or, The Seizer of the Seas. Wallack's (N.Y.), October 5, 1858.

Night and Morning. Wallack's (N.Y.), January 15, 1855.

O'Donnell's Mission. Winter Garden (N.Y.), August 13, 1866.

Orion the Gold Beater. Bowery (N.Y.), November 29, 1856. (Originally *False and True*.)

A Peep from a Parlour Window. Burton's (N.Y.), October 11, 1849.

The Pirates of the Mississippi. Bowery (N.Y.), July 21, 1856.

Playing with Fire. Wallack's (N.Y.), October 2, 1860.

Pocahontas; or, The Gentle Savage. Wallack's (N.Y.), December 24, 1855.

Recollection of O'Flannigan and the Fairies. Broadway (N.Y.), 1856. (Originally by Tyrone Power.)

The Red Light; or, The Signal of Danger. Wallack's (N.Y.), June 6, 1870.

The Red Mask; or, The Wolf of Bohemia (or *Lithuania*). Bowery (N.Y.), November 3, 1856.

The Revolt of the Sextons; or, The Undertaker's Dream. Burton's (N.Y.), August 24, 1848.

Romance and Reality. Broadway (N.Y.), April 17, 1848.

A Row at the Lyceum. Brougham's Lyceum (N.Y.), April 22, 1851.

The Ruling Passion. Wallack's (N.Y.), October 19, 1859.

Shakespeare's Dream. Academy of Music (N.Y.), August 2, 1858.

Slander. 1877. (?)

The Spirit of the Air; or, The Enchanted Isle. Brougham's Lyceum (N.Y.), April 7, 1851. (Perhaps the same as the original burlesque of *The Tempest,* called *The Enchanted Isle*.)

Take Care of Little Charley. Wallack's (N.Y.), November 26, 1858.

Temptation; or, The Price of Happiness. Burton's (N.Y.), September 10, 1849.

This House to be Sold, the Property of the late William Shakespeare! Olympic (N.Y.), November 15, 1847.

Tom and Jerry in America. Bowery (N.Y.), 1856. (A revision?)

Tom Thumb the Second. London, 1841.

Valentine and Orson. Burton's Chambers St. (N.Y.), August 14, 1848. (Burlesque.)

Vanity Fair. Burton's (N.Y.), January 25, 1849.

The Veteran (with Lester Wallack). Wallack's (N.Y.), June 17, 1859.

While There's Life There's Hope. London, 1864.

The World's Fair in London. Brougham's Lyceum (N.Y.), February 10, 1851.

Ye Deville and Dr. Faustus. Brougham's Lyceum (N.Y.), March 10, 1851.

CAST OF CHARACTERS

CAPTAIN HENRI DE LAGARDERE

CARRICKFERGUS, *his friend*

PRINCE REGENT

PRINCE DE GONZAGUES

DUKE DE NEVERS

AESOP, *a hunchback*

HECTOR PEYROLLES, *steward to Gonzagues*

LEMUEL, *a gypsy chief*

DE BREANT
NAVAILLES } *noblemen*
CHAVERNEY

MALICOME
TONIO
BANNERMAN } *ruffians*
HERMAN

DIEGO, *an innkeeper*

TRUMPETER, *page to Lagardere*

NOTARY

COURTIERS, SERVANTS, RUFFIANS, GYPSIES, SOLDIERS, ETC.

BLANCHE DE NEVERS

PRINCESS DE GONZAGUES, *formerly Helen de Caylus, wife of Nevers*

ZILLAH, *a gitana*

MADELON

MARIANNA

MAID OF INN

LADIES IN WAITING, GYPSIES, ETC.

THE PROLOGUE OCCURS IN 1693 AND THE REST OF THE ACTION IN 1717.

PROLOGUE

SCENE 1: *Interior of an inn on the Spanish frontier (see property and scene plots). Malicome, Bannerman, Tonio, Herman and another Ruffian discovered seated around table. Music at rise. Loud laughter from Bravos at rise.*

OMNES. More wine! More wine! [*A female Servant enters with bottle on tray, which she places on table. As she passes to L., one of the Bravos attempts to kiss her; she slaps his face and exit, amidst the laughter of the band. Enter Peyrolles and Aesop*]

PEY. Silence! Silence, you set of ragamuffins! Body of Mars! Must *I*, Hector Peyrolles, the prince's shield and dagger, waste breath upon a set of curs!

OMNES. [*Rushing on him*] Curs!

PEY. [*Starts down R.*] Yes—curs! Rascally, cowardly curs!

OMNES. [*Starting again*] What!

AESOP. [*Interposing*] Be quiet, you don't know him. [*Carrickfergus enters*]

CAR. Not know him? Oh, yes, we do—some of us, at least. His fame has reached us even here. We honor the courage of the man who saved his master's life by slaying so many of his assailants, and we are proud of the great teacher of fence who has made so many swordsmen almost as skilful as himself. [*Aesop shrugs his shoulders, and crosses behind to footstool by fire, and sits*]

PEY. Hold your tongue! [*Carrickfergus bows, sits on table, around which the Bravos are now gathered*] Are these your comrades?

CAR. Yes; there they are, sir, the rejected of many countries, from bleak Sweden down to sunny Italy. Free lances and free livers; with no more conscience than a crowd of lawyers; no more mercy than a bench of country justices; and no more charity than a convocation of monopolizing prelates.

PEY. And may I ask what land has the honor of your nativity?

CAR. The land of lands, sir! Upon my native isle, sir, the warm sun loves to linger, kissing its mountain tops before it sinks to rest.

PEY. Yes, I've observed you Hibernians are very fond of your green isle—when you are *out* of it!

CAR. In or out of it, it's all the same—Paddy never forgets the Emerald Isle!

PEY. Now then for your instructions. A certain individual has become obnoxious to us.

CAR. I understand.

PEY. You will probably meet with him tonight.

CAR. How many will be with him?

PEY. He will be alone.

CAR. Alone! By Saint Columba-Kill, this looks a little too like assassination to be over palatable even to such a rough soldier as *I*.

PEY. But you don't know who this man is.

CAR. No—who is the giant?

PEY. Phillipe de Nevers! [*All start*]

CAR. Nevers? The idol of the people, and the fashion of the day; the very tradesmen name their wares after him, and, moreover, the very best swordsman in all France. I know but two men capable of standing up before him: one, our fencing master, my friend, the hunchback here, and the other, the little Parisian, Henri de Lagardere, of the King's Cavalry.

OMNES. Aye! Aye!

MAL. Oh! He's a devil at the play, as I know to my cost. [*Rubbing his arm*]

BAN. [*Rubbing his shoulder*] Lagardere! *I'm* indebted to him for a trifle of unnecessary surgery also.

CAR. [*Rises and comes forward*] This will be dangerous work.

PEY. Pshaw! What value do you set on your lives?

CAR. Faith, ours are worth little, it is true, but his is!

PEY. How much?

CAR. [*Glancing significantly at Bravos*] Well, his foes, perhaps might rate him somewhat low, but to us, who are his friends, his life is very precious. Suppose we say three thousand pistoles?

PEY. You shall have it.

CAR. The man is dead! But we must have earnest.

PEY. Oh! The hunchback keeps the purse, go with him—he'll satisfy you. [*Music. Aesop starts L., and beckons them*]

CAR. Away then and be quick—we haven't much time to spare. [*Exeunt all the Bravos after Aesop. Turning to Peyrolles*] And now, my little Goliath, we must have an explanation!

PEY. What! *You* seek an explanation of *me*! Body of Mars! [*Blustering up to Carrickfergus*]

CAR. Stop, stop! Don't crow so loudly, my fiery little bantam!

PEY. Ban—Body of Mars! Do you know who I am?

CAR. Perfectly. You are master Hector Peyrolles, steward to the Prince de Gonzagues.

PEY. Whose life I saved by the prowess of *this little arm!*

CAR. Yes—yes—I have heard of that gallant exploit, and I love to listen to deeds of valor—pray tell me, how did you accomplish it?

PEY. My master was attacked by three ruffians; he fought gallantly until stunned by a blow, when *I* valiantly—

CAR. Ran like a hound, while the only assailant hurried after you; in an agony of fright, you stumbled and fell; he fell over you and, as you thought, broke his neck; when the prince came to himself, he found you flourishing your sword over the fallen man, who thought it best to keep quiet.

PEY. How the devil did *you* know all this?

CAR. Simply, because *I* am the man you killed, my valorous friend.

PEY. [*Alarmed*] You are—then I'm off! [*Peyrolles turns to go. Carrickfergus catches him*]

CAR. [*Bringing him down C.*] No, you're not! It was from me you got your patent of bravery, and it is but fair that I should profit a little by it; so now, I'll make a bargain with you. Attach me to the prince's household, in any capacity, I don't care what, and if my natural diffidence does not totally eclipse my brighter qualifications, in time, perhaps, I may be enabled to shine; and in return I'll not only keep your secret, but I'll do all your fighting into the bargain, for a reasonable consideration.

PEY. [*Shaking hands*] I consent! I consent! Depend on me to place you in a very good position, for, to tell you the truth, my accidental character for bravery has led the prince to send me on some ticklish enterprises. [*Music*] Here come the fellows—not a word!

CAR. I'll shrink before your glance like a whipped schoolboy! [*Passing in front to R.*]

PEY. [*Drawing his sword*] Another word! And by the Body of Mars! I'll pin you to the wall! [*As Peyrolles is flourishing sword at Carrickfergus, Aesop enters, followed by the Bravos, who go up to the table*]

AESOP. Always rioting! A truce to this! The messenger is coming whose letters we must secure.

CAR. Why so?

PEY. It is only by them we can find out when and where we are to meet our man.

CAR. How?

PEY. Why, by an answer to a letter sent by an officer, asking a rendezvous, and who is now waiting at the inn for it.

CAR. It will be a service of some danger. [*Music*]

PEY. Silence! [*Exit Aesop*] He comes! [*Enter the Trumpeter. He comes down C., looking about him. As he enters, two of the Bravos drop down R. of him, the others and Peyrolles at his L. Carrickfergus, R. corner*]

TRUMP. The captain is not here—this certainly was the rendezvous.

PEY. Well; and who are you looking for, my fine fellow?

TRUMP. It's no business of yours!

PEY. Isn't it indeed? I'll soon show you that it is! Let us see what you have been stealing. [*Seizes the Trumpeter*]

TRUMP. [*Shaking him off*] I have stolen nothing; let me go!

PEY. Let us search the young rascal!

TRUMP. Don't come near me or I'll hurt you!

PEY. Ha! Do you hear the wolf's cub! [*Advances to him, he draws a dagger and uplifts to strike. Peyrolles starts back, placing a Bravo before him*] Ha! Take it away! Take the sting from the young wasp! [*The Bravos seize the Trumpeter, he struggles; enter Lagardere, and he throws them off. They all get downstage, L. Carrickfergus still R. corner. Peyrolles sneaks off*]

OMNES. [*At his entrance*] Lagardere!

LAG. ——Well known here it would seem!

CAR. Noble captain, we salute you.

LAG. ——away from their nests?

CAR. Merely a slight healthy trip across the mountains—but your humble servants, everywhere, most noble captain.

LAG. [*To Malicome*] ——Where have I seen you?

MAL. At Strasbourg, captain, faith, I have cause to remember it well. I carry with me a little souvenir of our last meeting. [*Rubbing his sword arm*]

LAG. ——Where is the answer?

TRUMP. I have it here. [*Holds out letter*]

LAG. [*Snatching it from him*] ——Give it me!

TRUMP. The duke confiding in your honor, has entrusted me with another to deliver to a noble lady near here, but I am afraid of these—

LAG. ——will dare to molest you! [*Music. Exit Trumpeter. Lagardere standing with sword drawn between him and Bravos. He then comes down C., opens letter, and reads. The Bravos crowd around him, peering over his shoulder*] ——Stand back, rascals! [*They all start back*] ——Thou art a true gentleman, Nevers! [*Carrickfergus and Bravos get up to table*]

CAR. [*Sitting on edge of table, to Bravos*] It is Nevers's letter!

LAG. ——I'm an exile!

CAR. An exile! *You,* captain?

LAG. ——heard of Phillipe de Nevers?

CAR. [*Significantly to others*] I should think we had.

LAG. ——some flavor of Nevers. [*As he rises and comes down C., the Bravos drop down R. and Carrickfergus, L.*]

CAR. Oh! How shocking!

LAG. ——through my brain Nevers! Nevers! Nevers!

CAR. I wonder how you could endure it.

LAG. ——did not get off so easily.

CAR. No?

LAG. ——pricked me on the forehead.

CAR. Painful cut, captain!

LAG. ——mark of infamy—*I*—Lagardere!

CAR. Faith, captain, it was hard to bear!

LAG. ——unhappily gave me the chance.

CAR. What! Baron Ballison?

LAG. ——Yes we met!

CAR. Well?

LAG. I tried to stroke.

CAR. Yes?

LAG. Oh! Succeeded surprisingly!

CAR. And Ballison the bully?

LAG. Is now Ballison the *quiet!*

CAR. Dead?

LAG. ——and I am an exile! [*Lagardere crosses to fireplace and sits; the Bravos get back to table, and Carrickfergus resumes his seat*]

CAR. What? An exile! And only for killing a little devil of a colonel? What is the law coming to? [*Aside to Bravos*] Now to find out about Nevers! [*Aloud*] This study may serve you sometime or other, captain.

LAG. ——It shall serve me now!

CAR. How so?

LAG. ——names the time and place.

CAR. Indeed! When is the time?

LAG. This evening.

CAR. And the place?

LAG. The fosse of the Château de Caylus.

CAR. And the hour?

LAG. Nine o'clock. [*All the Bravos burst into laughter*]

CAR. Ha, ha, ha! That's not so bad! Thank you, captain; that's all we want to know.

LAG. Why do you laugh, rascals?

CAR. [*Leaving table*] Simply to think that we should both be on the same errand.

LAG. What do you mean?

CAR. Why, we are here to meet with somebody.

LAG. And who is that somebody?

CAR. No other but the very man who marked you with that brand of shame!

LAG. [*Rising*] Nevers!

CAR. But trouble yourself no more about him, we'll throw your little account in along with our own and wipe off both together.

LAG. How?

CAR. Why, by—[*Touches the hilt of his sword*]

LAG. [*Seizes Carrickfergus and passes him to L. Bravos all down R.*] ——attempt to touch him!

BRAVOS. [*Advancing*] What?

LAG. [*Keeping them at bay*]. .——Those of dastardly assassins!

BRAVOS. Assassins!

LAG. ——and cage you here! [*Music. The Bravos have crossed in front to L. now*]——with the blade like curs!

BRAVOS. [*Advancing*] What!

LAG. ——Stand back! [*Exit. They rush at door, it is shut in their faces*]

CAR. He's right! He's a brave and noble fellow; and I love and honor him for it. Three thousand pistoles blown to the devil, on the breath of that fiery captain. [*Music*]

MAL. [*Has been examining window, finds rope*] Ha! The window over· looks the fosse; he must go round by the château to reach it! Hurrah! We shall yet be in time to earn our reward. [*To Carrickfergus*] Come, you will join us?

CAR. No! There are plenty of you without me—besides I have a savage attack of repentance on me!

BRAVOS. [*Laughing derisively at Carrickfergus*] Repentance! Ha, ha! [*Carrickfergus angrily rises, seizes a stool and threatens to throw it at them. Amid their laughter the scene closes in*]

SCENE 2: *Exterior of the inn. Enter Aesop followed by Gonzagues.*

GONZ. Where do these fellows loiter? The time is close at hand and should Nevers reach the château before they can, he will escape. Aesop— we must secure the child at any hazard. Send one of the bravos to me.

AESOP. [*Advances, enter Lagardere*] Here is one, prince.

GONZ. Hist! How imprudent to mention my title.

LAG. ——fight my way through the whole nobility.

GONZ. Come here.

Lag. [*Advancing*] ——He's rather cool!

Gonz. Have you a mind to gain fifty pistoles?

Lag. ——how are they to be earned?

Gonz. Easily enough. You have only to go to the oratory window of the château yonder, where you will see a lady.

Lag. ——a lady!

Gonz. Yes, Helen de Caylus. Phillipe de Nevers's wife.

Lag. ——a different kind. Well?

Gonz. She will hand you something, which you will take to the hotel in the village and the pistoles are yours.

Lag. ——with the lady's husband.

Gonz. I know. But there is time enough for both if you are expeditious. Get done with this and then attend to him. You have half an hour to spare.

Lag. ——so I'll undertake it.

Gonz. When you reach the window, knock gently; it will be opened by a lady to whom you will say, "I am here."

Lag. ——The Duke de Nevers motto!

Gonz. Yes. In fact, you will have to represent him.

Lag. [*Aside*] ——What's this?

Gonz. It is too dark for you to be recognized and when our man is dispatched—

Lag. ——Dispatched!

Gonz. Killed! You must make sure of that! Do not give him time to draw his sword but waylay and stab him to death without a moment's warning.

Lag. [*Aside*] ——Great heaven!

Gonz. Why, fellow, do you hesitate? Have I not promised you three thousand pistoles?

Lag. [*Aside*] ——What monstrous villainy!

Gonz. And are there not six of you?

Lag. ——conduct themselves as they may!

Gonz. Where are they?

Lag. ——They are close at hand.

Gonz. Away then at once. You have no time to lose. [*Music*]

Lag. ——I have not indeed.

Gonz. Do you know the window?

Lag. ——No.

Gonz. [*Pointing to Aesop*] He'll show it you. Do you remember the motto?

Lag. ——I am here.

Gonz. Right. And now, Nevers, take your last leave of earth, for the next chime will be your passing knell. [*Exit*]

Aesop. [*To Lagardere*] Come. I'll show you! [*Exit, followed by Lagardere. Change of scene. Lights all down*]

Scene 3: *The fosse of the château. Music. At opening of scene, all the Bravos are discovered, one leaving the rope hanging from window, and backing off through gateway, as if having escaped from the inn. Then enter Gonzagues, Aesop, and Lagardere on drawbridge. Gonzagues points for others to descend, and he crosses and exit. Aesop from C. on bridge, points to window.*

Aesop. There is the window. You know what to do?

Lag. ——Be assured of that! [*Aesop crosses drawbridge and exit*] ——Are you gone? He is! ——fortune has sent me here. [*Music. He ascends steps, claps hands three times. The window is suddenly illuminated; it opens and Helen de Caylus appears*]

Helen. [*Whispers*] Who is it?

Lag. ——I am here!

Helen. Phillipe!

Lag. ——It is Nevers's wife!

Helen. And do you still adhere to your intention?

Lag. ——Resolutely!

Helen. Thank Heaven for that, dear Phillipe. [*Disappears from window*]

Lag. ——is out of place. [*Helen reappears with Child and packet*]

Helen. Are you there?

Lag. Yes.

Helen. Here!

Lag. What's here?

Helen. Take my treasure, dear Phillipe, into no other hand but yours would I resign it; and here are the proofs torn from the register and sealed with your own motto. Oh! be careful of it, Phillipe, for on that may yet depend our name and fame. [*Music*] Ah! I hear footsteps! Save yourself, beloved! [*She gives Lagardere Child and packet and closes the window hastily. Lagardere descends steps*]

Lag. ——It feels soft and strange. [*Music and moonlight*]——By heavens! An infant! [*Remove the moonlight when he steps out of it*] ——have from lust of gain. [*Music. De Nevers appears on drawbridge*] ——saved both him and me!

Nevers. [*Descending steps*] Thank fortune, the darkness of the night is favorable for one of my purposes at least.

Lag. ——I hope, my lord duke.

NEVERS. Ah! Lagardere—I presume!

LAG. ———to that name, my lord duke!

NEVERS. [*Throws off cloak*] Well, sir, I have matters of importance to attend to and have but little time to spare. Defend yourself! [*Draws*]

LAG. ———rash and impetuous man!

NEVERS. On guard! [*Pressing upon Lagardere*]

LAG. ———Take care I say.

NEVERS. Come on, I say!

LAG. ———slay the infant?

NEVERS. What infant?

LAG. ———Your own, unnatural parent!

NEVERS. My child!

LAG. ———I mean, feel for yourself!

NEVERS. My daughter in your arms?

LAG. ———honor to salute you!

NEVERS. What mystery is this? I demand an explanation!

LAG. ———or you will wake her!

NEVERS. Do you wish to drive me mad?

LAG. ———first embrace your daughter. [*Nevers makes a movement to do so*] ———for a short time. [*Places child on bank*] ———unfit for ladies eyes!

NEVERS. What mean you, chevalier?

LAG. ———the noble lady, her mother.

NEVERS. Then you have seen Mademoiselle de Caylus?

LAG. ———the Duchess de Nevers.

NEVERS. I am justly reproved; and she confided to you—

LAG. ———had given it to you!

NEVERS. [*Surprised*] How?

LAG. ———having your hands full.

NEVERS. An attack?

LAG. ———No—an assassination.

NEVERS. Assassination! Organized by whom?

LAG. ———with a hunchback follower!

NEVERS. He! Then my life is of little value!

LAG. ———bit of personal criminality.

NEVERS. The villain aims then at my estate as well as life!

LAG. ———come round by the village here. [*Music*] ———a rope! They have escaped.

NEVERS. Hark! I hear the sound of footsteps. [*Murmur and noise of swords*]

LAG. ——Save in some righteous cause!

NEVERS. What, chevalier! Will you then fight for me?

LAG. ——with all my soul!

NEVERS. Lagardere, from this time forth our interests are joined whether I live or die. If I live, you shall be my brother! If I die, promise me that you will be a father to my child! [*They clasp hands*]

LAG. ——this side of Paradise!

NEVERS. Prepare yourself! I see the gleam of steel in the moonlight! [*Music. They stand in each corner of stage. Enter Malicome and four other Bravos cautiously, and all with swords drawn*]

MAL. Hist! Nevers!

NEVERS. [*Advancing*] I am here!

LAG. And so am *I!*

OMNES. Lagardere!

LAG. ——to look honest steel in the face?

MAL. Down with them both? [*Gonzagues enters on steps. Lagardere drives two Bravos off, during which Nevers disarms one and drives the other two upstage. Lagardere returns and disengages one of them, and drives him off*]

GONZ. By heaven! The cowards fly! He will escape at last!

NEVERS. [*Kills his man and comes down C., exclaiming*] Victory! Victory!

GONZ. Yes, for me! [*Fires at and hits Nevers*]

NEVERS. Ha—my cousin! Treachery! [*Staggers, and Lagardere catches him*] Brother, sworn brother, avenge my murder, and protect my child! [*Dies*]

LAG. ——recognize you yet by *this!* [*Rushes up steps, disarms Gonzagues, who has drawn his sword, and wounds him on wrist. Lagardere then rushes over to R. and picks up child, taking stage again, C. Malicome and two others reenter*]

GONZ. Ha! It is the child! A hundred pistoles to him who cuts him down! [*Flashes pistol*]

LAG. ——Heavens! Is there no escape?

CAR. [*In inn window*] This way, captain! [*Lagardere fights through the Bravos and seizes rope. Moonlight on him now. He is drawn up and gets in window*]

LAG. ——after the hirelings, the master! [*The moonlight on Lagardere in window. Ring in picture. Quick drop*]

ACT I.

SCENE: *A mountain gorge on the Spanish frontier. Set tent on an eminence. Music at rise. All the Gypsies discovered, male and female; Blanche and Zillah seated on bank. Enter Carrickfergus and Peyrolles. Carrickfergus throws some money to Gypsies.*

CAR. [*Coming down, L.*] Well, Peyrolles, my old friend, it is just twenty years ago since you and I entered into partnership.

PEY. So it is; and our mutual interests have bound us together like a pair of brothers.

CAR. Yes; our contract has been kept with singular fidelity. I have fought your battles for you until your name rings amongst the bravest in Christendom.

PEY. And I have lied for you—oh! how I *have* lied—until you rank amongst the prince's most favorite intimates.

CAR. Yes, we have worked together pleasantly and not unprofitably; but these fruitless expeditions in search of the Lady Blanche are not amusing and I'm not sorry that our faces are turned toward Paris once more.

PEY. Faith! Nor I! These mountain savages are dangerous companions! [*Two gypsy Boys run down, R., and shake their tambourines at Peyrolles, who starts*] Ha—a! What the deuce are these?

CAR. Pshaw! Don't be frightened—they are nothing but a few Zingari seeking alms.

PEY. [*Reassured*] Is that all? [*Drawing sword and blusteringly to boys*] Disperse, you ragged rascals! [*Drives them around in front of him and up L. He then comes down bravely to Carrickfergus, when Zillah rises and crosses to Peyrolles, shaking tambourine in his ear. He clings to Carrickfergus for support*]

ZIL. Bestow a trifle on the poor Zingara, señors!

PEY. Back, daughter of perdition!

ZIL. The Zingara can read the stars of your nativity, brave señor.

PEY. Can they?

CAR. Can they? Of course they can; as easy as an Irish bobby can read Greek.

PEY. Well—what do they say? But beware of lying.

Car. Oh! Gypsies never lie—in the daytime—when they are awake!

Zil. The voices of the stars are truthful as their brightness is eternal. [*Examines Peyrolles's hand*] Here's a line—

Car. I think I see that line! It's a strong one with a noose at the end of it.

Zil. Saturn and Mars ruled conjunctive at your birth, inspiring deeds of more than common valor. Your name will live amongst the heroes of the earth. Speak they not truly, señor?

Pey. True as an oracle, sweet gypsy! Somewhat orientally explained, to be sure, but in the main correct, and therefore worthy of requital. [*Gives her money*]

Zil. Thanks, brave, beautiful señor.

Car. [*Aside*] Beautiful—oh, dear! Beautiful as a hedgehog.

Zil. [*Crosses to Carrickfergus*] Shall I cast your nativity, gentle sir.

Car. No, thank you! I have heard enough to guarantee your skill; besides, I was born in the daytime—when the stars were out! [*Music*] Ah! The prince! [*Enter three Valets. Then Gonzagues followed by Aesop. Gonzagues throws money to Gypsies, who scramble for it. Aesop remains R. Carrickfergus and Peyrolles remain R.C. Gonzagues sends the Valets off*]

Gonz. Peyrolles! [*Peyrolles advances*] Be near at hand; I may have some work for you. [*Zillah, who has been speaking to Blanche, now goes into tent*]

Pey. [*Aside to Carrickfergus*] Oh! Law! Did you hear that?

Car. Fear nothing! I shall be near you.

Gonz. Carrickfergus.

Car. [*Crosses to Gonzagues*] Yes, my lord.

Gonz. Within the hour you must start for Paris. The family council which is to determine the succession of Nevers's estate will shortly meet; take an opportunity of spreading amongst them the intelligence that the supposed lost heiress, Blanche, is found.

Car. Found, my lord?

Gonz. Yes. I have discovered her at last!

Car. You shall be obeyed, my lord. [*Aside to Peyrolles*] That's a lie!

Pey. But what am *I* to do? But what *am I* to do?

Car. Wait! [*Music. Carrickfergus and Peyrolles converse a second, and Peyrolles then goes off. Carrickfergus saunters about at back*]

Gonz. Aesop! [*Aesop down R. of him*] I dare not trust these pliant tools with more than words; my secret thoughts I put into your keeping. The proofs of this girl's death I cannot find, and to face the council without them, or the girl herself, would be my ruin. A curse upon their legal niceness! When by a simulated zeal for Nevers's cause I at last induced his widow to become my wife, it was only in the hope of gaining the estate as well; but it was sequestered in favor of this girl, whom dead or alive—I hate—oh! with what a bitter hatred! Now, listen! I have found a girl about the age that Blanche would be; she must be presented to the council as the true heiress; her mother not having seen her from her infancy, it will be easy to impose upon her; and once the succession is established—the rest I leave to *you!*

AESOP. I understand! The drugged bouquet.

GONZ. Secures me the inheritance. Now for the gypsy girl! [*Music. Aesop goes up R. and remains at back. Lemuel enters from tent, beckons to Blanche, who crosses over to him. Zillah enters R. as Gonzagues finishes his speech*] Yes! Yes!

ZIL. [*Running to Gonzagues*] Do you want your fortune told, noble señor?

GONZ. No, I think I could tell yours.

ZIL. It must be a sad one.

GONZ. Perhaps not. Would you be willing to abandon your present occupation?

ZIL. Kind as the brotherhood has been to me, I would bless the means that took me from this life of false and wearying excitement.

GONZ. If I err not, such means are close at hand. It may be that a sudden and a happy change awaits you. Send the chief of your band to me.

ZIL. Directly, señor! [*Music. Aside*] What can he mean? His words have set my heart beating with anxiety and hope! [*Zillah runs up to Lemuel who is conversing with Blanche. She points to Gonzagues; Lemuel drops down L. Zillah and Blanche reseat themselves on bank*]

GONZ. [*Musing*] Yes, she'll look like a princess, at least; that is all we require! [*Crossing to R. and turing to Lemuel*] This gypsy girl is very beautiful!

LEM. What— Zillah? Our queen—our goddess! That she is, Señor Magnifico; and as clever as she is beautiful!

GONZ. That I can see. Is she your daughter?

LEM. No, señor. She is an orphan found by our band some twenty years ago, so that you see there is no monopoly of affection by any single one. Mistress of all our hearts, we share her love amongst us.

GONZ. Have you never suspected that she was of better birth than her companions?

LEM. As the queenly rose is to the vulgar nettle! If there ever was a born princess she is one.

GONZ. You are right. She is. I know it!

LEM. You, señor! You make me tremble and rejoice at the same time.

GONZ. Yes—for years I have been searching for that girl; and it is now in my power to reinstate her in her true position.

LEM. It will fall like a thunderbolt on our band.

GONZ. But if you love her as you profess, you would share in the joy of her restoration. Wealth—rank—position—and, above all—a mother's anxious heart awaits her.

LEM. You have said enough, señor; though she is our pride—our purse—our treasury of love and profit, there is not a Zingari of our band but will weep tears of happiness at her good fortune.

GONZ. In common justice, I shall indemnify you for the loss of her services.

LEM. You cannot, señor, if you were to lay down her weight in gold. You should not if you could. We can afford to give her to you freely. I, the chief of the band, say, take her, laden with our tears and blessings—but to weigh her welfare against dross? No! No! The Zingari does not make a barter of his love.

GONZ. You will at least accept a gratuity as a testimony of my esteem?

LEM. The Zingari is poor, señor, and if our show diverted you, we shame not to take payment.

GONZ. I shall require you to sign a document to the effect that you found and protected the child; but at once, for I have no time to lose. [*Music. Gonzagues and Lemuel exeunt into tent, followed by Aesop. Blanche rises, goes up L., meets Lagardere; they come down, sit on bank. Zillah gets C. with Gypsies*]

CAR. [*Coming forward*] So—so—I thought as much. That's the sweep the current's taking! A false Blanche since we can't find out the real one. A precious plot—but it's no affair of mine! [*Goes up again*]

LEM. [*Appears at tent and calls*] Zillah!

ZIL. Here, father!

LEM. Come hither, child. [*Zillah goes into tent with Lemuel*]

BLAN. Dear, good, kindhearted Zillah! I love her like a sister, Henri!

LAG. ——be sure that she deserves it.

BLAN. Why so, Henri?

LAG. ——attracted towards each other. [*Enter Aesop from tent*]

AESOP. Well, he knows best, but I fear this scheme. There's not a trace of the princely Nevers in that gypsy's face. Now yonder—[*Points to Blanche*] is a young girl more like what we require—ha! [*Seeing Lagardere*] Who is this? I'll swear I know him! [*During Aesop's speech Blanche leaves Lagardere and goes up to the Gypsies*]

CAR. [*Aside*]   Who is that fellow scowling at, I wonder; it bodes him no good, whoever he is. [*Sees and recognizes Lagardere*] As I live, it's our little Parisian turned Spaniard—he little knows the danger he's in. I will give him a hint—but no—it's no affair of mine. Yes, it is—I *will* give him a hint. [*Saunters up to return piece, and putting his foot on rock, while pretending to fasten spur, whispers*] Lagardere!

LAG. ——Who's there?

CAR.   Hush! Don't look but listen. You are watched by a tiger—look over your shoulder—you can see the beast crouching ready for a spring. Have a care—he's a merciless fiend.

LAG. ——The hunchback!

CAR.   Yes, the prince is here. Failing to discover proofs of the Lady Blanche's death, he is going to substitute a false heiress at the council which is to meet at Paris.

AESOP. [*In R. corner*]   It *is* Lagardere!

CAR.   Ah! The hunchback has recognized you! I see by the vicious glare of his eye! Have a care! Have a care! [*Carrickfergus exit*]

AESOP.   Then that girl must be the true Blanche. This will be rare news for the prince. [*Crosses to C. and turns to go; meets Lagardere*]

LAG. ——Seem to be merry, sir? [*Aesop has been rubbing his hands*]

AESOP.   I am!

LAG. ——somewhat in haste.

AESOP.   As you perceive.

LAG. ——compelled to check both.

AESOP.   How!

LAG. ——serious words to say to you.

AESOP.   I have no time to hear them.

LAG. ——But you must.

AESOP.   Must?

LAG. ——You know me?

AESOP.   Perfectly. Lagardere!

LAG. ——Lady who was by my side?

AESOP.   Well—I—

LAG. ——Blanche de Nevers!

AESOP.   It is she then—I thought so!

LAG.   You were quite right!

AESOP.   That's all I want to know! [*Aesop starts to go, Lagardere stops him*]

LAG. ——not all you have to hear!

AESOP. [*Sulkily*]   Well—then—go on!

LAG. ——tell him you have found her?

AESOP. It certainly is!

LAG. ——But you won't.

AESOP. What will hinder me?

LAG. ——a simple thing!

AESOP. And that is—

LAG. ——I mean to kill you! [*Music*]

AESOP. Kill me! Your master! Fool! I gave you your first lesson! [*Exit*]

LAG. ——After the hirelings, the master! [*Exit. Enter Gonzagues, Zillah, and Lemuel. Lemuel goes to Blanche, C. Gonzagues down L.*]

ZIL. Oh! It must be a dream! A delightful dream! I cannot be awake. What! I—the poor Zingara, whose place of rest has been the open field— to whom the meanest hovel was a palace—shall I live in a house? A real house, with fires in it—and have food and clothes, that I may not shudder at the thought of winter as I used to?

GONZ. You shall. You will also meet the noble lady, your mother.

ZIL. Have I then a mother? Oh! Heaven has no greater blessing left me on earth.

GONZ. You will soon see her now, so take leave of your hitherto companions and get ready to depart. I have a few directions to give, and will rejoin you presently. [*Music. Exit Gonzagues up L. Zillah turns to Blanche, who comes down C.*]

ZIL. O Blanche, my dear, good, kind friend, for so I shall ever call you— have you heard? Do you know I'm a princess? Blanche! A real princess— what do you think of that? And what's dearer still—I have a mother! Blanche! A treasure that my lonely heart has hungered for through all my life.

BLAN. What a happy change. Believe me, Zillah, my heart shares in the joy of yours.

ZIL. Oh! How I wish *you* could be a princess, too! Don't *you*, Blanche?

BLAN. No!

ZIL. Why not? To live in a palace!

BLAN. It might divide me from Henri; where he lives, is palace enough for me, Zillah.

ZIL. You love him, Blanche?

BLAN. With all my soul!

ZIL. And does he love you?

BLAN. Ah! There lies my hope and fear. I think he loves me, but then it is only as a child.

ZIL. What folly! Depend upon it, if he does not love you to desperation, it is because—

BLAN. Because?—

ZIL. He loves someone else!

BLAN. Someone else?—Yes—yes! It must be that which keeps him quiet.

ZIL. Why how you blush! Blanche, you are jealous!

BLAN. I *am* jealous, Zillah! Jealous of the sun that warms him—of the wind that breathes upon his face—of his very shadow, for that is always with him. O Zillah! While he is away my heart stands still, till he comes back again. [*Turns up C.*]

ZIL. Mercy on us! Now fate preserve me from such a devouring love! But the poor world workers, such as I have been, have little time for the indulgence of such luxuries. Love is a hothouse plant, and does not thrive well in the open air—but now that I'm a princess—perhaps I may be able to cultivate it. [*Music. Enter Gonzagues, Peyrolles and Carrickfergus*]

GONZ. Yes, Peyrolles, she is found. Here is Mademoiselle de Nevers.

PEY. [*Bowing*] I humbly salute her ladyship!

GONZ. We must set out at once for Paris. I will be your protector and have the happiness of restoring you to your mother, the Princess de Gonzagues.

ZIL. [*Running to Blanche*] You hear, sister!

GONZ. Peyrolles! [*Peyrolles advances*] You must go at once, so as to precede me. I'll write a few lines to his royal highness. But where's my shadow? My living desk? Aesop! [*Taking out notebook and pencil. Enter Lagardere as Aesop*] Carrickfergus. [*Carrickfergus advances L., while Gonzagues is writing in notebook on Aesop's back*] You have your instructions.

CAR. Perfectly, my lord. I cannot see Lagardere anywhere. [*Exit. Blanche, Zillah, and Lemuel are up C.*]

GONZ. Peyrolles, give this letter to the regent; I shall be at the council to defend myself from all accusers, and with this living proof, baffle my calumniators. Away at once! [*Exit Peyrolles*] And now, my dear girl, take a hasty leave of your companions and be ready to depart with me. [*Music. Exit up L. Lagardere is seated on bank, L. Enter Carrickfergus hurriedly*]

CAR. I cannot find our little Parisian anywhere. He left here just now with that scoundrel Aesop—*he's* come back and—[*Crosses to Lagardere*] There has been some foul play. Aesop—

LAG. ——my antagonist is dead!

CAR. Dead!

LAG. ——I killed him!

CAR. You! Then by the Fates and Furies one of us shall keep him company—[*About to draw his sword. Lagardere takes him down C.*]

LAG. ——don't you know me?

CAR. Lagardere?

LAG. ——Posada dell Torro on the road. Farewell. [*Music*]

GONZ. [*Appears L.*] Zillah!

LAG. ——Hush! [*Ring on picture. Lagardere and Carrickfergus in front. Gonzagues on rock. Blanche, Lemuel and Zillah up C., Gypsies surrounding Zillah. Quick drop*]

ACT II.

SCENE 1 : *Interior of the inn. At rise, enter Peyrolles.*

PEY. My fictitious bravery will get me into some horrible scrape at last. I know it will. To think of my traveling alone through this country of barbarians. This solitary inn would be a lovely spot to cut a poor devil's throat in. I'll lay a wager there are trapdoors in every floor. [*Music*] Ah! [*Starts*] I thought I felt it shake under my feet. I don't know which is worse—this solitary mountain road, with convenient chasms here and there, that make you shudder as you approach them, and hold your breath as you gallop by, or—[*Enter Diego, the landlord. Diego should be a jolly, little fat man. Seeing Diego*] Ah! [*Starts back into R. corner; Diego also starts to L., frightened at Peyrolles*] What the devil do you want? Who are you?

DIEGO. [*Obsequiously*] I—I—co—come to—to—tell you, señor, th—that your mule is ready!

PEY. [*Aside*] Ah! This is one of your placid bravos. Your sweet-voiced assassins are always more dangerous than your brawling rascals. [*Aloud and keeping as far away from Diego as he can*] My sweet, excellent friend, will you be so obliging as to prepare a repast for my master the Prince de Gonzagues, and his ward the Lady Blanche de Nevers, who will be here shortly? [*Diego advances as if to show him out*] Stay where you are, if you please!

DIEGO. [*Bowing and retreating*] It shall be done, señor.

PEY. I am infinitely grateful. And now, have the great goodness and politeness to show me to my mule.

DIEGO. [*Opening door*] This way, señor; I attend you. [*Music*]

PEY. No! You go first. *First,* if you please. I have no petty vanities in my disposition—please to go first. [*Exit Diego, bowing very obsequiously, Peyrolles watching him narrowly. When Diego off*] A cutthroat! I'll take my oath, a cutthroat! [*Music. Exit Peyrolles. Sleighbells are heard, as if the mule were galloping away. They cease and Diego reenters*]

DIEGO. [*Smiling and rubbing hands*] By Saint Boniface! We have right noble guests at the Posada today! [*Bells again*] Ha, ha! more arrivals! [*Enter Lagardere*]

LAG. ——within the past half hour?

DIEGO. Yes, señor, you will find them in yonder room. [*Points to L.*]

LAG. ——Prepare dinner as quickly as you can. [*Exit Diego. Enter Carrickfergus. Taking his hand*] ——Blanche?

CAR. Is there. We passed Peyrolles on the road, but I frightened him with a shout and he never opened his eyes till we were out of sight.

LAG. ——keep watch for the prince. [*Exit Carrickfergus*] ——sacred charge must be fulfilled! [*Music. Carrickfergus appears L. He motions to Lagardere, turns and hands Blanche on. Enter Blanche. She runs to and embraces Lagardere. Exit Carrickfergus with sign of caution to Lagardere*]

BLAN. Henri, why was I brought here so suddenly? Explain this mystery!

LAG. ——time and circumstance divide us?

BLAN. Divide us, Henri—Oh! what do you mean?

LAG. ——last day of happiness and hope.

BLAN. Henri—for heaven's mercy—explain yourself!

LAG. ——and noble of the earth?

BLAN. Yes, Henri, with you.

LAG. ——and without me?

BLAN. Without you! It would be nothing!

LAG. ——been happy, then, with me?

BLAN. Oh! Most happy!

LAG. ——Why do you weep?

BLAN. At your absence, Henri, and when—when—

LAG. ——When—what?

BLAN. When I think—that is—when I fear—you—you love someone else!

LAG. ——What do I hear?

BLAN. And that would kill me!

LAG. ——ask the question of your heart.

BLAN. Henri, it is my heart that speaks!

LAG. ——have other ties—a family!

BLAN. Thou art my family!

LAG. ——A mother!

BLAN. A mother! Ah! That is the only treasure for which my soul has longed. After *thee,* Henri, it is my mother I have thought the most [*sic*]. And if I have a mother she must call thee son. Oh, that would be happiness beyond expression.

LAG. ——choose between her and me?

BLAN. Between my mother and thee—O Henri—I—I—I love *thee!*
[*Throws herself into his arms*]

LAG. ——wakes to youthfulness again! [*Music. Enter Carrickfergus
hurriedly*]

CAR. The prince!

LAG. ——my life is in your hands!

CAR. [*Shaking his hand*] Aha! Those are the words that make men honest, as the end will prove. Have no fears for me!

LAG. ——Heaven watch over and protect thee!

BLAN. O Henri, is there danger to you?

LAG. ——Loved by thee, I am invincible!

CAR. Away! Away! [*Exeunt Lagardere and Blanche. Enter Gonzagues*]

GONZ. Where is Aesop?

CAR. He's close at hand, my lord. He's here! [*Enter Lagardere as Aesop.
Exit Carrickfergus*]

LAG. Well! Where's your gypsy ladyship?

GONZ. She's here. Well, Aesop, how like you my plan?

LAG. ——I like it!

GONZ. I see success before me.

LAG. So do I!

GONZ. [*Going*] You must go with us. I may want you near me.

LAG. I shall never leave you.

GONZ. Your fidelity shall be amply rewarded.

LAG. ——With the aid of Heaven!

GONZ. [Turning to him] Eh?

LAG. I follow your worship. [*Exeunt*]

SCENE 2: *The oratory of the Princess de Gonzagues. Opening backed by a
garden, etc. Tapestry hangings, R. and L., facing audience. Large table, R.C.,
six chairs R. of it; arm chair L. of it; state chair down R.; prayer desk against
siding, over which is a full length portrait of Nevers. Peyrolles, whip in hand,
and three Valets discovered. They are arranging chairs, etc., at opening; he
thrashing them.*

PEY. Ha! You miserable scum of kitchen-bred rapscallions, have I made
you feel that I am back amongst you? I know it's beneath a man of my repute
to cudgel your poor hides; but when I haven't nobler game to hawk at—I
must e'en cudgel your poor hides! [*Flogs them*] Don't you know, varlets, that
the family council, to be presided over by his royal highness, takes place tonight—almost immediately, here, in the oratory of the princess—now, just

arrange those chairs—[*In doing so, they tumble over each other*] That's right! Run over each other—do! [*Flogs them*] The princess wouldn't have the meeting held in the grand saloon because she wished to have it take place here in the presence of the portrait of her former husband, with which she has so often communed in secret, prayed to, and told her thoughts to, till she almost fancies it a living thing. [*Bell outside. Peyrolles starts*] Ah! What the devil do you stand there for? [*Runs at them, flogs them off. Comes down C. Lagardere enters at back*] Ah! This will be a night of astonishment to some.

LAG. ——It will!

PEY. [*Paralyzed with fear*] Eh! Who spoke?

LAG. ——Scoundrel! [*Exit*]

PEY. Somebody knows me! [*Looks up cautiously and sees portrait*] Oh! Confound that portrait! I always am afraid when in the presence of that; but, fortunately, here comes the prince and mademoiselle. [*Music. Enter Gonzagues, leading Zillah. She is dressed in handsome riding habit; Peyrolles bows them on, and exit. Gonzagues hands Zillah down C. and crosses to armchair R.*]

GONZ. Yes! This is to be your future home: are you pleased with it? [*Sits L. of table and writes*]

ZIL. [*Amazed and delighted*] Pleased with it? I think I shall go out of my senses with delight and joy. I never dreamt there was so much splendor in the whole world. Oh! What a beautiful place—[*Going to prie-dieu*] What lovely ornaments—[*Looking up at portrait*] And that noble portrait—who is it?

GONZ. [*Looks up, starts*] Oh, that? That was your father.

ZIL. My father! Oh! It can't be possible! And my mother? Shall I see her soon? And will she recognize me—the poor gypsy girl?

GONZ. [*Rising*] Aha! [*Reprovingly*] You must forget all that now, and endeavor to adapt your thoughts to your new position.

ZIL. I will, if I can! But I am so bewildered with excess of happiness, I do not know what to do or say—but when shall I see my mother? My heart yearns to embrace her. [*Enter two lady Attendants*]

GONZ. Be patient—you shall see her soon. Ah! Here are your attendants— go with them, and wait for me in the antechamber. [*Zillah crosses in great glee to R., tripping on her train* as she does so*]

ZIL. [*Bowing to ladies*] Please to go first, ladies. [*The Attendants curtsy and exeunt, R.; Zillah is following them*]

---

* Apparently a blunder in stage business. When Zillah entered in this scene she wore a riding habit as indicated above.

GONZ. Stay! You must make some slight alteration in your toilet, for after the council, it is my intention to take you to the regent's ball!

ZIL. A ball! Shall I go to a ball?

GONZ. Yes—a ball—and at the court of France.

ZIL. What! Amongst all the nobles and fine ladies? Oh! That makes my heart sink with apprehension.

GONZ. Remember you bear a name equal to the most illustrious of them all. Your father was a duke; your mother *is* a princess; you are cousin to the king of France.

ZIL. The poor Bohemian—daughter of a duke—mother of a princess—no I mean a princess for a mother and cousin to the king of France—O Blanche—if you could only see me now! [*Struts around stage, tripping and stumbling over train of her dress*]

GONZ. Blanche! What Blanche!

ZIL. My sister! No not exactly my sister but a friend as dear.

GONZ. Where did you meet her?

ZIL. At Barcelona, where we were staying with the gypsies.

GONZ. How old is she?

ZIL. About my age; and like me an orphan—stolen in her youth and—

GONZ. With whom did she reside?

ZIL. With a young French officer, who had been a captain in the royal service! [*Lagardere enters at back*]

GONZ. [*Aside*] Ha! In the royal service! [*Aloud*] Do you know his name?

ZIL. Yes—no! [*Aside*] I forgot—he is in exile! [*Aloud*] I saw them as we came along.

GONZ. Saw! Whom?

ZIL. Hen—I mean him—the young French officer and Blanche.

GONZ. Where did you see them?

ZIL. At the inn on the road where we stayed to dine—yes, and since we have been in Paris I'm sure I've seen him again.

GONZ. In Paris?

ZIL. Yes.

GONZ. Oh! Impossible!

ZIL. Oh! I could never mistake those eyes!

GONZ. He was disguised then?

ZIL. Oh, yes—and so strangely.

GONZ. How? As what?

ZIL. Why, as—

LAG. ——The regent has arrived! [*Music. Zillah starts on seeing Lagardere, but her surprise is suppressed at a warning from Lagardere*]

GONZ. [*To Lagardere*] Yes—yes—I'll attend to it presently. Well, child, go on—go on—disguised you said.

ZIL. Did I—but pray pardon me—I must go and get ready for the ball! [*Going*]

GONZ. [*Stopping her*] One moment. How was this officer disguised?

ZIL. I—I—don't know. My head was so giddy—I was dreaming, I believe.

GONZ. You said you saw him here in Paris! Now *did* you see him?

ZIL. [*Hesitates, looking furtively at Lagardere; he shakes his head. She deliberately answers*] No!

GONZ. [*Holding her a moment; aside*] There's something very strange in this. [*Leaving her and crossing slowly to L.*] Get ready for the presentation.

ZIL. Yes, my lord! [*Aside, quickly*] Lagardere here! Then there's some mystery for me to unravel! [*As she goes R., she turns and throws a kiss to Lagardere and exit*]

GONZ. [*Turning from L.*] Aesop, you heard what that girl said.

LAG. ———I did my lord.

GONZ. Is there any meaning in it?

LAG. ———he is in Paris.

GONZ. Who?

LAG. ———Lagardere!

GONZ. And why did you not inform me?

LAG. ———your mind on this occasion.

GONZ. Why should it trouble me?

LAG. ———none left now but *you* and I!

GONZ. [*Starts, but recovers himself*] Well, I think I can safely lead him to you. [*Going up C.*]

LAG. ———closer than his own shadow! [*Music*]

GONZ. We'll find a way to break his invincible sword!

LAG. ———How?

GONZ. By the hands of the executioner! [*Exit*]

LAG. ———the end is coming. [*Enter Carrickfergus*] ———Blanche safely bestowed?

CAR. At your house, and impatient to see you. We reached there unobserved by anyone.

LAG. ———been in great peril—[*Carrickfergus stops*] ———but it is past.

CAR. I expect the princess here shortly. [*Looking off C. and L.*] Ah! She comes! [*Music*]

LAG. ———how sad she looks!

CAR. Hers is indeed a life in mourning; she scarcely ever quits this apartment—that portrait is her only companion. [*Exit Lagardere behind tapestry.*

Enter Princess Gonzagues. She bows to Carrickfergus, who removes his hat, bows and exit]

PRIN. How long must this great martyrdom endure? And thou [*To portrait*], the silent sharer of my thoughts—thou, whom in my heart's agony, I have addressed; until the pictured memory became instinct with life—those eyes to beam on me with love ineffable—those lips to part, while my soul listened for the sound to come from them once again—ah! if my child is with thee, give me some assurance. [*Pause*] Silent! Silent! [*Music. She goes to prie-dieu and bows her head dejectedly on book, then raising her head discovers the paper left there by Lagardere*] What's here! A letter addressed to me! [*Comes forward*] What strange feeling is it that thus oppresses me—is it hope or fear? [*Reads*] "Heaven will have pity, if thou hast faith! Your daughter lives."——My daughter lives! "Fear not Gonzagues, but remember Nevers's motto. At the proper time, for thee only, the dead will speak. Signed Henri de Lagardere." Merciful Heaven! I thank you! [*Stands near prie-dieu, reading paper. Enter two Valets who stand across back. Enter Gonzagues. He bows to Princess*]

GONZ. Madame! [*She starts and conceals paper in book*] The council has assembled and waits your permission to attend you here.

PRIN. [*Curtsys profoundly*] I am quite prepared to receive them. [*Music. Exit Gonzagues followed by two Valets*] At the proper time, for thee only, the dead will speak! The dead will speak! [*Enter Carrickfergus and Peyrolles and cross down to R. corner. Then the procession in following order:*

1. Four regent's Servants with halberds; they range across back.

2. Two Gonzagues's Guards with drawn swords.

3. Five Nobles: Navailles, Chaverney, De Breant, etc.

4. Notary and three Judges to table.

5. Gonzagues, bowing Prince on.

6. Regent.

7. Valets, Madelon and two lady Attendants remain at back.

As the Regent enters all bow. He advances at C. and turns to Princess, who is absorbed, L.]

REG. Madame! [*She starts, turns and curtsys*]

PRIN. Pardon me, your royal highness. [*The Regent bows and goes to state chair, R., and sits, his hat on. All the others uncover, except Servants and Guards*] Pray be seated, gentlemen. [*They all sit except Peyrolles and Carrickfergus*] I thank you for according me the favor of meeting me in my apartment.

REG. Madame de Gonzagues, the great friendship which I had for your former husband, Phillipe de Nevers, together with the weighty interests which depend on the issue of this family council, have induced me to preside in person. The Prince de Gonzagues having solicited this convocation, we are now prepared to hear him.

GONZ. [*Seated L. of table. Rises*] Your royal highness has received my letter?

REG. Of tonight? Saying that you could fully meet all accusers? We are at your service.

GONZ. I thank your royal highness for the solicitude you have expressed about my family. Permit me also to tender my acknowledgements to the princess, my wife, who, notwithstanding her feeble health, and love of retirement, has descended from her spiritual elevation to mingle in affairs of merely human interest.

CAR. [*Aside*] What a beautiful exordium!

GONZ. Phillipe de Nevers was my cousin in blood—my brother in heart— yes—we were truly brothers.

CAR. [*Aside*] As Cain was to Abel!

GONZ. Phillipe was treacherously murdered. Twenty years have not softened the bitterness of my regret. Unfortunately justice has not punished the assassin.

CAR. [*Aside*] Not yet!

GONZ. I shall come now, your royal highness, to the question to be decided by this tribunal. The marriage of the princess with the late duke was secret but legitimate; a daughter was born to that union who disappeared on the night of her father's assassination; and, as her existence was in doubt, the Parliament of Paris suspended my claim to the Nevers inheritance in order to conserve the interests of his daughter, should she be alive. It was just that they should do so; but that suspension gave occasion for calumny to fling its darts at me. It was hinted that one sole obstacle intervened between me and the possession of an immense estate. I was suspected of a crime. [*The Nobles made an indignant movement*]

CAR. [*Aside*] Poor, innocent lamb!

GONZ. Yes, a crime! Have they not told you, madame, that it would be vain to search for your daughter, as some mysterious hand spirited her away?

PRIN. They have told me so!

GONZ. They told you also that the perfidious hand was that of your present husband.

PRIN. They told me so!

GONZ. And you believed them?

PRIN. I believed them! [*General movement. Nobles rise*]

GONZ. Well, madame, I responded to all these infamous accusations by the most ardent and obstinate pursuit. I sought for the daughter of Nevers, unceasingly sought for her with my heart, with my gold, and this night—

PRIN. You come to tell me she is dead?

GONZ. This night I come to tell you—I—Gonzagues, whom you so doubt —despise—while I respect and reverence you—that I have found your child. [*Music*]

PRIN. [*In great agitation*] My child! [*Clutching prie-dieu to support herself. General movement of all on stage*]

GONZ. Yes, your child, whom you so vainly searched for, *I* have found, and she is now beneath this roof.

PRIN. My daughter here—beneath this roof? And it is *you* who give her to me? Oh! Let me see her! [*He advances to support her*] Fear not for me. I can support this sudden joy! [*Gonzagues bows and exit. General anxiety and interest expressed by all*] My daughter rendered back to me—through his hands! [*Enter Gonzagues leading Zillah, who has changed her dress*]

GONZ. Mademoiselle de Nevers—go and embrace your mother.

CAR. [*Aside and quickly*] Will she receive her?

ZIL. [*Rushing down L.*] My mother—my dear mother!

PRIN. My child! [*Rushing to meet her, they both stop. Zillah, pale and trembling. The Princess in doubt and disappointment*]

CAR. [*Aside*] I thought not!

PRIN. [*To Zillah*] My heart beats not in response—no—no—you are deceived!

ZIL. [*Sadly*] It is a kind of awe that fills my soul, and not the love a daughter should feel.

GONZ. [*Who has been nervously watching the meeting*] Remember, your royal highness, they have not met since her infancy; it is not likely that they would recognize each other.

CAR. [*Aside*] Not at all!

REG. I have but little belief in what is called the voice of nature.

GONZ. [*At table R.C.*] No—no—your highness—nor I!

REG. But in this case we must be guided by the evidence alone. Of course, you have in your hands the proofs of mademoiselle's birth.

GONZ. Proofs?

PRIN. Yes. The paper torn from the register and given by me to Phillipe, and sealed with the duke's motto.

GONZ. No, but I have the declaration of the Bohemian who found and brought up the child. No further proof is necessary. Here it is. [*Produces it and hands paper to Regent, who reads it, Gonzagues watching him closely*]

PRIN. [*To Zillah*] Have you those proofs?

ZIL. Alas, madame, I have nothing. I only know that I was a poor orphan subsisting on charity; they told me they would restore me to my mother. O madame, the poor gypsy girl seeks not for grandeur or for wealth; she only asks the priceless blessing fate has yet denied her—a mother's love.

GONZ. [*Taking Zillah's hand and turning to Regent*] It is the voice of nature that thus pleads.

CAR. [*Aside*] The voice of nature slipped up that time!

PRIN. [*Aside*] Inspire me, Heaven, for I am much perplexed. In this my great misery I turn to thee! and thou [*To portrait*] who promised at the proper time to speak—speak now! [*Music. Lagardere appears, lifting drapery*]

LAG. ———I am here!

PRIN. [*Starting. Aside*] Ha! The miracle is wrought and I am strong again!

GONZ. Forget, madame, if you so will it, the hand that restores to you this treasure, but at least regard the trembling girl who wonders at your coldness. Is she not your daughter?

LAG. ———No! [*Music*]

PRIN. [*Firmly*] No!

OMNES. [*Astonished*] No?

GONZ. This is too much for human patience. [*Seizes up the paper from table*] You should have strong testimony to oppose this evidence! Have you any?

LAG. ———Yes! [*Chord*]

PRIN. Yes! [*Chord*]

OMNES. Yes? [*Chord*]

GONZ. [*Starts*] Where is it then? Produce it at once! Ah, monseigneur, the fortune of Nevers is a fine prey. Some desperate adventurer speculating on a mother's weakness has told her he has found her daughter. Is it not so?

REG. Answer, madame. [*Music*]

LAG. ———She lives!

PRIN. My daughter lives! Lives through the merciful protection of Heaven. Lives! and in your despite!

GONZ. [*Appealing to Regent*] Monseigneur, I blush to answer by a single word. It is for you to decide between the princess and myself!

REG. Since Madame de Gonzagues refuses to acknowledge the daughter you present, it will be necessary to produce the pages of the register abstracted from the chapel at Caylus; for which purpose we adjourn this court for three days. [*Rises*]

PRIN. I am agreed! I shall then have my daughter and my proofs! [*Music*]

LAG. ——Tonight!

PRIN. [*Aside*] Tonight!

LAG. ——At the Regent's Ball!

PRIN. [*Aside*] At the Regent's Ball!

GONZ. [*To Zillah*] Poor child! May Heaven restore to you your mother's heart.

ZIL. Ah, madame, I don't pretend to know the secrets of Providence; but whether *you* believe me to be your daughter or not—*I feel* nothing but respect and love for *you.*

PRIN. Ah! Thou art no accomplice, child. I can see that. You must remain here with me. [*Kisses Zillah*] Madelon! [*Madelon advances at entrance*] She will see to you; and, Madelon, tell them to get my carriage ready tonight! [*Madelon curtsys; exit Zillah slowly*]

GONZ. [*At table*] Your carriage! You? Who for so many years have scarcely ever quitted this apartment?

PRIN. [*To Madelon*] And prepare my jewels and my best apparel. [*Exit Madelon*]

GONZ. Jewels! Where are you going tonight, madame?

PRIN. To the Regent's Ball!

GONZ. You?

PRIN. Yes! This is my last day of mourning, for I shall recover my child tonight.

REG. [*Crossing and taking her hand*] Madame, we shall feel much honored by your presence! [*Escorts her off, followed by Nobles, etc., Soldiers and Servants last. All exeunt except Gonzagues, Peyrolles, and Carrickfergus. Lagardere enters as Aesop and remains up C.*]

GONZ. [*Aside*] That girl was right! Blanche must be in Paris, and her mother has by some means discovered it. Peyrolles!

PEY. [*Advancing*] My lord!

GONZ. A lady traveled from the frontier at the same time with us. You must track her. You *must!* And have her conveyed to my house in the Rue St. Magloire!

PEY. I shall do my utmost, my lord. [*Aside*] Oh! Law! [*Exit*]

GONZ. [*Crossing into L. corner*] Who? Who could thus so utterly confound my plans?

LAG. ——Lagardere!

GONZ. Lagardere?

LAG. ——deliver him up to you tonight!

GONZ. You?

LAG. ———I!

GONZ. And where?

LAG. ———At the Regent's Ball!

GONZ. Aha! At the Regent's Ball! [*Ring on word. Exit*]

LAG. ———After the hirelings, the master!

ACT III.

SCENE I: *A room in Lagardere's house. Table and one chair, R.C. Toilet table, L.C. up. Lighted candelabra on table, R.C. Music. Blanche discovered seated at R.C. table. Marianna, her attendant, standing L. of her, just completing the arrangement of her hair.*

BLAN. Thanks, a thousand thanks for your kindness; leave me now, there's a good girl, and let me endeavor to collect myself. [*Exit Marianna*] Will my heart never cease this painful throbbing? How I got dressed I cannot tell. A crowd of new sensations fill me with hope, joy, fear and apprehension. But Henri will be here presently, and to be worthy of his love I must be brave and calm. [*Picks letter up from table and reads*]

"I have seen your mother and have witnessed the touching fidelity with which she cherishes her husband's memory. She knows you are in Paris, and now waits impatiently to see you. I have promised that you should meet at the Regent's Ball. Be ready as quickly as you can in the dress I send and I will come for you.   Henri."

Mother, my dear mother—shall I see you so soon—tonight! [*Lagardere enters*]

LAG. ———Blanche! [*She rises and meets him*] ———then you must forget me.

BLAN. Forget you? Am I to die tonight?

LAG. ———I am an outcast—exile!

BLAN. Do you no longer love me, Henri?

LAG. ———rob you of your birthright.

BLAN. O Henri! Why did you bring me here?

LAG. ———until you are ready to depart! [*Music*]

BLAN. I hate it, Henri, hate it like a living foe! I could destroy it and abandon all the wealth it promises if in exchange I could get back your love. [*He leads her to door. She turns, they embrace, and she goes*]

LAG. ———and redeem my word. [*Enter Carrickfergus*]

CAR. Well, my little Parisian, here I am at your service. What are your commands? Why—what has happened?

LAG. ———Nothing.

CAR. All goes well, does it not?

LAG. ———granted me an interview.

CAR. What—to you—Lagardere?

LAG. ———and death for me!

CAR. Have no fears for me. If I am alive she shall be there! [*Shaking Lagardere's hand*]

LAG. ———Let your glove fall.

CAR. I shall obey your instructions to the very letter.

LAG. ———Now for his royal highness! [*Exit*]

CAR. Good fortune go with you! Aha! Our little Parisian is a prince of princes. By Saint Patrick, I owe him something for my soul's recovery! Faith, it was more than half way down before he fished it up! Ha! What do I see? One of Satan's most effectual soul-jeopardizers—a woman! [*Enter Zillah*]

ZIL. Is this No. 7 Rue de Chantres?

CAR. It certainly is! [*Aside*] What do I see? Gonzagues's gypsy girl! There's mischief in the wind—mischief!

ZIL. [*Eagerly*] The Lady Blanche is here, is she not?

CAR. The Lady who? Never heard of such a person, I can assure you, mademoiselle. Nobody in this house but a most respectable elderly lady—a relative of mine—in fact—my grandmother.

ZIL. Dear, dear! How very unfortunate. Can I see Captain Lagardere?

CAR. Captain Lag—Lag—who? Lager Beer.—Totally unacquainted with the gentleman. We don't indulge in captains here.

ZIL. But I have seen you with him, surely.

CAR. Utter impossibility! Mistaken identity, madame, that's all, upon my life. Ah! By the bye—there's another street of the same name in the suburbs. Perhaps you may find your military friend, the lieutenant, there.

ZIL. O sir, are you quite sure she is not here?

CAR. Who—my grandmother?

ZIL. No, sir—the Lady Blanche.

CAR. Positive, my dear madame! This house is wholly and solely occupied by myself and the venerable individual. [*Enter Blanche hastily, pauses at seeing Zillah*] May I have the inexpressible mortification of showing you the door! [*Is about to lead her out, when Blanche exclaims*]

BLAN. Zillah!

ZIL. Blanche! [*They embrace*]

CAR. [*Has opened door*] I trust you will find your—[*Turns and sees them*] Oh! this is delicious! I must look considerably like an ass!

ZIL. And you to tell me they were not here!

CAR. How did I know you were such brothers?

ZIL. Oh! You don't know what mischief you might have caused! [*To Blanche*] Where's Lagardere?

BLAN. I don't know. I left him here a moment since.

CAR. He's just gone out for a quiet walk.

ZIL. Out! Then he's lost! [*Aside to Blanche*] Let me speak with you alone, dear.

BLAN. Zillah, you terrify me. Do not fear to speak before him—he is his friend.

CAR. Yes, his most devoted friend. What has happened?

ZIL. O Blanche, you have a cruel and relentless foe! From the moment I saw Lagardere at the palace, inspired by my love for you, I watched and listened and I now know all!

BLAN. What do you know, Zillah?

ZIL. I know that you are the true Blanche de Nevers, and I am nothing but a cheat, a counterfeit, set up to rob you of your mother's love, and your inheritance. You are going to the ball tonight?

BLAN. Yes.

ZIL. Oh—no—no—remain here, or anywhere—where you may be safe. You will be seized on the road!

CAR. Seized—by whom?

ZIL. The prince! I overheard him give orders to Peyrolles. O Blanche, to think that *I* should be the instrument of your destruction—*I* who would rather lose my life than harm should come to you! Don't—pray don't go to this ball!

CAR. [*Has been walking about excitedly during the past speech. Now comes down between them*] Oh, she must! I have promised Lagardere and—what is to be done? Stop! I have it! [*To Zillah*] *You* were going to the ball?

ZIL. Yes.

CAR. How?

ZIL. In the prince's carriage.

CAR. I thought so! That will do famously—it is *you* who must stop at home. I'll bring the prince's carriage here, and take the Lady Blanche—they will not dare to stop us then!

ZIL. I will do anything you please if it can only shield her from harm.

CAR. Yes, I see my way clearly now. I will first attend you to the palace; then return for Lady Blanche—but be quick, we have no time to spare. [*Goes up and opens door, waiting for Zillah*]

ZIL. [*Embracing Blanche*] Bless you, bless you, my darling! [*Carrickfergus comes down and tries to lead her upstage; she swings round and breaks from him and once more embraces Blanche*] You know that I would lose my life sooner than any harm should come to you. [*Carrickfergus once more attempts to lead her up. Business* ad lib—*until Carrickfergus throws himself despairingly into chair*] But don't be cast down, Blanche, don't be cast down, for the poor gypsy girl whom he thought to make his instrument will watch over you like a sister! [*Music*]

CAR. [*Rising hurriedly*]   Yes—yes—but there's really no time for this sort of thing now—some other time you will have plenty of opportunity. Come, mademoiselle! [*He hands Zillah out door, and turns to Blanche*] Expect me shortly. I must keep my promise with Lagardere! [*Exit after Zillah*]

BLAN. [*Calls*]   Marianna! [*Enter Marianna*] Remain below, Marianna, and be sure to admit no one but Carrickfergus. [*Exit Marianna, closing door after her. Taking candelabra from table*] Now to get these papers. Shall I see Henri at this ball? If so—I shall laugh at danger. Oh, why was I not left in my contented loneliness. I was happy then—he loved me! [*Exit. Music changes. Lights all down. A slight pause before a ladder is seen to be placed outside of window. Presently one of the Valets disguised ascends and gets in, followed by two others. Peyrolles then appears*]

PEY. [*At window*]   Is anybody there?

FIRST RUFF.   Not a soul!

PEY.   Then what are you afraid of! [*Enters cautiously, with dark lantern, turns as he gets inside, and in backing away from window runs against table*]

PEY.   Aha—ha! What's that?

FIRST RUFF.   It's only a table.

PEY.   Look under it! [*The Valet does so*] Anybody there?

FIRST RUFF.   No!

PEY.   Then what are you afraid of? Cowards! Follow me! [*Crosses on tiptoe to L., and the glare of the lantern illuminates the mirror on dressing table. He staggers back in fear*]

PEY.   Who's that?

FIRST RUFF.   Why, it's yourself!

PEY. [*Looking in glass*]   Eh? I thought I was better looking! What are you afraid of? [*Goes to door L., and peeps in*] There she is—alone! [*Comes forward, the Valets all near*] This is a deed of daring *I can* accomplish. But stop! Women have sometimes cat-like talons, and a scratched face would be rather humiliating—so—[*To Valets*] go in—go in! [*They hesitate*] Fear not! *I* will *follow* you! [*They exeunt softly. Peyrolles remains on, looking after them, a pause, then a scream is heard from Blanche, and Peyrolles darts off into the room. Change*]

Scene 2: *Lights up. The Regent's cabinet. Bell pulls and tassels, R. and L. Music. Enter De Breant, followed by Regent.*

De B. May it please your royal highness—there is a person here who says you promised him an interview.

Reg. Oh, yes—by the bye—I did so. Admit the gentleman.

De B. Gentleman! [*Aloud*] He comes, your royal highness. [*Enter Lagardere. Exit De Breant*]

Reg. A hunchback! Was it you who wrote to me?

Lag. ———No, monseigneur.

Reg. I scarcely thought you could be Captain Lagardere.

Lag. ———Cavalry officer, your royal highness.

Reg. That I confess. Who are you? What is your name?

Lag. ———I am called Aesop.

Reg. With whom do you reside?

Lag. ———Prince de Gonzagues, monseigneur.

Reg. Gonzagues!

Lag. ———At present.

Reg. This Lagardere was a determined reprobate. What can he hope from me?

Lag. ———for his former follies.

Reg. But were I disposed to see him, where can he be found?

Lag. ———answer that question, monseigneur.

Reg. Being an exile he is still answerable to the law which condemned him; why does he wish to jeopardize his safety?

Lag. ———To keep his oath.

Reg. His oath—to whom?

Lag. ———To one long dead!

Reg. What was he called?

Lag. ———Duc de Nevers!

Reg. [*Eagerly*] Nevers! Well, what of him? And why has Lagardere been so tardy in addressing me?

Lag. ———to claim her inheritance!

Reg. Was it not the Prince de Gonzagues who restored her to her mother?

Lag. ———No, monseigneur.

Reg. He was mistaken, then?

Lag. ———substituting a false claimant!

Reg. [*Loudly and angrily*] What!

Lag. ———I am nothing.

Reg. And can he prove what you have now insinuated and what he has written?

Lag. ———He can and will!

Reg. That he was at Caylus when Phillipe was assassinated, and can point out the murderer?

Lag. ———from your royal highness.

Reg. Aha! Then he is in Paris and my prisoner! [*Rings bell violently*]

Lag. ———can be given to follow him!

Reg. [*Smiling*] Faith! He's a rare diplomatist! [*Enter De Breant*] Bring me a safeguard, sealed and signed! [*Exit De Breant*] This rascal treats me right royally through his ambassador!

Lag. ———humble one, your lordship! [*Reenter De Breant with safeguard, hands it to Regent, bows and retires*]

Reg. He has committed no fault I cannot pardon. Here is the safeguard. But remember, the slightest violence on his part will forfeit this protection.

Lag. ———five have already fallen!

Reg. By whom?

Lag. ———By him!

Reg. And the sixth?

Lag. ———Master villain waits his turn!

Reg. And he is—

Lag. ———I have no more to say.

Reg. It is very strange. However, I will see him, but let him remember, if this be only a plot on his part to regain his freedom he shall bitterly repent the trick! [*Music. Motions to De Breant to dismiss Lagardere, and exit*]

De B. Well, Aesop, have you been successful?

Lag. ———Perfectly! Perfectly!

De B. Then, as the ball is about to commence, you had better go!

Lag. ———I don't want to go.

De B. Thank you, but you really cannot stay!

Lag. ———I think I can!

De B. What for?

Lag. ———to see the splendid show.

De B. Oh! That's utterly impossible!

Lag. ———I don't think it is!

De B. Well, I *might* manage to *hide you* somewhere.

Lag. ———don't want to be hidden!

De B. What! *You* walk about amongst the company?

Lag. ———I'll be very quiet!

De B. But in this dress?

Lag. ——to find me another?

De B. Well, perhaps I might.

Lag. ——A place to change?

De B. Your arguments are irresistible. Come!

Lag. ——I thought so! [*Exeunt, De Breant bowing him off. Change*]

Scene 3: *Lights down. Moonlight. The gardens of the Regent's palace. Illuminated cloth at back. Guards discovered at various entrances. Servants passing to and fro. Ladies and Gentlemen, Courtiers promenading. Music. Gonzagues enters at L. and crosses up to platform at back, speaking as he crosses.*

Gonz. I can't find my gypsy girl anywhere! [*Exits. Enter the Regent, conducting the Princess from L. She is magnificently dressed. All bow and curtsy as they pass*]

Reg. Pray accept the support of my arm; after so lengthened a retreat, the noise of this crowd and the glare of the lights may be too much for you to bear.

Prin. [*Going to seat at R.*] I most gratefully thank your royal highness; but it is only for this night that I visit the gay world again.

Reg. [*Standing left of Princess*] You expect someone, who, in the name of Nevers, has promised to meet you here? [*Gonzagues reenters, and remains listening to their conversation*]

Prin. I do, monseigneur!

Reg. I presume it is the same person who has written to me—Captain Henri de Lagardere.

Prin. Lagardere!

Reg. Yes, is it not he whom you hope to meet?

Prin. It is indeed, your royal highness, for he has promised to restore to me my daughter.

Gonz. [*Aside at L.*] Lagardere! Oh! impossible—my people guard every avenue—besides the hunchback promised to secure him for me. I am safe.

Reg. I would put little trust in the promise of such a man. He wrote to me that he would denounce the murderer of Nevers tonight and hinted that he was a man of high station, and though I have sent him a safeguard, upon the merest hope that he *might* reveal that hideous crime—depend upon it, he will not appear! [*Enter De Breant who announces*]

De B. Captain Henri de Lagardere! [*Music. General movement. Enter Lagardere. Exit De Breant. Gonzagues down L.*]

Lag. ——here to redeem my word!

PRIN. [*Rises*] And my child? Pardon me, your royal highness, but you remember his promise.

REG. To restore to you your daughter. [*To Lagardere*] You said, sir, that you could restore the Lady Blanche de Nevers. Can you do so?

LAG. ——she will be here presently.

GONZ. Your royal highness already knows that *I* have restored the Lady Blanche to her mother, but, swayed by an influence I cannot understand, she refuses to acknowledge her, in spite of the plain evidence I bring. If this man has suborned some poor creature to represent the daughter of Nevers, surely my character and position will outweigh the testimony of an outlawed criminal!

LAG. ——Should not be here!

REG. What testimony?

LAG. ——from the register at Caylus.

PRIN. Ah!

REG. Have you those papers?

LAG. ——hand them to your royal highness.

GONZ. These are the ravings of a lunatic, or the subtle plottings of some desperate adventurer; how can we tell by what act of violence or chicanery those papers came into his hands?

LAG. ——by the princess herself.

PRIN. By me?

LAG.——the château at Caylus.

PRIN. I gave them to my husband, Phillipe.

LAG. ——With your infant child.

PRIN. Yes—yes—

LAG. ——to *me* you gave them!

GONZ. [*Aside startled*] What's this?

LAG. ——think of the duke's motto!

PRIN. Ah! I remember. It was the signal agreed upon between us. Well, sir, go on—go on—

LAG. ——delivered up to me!

PRIN. And Phillipe, my husband—

LAG. ——treacherously slain!

REG. And can you name the assassin?

LAG. I can! [*General movement. Gonzagues trembling*]——and *mark the murderer!* [*Gonzagues nervously hides his wrist. Enter Carrickfergus quickly through the crowd and down between Lagardere and Gonzagues*] ——Nevers's assassin is—[*Carrickfergus throws his glove before Lagardere, who starts. A slight pause*]

PRIN. Why do you pause and change color?

REG. Proceed, sir, whom do you accuse?

LAG. [*Carrickfergus stands a little above him, his finger on his lips and despair depicted on his face*] ——No one! [*Gonzagues resumes his former bravado*]

REG. But you said you could name the murderer.

LAG. [*After business*]——I cannot! [*Music. Enter Peyrolles hurriedly*]

PEY. [*To Gonzagues, in whisper*] I have secured the girl and papers—she is at the Rue St. Magloire!

GONZ. [*Aside*] Aha! Then all's regained!

REG. [*To Lagardere*] Why do you not speak, sir?

LAG. ——I have no more to say.

GONZ. [*Boldly*] Oh! I can interpret his confusion, your royal highness. It is because he knows that he has been lying! [*Lagardere starts but Carrickfergus signs to him to restrain himself*] Yes—lying! The proofs he boasts of I defy him to produce and the monstrous accusation he has made, against whom I can't conceive, was uttered but to shield himself. I now denounce that man as the assassin of Nevers! [*Music. General movement from all on stage. Exclamations heard of "Murderer," "Assassin"*] And I pledge the honor of my name that I can fully prove the truth of my assertion!

REG. [*To Lagardere*] What have you to say to this?

LAG. ——Nothing!

REG. Nothing, sir? Then you must be content to remain in close imprisonment until the courts of justice can determine this. Deliver up your sword!

LAG. ——My sword!

GONZ. [*Quickly to Peyrolles*] Peyrolles, he must never leave those prison walls alive!

LAG. ——O Blanche! Blanche! [*As his sword falls on stage, ring on picture. Quick drop*]

ACT IV.

SCENE 1: *Interior of a prison. Music. Lights down. Lagardere discovered.*

LAG. ——the redemption of my word! [*Enter Carrickfergus*]—— Who's there?

CAR. Carrickfergus, your friend. Hush! You are in danger!

LAG. ——How?

CAR. I heard the prince give orders to Peyrolles to kill you.

LAG. ——Poor Blanche!

Car. Here, take my sword. I have my knife and if we cannot cut our way out, we can at least die like soldiers.

Lag. ——in my good fortune still!

Car. Well, I have more faith in my sword. Hush! They come! [*Music. Enter Peyrolles and three Ruffians*]

Pey. You have lodged the girl safe in the Rue St. Magloire?

First Ruff. Safe as an oyster in his shell.

Car. [*Aside to Lagardere*] Do you hear?

Pey. Be near at hand, and when you hear this signal [*Slaps his hand three times*], rush in and finish him! Don't let him speak a word, for there's something in his voice that's dangerous.

First Ruff. Pshaw, man, don't fear us! [*Exeunt three Ruffians*]

Pey. My bravery has brought me into a beautiful predicament at last. The prince says "Go! Kill me this man," as if it was as easy as slicing a lemon or a cucumber. If I could only persuade him to hang himself, it would save a deal of trouble. [*Sees Lagardere*] There he is. I think I might do it—if he were asleep! [*Approaches Lagardere cautiously, is very near him, when Lagardere turns quickly. Peyrolles starts back to C., very much frightened*]

Lag. ——Who's there?

Pey. [*Trembling*] No—nobody! Only I—Peyrolles, your *friend*.

Lag. ——What do you want?

Pey. Hush! Don't disturb yourself! The jailors are without and they'd hear the slightest noise. You—you are aware, I suppose, that you have to die?

Lag. ——To die—poor Blanche!

Pey. Yes. The prince has sent *me* here to kill you.

Lag. ——What?

Pey. [*Retreating to L.*] But I'm not agoing to do it. Do you suppose I would raise my arm against an unarmed man? Not likely, indeed. But there are plenty for the work outside. Now I know you are a brave fellow, and since it is quite impossible for you to live, why a few moments can't much signify. Therefore, if you'll do me the favor to hang yourself, it would be a great deal pleasanter for *you* than to have your body made a pincushion for these fellows' daggers. Now, do! There's a beautiful beam over your head—a sweet thing—

Lag. [*Business*] ——or be killed—which?

Car. [*Down L.*] The rat is in the trap!

Lag. ——unless you're sick of life!

Pey. Oh! Why did I venture into this tiger's den?

Lag. ——Take off your coat!

Pey. [*Obeying him*] Oh! You're not going to murder me?

LAG. ——Be quick!

PEY. What are you going to do with me? I'll kneel before you! [*Does so*] Grovel at your feet—lick the very dust. Kick me—cuff me—stab me! [*Carrickfergus does so*]—a *little*—if you like, so long as it is not in a vital part, but don't, oh, don't cut me off in the flower of my days!

LAG. ——or you're a dead man! [*Forces Peyrolles into cell*]

PEY. [*As he disappears*] Oh! What'll my poor mother-in-law do without me? [*Exit*]

CAR. Now, then, to get out; it's rather a ticklish movement, as there are four outside—but here goes! [*Claps his hands three times. Three chords. Enter Jailer and three Ruffians*]

JAILER. [*In whisper*] The prisoner?

LAG. ——There! [*Exeunt Lagardere and Carrickfergus. Jailer and Ruffians exeunt. Then change*]

SCENE 2: *Lights up. Chamber in the hotel Gonzagues. Enter Princess and Zillah.*

PRIN. Girl, you amaze and terrify me!

ZIL. Madame, I have told you nothing but the simple truth; and two innocent people, whom I love, are sacrificed through me. One, *your* daughter, and the other her devoted friend, her champion and protector.

PRIN. But why did you not reveal this fearful plot before?

ZIL. Alas, madame, I knew it not myself until too late; for when I heard that Blanche was to be waylaid, I hurried to prevent it, but fortune was against us.

PRIN. You are certain, then, that the Blanche you speak of is my child?

ZIL. I heard the prince himself confess. Indeed, the words of Lagardere were correct; she had the proofs in her possession.

PRIN. But these he will return to me together with my child as he has promised.

ZIL. Madame, believe it not. [*Aside*] O Heaven! How can I impart to a mother the knowledge I have gained?

PRIN. He cannot! He dare not! dream of violence to her? Girl, answer me!

ZIL. Madame, I have not the courage or the cruelty to tell you what I fear.

PRIN. Ha! then he has some terrible intention! You know it. It would be better to be told the worst than to endure this frightful agony of suspense. There! I will listen calmly now. Speak! Speak! I command you.

ZIL. Madame, I only know your daughter Blanche is in the power of her gravest enemy, while he who can alone defend her and maintain her right is now a prisoner!

PRIN. Heaven counsel me! What *is* to be done? Come, girl, to the Regent! [*Music*] He will prevent the consummation of this crime. [*They are going. Enter Lagardere*]

ZIL. Lagardere!

PRIN. Ah! Then there is hope!

LAG. ——Where is Blanche? Your daughter?

PRIN. Alas, sir. I cannot tell!

LAG. ——Where can he have conveyed her?

ZIL. Ah! I know!

LAG. ——You do?

ZIL. He is to be up tonight at the Rue St. Magloire.

LAG. ——that *we* shall yet prevail!

PRIN. My prayers are with you, sir. [*Exeunt Zillah and Princess, L. Exit Lagardere, R. Change*]

SCENE 3: *La Petit Souper at the Rue St. Magloire. Gallery across stage at back, with stairs descending R. and L., with a curve. Archway beneath C. Table, L., and one chair. Lighted candelabra on table, bell, also writing materials. Arm chair, R. Lights all up. Music. At opening, Gonzagues, Navailles, Chaverney, and Notary discovered, C., drinking. They place glasses on salver, and a Servant, who is holding it, goes out under arch.*

GONZ. I tell you that this very night you shall be satisfied.

NAV. You have said this so very often, Gonzagues. You know we have heavy interests in settlement of the Nevers estates.

GONZ. The money that I owe you, shall be repaid; in proof of which I have brought my notary to prepare the deeds of transfer. [*Aside*] Lagardere must be dead ere this. [*The Notary and two Nobles go up to table. Enter Lagardere, R.*]

LAG. ——No trace of Blanche.

GONZ. Aesop, you seem agitated.

LAG. ——news for you, my lord.

GONZ. Of Lagardere?

LAG. ——that set his spirit free.

GONZ. Yours!

LAG. ——Grant me private audience.

GONZ. Willingly, my deliverer. [*To Gents*] Friends, leave us together for a few moments. [*Navailles and Chaverney exeunt under arch. Aside to Aesop*] We are safe now. [*To Notary*] You can prepare those deeds, I'll sign them presently. [*Notary goes upstairs*]

LAG. ——how can I discover?

GONZ. Aesop, I owe you a heavy recompense. How can I repay you?

LAG. ———*one I* have removed—the other—

GONZ. Blanche?

LAG. ———If she has escaped—

GONZ. Escaped! Ha, ha! She's here!

LAG. ———In this house?

GONZ. Yes! [*Surprised at his manner*] Why—

LAG. ———In this house?

GONZ. Whence she shall never depart alive.

LAG. ———Why?

GONZ. Why? Don't you know that I cannot succeed to the Nevers inheritance save by her death?

LAG. ———Give her to me.

GONZ. To you? You must be mad!

LAG. ———I love her!

GONZ. Love! Love Blanche de Nevers!

LAG. ———and his final doom.

GONZ. The thing is simply impossible. Give Blanche to thee?

LAG. ———be to her a living death!

GONZ. [*Musingly*] And so it would.

LAG. ———You consent?

GONZ. Of what avail would be my consent, since it is quite impossible you can gain hers.

LAG. ———leave her to me!

GONZ. Well, I'm not over-scrupulous, and if you can save me an unnecessary murder, so be it—but if she refuses—

LAG. ———She dies! [*Music*]

GONZ. Make sure of that. But come, we'll make this your wedding feast, and sign the marriage contract. [*Rings bell on table*] I'll give you all the aid I can. My notary is here. [*Enter Valet from gallery*] Tell Angelique to bring here the lady who was given to her charge. [*Exit Valet*] Navailles! Chaverney, come here all of you. I have a comedy that will amuse you! [*Enter Navailles, Chaverney, Carrickfergus, and three Nobles, from under the arch. Notary from gallery downstairs, down L.*]

LAG. [*To Carrickfergus*] ———what you have to urge?

CAR. The influence of magic! I'll urge it at the proper time.

GONZ. Ha, ha, ha! If you don't die with mirth you must be laughter-proof. Sirs, we are to have a wedding here tonight to which you shall be witnesses.

ALL. A wedding!

GONZ. Yes. With two of my protégés.

Nav. Indeed! Who are they?

Gonz. [*Laughing*]   Here is one! [*Points to Lagardere*]

Car. What! The hunchback? That's capital! He'll make a precious bride-groom. [*All laugh sneeringly at Lagardere*] And the other—who is she? The kitchen wench?

Lag. ——Laugh away, gentlemen! [*They continue laughing until*] ——At apes, for instance! [*They cease suddenly and half threaten him*] ——You cannot anger me!

Nav. If we could only put him in a passion now, how superb he'd be!

Lag. ——about to make my wife!

Car. Lady? Ha, ha, ha! That's capital!

Lag. ——Yes, every lord must have his lady!

Gonz. Yes, and I can vouch that she *is* a lady.

Car. A lady marry with a hunchback! It must be through magic then! [*Music*]

Lag. ——Through magic!

Gonz. What! Do you deal in sorcery?

Lag. ——By natural means!

Gonz. Well—ah! Here is Blanche! [*Enter Blanche on gallery*] If you can overcome her repugnance, I'll hail you a master of the black art! [*Goes upstairs, meets and conducts Blanche down to C. Carrickfergus, R. The Nobles, extreme L. Lagardere, up C. Gonzagues, L.C.*]

Nav. By heaven! A pearl of rare beauty, and this abject wretch to think of wedding her—it's monstrous!

Blan. What is to be my fate?

Gonz. Fear nothing. We design to do you a great service. You are a poor and friendless orphan. Any change must better your condition. We now offer you a husband and a fortune.

Blan. Merciful powers! Have my great sorrows driven me mad already? I do not understand you!

Gonz. You will need a protector. Here is one.

Blan. A protector? Ah! I had one, once, but he is dead! Yes, they have killed him, or he would have been here to defend me.

Gonz. Defend thee, child, from whom?

Blan. From thee! I know thee not and yet I feel that you are my secret enemy! 'Twas you who caused me to be brought here! 'Twas you who murdered Lagardere! Spare me! I know not what I say—my brain is distracted! Oh! if you would have pity—kill me and let this torture end! [*Faints. Music. Lagardere moves armchair over and Blanche sinks in it*]

Nav. Poor girl! Master Hunchback, your chances are but small!

LAG. ——Is the notary at hand? [*All laugh at him*]

NAV. Upon my word, his impudence is superb!

GONZ. Well, let us see what his five minutes will do at all events! [*Music. Gonzagues, Navailles, Chaverney, Notary, etc. go well up steps, L. Carrickfergus up R. Blanche recovers from swoon, but remains in chair*]

LAG. ——Blanche! [*Chord*]

BLAN. [*Half rising*] Ah! Who speaks! [*At his "Hush" sinks back*]

LAG. ——recognize my voice?

BLAN. Is it a dream—a happy dream?

LAG. ——and we are lost!

BLAN. O Henri, is it you indeed?

LAG. ——Silence!

GONZ. [*On gallery*] Why, what spell is he working now?

LAG. ——though some witchery controlled you.

BLAN. Henri, dear, dear Henri!

NAV. [*On gallery*] Look! Look!

LAG. ——fall gently into mine! [*Blanche slowly raises her hand in mesmeric manner and lets it fall into Lagardere's*]

NAV. She has given him her hand!

GONZ. Oh! This man's a demon!

LAG. ——look me in the eyes! [*She turns slowly to him*]——do you consent? [*Slight pause, then Blanche falls gently into his arms. He holds up his left hand*]

CAR. [*Coming down*] It's positive witchcraft! And in the five minutes he demanded. He must have courted her in Irish.

LAG. ——Where is the notary?

NAV. But this is infamous! Mademoiselle, do you clearly understand the nature of the contract you are about to sign? [*Gonzagues and others are now down L.C.*]

BLAN. I do! I am his and his alone!

CAR. Well, talk of miracles! This is one that caps a nightcap on old Friar Bacon's head.

GONZ. [*To Notary*] Have you a contract of marriage duly prepared?

NOT. [*Back of table*] Is quite unnecessary. It only requires the signatures of all the parties.

GONZ. [*To Lagardere*] Now, then, your name!

NAV. Has he one?

LAG. ——set them an example, my lord.

GONZ. With all my heart. Where is the pen? [*Music. Notary hands him pen. He signs, stands R. of table, then turns*] Now for the witnesses! [*Hands pen to Chaverney. Chaverney signs and hands pen to Navailles, passing to his L. Navailles signs and then turns to Blanche*]

NAV. Now for the bride. Will *she* sign? [*Pause*] No! She hesitates!

LAG. ———to share it with me?

BLAN. For life and death!

LAG. ———it shall be united! [*Passes Blanche across in front of him. Navailles hands her pen. Blanche takes pen and is about to sign, pauses and turns and looks at Lagardere, then she turns and signs quickly; Lagardere then passes her to R. again. Notary raises paper and reads*]

NOT. [*Reading*] Blanche de Nevers!

NAV. and OTHERS. What?

LAG. ———to the Prince de Lorraine!

GONZ. Now yours! [*Bell strikes twelve times, clear and distinct. Music*]

NAV. Now we shall find out his real name!

CHAV. I am curious to know what it is!

LAG. ———Behold it sirs!

NOT. [*Reading as before*] Henri de Lagardere!

OMNES. Lagardere! [*Drawing*]

LAG. [*Down R.*] ———Aye! Lagardere!

CAR. [*Down R., drawing*] With Carrickfergus by his side!

GONZ. [*Furiously*] Lagardere! Down with him! Slay him! [*They are about to rush on him when Regent appears on gallery from R.*]

REG. Hold! [*The Nobles drop points of their swords. The gallery and archways become thronged with Nobles, Soldiers, Servants, Ladies. The Princess and Zillah enter, following Regent. The Princess comes partly down R. stairway, the Regent down C.*]

LAG. ———go and embrace your mother! [*Blanche rushes upstairs. The Princess meets her and they embrace*]

PRIN. It is—it is my child! Merciful Heaven, be thanked! And you, chevalier! I need no further evidence, for in these features my Phillipe lives again!

GONZ. [*With suppressed rage*] Monseigneur, I demand the arrest of this audacious criminal!

REG. This man is not a criminal, Gonzagues. If he were he might have been far away ere this. He has my safeguard in his possession. Gonzagues, what am I to believe?

GONZ. Believe, monseigneur? In these proofs which I now hold in my hand. [*Produces them*]

LAG. ———name of the murderer!

GONZ. What?

LAG. ———and the dead will speak! [*Music*]

REG. Gonzagues, you tremble!

LAG. ———yours or mine! [*Gonzagues turns to table suddenly and ignites the packet at the candelabra*]

PRIN. [*On stairs*] See! See! He would destroy the proofs!

LAG. ———you have written your own! [*Gonzagues dashes the packet to the ground and stands baffled and confounded*]

CAR. Yes! In a fine, bold Roman hand!

LAG. ———here it is! [*As Lagardere reveals his wrist, Gonzagues tries to cover it without avail*]

REG. Miserable man! You have indeed denounced yourself! Let him be removed!

LAG. ———satisfied your royal highness?

REG. Fully!

LAG. ———grant me one boon!

REG. Freely—what is it?

LAG. ———After the hirelings, the master!

REG. You have my word!

GONZ. [*Drawing*] Ha! Then I have still a chance!

LAG. ———your hour has come!

CAR. Oh! Five minutes will do for him!

GONZ. I defy you to the last. [*They cross swords. Movement of Nobles to interfere*]

REG. [*Waving them back*] Let justice be done! [*Very short fight. Gonzagues is killed*]

LAG. ———After the hirelings, the master! [*Blanche rushes to Lagardere, who embraces her exclaiming*] Blanche! Blanche! [*Ring quick curtain. Picture*]

THE END

America's Lost Plays